Charles Hardwick

Christ and Other Masters

An historical inquiry into some of the chief parallelisms and contrasts between

Christianity and the religious systems of the ancient world. Vol. 2

Charles Hardwick

Christ and Other Masters
An historical inquiry into some of the chief parallelisms and contrasts between Christianity and the religious systems of the ancient world. Vol. 2

ISBN/EAN: 9783337063535

Printed in Europe, USA, Canada, Australia, Japan

Cover: Foto ©Lupo / pixelio.de

More available books at **www.hansebooks.com**

CHRIST AND OTHER MASTERS:

AN HISTORICAL INQUIRY

INTO SOME OF

THE CHIEF PARALLELISMS AND CONTRASTS BETWEEN CHRISTIANITY

AND THE

RELIGIOUS SYSTEMS OF THE ANCIENT WORLD.

With special reference to prevailing Difficulties and Objections.

BY

CHARLES HARDWICK, M.A.

LATE ARCHDEACON OF ELY, AND CHRISTIAN ADVOCATE IN THE
UNIVERSITY OF CAMBRIDGE.

SECOND EDITION.

VOL. II.

"Are not Abana and Pharpar, rivers of Damascus, better than all the
waters of Israel? May I not wash in them and be clean?' So he
turned, and went away in a rage."—2 KINGS v. 12.

London and Cambridge.
MACMILLAN AND CO.
1863.

Cambridge:

PRINTED BY JONATHAN PALMER, 58, SIDNEY STREET.

CONTENTS OF VOLUME II.

PART III.

RELIGIONS OF CHINA, AMERICA, AND OCEANICA.

PART IV.

RELIGIONS OF EGYPT AND MEDO-PERSIA.

CHAPTER I.

CHAPTER II.

CHAPTER III.

CHAPTER IV.

Contents.

PART III.

RELIGIONS OF CHINA.

RELIGIONS OF CHINA.

‹ Behold, these shall come from far; and lo, these from the north and
from the west; and these from the land of Sinim.’

A REVIEWER of the second Part of ‘CHRIST AND
OTHER MASTERS’ put on record his conviction that
‘the very centre of the controversy’ now waging between the Christian faith and its assailants is the
point I have been hitherto attempting to elucidate.
‘Discussions of particular doctrines are,’ he argues,
‘secondary to this deeper question,’ touching the
main relations of the Gospel to other ancient systems,
and the cogency of claims, which it advances, not as
a philosophy among philosophies, but rather as the
living and life-giving ‘Word of God,’ which offers
a continuous attestation of its supernatural origin by
working mightily in them that believe (1 Thess. ii. 13).
Assured that all solutions of this problem, which
deserve the name of rational and philosophic, must
materially depend upon the clearness of our insight
into the distinctive genius of each system, or, in
other words, involve an accurate knowledge both of
what it really was and what it actually achieved,
I shall endeavour in the following pages to conduct
the reader through a fresh department of heathendom,
selecting for review those wild and multifarious creeds
which flourished in localities remote from the original

haunts of man, and in all likelihood completely foreign to the sphere of Hebrew influence. When the mind is once familiarized with characteristic principles of such outlying systems, we shall find ourselves more able to discuss the several points of correspondence which are said to have resulted from long years of intercourse between the earlier Hebrews and Egyptians on the one side, or the later Hebrews and the Medes and Persians on the other.

Particular field of inquiry. As I cannot hope to furnish satisfactory reports from all the single provinces of ancient heathendom, my plan is to devote one special chapter of this Part to China, a second to Mexico, and a third to some of the more dominant islands of the Eastern and Southern Ocean, in the hope that by so doing the important phases of religious sentiment will each in turn have been submitted to the reader for reflection and comparison.

If ever it be possible to ascertain the independent workings of the natural heart of man, such knowledge may especially be sought in regions now before us. There whatever forms of civilisation have existed seem the native and, as one might think, spontaneous products of the soil. The glimmerings of tradition are more faint and more unsteady. They who knowing God refuse to glorify Him as God, are eventually abandoned to their own devices; and amid the anxious gropings after truth which follow that terrific obscuration of the moral consciousness, we see a fresh exemplification of the sacred story, where the younger son, having gathered all together, takes his journey into a far country; yet too often when the land of his adoption has been stricken by some 'mighty

famine,' none is found to answer his despairing cry
for bread, nor fill the aching void within him.

There are still, indeed, sufficient indications in the
darkest depths of heathendom, that man is everywhere the self-same being, open to the same appeals,
and giving utterance to the same emotions, conscious
of incurable discord in the elements of his moral
nature, lifting up his heart to heaven, and yearning
after some emancipation from the iron yoke of evil.
Hence it is that in all creeds whatever certain points
emerge where natural and revealed religion seem to
touch, and where they almost promise to embrace
each other. Yet on close examination nearly all the
chief suggestions which they offer in the hope of
healing and exalting our depraved humanity are found
to be divergent, not to say antagonistic. They proceed from very different thoughts of God, of man, and
of the universe; and therefore differ both as to the
meaning and the method of redemption. If I here
abstain from dwelling largely on these numerous contrasts and divergencies, the reader who possesses any
adequate knowledge of Christianity will hardly fail,
in passing, to remedy the defect. For such a class
of persons, it should be remembered, I am now
engaged in writing. It is not my leading object to
conciliate the more thoughtful minds of heathendom
in favour of the Christian faith. However laudable
that task may be, however fitly it may occupy the
highest and the keenest intellect of persons who
desire to further the advance of truth and holiness
among our heathen fellow-subjects, there are difficulties nearer home, which may in fairness be regarded as possessing prior claims on the attention

of a Christian advocate. My aim, accordingly, will be to shew by strict analysis of ancient systems that as none of these could possibly have given birth to Christianity, so neither does the knowledge thence derivable of what has been attained by man's unaided efforts warrant a presumption that any merely human agent could originate that system of harmonious mysteries, whose life and centre is the Crucifixion of the ' Lord from heaven.'

Modern heathenism. I may also be allowed to add, that in the present chapters the more thoughtful reader will not fail to recognise the proper tendency of certain current speculations, which are recommended to us on the ground that they accord entirely with the last discoveries of science, and embody the deliberate verdicts of the oracle within us. Notwithstanding all that has been urged in their behalf, those theories are little more than a return to long-exploded errors, a resuscitation of extinct volcanoes; or at best they merely offer to introduce among us an array of civilising agencies, which after trial in other countries have been all found wanting. The governing class of China, for example, have been long familiar with the metaphysics of Spinosa.[1] They have also carried out the social principles of M. Comte upon the largest possible scale. For ages they have been 'what people of the present day are wishing to become in Europe,'[2]—with this difference only, that the heathen legislator who had lost all faith in God attempted to redress the wrongs and elevate the moral status of his subjects, by the study of political science or

[1] Cf. Hegel, *Phil. of Hist.* p. 69, Lond. 1857.

[2] Huc, *Le Christianisme en Chine,* &c. I. 358, Paris, 1857.

devising some new scheme of general sociology : while the 'positive' philosopher of the present day who has relapsed into the same positions is in every case rejecting a religious system which has proved itself the mightiest of all civilisers, and the constant champion of the rights and dignity of man.　He offers in the stead of Christianity a specious phase of neo-paganism, by which the nineteenth century after Christ may be assimilated to the golden age of Mencius and Confucius; or, in other words, may consummate its intellectual freedom, and attain the highest pinnacle of human progress, by reverting to a state of childhood and of moral imbecility.

CHAPTER I.

Religions of China.

'Die Chinesische Religion ist eine schlechterdings selbstgemachte
des natürlichen Menschen, so ungestört von fremden Einflüssen,
wie keine andere. Wir dürfen uns daher auch nicht wundern,
wenn wir in ihr merkwürdige Berührungs-punkte mit den Lehren
eines modernen Heidenthums unter christlichen Völkern finden.'

CHAP. I.

Importance of the sub-ject.

IF China were regarded simply as one spacious hive of human beings, all proceeding with instinctive art and order to fulfil the various tasks prescribed by the superior powers, the investigation of successive phases in its mental history might well attract the interest and excite the musings both of statesmen and philanthropists. They see unrolled before them the eventful annals of an empire whose prodigious population far outnumbers that of all the Indo-European family.

Antiquity of Chinese civilisation.

But inquiries such as we are prosecuting in these chapters will have stronger and more sacred claims upon the sympathies of every philosophic Christian. China, he remembers, is the birthplace of the oldest institutions known to history, the centre of the most enduring civilisation in the world. However much of wild pretension has in course of time been pruned away by critics from the semi-legendary archives of most other countries, those of China, it is still conceded even by the more sagacious of our modern scholars, have not suffered in their passage through the literary ordeal. There is reason to believe that portions of her present territory were the seat of thriving and of fully organised communities not less than two thousand years before the Christian era.[1] It is true, indeed, that of surviving records none may in their extant form be much anterior to the birth of Herodotus. It may be questioned also whether the Chinese have ever had a series of regular annals stretching to a more remote antiquity than the commencement of the Greek Olympiads or the first Assyrian conquests in the Holy Land; but inasmuch as all accounts which have been left us, from that epoch downwards, bear a perfectly historic impress, it is probable that fragmentary notices of ancient China which profess to have come orally from very primitive ages, are, at least in all their broader outlines, worthy of the credit which has been awarded to them by the modern sinologue. Before the name of the Middle Kingdom had been ever uttered in the learned halls and avenues of the Athenian Academy; before the eagle of the Roman legions, thirsting after universal sway, had tried its earliest flight across the Central Apennines; before the English of that ancient world, the colonising merchants of Phœnicia, had unfurled their sail upon the waves of the Atlantic, and trafficked in the precious metals on the coasts of Albion and Ierne,—large communities of settlers stretching far across the plateau of Upper Asia were

---

[1] See, for instance, Prof. Neumann's paper in the *Journal Asiatique* (1834), tome xiv. pp. 50 sq.; and Prichard's *Researches*, iv. 476—480. Gutzlaff, in like manner, dates the commencement of the historical period from the accession of the Hëa dynasty B.C. 2207: *Chinese History*, i. 75.

already living under the patriarchal rule of great and powerful princes. Chinese ports were even then frequented by adventurous traders from Ceylon, from India, from the Persian Gulf. A knowledge of Chinese astronomy found its way beyond the mountains and took root in northern Hindústán.[1] The products of the almost fabulous industry of China had established their reputation in countries lying farther to the west; nay, cups of Chinese porcelain, inscribed with her peculiar symbols, had been buried *Permanence* in the ancient sepulchres of Egypt.[2] Or, looking *and wide* from our modern point of view, we find that ages *diffusion of* after the distinctive nationality alike of Egypt and *Chinese* Phœnicia is obliterated, or absorbed in that of their *civilisation.* oppressors; when both Nineveh and Babylon are swept away, and other races strange in tongue and stranger still in spirit are exploring the vast pile of ruins and are bent on disinterring one by one the trophies of the former masters of the eastern world, few changes have come over the ideas, the habits, or the institutions of the Middle Kingdom. China is China still. Her arts, her laws, her customs, the more sacred and more classic portion of her writings, most of all her marvellously characteristic language in its various dialects, continue to be everywhere diffused;[3] while far beyond the proper limits

---

[1] Lassen, *Ind. Alterth.* I. 742.
[2] Gfrörer, *Urgesch. des menschlichen Geschlechts*, p. 214, Schaffhausen, 1855, in his allusion to this fact, exclaims most naturally, 'Welcher Blick in die graue Urzeit öffnet sich uns hier!' The subject is discussed at length in Sir John F. Davis's *China*, II. 72 sq. Lond. 1841.

[3] A few mountaineers, however, still continue to hold out against the civilisation of the great mass of the Chinese: Prichard, IV. 487 sq. According to Duhalde, there cited, the unconquered Miao-sse 'have not adopted the religion of the Lama, but still remain devoted to the superstition which appears to have been the

of her empire she impresses the peculiar genius of her
policy and civilisation, from the borders of Siberia to
the snowy chain of Shang-gan-Alin and the eastern-
most extremity of Japan. It is computed that the
circle of Chinese influence at the present day embraces
a population of not less than four hundred millions
of human beings.

We cannot urge, indeed, that China has been *External*
utterly exempted from all foreign perturbations. The *and in-*
ternal dis-
great wave of Huns, which propagating itself beyond *turbances.*
the Don and Danube, had ultimately, under Attila,
produced confusion in the capital of the Roman
world, originated in the upper valley of the Hoang-
ho, from whence it had been forced in new directions
by the vigorous unity of Chinese rulers; and at last,
when their dominions were invaded, and in part subdued, by hordes of Mongols and Mandshurs, it is remarkable that like the Visigoths and Lombards, who
ravaged all the fairest plains of southern Europe, the
invader found the reigning civilisation far too strong
for him; he was himself led captive; he bowed
before the ancient language and majestic institutions
of the very nation he had spoiled. The Chinese
empire has moreover experienced the disturbing influence of religious controversy, and a large proportion
of the people have been fascinated by a creed whose
birthplace was in central India: yet here again the
genius of the Chinese state-religion proved itself so
dominant that no sensible changes have been thus
effected in any part of the political or social machinery.

And corresponding to the wide extent of China,

primitive one in all eastern Asia,   see above, Vol. i. p. 376.
namely, that termed *Shamanism.*'

CHAP. I.

Moral and spiritual isolation.

to the permanence of her institutions, and the consciousness of her superior rank among the Asiatic tribes, has been her tendency to look on others with indifference or contempt and her unconquerable isolation. Long before the inroads of the Tatars made it necessary to protect her people by building the Great Wall, a spiritual barrier was in process of erection. China grew into a kind of homogeneous world within herself: the China-man was virtually cut off in sympathy from every other nation, just as much as if his lot were cast in some distant planet. The Middle Kingdom was and is to him the centre of the universe; all others, they of the 'Great Western Ocean'' not excepted, being mere extremities or pendants. Hence had sprung not only the distinct and thoroughly national character of almost everything which called itself Chinese, but also the monotonous air pervading every single feature of that nationality. Arts, manners, and religion in so far as it is really indigenous, appear to have been cast in precisely the same mould. As in the physical characteristics of the nation, the old traits almost universally recur, the same dark eye with its oblique expression, the same black hair, the same tawny skin, so in their mental temperament and moral qualities the uniformity is no less manifest. As a people the Chinese are shrewd and clever, calculating, sordid, plodding, and prosaic,[2] enterprising, fraudulent, and

Natural characteristics of the Chinese.

---

[1] A specimen of Chinese impressions respecting Europeans (who are called the people of 'Ta-se-yang,' = 'the Great Western Ocean,') may be seen in Prof. Neumann's *Preface* to his version of the Chinese *History of* *the Pirates*, pp. xxii. sq.

[2] 'A partir de l'époque historique, on ne rencontre plus que ce qu'on pourrait appeler de la prose, et du sens commun.' Pauthier, *Chine*, p. 43, Paris, 1839.

gambling, strong in worldly wisdom, wanting in religious fervour and in moral sensibility; while, in spite of the unparalleled extent of popular education, all the higher intellectual faculties, with very rare exceptions, have remained from age to age imbecile and inert.

These properties of the China-man are best appreciated on contrasting him for a moment with his Hindú neighbour.[1] In the Áryan race, as early as their first descent on northern India, the imagination is ever asserting its predominance. Their favourite mythes are all of a peculiar wildness and exuberance; they revel in the vague, the vast, the allegorical, the

China-man and Hindú contrasted.

---

[1] We have a curious account of the Chinese and their ancient civilisation, written by one of themselves (in the *Vie et Voyages de Hiouen-Thsang,* pp. 230, 231; ed. Julien, Paris, 1853):

The Buddhists of India wished to detain this pilgrim, urging that the Buddha was not born in China, and that the Chinese were *Mie-li-tch'e* (Mléch-chhas,' barbarians'). It was also added, that 'les vues des habitants sont étroites et leurs souillures profondes.' Then comes the answer of the China-man:

' Le roi de la loi [*i. e.* the Buddha] a fondé sa doctrine pour qu'elle se répandit en tous lieux; quel est l'homme qui voudrait s'en abreuver tout seul et délaisser ceux qui ne l'ont pas encore reçue? Or, dans ce royaume (en Chine), les magistrats sont graves et les lois sont observées avec respect. Le prince se distingue par sa haute vertu et ses sujets par leur loyauté; les pères par leur affection, les fils par leur pieuse obéissance. On y estime l'humanité et la justice, et l'on place au premier rang les vieillards et les sages. Ce n'est pas tout: la science n'a pas de mystères pour eux; leur pénétration égale celle des esprits; le ciel leur sert de modèle et ils savent calculer les mouvements des sept chartés (du soleil, de la lune et des cinq planètes). Ils ont inventé (toutes sortes) d'instrumens, divisé les saisons de l'année et découvert les propriétés cachées des six tons de la musique. C'est pour cela qu'ils ont pu expulser ou soumettre les animaux sauvages, toucher et faire descendre les démons et les esprits, calmer (les influences contraires du) *In* et du *Yang* [the male and female principles in nature, the harmony of which is essential to the well-being of creation], et procurer la paix et le bonheur à tous les êtres.' In the *Laws of Manu* (x. 43, 44) the *Chinas* are reckoned among those Kshatriyas, who had been debased through their neglect of sacred rites and through their want of intercourse with Bráhmans.

shadowy, the mysterious. In China, on the contrary, imagination exercises very little influence. Relics of the early poetry, in which, if ever, we might hope to trace the operation of this class of faculties, are seldom more than tame and frigid representations of ordinary life. Excepting one important school[1] whose Indian tastes and predilections are continually betrayed, the Chinese have no primitive mythus, corresponding to the vivid and romantic imagery in which different tribes of man had veiled their worship of external nature, or idealised the legends of their simple forefathers. All in China is more commonplace, more tangible, more practical, more real. 'What the Chinese cannot comprehend with the natural understanding exists not for them, and is an object of their derision.' Hence the Bráhman comes to be esteemed by learned followers of Confucius a mere dreamer and fanatic; while in his opinion they are abject and plebeian spirits, selfish, sordid, and materialistic. He disparages the world around him on the plea that it is only an illusion, acting as the transient mirror of the supernatual and enduring: they as absolutely yield themselves to the dominion of the seen and temporal; they long for nothing higher.

Primeval traditions of the Chinese.

On proceeding to investigate the early history of 'these utilitarians of the ancient world,' their own

---

[1] This school, the *Tao-sse* (respecting whom, see below, § 2) had a mythology in many points resembling that of the Greeks and Romans. A judicious writer on Chinese institutions in the *Nouveau Journal Asiatique* (1854), v. série, tome IV. p. 314, says that he has read some of the Tao-sse dramas, and found in them the fable of Epimenides, the fable of Niobe, the fable of Venus issuing from the sea after Saturn had thrown into it a magical composition, the representation of Neptune armed with a trident, &c.

traditions[1] uniformly point us backward to the mountains of the west,—the sources of those mighty streams that fertilize the whole of central China, and the spot to which the memory afterwards reverted as the paradise of primitive man and as the cradle of all natural and preternatural being.[2] When the Chinese issued from their native highlands they appear to have first occupied the numerous valleys of the Kwan-lun, and most writers on the subject have conjectured, from the simple genius of their language, its monosyllabic forms, its want of organisation, and its very limited affinities with foreign idioms,[3] that their isolation from the rest of men was dated from a very distant period. In the earliest dawn of history, we see them like the other shepherd-tribes of central Asia, wandering onward with their eyes directed to the pastures of the south and east; yet in the meanwhile little higher in the scale of civilisation than the Bushmen of the present century.[4] Their dress consisted of the skins of animals; their food of roots and insects. From this depth of barbarism the legends tell us how they finally emerged at the command of early emperors,—a representation savouring, it is true, of ages when the state-machinery was fully organised, but well adapted to convey the notion, that material progress flowed in their case from administrative ability. When due allowance

---

[1] Prichard, iv. 478 sq.; Gfrörer, pp. 217 sq. The latter is of opinion that the Chinese have all sprung from a Turanian stock.

[2] Cf. Vol. i. pp. 300 sq. on the Mahá-Méru of the ancient Aryans, corresponding to this legend. Other features of the Chinese paradise will be found in Lüken's *Traditionen*, p. 67, Münster, 1856.

[3] Prichard, iv. 481: cf. the 'Introduction,' prefixed to M. Biot's edition of the *Tcheou-Li*, Paris, 1851, pp. v. sq.

[4] Gutzlaff, i. 124 sq. Pauthier, pp. 33 sq.

has been also made for some of the ideal excellencies ascribed to early kings and statesmen, it is obvious that the march of ancient China in acquiring all the arts of settled life was most extraordinarily rapid.

Culmination of Chinese civilisation. The whole empire seems as if it sprang directly from a savage to a civilised condition by one mighty bound; but, having exhausted all its elasticity in this single effort, had been afterwards reduced as rapidly into a stiff and spiritless automaton. The borders of the Chinese empire were at first indeed comparatively narrow. In the seventh century before Christ they had extended only so far as to embrace five out of the present eighteen districts; while beyond them and around them lay a multitude of barbarous people whom it was their object to subdue and humanize. As early, however, as the second century of the Christian era, the huge system of Chinese administration had received its finishing touch. The emperor was everywhere regarded as the centre and moving principle of the whole machinery: government-schools, which had been planted long before, were now enlarged and multiplied in every quarter: while literary merit, tested by competitive examinations[1] in a number of accredited books, became the single passport to promotion in the public service.

Religious phases. With these cursory observations on the state of ancient China, I proceed to notice the peculiar forms and phases under which religion has been there diffused among the people.

The number of such forms is three:

1. The State-religion, as re-modelled by Confucius.

---

[1] Meadows, *The Chinese and their Rebellions*, pp. 402 sq. Lond. 1856.

2. Tao-ism, or School of the fixed Way.
3. Fo-ism, or Chinese Buddhism.

§ 1. *Confucianism.*

The civilisation of ancient China, as of other Sacred
Eastern states,[1] is founded mainly on one class of books.
writings, which are held to be deserving of especial
honour. These the China-man entitles *king*, or, with
peculiar emphasis, 'the books.' As might perhaps
have been predicted from the general texture and
constitution of his mind, he never thinks of God as
of a Being who reveals Himself objectively to man,
and therefore manifests no faith in any kind of supernatural religion. Yet the Chinese seldom fail to
draw distinctions between the authority of the *king*
and every other class of ancient writings. The 'holy
man'[2] (*shing-jin*) is said to have possessed instinctively
the power of diving to the bottom of metaphysical
discussions, and of yielding a spontaneous obedience
to the promptings of the pure and perfect nature he
inherited in common with the rest of men. His
teachings therefore on their first enunciation are all
absolutely true : they rank far higher than the works
of those who are entitled 'sages' (*heen-jin*), but who
only rise to full perception of religious truth, and
practise all the higher virtues, after painful and assiduous cultivation.

[1] Differing, in this respect, from
Greece and Rome, where, in the
absence of 'sacred' books, there
was a much freer development of
human thought. Pauthier seems
to be of opinion that the *king*
bear a strong resemblance to
the *Védas* in the general character of their contents ('non
pour le contenu mais pour l'espèce
du contenu') ; and adds that this
conformity 'n'est peut-être pas
purement due au hasard.'
[2] Meadows, as above, pp. 347,
348.

In this chain of 'holy men' the foremost link was Fuh-he, the reputed founder of Chinese civilisation and author of the oldest of the 'sacred' books,—the *Yih-king.*[1] It is not my purpose to insist at present on the legend where Fuh-he, escaping from the waters of a deluge, re-appears as the first man at the production of a renovated world, nor on the fact that he is there attended by *seven* companions, his wife, his three sons, and three daughters,[2] by whose inter-marriage the whole circle of the universe is finally completed. His work is even more mysterious than his personal history. 'The wisest among the Chinese have entered this labyrinth, but only to come out of it more bewildered.' It may be described as an expanded form of ancient and recondite speculations on the nature of the universe in general, the harmonious action of the elements and periodic changes of creation. These ideas were primarily expressed by means of eight peculiar diagrams (*kwa*), which constitute the basis of natural philosophy as well as of religion. Yet the work professing to unriddle all the mysteries which are believed to have been latent in those venerable signs, was treated as a series of enigmas in the classic age of Chinese literature; and so capricious were the expositions to which the

---

[1] The best edition 'ex inter-pret. Regis' is that of Mohl, Stuttg. 1834—1839. This anno-tator was Wán-wang, 'the liter-ary prince' and founder of the Chow dynasty, who during his imprisonment (B.C. 1144—1142) arranged the diagrams of Fuh-he on different principles. His re-arrangement and expositions, as completed by his son, Chow-kung, became the text of the earliest of the Chinese sacred, or canonical, books.

[2] See Mr. McClatchie's paper in the *Journal of the Asiatic So-ciety* (1856), XVI. 403, 404, where it is contended that in Fuh-he and his family we may recognise Noah and the second parents of the human race: cf. Gutzlaff, I. 129, 130, Wuttke, II. 100, 101.

Yih-king was submitted, that instead of being as at first a cosmological essay it became eventually a standard treatise on ethical philosophy.

The second of the Chinese 'sacred' books is called the *Shoo-king*,[1] which, as more historic and intelligible than its predecessor, has been everywhere esteemed the chief authority in tracing out the spiritual development of the Middle Kingdom. It commences with the reign of Yaou, one of the very earliest emperors, and stretches onward to the life-time of Confucius: while the moral and political maxims it contains have formed the text on which the ingenuity and erudition of the native commentators have been exercised for ages. The vast importance of the *Shoo-king* in directing the national mind of China was never more evinced than in the desperate efforts to suppress it during the reign of Che-hwang-te, the scourge of the barbaric Huns and the projector of the Great Wall (about 240 B.C.). This able tyrant, anxious to uproot the old traditions and to render everything Chinese dependent on his beck, had spared the copies of the enigmatical *Yih-king;* but all other books, both secular and sacred, had, with very rare exceptions, been committed to the flames.[2]

The *She-king*[3] is the third authoritative document that serves to illustrate the general course of Chinese civilisation. It comprises 311 odes and other lyrics, for the most part moral in their tone, and sometimes

---

[1] See *Le Chou-king*, ed. De Guignes, Paris, 1770; and *Livres Sacrés de l' Orient*, par Pauthier, Paris, 1842. Gutzlaff, speaking of the *Shoo-king*, says that 'it forms the great text-book, upon which all Chinese literati have expatiated: '(I. 127).

[2] Gutzlaff, I. 223, 224: Meadows, pp. 333, 334.

[3] See *Chi-king, sive Liber Carminum*, ed. Mohl, Stuttg. 1830.

CHAP. I. breathing in the midst of tender sentiments and deep regrets a freshness and simplicity entirely character- istic of the earliest ages of mankind. The ancient bard appears more conscious than the modern China- man of some corruption cleaving to the human family as a whole ; and here and there we trace an ardent aspiration after some more lofty stage of being, which, as time went over, was completely stifled by the growing love of pelf, and the incurable self-sufficiency engendered in the heart of the Chinese.

Other sa- cred books. Inferior only in authority to works already men- tioned, is the Chinese book of rites and manners, *Le-ke*,[1] which, prescribing as it did for all relation- ships of life and all the various orders of society, established everywhere unnatural stiffness and fas- tidious decorum. Other writings,[2] nearly if not al- together standing on the same superior level, might be added to this series; but in it we have the principal monuments of the older race of 'holy men,' and therefore the great bases of all Chinese history and ethics, politics, philosophy, and religion.

Rise of Confucian- ism proper. It appears, however, highly probable that several changes were effected in the ancient creed of China during the fifth and sixth centuries before the pro- mulgation of the Gospel. In Kong-fu-tse (a name

---

[1] See *Le Li-Ki, ou Mémorial des Rites*, ed. Callery, Turin, 1853.

[2] It is usual to speak of the four works above noticed, together with the *Tsun-tseu*, (an historical composition of Confucius), as the Five Sacred writings (*Woo-king*): see Mohl's *Pref.* to the *Yih-king*, pp. 79 sq. But the *Ta-heo* (or 'great doctrine,' ed. Pauthier, Paris, 1837), the *Chung-Yung* (ed. Abel-Rémusat), the *Lun-yu* (ed. Schott), and the *Hi-tse*, all eman- ating directly from the school of Confucius, though not always written by himself, are held to be co-ordinate authorities in fa- vour of the state-religion. Next in order stand the works of Men- cius (Meng-tse), who died about 317 B.C. His various treatises are edited by M. Stanislas Julien, Paris, 1824.

which missionaries from the west have Latinized into Confucius), we behold the 'prince' of Chinese 'wisdom,' or the second founder of the state-religion; and as all the ancient documents were then submitted to inspection and revision,[1] it is rather to Confucius than to Fuh-he, or to other ancient worthies, that the ruling forms of civilisation in the Middle Kingdom must be ultimately referred.

The labours of Confucius constituted a fresh *General aim of Confucius.* epoch in the mental progress of the Indo-Chinese world. He comes upon the theatre of history soon after the demise of a reformer, who in various points is most unlike him. Sákya-muni died, as we saw reason to believe,[2] in 543 B.C.: Confucius was born in 551 B.C. Addicted in his early boyhood to the study of the ancient records,[3] he acquired a habit of contrasting the disorders and demoralisation of his age with the ideal pictures there presented of the primitive line of Chinese kings. The heavenly maxims of a Yaou, the stern and simple virtues of a Shun, the perfect system of administration that had characterised the golden age of Yu, these all excited the unbounded admiration of Confucius; and at the early age of three-and-twenty he conceived the thought of leading back his fellow-subjects to the ancient

---

[1] Meadows, p. 332, who remarks : 'It is well known that he expressly repudiated portions of the ancient literature, as containing doctrines adverse to the views which he held and strove to diffuse. The names only of some celebrated ancient books, one dating from the times of Fuh-he himself, have been preserved.'

[2] Vol. I. pp. 218, 219.
[3] See the ample sketch of his life and writings in Pauthier's *Chine*, pp. 121—186. The collected works of Confucius were published, with an English translation, by Marshman at Serampore, in 1809; and with a German translation at Berlin (1826-1832), under the editorship of Dr. Schott.

models. It was the predominant force of this idea that afterwards impelled Confucius during his long life to visit several courts of Chinese princes, among whom the country had been subdivided, and in some few cases he was actually allowed to try his grand experiment as a political and social reformer. But his course as he advanced was very far from prosperous. The importance given to virtue as the proper basis of good government exposed him to the scorn of some and the malignity of others. The last words he uttered savour not of hope and exultation, but of bitter disappointment. During his life, however, an enthusiastic band of followers had begun to cluster round him; and after rearing his modest tomb upon the banks of the Soo river, they proceeded with untiring industry to methodise his principles and circulate his writings. 'My doctrine' he had constantly declared[1] 'is that which all men ought to follow. It is the doctrine of Yaou and of Shun. As for my way of teaching, it is perfectly simple. I cite the patterns left us by the ancients. I counsel men to read the sacred books (*king*), and I require them to form the habit of reflecting on the various maxims there preserved.' Accordingly the principal ground on which Confucianism has ever rested its appeal is narrow, and the ruling spirit of the system cautious and conservative. It promised that the old traditions of the country should be sacredly collected and as sacredly embalmed; and very much of the success it ultimately won is due to its profession of respect for social and political precepts current in the governing class, and the effectual aids it thereby rendered

---

[1] In Pauthier, p. 134.

in maturing and consolidating the nationality of
China.

But although the fashion was to eulogize the *Alleged*
founder of this system as the last and brightest of the *finality of*
his changes.
Chinese 'holy men,' and though an obvious tendency
of all the 'reformations' he promoted was to deaden
the activity of the human intellect, and make the
future ages a mere reproduction of the past, we are
not justified in arguing that the mind of the Chinese
did actually subside at once into a state of apathy
and torpor.[1] On the contrary it seems as if the
fluctuations of religious thought were not less numerous in Peking than in the eastern capital of the
Cæsars.

Taking no account of those great movements *Intellectual*
activity in
which ran counter to the state-religion, and as such *China.*
will be considered separately, we find that under the
nineteenth or Sung dynasty (extending from A.D. 960
to A.D. 1279), the general tone of Chinese 'orthodoxy'
had experienced an important modification. As the
earlier changes synchronized with various tokens of
activity in the western world, Confucius being the
contemporary of Pythagoras and his greatest follower
Mencius the contemporary of Aristotle, so the epoch
that beheld the first advances of the Christian school-
men and the growth of speculative Judaism in writers
like Maimonides, was also that in which the doctors
of the Middle Kingdom laboured to evolve a definite

---

[1] Prof. Neumann's remark is perhaps exaggerated, but there is no reason for doubting its sub- stantial truth : 'Das Mittelreich zeigt nicht weniger *geistige* und politische Revolutionen als andere Theile der Welt.' See his valu- able contribution on 'Die Natur- und Religions-philosophie der Chinesen,' in Ilgen's *Zeitschrift für die historische Theologie* (1837), VII. 19.

CHAP. I. and coherent system of philosophy from the writings of their ancient sages. Whether traceable, as some conjecture,[1] to the agency of printing which had been invented and established with imperial sanction as early as the middle of the tenth century ; or whether, as might also be conjectured, some at least of the new impulse was communicated to the governing classes by the rapid growth of Buddhism and the consequent infusion of a Hindú spirit, there can be no doubt that China was producing a new race of scholars marked by greater aptitude for metaphysical speculations. Their philosophizings, it is true, were based on the received traditions of the ancient writers, with whom at every turn they claim a spiritual fellowship ;[2] yet all had grown more conscious that in order for the state-religion to retain its old supremacy and crush or counteract the innovations now rampant in all quarters, it must coin a more scholastic terminology, must grapple with a harder class of questions, and must speak out far more plainly not on matters of finance, economy, and etiquette, but on the nature of the world and its inhabitants, and the

---

[1] *e. g.* Meadows, p. 334, who remarks : 'The originative capacities of many minds, which would otherwise have lain dormant in unlettered ignorance, must have been brought [by the cheapening of books] into fruitful action in the fields of philosophical speculation and historical inquiry.'

[2] The following clear testimony is from the philosopher, Choo-he (Tschu-hi), translated by Neumann, as above, p. 21 : 'Kong [Confucius], Meng [Mencius], Tsching und Tschang [both of whom flourished 1000 years after Christ] sind die vier berühmten Stützen unserer Lehre. Die Weisheit und die Untersuchung des Grundes aller Dinge ruht auf diesem festen Fundament : alle jene andern Lehrer haben sicherlich geirrt. Nur diese vier verehrt man als die Grundpfeiler der Weisheit ; ihre Entfernung [in der Zeit] von Fohi [Fuh-he] will wenig sagen : *sie verbindet das gleiche Princip.*'

true relation of the seen and temporal to the Absolute
and All-embracing.

The philosopher who guided this great movement to a prosperous close was Choo-he, termed by European scholars the Aristotle of the Middle Kingdom, and revered by all the governing class of China as 'the prince of sciences.' The commentaries he has left behind on all the Chinese classics are a fraction only of his multitudinous writings; yet in them especially it was that Choo-he shaped the course which Chinese thought has very generally followed from his day to our own.[1] All statements on religious subjects which are not supported by appeals to his authority are branded as injurious and heretical; and since the millions who present themselves as candidates for office under government are constantly employed in learning his works by heart, it is most obvious that the influence he still exercises, whether as a guiding or a cramping agent, is incalculably vast. If the intelligence of China only reached its prime when first awakened by Confucius, it was passing through the phase of manhood, if not verging to a state of absolute senility, when Choo-he breathed his last in A.D. 1200.

What, then, may be deemed the leading features in the practical working of Confucianism, a system planted, there is reason for believing, in the twilight of the world's history but perfected as late as the concession of our Magna Charta?

In that system, as administered in every age, the emperor of China is the foremost object. Mounted

---

[1] See Neumann, as above, pp. 22 sq., Meadows, pp. 335 sq., and   McClatchie in *Journal of As. Soc.* (1856), XVI. 433.

on the 'dragon-throne,' as it is called, he is the main-spring of the whole machinery, whether his empire be regarded as a civil or religious institution. The laws indeed distinguish very clearly between the private and official status of the emperors; for as individuals they enjoy a privilege, granted also, with conditions, to their subjects, of choosing for them-selves a second or subordinate creed, and emperors have at different times made very different choices.[1] But as every father of a Chinese family is constrained to recognise the state-religion by some special acts of homage, so the emperor himself, officially con-sidered, must be always 'orthodox,' devoted to the maintenance of the sacred books, as well as to the vindication of all ancient usages. These jointly form the rule according to which the various functions of the government must be directed; and so long as any emperor abstains from innovations in perform-ing his public duties, he is honoured as the 'Son of Heaven,' the source and champion of established order, the exponent of mysterious principles which underlie the course of nature, and the organ of some powerful but impersonal energy that lingers round about us and above us. Heaven itself is present in him: he becomes in virtue of that presence a celestial potentate, not only the great chieftain of the Middle Kingdom, but a pattern of ideal excellence for every member of the human family.

---

[1] Thus, at the present day, the emperor as a private person ad-heres to Buddhism, which (so to speak) had mounted the imperial throne of China, as far back as the Ming dynasty: while under the Sung monarchs, the Tao-ists were equally in the ascendant. See an interesting article on Chinese institutions in the *Nou-veau Journal Asiatique* (1854) IV. 292 sq.

It should also be observed that ever since the patriarchal times of Yu,[1] the emperor has been invested with a twofold character. He is king and also priest of China: standing in the latter capacity at the head of a peculiar cultus, and declaring of himself in that relation, 'I am one man,' *i. e.* the only being of my kind.[2] As such he only has the privilege of uttering some hereditary form of prayer, and offering a more costly and more potent sacrifice than any other mortal.[3] The large group of mandarins, who form his agents in the task of government, have also, it is true, been each invested with a quasi-sacerdotal power; yet the objects whom they have the right to worship are esteemed of lower dignity,—as genii of the soil, the streams, the mountains; or malignant demons, haunting this or that locality; or elements and atmospheric agencies regarded in their nudest form, of wind, of drought, of rain, of lightning or of tempest. Accessories of the mandarinic worship also correspond to this idea of fundamental subordination and derived authority. The emperor, for example, sacrifices at the seat of government in temples which have been devoted to that special use: the mandarins officiate, on the contrary, in the provincial temples. The emperor is attired in sacerdotal vestments of peculiar hue and texture, and embroidered with numerous symbols of the sun, the moon, the planets, to betoken his exalted

---

[1] Gutzlaff, i. 142, 143.

[2] See Mr. S. C. Malan's recent volume entitled *Who is God in China?* pp. 186, 187.

[3] 'L'empereur a le droit de sacrifier au Ciel et à la Terre: les seigneurs sacrifient aux dieux tutélaires de l'empire,' &c.' *Li-ki,* ed. Callery, p. 16. It also would appear as though fresh solemnity were given to the imperial sacrifice by offering on some occasions *in the open country. Ibid.* pp. 47, 60, 62, 119.

mission as the Heaven-born pontiff; while the mandarins in acts of public worship still preserve their ordinary dress. To sacrifice aright it is contended that the emperor must undergo a special course of training: he must fast on three consecutive days; he must abstain from every kind of sensual gratification, and in order, as it seems, to check the least intrusion of a secular spirit, he must during those days take no part in the administration of public justice. On the contrary, the mandarins are bound by no such stringent regulations: they appear to act as civil rather than as sacerdotal functionaries. The disparity again is noticeable in the different kinds of sacrifices they are authorised to offer. When the emperor once a year, or in some grand emergency, comes forth to sacrifice, the victim chosen is a goodly ox, and not this merely, but an ox submitted to a searching process of purification,[1] with the view, it is believed, of marking more distinctly the exalted nature of the rite and the superior dignity of the object in whose honour it is consumed: while in the various branches of the mandarinic cultus, incense and libations are the common offerings, or if otherwise, anxiety is seldom felt to offer up the costliest victim of its kind.

Want of moral sensibility in the established worship.

Yet even where the rites of China are most solemn and most obviously religious in their purport, it is difficult to trace in them a particle of zeal or fervour, least of all the consciousness of personal demerit.[2]

---

[1] 'Il est assez curieux' says M. Callery (*Li-ki*, p. 63, n. 2) 'que les anciens Chinois aient admis, dans cette circonstance, la nécessité d'une purification, eux qui n'ont jamais attaché à rien aucune de ces idées *de souillure légale si communes chez les peuples sémitiques et chez les Hindous.*'

[2] 'In China trennt keine Sün-

The heart-broken ejaculations of the Hebrew penitent, gazing through his tears on symbols of the temple-worship which announce the unapproachable holiness of God and whisper also of His love and placability; the spectral gloom of the ascetic, pining year by year beneath the shadow of some Indian fig-tree, in the hope of torturing out the remnant of his earthly passions, and so hastening the hour of ultimate re-absorption;—these are things entirely foreign to the cold and callous nature of the Chinese. Whenever their great model, the imperial pontiff, offers up the yearly sacrifice to Heaven, it savours less of awe and ador-ation than of pride and self-complacency: it pub-lishes the fact that harmony continues to subsist as heretofore between celestial and terrestrial powers: it certifies the oneness of the emperor in act and interest with the unseen spirit which pervades the universe and is directing all the fortunes of the Middle King-dom. An exception to this general statement does *The em-* exist, however: for, on one or more occasions in *peror a* *penitent.* the lifetime of an emperor, we see him driven to adopt the lowly posture of the suppliant, and offer a more genuine sacrifice to Heaven. An army of barbarians, for example, hover on the frontiers; or an earthquake threatens to engulf some fertile dis-trict; or a pestilence is raging in the capital; or famine rouses and inflames the angry passions of the populace; rivers overflow their margin, crops are blasted, heaven and earth appear at enmity; or,

denschuld die Menschheit von Gott; das menschliche Geschlecht ist nur in vereinzelten Erschein-ungen abgewichen; und der Mensch ist ja seinem Wesen nach mit Gott eins, hat kein selbststan-diges Dasein Gott gegenüber, ist noch nicht wahrhaft persönlicher Geist, der als solcher auch sündi-gend von Gott sich lösen könnte.' —Wuttke, II. 63.

worst of all, some brilliant comet, the precursor of dynastic changes, sheds a baleful light across the firmament. Excited and dismayed by these portentous incidents, the ruler of the Middle Kingdom seems to hesitate for once respecting the validity of his claim to be entitled 'Son of Heaven:' he fears lest, owing to some former negligence or present incapacity, his high commission is about to be withdrawn.[1] The only refuge open to him is in bowing to the terrible scourge by which he is chastised: 'he humbles himself before Heaven and his subjects, by publishing those self-accusatory and repentant documents, which Europeans peruse with surprise and ridicule, but which are wrung from his pride by his fears, and are earnest, trembling efforts to avert the execution of Divine justice.'[2]

Worship of Earth as well as Heaven. But the sacrifices offered up to Heaven were not the only rites, in which the Chinese emperor was seen invested with pontifical authority. A second temple where he had been long accustomed to officiate was dedicated in honour of the Earth, the great correlative divinity of ancient China. Hope, and joy, and gratitude, were periodically awakened in all quarters by the contemplation of the genial processes of nature. 'Earth,' men felt, 'is bearing in her lap whatever is found needful to our life: as Heaven suspends the luminaries overhead. From Earth we gather riches; to Heaven we look for good examples. It is fitting therefore to evince respect for Heaven, and pay a tribute of gratitude to Earth.'[3] In other words, as we shall see hereafter, the Chinese have

---

[1] Meadows, p. 18. De Guignes, pp. 141, 142.
[2] *Ibid.* p. 19 : cf. *Chou-king*, ed. [3] *Li-ki*, Ch. x. ed. Callery, p. 16.

learned to worship two great Powers or Principles,
the former ruling in the active and paternal province
of creation, the second in the passive and maternal;
and thus constituting, in popular phraseology, the
Father and the Mother of all things.

Passing by the manifold objects of religious wor- *Practical*
ship which originated in the non-official creeds of *polytheism.*
China, we discover that Confucianists have also been
accustomed from very early times to offer prayers
and sacrifices to a multitude of minor deities. The
parent-gods, or Heaven and Earth, were, so to speak,
resolved into their various elements, in such a manner
that the populace, who felt no inclination to adore
them as a whole, might choose some favourite aspect
or some special energy of nature, and so concentrate
on it the principal share of their devotion.

In this pantheon it would seem as though the *Worship of*
highest place, in theory at least, had been allotted to *genii and*
demons.
a class of spiritual or quasi-spiritual intelligences,
like the genii and the demons of other heathen
systems : but the period when such modes of worship
took their rise it is impossible to determine. The
Shoo-king, as edited by Confucius, is not wanting in
examples where the early emperors[1] of China sacrificed to spirits of the hills, and rivers, as well as to
the shining host of heaven;—thus intimating that
the usage may have been a remnant of the old
' Turánian' creed which lingers still as devil-worship,
under many of its most appalling aspects, on the
plains of upper Asia and apparently among a handful
of the Chinese mountaineers. So deeply rooted was it

---

[1] Gfrörer, pp. 277 sq. Gutzlaff, I. 134.

CHAP. I.

in the heart of the people that Confucius was unable, or unwilling, to dislodge it.[1]

Hero-wor-ship.

But popular as every kind of spirit-worship is in China, she is even more addicted to the worship of departed men. This superstition forms a very prominent article in the creed of the Confucianist. Originally suggested by the feelings of respect, of admiration and of gratitude, it issued in the deification of each man who had stood foremost in promoting the diffusion of some useful art, or who communicated some extraordinary impulse to the intellect of China

Confucius an object of worship.

by the fruitful produce of his pen. Confucius was himself an instance of the latter kind of deification. 'His fame,' writes one of his devoted followers,[2] 'overflowed all China like a deluge, and extended to the barbarians. Wherever ships or carriages reach, wherever human strength penetrates, wherever the heavens cover and the earth sustains, wherever the sun and moon shed their light, wherever frost or dew falls, wherever there is blood and breath, there were none who did not approach and honour him: therefore, he is equal to Heaven:' *i. e.* co-ordinate and on a level with the very loftiest form of being. The whole empire is at present dotted over with temples sacred to the memory of Confucius, and a very large number of animal sacrifices (more than sixty thousand) are provided annually by the government for immolation to his manes, in addition to the multi-

---

[1] Medhurst's *China*, pp. 193, 194, Lond. 1857: "When one of his disciples asked him how he was to serve spiritual beings, he replied: 'Not being able to serve men, how can you serve spirits?'" In other words he chose to speak exclusively on different subjects.

[2] *Ibid.* p. 192. Dr. Medhurst adds: 'Thus have these atheistical people deified the man who taught them that matter was eternal, and that all existences originated in a mere principle.'

tudinous offerings brought by earnest individuals.
Similar feelings are betrayed in the devotions which *Worship of*
the more accomplished China-man perpetually ad- *Kwan-yu.*
dresses to Kwan-yu, the model of fidelity, of courage, *and others.*
and of magnanimity: and every age contributes a
fresh stock of inmates to the crowded pantheon,[1] or
displaces this or that divinity whose worship had
been general in the age preceding.

Another feature of Chinese mythology, if such it *Goddess-*
can be called, is the comparative absence from it of *worship.*
licentious stories and revolting rites, like those already noticed[2] in the old religion of Phœnicia, and
in fact pervading, more or less, all other dualistic
creeds. The goddess-worship of *modern* China (for
to this alone our evidence refers) has mainly found
expression either in the deification of chaste wives
or else in that of virgins. It is stated[3] even that

---

[1] See *Li-ki,* ed. Callery, p. 114.
A very remarkable instance, shewing that this kind of apotheosis
still goes on among them, will be
found in the native *History of the
Chinese Pirates,* translated by
Neumann. We there read (pp.
43, 44) of a brave man, Shaou-
yuen, who was killed A.D. 1809,
while engaged in defending the
citadel of Lan-shih : 'The villagers
were greatly moved by his excellent behaviour; they erected
him a temple, and said prayers
before his effigy. It was then
known what he meant [when he
said] that he should be glorified
in the course of the year. Now
that twenty years are passed,
they even honour him by exhibiting fireworks.'

[2] Vol. I. pp. 97, 98.

[3] The French writer in *Nou-
veau Journal Asiatique,* as above,

p. 295, is of opinion that this
worship of the virgin, Kwan-yin,
is more popular than any other.
A mysterious reverence attaches
to her name, and she is said to be
the tutelary goddess of women.
Her 'nativity' and 'assumption'
are both celebrated. Gutzlaff (in
the *Journal of the Asiatic Society,*
XVI. 79, 80) distinguishes between
Kwan-yin, the goddess of mercy,
who is thought to be of Hindú
origin, and Ma-tsoo-poo, 'the
holy Mother,' of Chinese origin.
The worship of the latter was introduced, he writes, 'some centuries ago. She is so strikingly
akin, in her whole character and
figure, to the Virgin [of the
Roman-catholic Church], that the
Chinese at Macao call her *Santa
Maria de China.* The sailors
make her especially an object of
adoration; and there are very

CHAP. I.   the worship of one particular virgin, who is made the tutelary goddess both of women and of sailors, is the dominant superstition into which the heathenism of China is subsiding at the present day. How far such modification of religious thought may be connected with some slender knowledge of the Roman-catholic version of Christianity, I do not pause to determine.

Worship of ancestors :   But the phase of creature-worship, which from very ancient times has constituted the special characteristic of heathenism in China, is the worship of departed ancestors. According, it would seem, with those ideas of clanship and those strong domestic instincts which have ever operated with peculiar force upon the spirit of the China-man, the custom of preserving some memorial of his forefathers grew at last into the custom of paying them religious honours. It was felt that 'as all created beings owe their origin to Heaven,' which is accordingly an object of the deepest veneration, 'so man owes his existence to his ancestors,' and ought to give them worship for this reason.[1] To restore and justify the practice, *its universality :* which had previously been falling to decay, was one of the earliest reformations[2] attempted by Confucius : and at present it has been so universally recognised in China, by the learned and unlearned, by adherents of the state-religion and of non-official creeds,[3] that

few junks that have not an image of her on board. She is also accompanied by very dismal satellites, the executors of her behests.'

[1] *Journal Asiatique,* as above, p. 298.

[2] Pauthier, *Chine,* p. 127. The same practice, we may have occa-sion to remark hereafter, is also found in records of ancient Egypt.

[3] 'The Buddhists have taken advantage of this prevailing sentiment, and have grounded on it a variety of superstitious services.' —Medhurst, p. 212.

we may point to it as to a common principle which
more than any other penetrates the moral life of all
Chinese society. 'Building a tomb in the form
of a horse-shoe, they inscribe thereon the name of
the deceased, erect a tablet to his memory in the hall
of his ancestors, and repair annually to the graves, in
order to prostrate themselves before the manes and to
offer victuals to those hungry spirits.'[1] The precise *its mean-*
intention of the sacrificer has been differently estimated *ing.*
by different writers. All agree, however, that no
reference is made by him to moral guilt or to the re-
instatement of departed souls in a position of primeval innocence. On the contrary, they are addressed
as beings capable of giving aid and counsel to the
meritorious of their progeny, and also of inflicting
vengeance on the fallen and unworthy.[2] To their
own they occupy the place and wield the high prerogatives of the Supreme Being. The vulgar seem,
indeed, to fancy that the appetite of the deceased
is really gratified by feeding on the subtler portions
of the food presented at his grave; and notions *Sacrificial*
equally absurd appear, in later times at least, to be *paper.*
profusely indicated by the offering of a species of
gilt-paper, covered with figures of houses and utensils,
which becomes, on passing through the fire, available
as the currency of the unseen world.[3] But other and

---

[1] Gutzlaff, 1. 60, 61. On the ancient ceremonial, see the *Li-ki,* ed. Callery, p. 42.

[2] *Chou-king,* ed. De Guignes, pp. 116, 179. At other times, however, nothing is said of their immortality and present influ-ence: they are commemorated or deplored as beings altogether of the past.

[3] *e. g.* Medhurst, pp. 213, 214, who adds: 'Besides transmitting money to the distressed and indi-gent spirits, the Chinese think it necessary to provide their ghostly friends with clothes, and other articles, adapted for their use in the shades below. With this view, they cause coats and gar-ments to be delineated on paper,

more philosophic minds have uniformly repudiated this debased interpretation of their ancient customs. For example in the *Le-ke,* or authorised ritual of Confucianism, it is declared that the oblations to the manes should be understood *symbolically,* as meaning, 'That we ought to keep the dead before our eyes, and honour them as if they were still living.'[1] On earth the father and mother were revered by all the members of their family, who saw in them an image of the two divine Principles in nature; and similarly on their removal hence they were regarded as the chosen deputies and ministers of Heaven, as watching with affectionate interest all the varied fortunes of their progeny, and urging them along the beaten road of duty to a higher and a happier stage of being. These relations with the world invisible were not unnaturally held to be most real in the case of the emperor himself, who as the Son of Heaven and father of his people had become an object of especial favour and solicitude to all his royal predecessors; yet the humblest China-man believes, and has believed from ages out of memory, that his welfare both in this world and the next is made to hinge

which pass through the fire, as certainly and as regularly as the paper-money, into the abodes of spirits.'

[1] *Li-ki*, ed. Callery, p. 121. Wuttke (II. 65, 66) has the following remarks on the rationale of this strange custom of offering gold and silver paper: 'Falsch ist es, dass diese Sitte an die Stelle früherer Menschenopfer getreten wäre, oder dass man den Seelen der Gestorbenen durch das Verbrennen die auf dem Papier gezeichneten Dinge zum Gebrauch im Jenseits verschaffen wolle, wenn auch zur Zeit der Mongolen, welche den Todten Menschen und Thiere nachsandten, solche für das chinesische Bewusstsein ungereimte Dinge vorgekommen sein mögen. . . . . .Das Gold- und Silber-papier mit seinen Bildern bedeutet dann den Reichthum, und das Verbrennen des Papiers ist dann freilich *die verdünnteste und abgeflachteste Weise des Opfers,* welche ein prosaisches, den Besitz leidenschaftlich liebendes Volk ersinnen kann.'

almost entirely on the due discharge of filial obliga- tions, and the offering up of periodic sacrifices to the manes of his ancestors.

From this account of the external aspects of Con- fucianism as a religious system, I pass forward to a more minute investigation of the primary article of faith and of ideas which had been silently moulding the established forms of worship. Ever since the western missionaries came in contact with the literati of the Middle Kingdom, two important questions have been agitated in reference to these subjects. It was asked, in the first place, Do Confucianists believe in the existence of a Supreme Being? and, secondly, What words or phrases in the Chinese language form an adequate rendering of the 'God' of Christianity? Upon the latter question,[1] though hardly separable

Confucian idea of God.

Difficulties of the ques- tion.

---

[1] The principal word selected by the early Roman-catholic mission- aries as equivalent to אֱלֹהִים and Θεός, was the Chinese *Teen*, which means, however, nothing more than 'Heaven,' the visib'e and invisible 'Heaven,' as construed in its broad indefinite sense. To give a greater personality to the idea intended by it, the word *Choo* (= 'Lord') was subsequently added by authority of the Inqui- sition; and the phrase 'Teen- Choo,' 'Heavenly Lord,' or 'Lord of Heaven,' became the recognised appellative of God for all Romish converts in the empire. Among the Chinese missionaries of other communions who rejected *Teen*, the general practice was to render the biblical name of God either (1) by *Shin*, or (2) by *Shang-te*, both of which have found a num- ber of determined advocates, es- pecially since the missionary con- ference held at Shanghae, in 1847.

It is contended on the one side that *Shin* is not a faithful render- ing of Θεός, because it is really a collective noun, is never used with a numerical affix, and there- fore cannot possibly mean *one* Shin. (See Mr. S. C. Malan's re- cent volume, entitled *Who is God in China?* He pleads earnestly and learnedly in favour of the phrase *Shang-te*.) On the other hand it is maintained with equal earnestness that *Shang-te* is an ethereal ψυχὴ κόσμου, 'not a per- sonal Being distinct from matter;' and warnings are accordingly held out to the effect that by sanction- ing the worship of *Shang-te*, we should be virtually dethroning the Great Self-existent Spirit, whom the Hebrew and Christian have equally worshipped under the adorable name Jehovah. (See, for instance, Mr. McClatchie's paper on *Chinese Theology*, in the *Journal of the Asiatic Society*,

from the first, I shall decline to enter; feeling that the only persons who can claim to speak about it with any semblance of authority are those who have acquired a competent knowledge of Chinese. It is somewhat different with regard to the more general subject of enquiry, 'Are the governing class of China atheistic?' for the right solution of that problem is derivable not so much from the discussion of particular terms, as from the main complexion of her history and sacred literature. Yet rich as the materials are for such investigation, and accessible as they have now become to ordinary scholars, the difficulties experienced in turning them to good account are of no common magnitude. The ardour of the Christian missionary, who in this case as in others proved himself the pioneer of art and science and philosophy as well as of the Gospel, not unfrequently propelled him into serious errors and exaggerations; and owing to the way in which he has misread the monuments of eastern paganism and overcoloured both its truths and untruths, the first duty of dispassionate students is to subject his reports to close and rigorous criticism, by going back, wherever it is possible, to the original authorities.

Reports of Jesuit missionaries. When Ricci headed the first regular mission of the Jesuits in China, opening his great campaign at Nanking in 1590, it became a leading feature of his project to disarm the opposition of the governing class[1] by making common cause with them against

---

XVI. 427 sq.) As far as I can judge, the verbal controversy is at last resolvable into a question of metaphysics, 'Have the Chinese any conception of a pure spirit, or of incorporeality in the Christian sense?'

[1] 'Il était en quelque sorte de mode d'être son partisan et son apologiste. Les lettrés en parti-

the popular forms of misbelief. To justify this questionable measure, and so facilitate the arduous work of the evangelist, he uniformly pleaded that Confucius was the brightest luminary of the ancient world,— a genuine philosopher, whose tenets harmonised in almost every point with those transmitted in the sacred family from antediluvian times, and consequently that the Gospel, so far from advocating any kind of novelty, was in substance a revival of the primitive faith of China. The missionary at the same time ventured to take part in sacrifices offered to Confucius, on the ground that honours thus awarded to the great philosopher of China were all purely civil.[1] It was felt indeed by Ricci, as by many of his coadjutors, that a meeting-place might be established between the Gospel and the authorised religion of the Middle Kingdom by laying stress upon the doctrine of one infinite, all-embracing Spirit,[2] whom

some ascribing theistic priniciples,

---

culier n'hésitèrent pas à se déclarer pour lui, parce que, dans ses discours, il attaquait avec un succès complet les doctrines des bonzes [*i.e.* of the Buddhist monks] et des docteurs de la Raison (Tao-Sse), et que, d'autre part, il professait toujours un profond respect et une grande admiration pour les enseignements de Confucius. Le docteur européen était à leurs yeux un vrai membre de la corporation des lettrés, un Confucéen un partisan de leur doctrine, un ennemi des superstitions des bouddhistes et des rêveries des sectateurs de Lao-Tze:' Huc, *Le Christianisme en Chine,* &c. II. 154, 155.
[1] *Ibid.* p. 155. Other missionaries of a kindred spirit, and professing the same admiration for

Confucius, travelled about the country in the disguise of watchmakers, astronomers, artists, and engineers.
[2] We are told of Ricci in particular: 'Negabat religionem, quæ unum sine consorte Deum doceret, peregrinam esse. Hanc probabat fuisse a Sinensibus philosophis et eorum principe Confucio traditam, sed obliteratam paulatim temporum vitio.' Hardwick's *History of the Reformation,* p. 443, n. 6. It was even pretended in some quarters that the Christian doctrine of the Holy Trinity had been anticipated by three horizontal lines, made use of in the *kwa* of Fuh-he (above, p. 18), to represent Heaven; or else by the triplication of *Shang-te* into Heaven, Earth, and man.

the China-man appeared to worship as *Teen*, or *Shang-te*. The two great temples at Peking, in which, as we have noticed, the emperor himself was in the habit of sacrificing to Heaven and Earth respectively, were held to be alike the sanctuaries of this one eternal Spirit: the Creator and Conservator of the universe was merely worshipped under different titles.[1]

others athe-istic prin-ciples to the Chinese.

On the contrary it was alleged with equal firmness by a learned member[2] of the same fraternity (the Jesuit Longobardi), that many statements of his predecessors on this subject were devoid of all foundation.

Verdict of modern si-nologues.

According to his view the Chinese literati had never during the historic period worshipped one supreme and spiritual Intelligence,—a God whose being is entirely independent of the visible and sensible universe: and notwithstanding all the fervid eulogies which, half in ignorance and half in malice, have attempted to exalt the 'wisdom' of the Middle Kingdom to equality with that of Palestine, the verdict of Longobardi is continually corroborated by the disquisitions of our modern sinologues. They hold that, theoretically at least, the followers of the Chinese state-religion are all atheists to a man.[3]

---

[1] See *Nouveau Journal Asiatique* (1854), tome IV. p. 300.

[2] His essay, first printed at Madrid in 1676, was translated into French, in 1701, with the title *Traité sur quelques points de la religion des Chinois*, par le R. Père Longobardi.

[3] See, for instance, Meadows, p. 361. Prof. Neumann, whose opinion as a very accomplished Chinese scholar is peculiarly valuable, had already expressed himself with even greater emphasis: 'Nie und nimmermehr ist dem Chinesischen Volke ein Gott erschienen; von einer Offenbarung ist keine Spur bei dieser prosaischen Nation. Die Wörter *Gott, Seele, Geist*, als etwas von der Materie ganz Unabhängiges und sie willkürlich Beherrschendes, *kennt die Chinesische Sprache gar nicht*. Ein einziges Band umschlingt, nach den Ansichten der Weisen dieses Landes, alles Seyende, das Reich der Natur und das Reich des Geistes; der Bruch, die Störung der angemessenen Thätigkeit eines Gliedes bringt

However much the instincts of their moral nature must rebel against this blank and desolating creed; however much they are impelled when bending under some disastrous visitation to take refuge in the thought of a superior *Teen*, or ' Heaven,' and recognise in him the attributes of justice and of mercy, of father-hood and special providence, the highest efforts of their reasoning faculties all stop at the conception of an ' unintelligent and will-less principle,' from which the universe, its laws and its inhabitants have been eternally projected or evolved.

How long these modes of thought and feeling *Was the* have been prevalent in China; whether as one class *oldest creed of China* of writers are disposed to argue they may be regarded *theistic?* as the earliest product of a national mind absorbed entirely in the love of pelf, or whether they resulted gradually from the adoption by the learned orders of a system of philosophy akin to that which we entitle ' naturalism,' it is not easy to determine. In the *Shoo-king*, which Confucius (we have seen) remodelled out of older documents, allusion is made as many as eight-and-thirty times[1] to some great Power or Being, called *Shang-te*. The name itself imports ' august'

Unordnung in die ganze Kette des Seyenden. Die geistigen und moralischen Kräfte gebieten aber den physischen; wer Tugend und Sitte beleidigt, stört die glück-liche Ordnung der Elemente, er bringt Unheil über die Gesell-schaft und ist ihr deshalb verant-wortlich. *So innig ist dieser Ideengang mit der Sprache selbst verwachsen, dass es unmöglich ist, den ersten Vers der Genesis ohne weitläuftige Umschreibung ins Chinesische so zu übersetzen, dass er wirklich Chinesisch ist.* Denn

hoa, das Wort für *schaffen*, be-deutet eigentlich auf eine spontane, unbewusste Weise vom Nichtseyn zum Seyn übergehen; und *tsáo*, welches in der Bibelübersetzung von D. Morrison vorkommt, wird von den Chinesen bloss in der Bedeutung von anders machen aus einem Etwas, nie aber in dem Sinne von *schaffen*, dem *Machen aus einem Nichts*, gebraucht:' *Naturphilosophie der Chinesen*, as before, pp. 11, 12.
[1] Malan, *Who is God in China?* p. 167.

or 'sovereign Ruler.' As there depicted he possesses a high measure of intelligence, and exercises some degree of moral government: he punishes the evil, he rewards the good. To him especially is offered the sacrifice *Loüe;* while other ceremonies are performed in honour of 'the six Tsong, the mountains, the rivers, and the spirits generally."[1] These beings of inferior rank appear to constitute the court, or retinue, of the celestial Ruler; and elsewhere he is attended by 'five heavenly chiefs, members also of his council, who are set over the presidents of heaven, of the earth, and of the sea. These, in turn, range in the world of *shin* (or spirits of the air), of *kwei* (souls of the deceased), and *ke* (spirits of, or from below, the earth).'[2] It is again expressly stated in the *Shoo-king*, and perhaps with reference also to the nature of *Shang-te:* 'Heaven is supremely intelligent: the perfect man imitates him (or it): the ministers obey him (or it) with respect: the people follow the orders of the government.'[3] And, finally, it is enjoined[4] by fresh authorities that, on these sacred

[1] *Le Chou-king*, ed. De Guignes, pp. 13, 14. The editor is unable to determine accurately what is meant by the six *Tsong* (= 'worthy of respect'). They seem to be different kinds of spirits. As for the sacrifice *Loüe*, it is explained by Choo-he (in Neumann, as above, p. 64) to mean the sacrifice of the inexorable death, 'because Heaven and Earth feel no pity.'

[2] Malan, as before, p. 166. On the *five* chiefs here alluded to, as relieving *Shang-te* in his administration of the world, see the *Notice de I'y-king*, appended to the *Chou-king*, as before, p. 432.

May they not correspond to the *fire* planets of ancient China? See above, p. 13, n. 1.

[3] *Le Chou-king*, pp. 124, 125. One of the native commentators there cited (n. 3) says that 'Heaven is simple, intelligent, just, spiritual, and all-seeing.' And another adds: "To be able to chastise the bad, to recompense the good, to be truth itself, to be a spirit incomprehensible, immutable, permanent, just, devoid of passion,—all this is contained in the two Chinese characters (*Tsong-ming*), which in this passage signify 'supremely intelligent.'"

[4] *Le-ke*, ch. vi. (quoted by Mr.

grounds, the 'people shall not hesitate to contribute with all their power to the worship of the sovereign Lord of Heaven, *Shang-te*, to that of celebrated mountains, great rivers, and of the *shin* of the four quarters.'

On the other hand, a second class of writers have *Or were the oldest Chinese worshippers of Nature?* contended, that in the very oldest products of the Chinese mind no proper personality has ever been ascribed to this supreme and all-embracing Power. Heaven is *called* the Father of the Universe, but only in the same way as Earth is called the Mother.[1] Both of them are said to live, to generate, to quicken: yet neither to have life inherent in itself. They both are made the objects of solemn prayers and sacrifices. Both may also be described as 'spiritual'; yet only in so far as spirits[2] of which they are in some sort the aggregate expression are diffused in every form of animated nature. 'Heaven' is in particular (these writers argue) a personification of the ever-present Law, and Order, and Intelligence, which seem to breathe amid the wonderful activities of physical creation, in the measured circuit of the seasons, in the alternation of light and darkness, in the ebb and flow of tides, in the harmonious and majestic revolutions of the planetary bodies. 'Heaven,' in other words, so far from being personal, or spiritual,

Malan, p. 185). Mention is also made of sacrifices to ancestors and to the tutelary gods of the empire (p. 28, ed. Callery).

[1] *Le Chou-king*, p. 151. '*Heaven*, therefore, has no higher meaning than *Nature*.' Hegel, *Phil. of Hist.* p. 138.

[2] 'Wenn man sagt: Himmel und Erde haben keinen Geist, so heisst diess so viel: Himmel und Erde *haben nur in so weit* Geist, als daraus die vier Jahreszeiten und alle Dinge hervorgehen.' Tschu-hi (Choo-he), translated by Neumann, as before, p. 61. The whole of the dialogue on 'Heaven and Earth' is well worth perusal.

or self-conscious, is a blind necessity inherent in all forms of life, a Law and not a Legislator, a Power without volition, and a Guide without intelligence.[1] Nay, many of these writers have gone so far as to contend that *Shang-te* himself, of whom the highest and most god-like qualities are predicable, is really no more than a great 'Anima mundi,'[2] energising everywhere in all the processes of nature, and binding all the parts together in one mighty organism, exactly as the soul of man pervades and animates the body : and in accordance with this notion they remind us how the *Le-ke*[3] had decided, that 'if we speak of all the *shin* (or spirits) collectively, we call them *Shang-te.*'

Most probable solution. After threading my way as far as possible among this tangled, and in many points conflicting, evidence, I am led to the conclusion that in China as elsewhere had lingered from primeval ages the conception of one living, bounteous, and paternal providence, whose earthly shadow[4] was believed to sit exalted far above his fellows on the throne of the Middle Kingdom ; but that ultimately this conception was broken and obscured, until the unity of God no longer formed the basis of the Chinese creed. Philosophy then came forward as in other countries, and attempted

---

[1] Thus in the *Hi-tse* ascribed to Confucius (IV. 4, appended to *Yih-king*, ed. Mohl) the author avows that while the sages act freely, it is different with the primary elements of the universe, the male and female principles in nature, or, in other words, the Godhead of ancient China. The action of these results from forces inherent in their very being.

[2] See the passages collected by Mr. McClatchie, as before, pp. 390 sq.

[3] *Ibid.* p. 401.

[4] *Le Chou-king*, p. 151: 'Le Ciel a établi un Roi pour conserver les peuples et pour les instruire. Ce Roi est le Ministre du Souverain Seigneur (Chang-ti), pour gouverner paisiblement et avec douceur l'Empire.'

to recover the idea of unity. 'Heaven' was made by the more thoughtful of philosophers a verbal representative of all the energies in nature: all were *said* to flow originally from it, as from the common source of life, and common principle of order: all were *said* to have been recapitulated and embraced in it as in the animating soul and ruling spirit of the universe: while, in the worship of the many, ' Heaven' was ordinarily confounded with the firmament itself, the blue ethereal canopy above our heads, the shining and the burning heavens.[1]

But whatever may be thought of the preceding summary, no one will deny that the absence of distinct allusion in the writings of Confucius to a God at all resembling the God of Christianity is very strange and startling. The few scanty notices which they afford are barely recognitions of some powerful and indefinite Heaven (*Teen*),—a cold abstraction of the logical faculty, whom the philosopher does not dream of clothing with moral and spiritual attributes, or of propounding as an object of man's love and adoration. He seems, in fact, to have been wavering more than once respecting the existence of this great abstraction ; for when questioned on the subject by his followers, he either evaded the inquiry

General scope of Confucian ethics and politics.

---

[1] "'Whom do you worship?' I asked. "I worship Heaven just as you foreigners do," he replied. "Who is the Heaven you worship?" "Why, Shang-te, of course," said he. "Can you *see* Shang-te or not?" I inquired. "Why," replied he, looking at me with surprise at my ignorance, and leading me to the door while he pointed up to the sky, "there he is!" "What!" said I, "Do you mean that *blue sky* up there?" "Of course," said he, "That is Shang-te, *the same as your Jesus!*" I have never yet asked the above questions without receiving *precisely the same answers ;* for *all* classes of Confucianists in China consider Shang-te to be the animated material Heaven.' McClatchie, as before, p. 397.

or else reprimanded them for prying into matters unconnected with their duties to society and lying far beyond their depth.[1] To him a personal Deity, the Maker, the Redeemer, and the Sanctifier, was theoretically superfluous. " You find yourself," he argued, " in the midst of a stupendous, yet most orderly piece of mechanism. That mechanism, so far as we can tell, is self-originating, self-sustaining. Change there is, but no creation : all things from eternity existed and were subject to a flux and re-flux, in obedience to initial laws impressed upon them, how and why we know not, by some stern necessity. Be warned and guided by this principle : devote yourself no longer to the fruitless study of theology : it brings, and can bring, with it no prac-tical advantage. Seek not to explore the doctrine of final causes : rather, if you speculate at all, confine your thoughts to the discussion of phenomena and the laws of phenomena. Such alone are useful and legitimate subjects of inquiry. It is possible indeed that laws may be connected somehow with the demons of the air, or else with other forms of spiritual agency : we cannot absolutely say that they are not. You may continue, therefore, on this ground, to follow the established ritual of your ancestors. ' Sacrifice *as if* your sacrifice were a reality : worship *Shin* as if *Shin* were really present.'[2] But meanwhile your chief concern is with the visible and palpable universe,

---

[1] Cf. *Journal Asiatique* (1834), XIV. 57.

[2] See above, p. 37, n. 1 ; and Malan, *Who is God in China ?* p. 14. Abel-Rémusat, *Chung-Yung*, c. XVI. § 3, compares the language of Confucius on these subjects with the corresponding language of Spinosa, of whom he thinks the Chinese a worthy pre-cursor.

and with the homely tasks of life. You constitute one little member in some mighty organism; you stand as part of some great moral order: strive to act on all occasions as such a being should act. Far from pausing to bemoan your weakness or unworthiness, remember that 'he who offends against Heaven has no one to whom he can pray.'[1] The past is gone and is irrevocable. Be more vigilant in time to come. Endeavour so to rule yourself, according to the sacred maxims, that you may be fitted first to rule a family, and lastly may attain the highest point of your ambition,—an office under government. To practical men the theatre of this present life gives ample scope for enterprise: it teems with stern realities and all-engrossing cares: perhaps,[2] too, it may prove your last, your sole possession. Be thoughtful, therefore, be industrious: make the most of what you have: be modest, sober, grave, decorous; cultivate the qualities which mark the men of 'the due medium;'[3] more particularly aim at that which forms the crowning excellence of all, be scrupulous in your devotion to the emperor, the Son and representative of Heaven. For is not he in very truth the father of his people? and as filial piety has ever been the source of joy and blessing to the single household, and as reverence for the memory of departed kinsmen is the glory, hope, and safeguard of survivors, so to venerate the emperor of the Middle Kingdom is to

---

[1] Medhurst, p. 186. In another passage, there cited, Confucius declares: 'Imperial Heaven has no kindred to serve, and will only assist virtue.'

[2] See Wuttke's investigation of this article in the Confucian creed, ii. 40 sq.

[3] This is the meaning of *Chung-Yung,* the title of the Confucian treatise on the duties, and transcendent dignity of the 'holy man,' who identifies himself completely with the fixed order of Heaven.

CHAP. I. aid in regulating the whole course of nature; every comfort which you prize or long for is involved in it,—domestic peace and social order and the safety of the commonwealth. And if," Confucius seems to have concluded, "if you wish to place your institutions on the very surest basis, educate the young, diffuse intelligence in every quarter; most of all insist upon the study of that science which surpasses every other, as enabling you to turn all other kinds of knowledge to a practical account,—I mean, the science of political economy."[1]

Chinese philosophy of the Absolute. Vast, however, as the influence of Confucius was in moulding the institutions of his country and imparting that distinctive air of regular animation which pervades the social life of China at the present day, he could not draw men off entirely from the deeper questions touching their connexion with supernatural powers and their relation to the world invisible. The human heart *must* muse and speculate on these momentous questions; for the plodding and prosaic China-man himself was not entirely dead to their importance. What then was the drift of ' orthodox' philosophy in reference to the subjects which Confucius had comparatively disregarded? The answer is furnished in the numerous works of Choo-he,[2] whom

---

[1] ' It is rather extraordinary that political economy constitutes the first science which all Chinese boys are taught.' Gutzlaff, I. 198. It was the wish of Confucius himself that his disciples should all become state officials, and therefore, as in the *Lun-Yu*, ' he confined his instructions to political economy, to which he reduces all the duties of life.' *Ibid.*

p. 196.

[2] My knowledge of his writings is derived chiefly from Prof. Neumann's translations, above cited. I have also profited by the recent work of Mr. T. T. Meadows, who devotes a chapter (ch. XVIII.) to the subject of Chinese philosophy; and also by the paper of Mr. McClatchie, as before cited, on ' Chinese Theology.'

we saw abundant reason for esteeming the approved expositor of Chinese metaphysics and theology. According to the views propounded by him, and in part at least transmitted from preceding ages, there is underlying all phenomena, however mixed and manifold they seem, a fundamental unity, of which the common name is *Tae-keih*, the Absolute, or literally the 'Great Extreme.' Beyond it, as the highest 'pinnacle of heaven,' the one ultimate power, the entity without an opposite, no human thought whatever is capable of soaring. Itself incomprehensible, it 'girdles' the whole frame of nature, animate and inanimate. From it alone as from the fountain-head of being issued every thing that is.[1] 'Creation' is the periodic flowing forth of it. 'The Absolute is like a stem shooting upwards : it is parted into twigs, it puts out leaves and blossoms : forth it springs incessantly, until its fruit is fully ripe : yet even then the power of reproduction never ceases to be latent in it. The vital juice is there ; and so the Absolute still works and works indefinitely. Nothing hinders or can hinder its activity, until the fruits have all been duly ripened, and activity gives place to rest.'[2]

[1] Tschu-hi (Choo-he), as above, pp. 46, 47. In reply to the question 'What is the Absolute ?' it is there answered, (p. 46) : 'Das Absolute ist die höchste, erhabenste, äusserste, grösste Fundamental-Normalurkraft ; alle Menschen sind durch das Absolute und alle Dinge sind durch das Absolute.' In another passage (p. 72) it is said that *Tae-keih* itself springs out of something higher, out of *Wu-keih* 'the Illimitable.'

[2] *Ibid.* p. 50. The following passage (also quoted from Choo-he, by Mr. M'Clatchie, p. 381) forms a good illustration of the Chinese theory respecting a succession of similar worlds : "Being asked, 'From the opening and spreading out (of the world from chaos) to the present time, is not 10,000 years ; how was it *before* that time ?' He (the philosopher) replied, 'Before that there was another (world) similar to the present one.' Being asked, whether Heaven and Earth are capable of being annihilated, he replied 'No,

It is, meanwhile, acknowledged by the great philosophers of China that this thought of one efficient Cause, or rather of one causative power and principle, was quite unable to retain its true ascendancy in opposition to the seeming contradictions of the outer and the inner world. The vision of the soul, the eye of faith, was gradually bedimmed, and hence those higher intuitions which had prompted Hebrew patriarchs to hold communion with the Self-existent, who converts all agencies whatever into means for carrying on His moral government, were lacking in the ordinary China-man. The God whom he adored was rather an ideal being than the living God of nature. ' All things in the world,' says Choo-he,[1] ' seem as to their primary tendencies to issue from the One: the One, however, is not really in a condition to bring them forth;' the meaning of which is probably that while our reason points us back to the hypothesis of unity, our senses are too apt to lead us in a different direction: multiplicity is everywhere apparent and so constitutes for us the law of the phenomenal universe.

In other words, the Chinese speculator found himself impelled to the conclusion that although the proper basis of all life is one, and though such unity may still by some mysterious process form the ultimate

---

but it is my opinion that *when men completely depart from correct principles,* then the whole will become chaos, and men and things will cease to exist, and then there will be a *new commencement.*' "

[1] *Ibid.* p. 71. The question had been asked ' Ist die Einheit Grund (*causa efficiens*) des Lebens?' To which it was replied, quoting

Hong-Khiu: ' Das Eins bleibt. . . immerdar das Fundament, auf dieselbe Weise, wie der Zehner in 100, 1000, und 10,000; das Zwei kann durchaus nicht als dasjenige betrachtet werden, wodurch ein Ding wird; es ist bloss der Grund des Hervortretens.' Choo-he then adds further explanations of his own.

principle of rest and motion, yet duality is the active
visible cause of all advancement, the foundation of
the present order of the world.[1] It thus resulted that
in spite of the idea of abstract unity which lingered
as an echo of some old tradition in the background
of their metaphysical system, the Chinese philosophers
were all addicted to the theory of two principles.
Their ordinary speech was *dualistic.* They rested
on two entities or essences, the one a power or cause,
the other a more passive something where that power
or cause could operate.[2] The former may be styled
the ultimate *immaterial* element of the universe (*Le*);
the second (*Ke*), consisting as it does of matter most
ethereal in its texture, may be styled the ultimate
material element of the universe. *Le* is, therefore,
only another name for *Tae-keih ;* it is the Absolute
regarded in association with material essences, and
manifesting itself in virtue of such association as
the cause of organisation and of order. Both these
elements as to their essence are held to be eternal ;
and so inseparably united that one is necessary to
the true subsistence of the other. 'If there were
no *Ke*, then *Le* would not have any thing to rest
upon.'[3] The predicates of *first* and *second* are in-
applicable to all such cases: but if we must speak
of order and priority, the immaterial element is

---

[1] 'Tschi-hiang sagt : Das Eins
ist der Lebensgrund, so wie es die
Ursache ist der Bewegung und
der Ruhe ; seine Grenze ist deren
Grenze ; das Zwei ist *die Ursache
des Werdens,* so wie der vollen-
deten Bewegung und der darauf
folgenden Ruhe, eben so der vol-
lendeten Ruhe und der darauf folgenden Bewegung.' *Ibid.* p. 72.

[2] Meadows, p. 68.

[3] See this and other extracts in
McClatchie, p. 384. The thought
of necessary interdependence between *Le* and *Ke* had sometimes
led men to speak of the primary
matter as identical with the Absolute : *Ibid.* p. 383.

CHAP. I.   worthy of the foremost place:[1] particularly since this element is the basis of all things viewed abstractedly, as destitute of form and figure; while *Ke*, the primary matter, acts as the substratum on which things endued with form and other qualities all take their stand, or out of which they have been gradually evolved.

Yang *and* Yin.

But *Ke*, again, if duly analysed, is found to be not singular but dual, not simple but compounded. The resolution of this primary matter into its constituent elements[2] gives birth to two opposite essences, to *Yang* and *Yin*, which therefore may be treated as the phases under which the Ultimate Principle[3] of the universe displays itself in the phenomenal world. As early as the *kwa*, or diagrams of Fuh-he, the symbolic mode of representing them was a broken and black line for *Yin*, a white and continuous line for *Yang*. The popular account of this duality, in which it was intended to express the parting asunder of the one chaotic *Ke* and the production of Heaven and Earth, is all the more remarkable, because it reappears not only in the story-books of other Chinese sects,[4] but also, we shall see hereafter, in the ancient mythus of New Zealand. *Yang* and *Yin*, thus gener-

---

[1] Choo-he, as before, pp. 32, 33.

[2] '*In* und *Yang* gehen aus der Urmaterie hervor; sie sind beständig in gegenseitigem Kampfe, und sie müssen immer im Kampfe seyn; daraus entsteht das Gute und das Böse, daraus der Ursprung des Verschiedenen:' *Ibid.* p. 78.

[3] 'Der Ausdruck: das *Absolute* (Tai-Ky), ist gleichbedeutend mit dem Worte *Urkraft* (Ly):' *Ibid.*

p. 42.

[4] *E. g.* of the followers of Taoism, who say that 'after chaos was settled, heaven and earth divided, and human beings were born:' in Medhurst, p. 198. Mr. McClatchie also notices (*Journal of As. Soc.* XVI. 386) the affinity between this representation and that of the Chaldean Bel, who was said to form light and darkness, &c. by *cutting himself in two.*

ated by the 'Great Extreme' of the Chinese theology when separating himself from unformed matter, are called the two *Ke*, and may be represented either by the names of positive and negative essences, or else in a more concrete form, as the paternal and maternal principles of nature. From the constant evolution and interaction of these opposite essences[1] resulted every species of formal matter and the mixed phenomena of the world. According to the different proportions in which *Yang* and *Yin* are blended is the character of every grade of creaturely existence. Every thing is *Yang* and *Yin* together. For the highest actual manifestation in which *Yang* preponderates we look to Heaven itself, which is accordingly to be esteemed the aptest image cognisable by the senses of the ultimate and all-embracing Principle. Earth is, on the contrary, the highest form of *Yin*. The same duality where one or other of the factors operated, either for the purpose of transforming or uniting, issued in the first production of the innate essences, which constitute the Five Elements of water, fire, wood, metal, and earth.[2] 'A transcendental union and coagulation now takes place of the Ultimate Principle, the Two Essences and the Five Elements. The Positive Essence becomes the masculine power, the Negative Essence the feminine power—conceived in which character the former constitutes the Heavenly Mode or Principle, the latter the Earthly Mode or Principle: by a mutual influencing, the two produce all things in the visible,

---

[1] 'It is here,' as Mr. Meadows well remarks, 'that Chinese philosophy slips over the much discussed, hitherto unsolved, and apparently unsolvable question of the existence of matter:' p. 344.

[2] Choo-he, as before, p. 43, pp. 82 sq.

CHAP. I. palpable world; and the double work of evolution and dissolution goes on without end :"[1]—*Yang* evincing its peculiar force in every kind of progress, *Yin* in every kind of retrogression: *Yang* determining commencement, *Yin* completion: *Yang* predominant in spring and summer, and the author of all movement and activity, *Yin* more visible in the autumn and the winter, passive, drooping, and inert.

Confucian theory of man.

These dualistic speculations on the constitution of the universe in general are consistently adopted in the framing of the Chinese theory of man. In popular phrase it was the marriage of Heaven and Earth, the male and female principles in nature, that gave rise to the production of the human species: or in other words, since *Yang* and *Yin* must always coexist as the material ground on which the Ultimate Principle takes effect, they enter into the composition of rational as well as of irrational beings. Man, however, in addition to his physical framework, is endowed with Five qualities or Virtues, corresponding to the Five Elements of the Chinese cosmogony. These constitute his mental and moral nature.[2] They

---

[1] Meadows, p. 345.

[2] They are *Jin, E, Le, Che,* and *Sin,* which are called the Five *Tih,* or Five Virtues: *tih* being a word that, like our English *virtue,* signifies first, qualities or characteristics generally, whether of man or of things; and then, collectively, the best qualities of man, or Virtue as opposed to Vice. In accordance with the dictionaries, *Jin* is usually rendered by *Benevolence* (or Charity in its widest sense); *E,* by Righteousness [Uprightness]; *Le,* by Propriety; *Che,* by Wisdom; and *Sin,* by Sincerity. But sinologues will perceive that as the Five *Tih*

embrace the *whole* of what we consider the better side of man's nature, it is not certain that these five English words are exhausted.' *Ibid.* p. 346.

In the *Li-ki,* ed. Callery, p. 45, the question is stated differently: ' L'homme émane (pour le moral) de la vertu du Ciel et de la Terre; (pour le physique, il émane) de la combinaison des (deux principes) *In* et *Jañ;* (pour la partie spirituelle, il émane) de la réunion des esprits et des dieux; et (pour la forme qui lui est propre, il émane) de l'essence la plus subtile des cinq éléments.'

unite him to the Absolute, the *Le*, from which pro- CHAP. I.
ceeded all ingredients both of rationality and order,
and with which the spirit of man is strictly one and
consubstantial. As the Chinese speculator had evaded
the great problem touching the origin of primary
matter, so he offers no intelligible explanation of
the rise and growth of evil. He affirms indeed that *Denial of*
every man is at his birth in the possession of a *Original Sin.*
nature radically good. Itself an efflux from the source
of Order, it gives proof of this celestial origin by
moving in obedience to the general laws on which
all other things are founded. 'Human nature,' says
a great Confucian authority,[1] 'is good, just as water
has a tendency to flow downwards; men are universally inclined to virtue, just as water invariably
flows downwards.' And the only qualification which
the author offered of this startling language is appended in the following extract : 'Water, by beating,
may be made to splash over your head, and by forc-
ing may be made to pass over a mountain; but who
would ever say that this is the natural tendency of
water? It is because violence is applied to it.
Thus men can be made vicious : but it is by no
means their nature.' Vice, in other words, is in the *Meaning*
system of the China-man a rare and casual deviation *of vice.*
from the path of rectitude, produced by strong solicitations of the outer sensible world, to which the
culprit, for some cause or other, finds himself attracted. And in manifest accordance with this pantheistic principle, evil is there said to punish itself,
or rather it is punished by the necessary operation
of the order which it dares to violate. With sin,

[1] Mencius, quoted in Medhurst, p. 196.

as it involves a painful consciousness of guilt, or
evil in the biblical sense of the expression, we very
seldom meet; for in the Chinese system, evil-workers
are not viewed as persons gifted with moral freedom,
and sin is never represented as ingratitude, or even
as rebellion against a personal and holy God. We
cannot say of evil that it ought not to be; it is a
something that must be. It enters, and must enter,
into a concatenation of causes and effects originating
from eternity: it is the shadow which gives harmony
and contrast to the picture of the universe: it is the
Yin of the moral world, as good is the *Yang*.[1] The
root of both is in the primary material essence.

No idea of regeneration. They are both the necessary modes in which the
Absolute comes forward into being, and conducts his
operations in the region of phenomena. And as
moral guilt is thus unknown to the Confucianist,
so neither does he manifest a wish or craving after
spiritual regeneration. He has no 'word of prophecy
that shineth in a dark place until the day break and
the day-star arise in the heart.' He offers up no
sacrifice for sin, in order to restore relations between
man and God, which are subverted by iniquity. He
lives exclusively within the sphere of nature: his
home is there, and he is wholly satisfied with his
condition and his prospect. He believes in no futurity, excepting, it may be, some reproduction of the
present forms of life and matter. What he worships

[1] Choo-he says expressly, as
before, p. 76: 'Das bewegende
Princip [*Yang*] est das Gute und
das ruhende Princip [*Yin*] est das
Böse, wie diess oft genug die
Vollkommenen und Weisen gesagt
haben; denn aus der aufrecht
stehenden absoluten Urkraft er-
folgen die zwei Entgegengesetzten,
gegenseitig in nothwendiger Beziehung Stehenden, und daraus
erfolgt nun Jegliches, das einem
Jeden Eigenthümliche.'

are the tutelary gods of China, or creation contemplated in its twofold character of Earth and Heaven,
or else, succumbing more completely under the dominion of the seen and tangible, his worship is degraded into hero-worship; he deifies humanity itself.[1]

How many are the points in which Confucian *Antagon-*
tenets are opposed to Christianity it were superfluous *ism to Christian-*
to enumerate. The opposition in respect of doctrines *ity.*
is entire and fundamental. It is the opposition of
nature and of grace, of unregenerate and regenerate
principles, of sight and faith, of earthy and of
heavenly. And how vast will therefore be the revolution in the moral nature of the China-man if he
shall ever learn to practise the unworldly lessons of
the Gospel, or to echo those heroic sentiments which
more than once have been propounded in his hearing
by the ardent and devoted missionary! 'I have had
no home,' exclaimed Capillas to the implacable mandarins, when they consigned him to the executioner in
1647, 'I have had no home but the world, no bed but
the ground, no food but what Providence has sent me
day by day, and no other object but to do and suffer
for the glory of Jesus Christ, and for the eternal
happiness of those who believe in His Name.'[2]

[1] According to Renan (*Études d' Histoire Religieuse*, p. 200, Paris, 1857) the Chinese were of all people the least supernaturalist, which may (he thinks) explain 'the secret of their mediocrity.' It is not unworthy of notice that M. Comte, of whom we are continually reminded in our study of Confucianism, has recently announced a new scheme of man-worship, which he ventures to predict will supersede Christianity, and form a kind of bridge to persons who are passing across the gulf between Theism and Atheism. The title of the tract is *Culte Systématique de l'Humanité*, Paris, 1850. All the benefactors of mankind are to be the objects of this cultus: Moses, Solomon, St. John, St. Paul, Buddha, Confucius, Muhammad; but, strange to say, the name of our blessed Lord does not appear in the catalogue!

[2] See the narrative in Mr. Kesson's work entitled *The Cross and the Dragon*, p. 112.

Contrast between Confucius and Lao-tse.

§ 2. *Tao-ism, or School of the Fixed Way.*

Although the tenets of the governing class appear to have accorded with the calculating and materialistic genius of the Chinese nation, individuals were never wanting in whose spirit the religious sentiment was ineradicably fixed. If the adherents of the state-religion frequently remind us of the sceptical and self-complacent Sadducee, we find existing side by side with them another Chinese sect whose mystic creed and fervid temperament especially resemble those of the Essene. The Chinese spiritualists had learned to recognise a head and champion many years before the origin of the Confucian movement: for Lao-tse, the founder of Tao-ism, seems to have been born as early as 604 B.C., and therefore was already hastening to the close of his career when the reformer of the state-religion entered on his first appointment as inspector of the corn-marts of his native province. Confucius shewed himself at every turn a politician and a sociologist, proceeding, it is true, on strictly moral grounds, yet hoping to recover and cement the unity of China most of all by the assiduous cultivation of political economy and by proficiency in general state-craft. Lao-tse, however, manifested an entirely different bias. He had always been a scholar and recluse, alive to the reality of the world invisible and to the presence of superior powers; of ardent and imaginative temper, subtle, penetrating, spiritual, unambitious; the unwavering preacher of inaction and retirement,[1] and as such exposed to the

[1] The Chinese themselves were not slow in perceiving the real bent of his philosophy. Thus Choo-he, as before, p. 27, declares:

reproach of inculcating apathy and moroseness, and CHAP. I.
of cherishing among his followers a dislike of human
kind, and a contempt for the well-ordering of Chinese
society.   In other words, the genius of Confucianism
was cold and worldly, that of the Tao-ists was more
earnest, soaring, and contemplative : the first inclined
to scepticism, the second to superstition : in the judgment of the former, man is bound to make the most
of the present life, while in the latter the chief aim
was to subdue all earthly appetites, and deepen a
desire for the unfading and immortal.

As we saw already in the case of Śákya-muni, *Superna-*
the oldest narratives[1] respecting Lao-tse agree in re- *tural attri-*
presenting him as a man and a philosopher : exalted, *cribed to*
it is true, but all the while a being subject to the *Lao-tse.*
ordinary conditions of humanity, and therefore such
as men might hope to imitate.   His ignorant disciples
have, however, added large embellishments to the
original story.   Anxious to place their master high

---

[1] 'Die Satzungen des *Lao-tse* zielen
durchaus auf das Leere; auf die
Ruhe und Unthätigkeit.   Die
Aufgabe des Lebens besteht (nach
ihm) in einer tiefen Selbstbe-
schauung.'   And in the 'Notice
Historique,' supplied by M. Stanislas Julien's edition of the *Tao-
te-king*, p. xxi. we have the following native criticism : 'Ceux
qui étudient la doctrine de *Lao-
tseu* la mettent au-dessus de celle
des lettrés ; de leur côté, les
lettrés préfèrent Confucius à *Lao-
tseu*.   Les principes des deux
écoles étant différents, il est impossible qu'elles puissent s'accord-
er entre elles.   Suivant *Lao-tseu*,
si le roi pratique le *nonagir*, le
peuple se convertit ; s'il reste dans

une quiétude absolue, le peuple
se rectifie de lui-même.'
[1] This subject has, for the first
time, been critically discussed by
M. Julien, as above.   Even the
Légende Fabuleuse de Lao-tseu denies (p. xxv) that he was 'a divine
and extraordinary being.'   It adds,
however : 'Dès le moment de sa
naissance, il reçut une pénétration
divine et fut doué d'une intuition
profonde.   La vie dont le ciel
l'anima ne ressemblait point à
celle des hommes ordinaires ; il
était destiné à devenir le maître
et le propagateur du *Tao :* c'est
pourquoi il put être protégé par
les esprits du ciel et commander
à la multitude des immortels.'
(p. xxvii.)

above the rank of mortals, and so gain themselves the power of competing with a host of foreign emissaries, who deified the founder of the Buddhist system, the Tao-ists had begun as early as the fourth century of the Christian era to assert for Lao-tse a supernatural origin. They celebrated the stupendous marvels of his birth:[1] they worshipped him as later Bráhmans worshipped the mysterious Krishña, on the ground that he was one of many *avatáras*, the 'exalted, precious, and most venerable Prince,' identical with him, who under different aspects is the 'incomprehensible Non-being.' 'Lao-tse inhabited,' according to a popular legend, 'the abode of matchless purity; he was, in other words, the great progenitor of the subtle and primordial elements (of creation): he was the basis of the earth and of the shining heaven. Before the dawn of the great be-

---

[1] 'Quelques auteurs disent que *Lao-tseu* est né avant le ciel et la terre; suivant d'autres, il possédait une âme pure émanée du ciel. Il appartient à la classe des esprits et des dieux. Certains écrivains racontent que sa mère ne le mit au monde qu'après l'avoir porté dans son sein pendant soixante et douze ans [others say, 81 years]. Il sortit par *le côté gauche de sa mère.* En naissant il avait la tête blanche (les cheveux blancs): c'est pourquoi on l'appela *Lao-tseu*(l'enfant-vieillard). Quelques autres disent que sa mère l'avait conçu sans le secours d'un époux.'.... *Légende Fabuleuse*, as above, p. xxiii. This legend is extracted by M. Julien from a Chinese 'History of the gods and the immortals,' by Ko-hong, who wrote about A.D. 350. It is most remarkable that the same story is in substance told of Śákya-muni by his later followers. St. Jerome, and after him Ratramnus, mention the story as current in their day (cf. Lassen, *Ind. Altert.* III. 370, 406, 411), and as early as the *Lalita Vistara* (assigned by M. Foucaux and Prof. Wilson to about 150 B.C.), Śákya-muni is said to have been miraculously born *from the side* of his mother, Máyá, who died seven days after his birth; see *Journal of the As. Soc.* (1856); xvi. 243. The feeling which gave rise to this peculiar theory of incarnations,—a wish to represent the incarnate one as free from all hereditary taint of matter and of evil,—was shared by Valentinian heretics, and in the 16th century by our Joan of Kent: see Hardwick's *Hist. of the Reformation*, pp. 278, 279, and n. 6.

ginning, he had taken root in the bosom of supreme
repose and in the deepest void. It was he, and he
alone, who from the height of his imperial throne
distributed the subtle elements of air and gave trans-
parency to ether. He extended and transformed
both heaven and earth, to bring about, in cycles of
incalculable period, the production and the death of
all created forms. His person was transfigured (by
assuming a mortal body); he submitted to the various
conditions of this soiled and dusty world; yet meanwhile bearing small resemblance to the crowd with
whom he came to sojourn. He appeared to men as
an illustrious sage. The good and evil of successive
generations were all noted by him: and his doctrine
had been shaped according to the times. He was
the great instructor of the generations: he inculcated
his principles with due measure. He attained unto
the nine heavens: he stretched himself as far as the
four seas. Since the period of the three kings, the
emperors and potentates of all successive generations
have bowed down before him and embraced his
teaching."[1] As the story runs, however, in the oldest *Primitive*
version, disengaged from wild and fabulous after- *account of him.*
growths which thickened with the lapse of ages,
Lao-tse is found to be an eminent Chinese sage, of
whom it was recorded that he ' loved obscurity,' and
who by dint of self-renunciation was believed to have
attained the highest point of moral and religious
eminence (or, in a word, to have acquired the *Tao*).
His early studies lay among the royal archives of
his native province, which were placed under his

---

[1] Translated in Pauthier's *Mé-* *tion de la Doctrine du Tao*, Paris,
moire sur l'origine et la propaga- 1831, pp. 20, 21.

Chap. I. immediate custody: but as the troubles of the age increased and deepened his dissatisfaction with the men and things around him, he appears to have at last retreated altogether to 'the passage of Han-ku," in order that he might devote the evening of his days exclusively to philosophic speculations.

Did Lao-tse travel westward? Owing to the mystery in which that period of his life has been enveloped, Lao-tse is thought by many writers to have travelled out of China into countries lying westward, and either to have learned or taught in them the leading articles of his creed.[2]

Received account: The chief authority in favour of this statement specifies[3] not only Hindústán and Parthia, but also districts bordering on the western or Caspian sea, and even kingdoms of Ta-thsin (the Roman empire), as alike included in the regions then explored by the Chinese philosopher. It is doubtless true that such external intercourse would best enable us to account for some points of contact which exist between the doctrines commonly ascribed to Lao-tse, and those which in the same eventful era occupied the thoughtful spirits of India and of Greece.[4] We also find in it a possible explanation of some Aryan and Hellenic mythes[5]

[1] *Notice Historique sur Lao-tseu*, prefixed to M. Julien's edition of the *Tao-te-king*, p. xx. The district to which he retreated was in his native province of Ho-nan.

[2] Abel-Rémusat *Mélanges Asiatiques*, I. 92, Paris, 1825.

[3] See the *Légende Fabuleuse*, as before, pp. xxx. xxxi.

[4] Abel-Rémusat (*Ibid.* p. 95) says, in speaking of the 'sublime reveries' of Lao-tseu, that they present 'une conformité frappante et incontestable avec la doctrine que professèrent un peu plus tard les écoles de Pythagore et de Platon.' Pauthier in like manner concludes, 'avec une espèce de certitude, that 'les doctrines, les croyances des sectateurs de Lao-tseu sont des doctrines, des croyances *empruntées de l'Inde.*' He then goes so far as to determine that the Chinese philosophy is to be connected with the Sánkhya and Védantine schools (*Mémoire*, as above, p. 49), and even (as he elsewhere argued) with the theorisings of the Gnostics and Neo-platonists, and last of all with those of Schelling.

[5] Above, p. 14, n. 1.

which reappear in various dramas of this Chinese sect, but are unknown to others. We may further trace with some degree of probability the origin of contradictions which are said to have existed from early times between historic legends of Confucianists and of Tao-ists, with reference to the founding of the Chinese empire and its ancient civilisation.[1] If Lao-tse had actually braved the perils of a journey to the far-off borders of the Mediterranean, and had really drawn his knowledge from a channel which was also open to the other doctors of the ancient world, we are prepared at once to recognise in such community of origin the ground of all the family-likeness which has been detected in the speculations of the East and West. But, on the other hand, the evidence in *how far* favour of this connexion is exceedingly precarious, *tenable.* and will never stand the test of rigorous criticism. The legend where the story first appears,[2] so far as we have any present means of judging, is taken from a mythological account of Chinese gods and heroes, not earlier than the fourth century after Christ; *i. e.* eight hundred years, and more, after the demise of Lao-tse. It also makes the great philosopher allude to his intention of visiting the Roman empire,[3] long before the deposition of the Tarquins and the plant- •

[1] See Prichard, IV. 486. According also to Prof. Neumann (as there quoted) the Tao-ists frequently charge Confucius with rejecting usages and ignoring facts that told against his own system.

[2] See M. Julien's 'Introduction' to the *Tao-te-king*, p. ix.

[3] Perhaps one of the earliest instances in which China manifested her acquaintance with the Roman empire, occurred in the time of Vespasian and Domitian, when a Chinese army marched victoriously as far as the eastern coast of the Caspian. Their own writers say that the leader of this expedition meditated an attack on the Tath-sin (Romans), but that on the advice of the Persians he changed his mind: Humboldt's *Cosmos*, II. 185, 186, Sabine's ed.

ing of the first republic: and what is still more noticeable as bearing on the foreign derivation of Tao-ism, it is said expressly that Lao-tse composed his principal work, 'consisting of something more than 5000 words,' *not* after his return from western countries, but upon the eve of the departure for his unknown resting-place.

The Tao-te-king.

That work, however, still remains (the *Tao-te-king*) the monument of his extraordinary power and penetration: for even if we hesitate to echo all the praises of an able sinologue, who finds in Lao-tse 'a genuine philosopher, a judicious moralist, an eloquent divine, and a subtle metaphysician,'[1] there is ample reason for assigning him a place indefinitely higher than the mass of his contemporaries, and superior also to the greatest of his disciples.

Theology of the Tao-ists.

What, then, was the substance of his teaching on the central truth of all religion,—the nature and the attributes of God? In other words, what is the meaning of the *Tao*, which among Tao-ists very soon supplanted both the *Teen* and *Shang-te* of the previous period? It were idle to insist on the resemblance of this appellation either to the *déva* of the Bráhmans, or the θεός of other countries. The primary meaning of the word, as given by Morrison and others, is 'a way,' or 'the fixed Way.' Its secondary meaning is 'a principle; the Principle from which heaven, earth, man, and all nature emanates.' Among Confucianists the word was chiefly used in its untechnical sense, but still with indirect allusion to the orderly course of human conduct. 'The way (*Tao*),' said Confucius himself, 'is not frequented: I know why.

---

[1] Abel-Rémusat, *Ibid.* p. 93.

Intelligent persons go beyond it, while the ignorant fall short of it."[1] As soon, however, as the term had been adopted by Lao-tse and his disciples, many writers have supposed that *Tao* at once became a synonym of 'the primordial Reason, the Intelligence, which having formed the world, still rules it as the spirit rules the body:'[2] and accordingly such writers are accustomed to describe Tao-ism as the 'rationalism' of China. But the recent publication of the *Real meaning of the Tao.* sacred book on which the whole of that religion is believed to hinge goes very far to modify the old hypothesis. The *Tao* of Lao-tse in its exalted meaning is declared to be entirely void of thought, of consciousness, of judgment, of activity, of intelligence.[3]

---

[1] Quoted in M. Julien's 'Introduction' to the *Tao-te-king*, p. x. I am indebted largely to the work of this distinguished scholar for the views here advocated on the subject of Tao-ism.

[2] *Ibid.* p. xii. 'Ce mot me semble,' wrote Abel-Rémusat, 'ne pas pouvoir être bien traduit si ce n'est par le mot λόγος, dans le triple sens de *souverain être*, de *raison* et de *parole*. C'est évidemment le λόγος de Platon, qui à disposé l'univers, la *raison* universelle de Zénon, de Cléanthe et des autres stoïciens,' etc. Pauthier goes still further, and connects the doctrine of Christianity itself with Tao-ism, (*Chine*, p. 114). He says that the attributes given to the *Tao* are those 'qu' ont donnés à l'Être suprême toutes les doctrines spiritualistes de l'Orient, transmises à l'Occident *par une voie juive et grecque;* par les thérapeutes et les esséniens, dont Jésus, le fils de l'homme, fut *le révélateur et le représentant;* doctrine dont les gnostiques furent aussi les représentants à l'état

philosophique.' He then continues, in a passage full of misrepresentations as to the real genius of Christianity : 'Tous ces théosophes, les esséniens, qui étaient en quelque sorte les stoïciens de la Judée, comme Lao-tseu et ses premiers sectateurs l'étaient de la Chine ; les thérapeutes, qui menaient en secret une vie contemplative et réglée sur une morale austère ; les gnostiques, qui furent les révélateurs et les continuateurs de la *philosophie orientale*, au dire de Clément d'Alexandrie [!]; tous, ou presque tous, partaient du principe "qu'il faut dégager l'âme des entraves et des influences de la matière ;" principe appelé *zoroastrien* par les écrivains des premiers siècles de notre ère, parceque ce furent les écrits de Zoroastre qui le transmirent de l'Asie orientale et centrale dans l'Asie occidentale, où, après avoir été interprété et appliqué de mille manières, il devint *le principe chrétien en Europe*' [!].

[3] *Tao-te-king*, ed. Julien, 'Introd. p. xiii.

It is the deification of that one transcendant *Way* by which all beings came at first into existence: it is fixed, impassible, eternal; and in proportion as mankind are more devoted to the doctrines of apathy and inaction, they are said to walk directly in the *Tao*, to approach the *Tao*, and eventually to gain the *Tao*.[1] 'This Way,' writes a native commentator,[2] 'whose level is high above the world, has neither colour, form, nor appellation. If you seek it with the eyes, you do not find it: if you listen, you do not hear it. The reason is, that it is not susceptible of utterance by the human voice, nor of being designated by the help of names.' The 'nameless' being is, however, styled by Lao-tse the origin of Heaven and Earth,[3] since all things are the fruit of its self-manifestation. 'O how profound the *Tao* is! It seems to be the patriarch of all existences...I cannot tell whose son it is: it seems to have preceded the master of the Heaven.'[4] 'Behold the nature of the *Tao:* it is vague, it is invisible.....Inside it, lies a spiritual essence. This spiritual essence is profoundly true.....It gives birth to all beings.'[5] 'Man imitates the Earth: the Earth imitates the Heaven: the Heaven imitates the *Tao:* the *Tao* imitates his own nature.'[6] Yet the *Tao*, in a certain sense, is represented as the fitting guide and model for all human

[1] *Ibid.* p. xv.
[2] *Ibid.* p. 121, where a distinction is clearly drawn between the ordinary *Tao*, 'the way of justice, of rites and of prudence,' and the sublime *Tao* of Lao-tse.
[3] *Ibid.* p. 1, p. 122.
[4] *Ibid.* p. 7.
[5] *Ibid.* pp. 29, 30, 165. In

p. 174 we have the supplementary idea of preservation. 'Il nourrit,' says a commentator, 'tous les êtres comme une mère nourrit ses enfans.' Elsewhere it is *Virtue* that nourishes what the *Tao* has produced (p. 75).
[6] *Ibid.* p. 37.

beings. 'He that imitates not the *Tao* will · die
prematurely.'[1] 'A prince that rules his empire by
the *Tao* is exempted from the malice of the demons.'[2]
'The *Tao* is the refuge of all creatures : (being universally diffused) it is the treasure of the virtuous
man, the ultimate resource and resting-point of the
unholy.'[3] In a word, the *Tao* is the most exalted
and most estimable being in the universe.

I feel disposed to argue from these various passages *How far*
and others like them, that the centre of the system *resembling the God of*
founded by Lao-tse had been awarded to some energy *Christians.*
or Power resembling the 'Nature' of modern speculators. The indefinite expression *Tao* was adopted
to denominate an abstract Cause, or the initial
Principle of life and order, to which worshippers
were able to assign the attributes of immateriality,
eternity, immensity, invisibility. They also felt that
human happiness was in some way or other connected
with assimilation to its likeness: without, however,
rising to a clear conception of its personality, volition,
or intelligence, much less of those peculiarly moral
attributes, as goodness, mercy, justice, which the
sacred family were uniformly taught to predicate of
the Supreme Being.[4] The will-less, unintelligent

[1] *Ibid.* pp. 45, 83, in both of
which passages, however, the non-
imitation of the *Tao* is explained
by the context to mean no more
than 'waxing old and impotent,'
and by the commentators, 'placing oneself in opposition to the
Tao' (p. 187).

[2] *Ibid.* p. 89. The gloss upon
this passage (pp. 246, 247) gives
us some of the chief characteristics
of the perfect prince who governs
by the *Tao :* 'Le Saint emploie
le vide et la lumière (c'est-à-dire

se dépouille de ses passions et
dissipe leurs ténèbres) pour nourrir sa nature, la modération et
l'économie pour subvenir aux be-
soins de son corps, la pureté et
l'attention la plus sévère pour
fortifier sa volonté, le calme et
la quiétude pour gouverner son
royaume.'

[3] *Ibid.* pp. 93, 251.

[4] M. Callery (*Li-ki*, pp. 142, 143)
has some judicious annotations on
the same subject. While conceding that the *Tao* of Lao-tse is

Tao of ancient China was thus something very different[1] from the personal God of revelation, very different also from the Logos of St. John, and from the Living 'Way' of Christians.

Tao-ist doctrine of the Trinity. Not content with offering violence to the words of Lao-tse, in order at all hazards to establish such affinity, some writers have gone further still, and have discovered in the 'doctrine of Reason' (as they term it) the anticipation of one high and central mystery of the Gospel,—the doctrine of the Holy Trinity in Unity. 'The principal object of the *Tao-te-king*,' a modern Chinese scholar has declared, 'is to establish a particular knowledge of one Supreme Being in Three Persons. Numerous passages so clearly speak of a Triune God, that no one who reads this book can any longer doubt that the mystery of the Most Holy Trinity was revealed to the Chinese more than five centuries before the advent of Jesus Christ.'[2] It was expected that a deeper knowledge of this singular resemblance would, as furnishing points of contact with the heathen mind, contribute largely to the spread of Christianity in China, and accordingly the triad of Lao-tse continues

---

properly rendered the 'Way,' and is sometimes described as actually possessing the qualities of a way, he thinks that the philosopher was led to the adoption of this term chiefly because it was general and obscure, in order to bring out more clearly the difficulties he experienced in giving any denomination to the Ultimate Principle of all things.

[1] 'Die Idee des christlichen Gottes ist das reine Gegentheil jener leeren Einheit, ist die lebendige Fülle alles Lebens selbst; und diese positivste aller Ideen wird wahrlich nicht durch blosse Verneinungen errungen:' Wuttke, II. 79.

[2] Montucci, *De Studiis Sinicis*, p. 19, Berolini, 1808 (quoted by Julien, *Tao-te-king*, p. iv.). The motive of this writer may be gathered from what follows: 'Studium ergo et vulgatio hujus singularissimi textus, *missionariis utilissima*, evaderent ad messis apostolicæ peroptatam coacervationem feliciter provehendam.'

to assume importance in the publications of the present day.[1] One writer even goes so far as to discover
in the Chinese triad the three principal characters
which enter into the formation of the ineffable name
of God,—or the JEHOVAH of the ancient Hebrews;
and from hence he has not only argued for some
actual intercourse between philosophers of Eastern
and Western Asia, but has also found in the supposed transcription of the Hebrew name 'indisputable
traces of the route which the ideas we call Pythagorean
and Platonic had pursued on their migration into
China.'[2]

The only passage of the *Tao-te-king* which sup- *Alleged*
plies a warrant for these grave conclusions is the *proof.*
following: 'You look for the *Tao*, and you see it
not: its name is *I*. You listen for it, and you hear
it not: its name is *Hi*. You wish to touch it, and
you feel it not: its name is *Wei*. These three are
inscrutable, and inexpressible by the aid of language;
we are therefore in the habit of combining (or confounding) them into one, (the three all seem to meet
in one single quality,—voidness or incorporeity).
Its upper part is not enlightened: its lower part is
not obscure (*i. e.* the properties of this entity are the
same throughout). . . . It is called a form without

---

[1] *e. g.* Wiseman's *Lectures on Science and Revealed Religion*, p. 402, Grant's *Bampton Lectures*, p. 268, Lond. 1844. The former says with great confidence: 'The doctrine of a Trinity is too clearly expounded in his (Lao-tse's) writings to be misunderstood.'

[2] Abel-Rémusat, *Mélanges Asiat.* I. 95, 96, and more fully in his *Mémoire sur la vie et les ouvrages de Lao-tseu*, pp. 43 sq. He affirms that the essential, or articulated, letters of יְהֹוָה, are I, H, V, and that these were combined into a Chinese trigram I-Hi-Weï, of which, he thinks, the several characters have no meaning in the Chinese language itself, and there-fore a meaning for them must be sought elsewhere. This he readi-ly finds in Judæa.

Chap. I. form, an image without image. It is vague and undefinable. Go before it, and you see not its face; follow after, and you see not its back."[1]

Explana-
tion.

I give this memorable passage exactly as it stands in the translation of one of the most illustrious living sinologues; but the reader will have scarcely failed to notice that, when so translated, there is little left in it to justify phantastic theories of which it was the strongest and the most explicit basis. I should also add, that so far from the three syllables (*I, Hi, Weï*) enshrouding any special mystery, like that ascribed to them by this hypothesis, they all are terms well-known to China, and were all expounded by disciples of Lao-tse before the Christian era. The first imports the absence of colour; the second, the absence of sound or voice; the third, the absence of form or body;[2] they are, therefore, all most fitly used to characterise the great 'Unnamed,' who is the ultimate Principle of Tao-ists.

Moral sys-
tem of Lao-
tse.

But the moral teaching of this school is even more remarkable than the stress which it has laid upon the thought of some transcendant unity in nature. The genuine convert or 'holy man,' as he is called, was ever anxious to conserve his primitive simplicity.

---

[1] *Tao-te-king*, p. 19, ed. Julien, and notes, p. 147. The version of Dr. Wiseman, who follows Abel-Rémusat, is different in some particulars. For instance, one passage is made to say: 'These three are inscrutable, and, being united, form only one. Of them the superior is not more bright, nor the inferior more obscure.' In a second passage of the *Tao-te-king* (p. 65) we read: 'The *Tao* produced one; one produced two; two produced three: three produced all beings:' —which is explained by the native commentators to mean, first, the self-manifestation of the *Tao* as unity, then, the separation of this unity into the male and female principles (*Yang* and *Yin*), and thirdly, the production of harmony between these two (p. 211).

[2] *Tao-te-king*, 'Introd.' pp. vii. viii.

He shrank from every kind of luxury, of bustle, and of competition. His leading aim was to 'make void the human heart;' to drain away from it whatever ministered to passion, to cast off the bondage of 'particular affections,' and convert his principal occupations into virtual inactivity.[1] He was anxious also to perform good deeds without the slightest sense of satisfaction or even with entire unconsciousness.[2] Each holy man who thus preserved the *Tao*, by destroying or ignoring self, was finally exalted into a model, and perennial source of blessing, for other members of the human family.[3] 'The man of a superior virtue is like water, of which one excellency is that it does good to all creatures. Water also does not strive (it flows into the empty spaces and avoids the full). Its home is in localities which have no charm for crowds (a proof of self-abasement). Therefore does the sage approach still nearer to the *Tao*. He is content with the lowliest positions. His heart is struggling to become as deep (and tranquil) as an abyss. If he distribute favours, his aim is to excel in humanity (his tenderness is not confined to individual favourites). If he speak, his actions do not afterwards belie his promise. If he govern, his desire is to establish peace. If he work, he shews capacity and aptitude. If he change his calling, he adapts himself completely to the times. He strives with no one : hence it is that he incurs no blame.'[4] ' I possess three precious things,' is the

[1] *Ibid.* pp. 5, 7, 9.
[2] *Ibid.* p. 58.
[3] *Ibid.* p. 31. It was not, however, contemplated that all persons were capable of understanding and appreciating the doctrine of the *Tao :* some would of necessity deride it as enveloped in darkness (p. 63).
[4] *Ibid.* p. 11, and notes, p. 136.

assertion of Lao-tse himself: 'these I hold and guard as I would guard a treasure. The first is called affection (tenderness for living creatures); the second is called economy (frugality and moderation); the third is called humility, which prevents me from wishing to become the first man of the empire. I have affection, and hence it is I am courageous. I have economy, and hence it is that my expenditure is large. I dare not be the first man of the empire; hence it is that I have power to become the chief of all men.'[1]

The Tao-ist Book of Rewards and Punishments.

But besides the moral truths occasionally enunciated in the 'Book of the Way and of Virtue' (the *Tao-te-king*), we have other and more copious means of understanding the ethical system of Tao-ism. The members of that sect have long been in the habit of printing by subscription, and circulating as a matter of religious duty, the collection of moral maxims known as the *Book of Rewards and Punishments.*[2] Each maxim is followed by a gloss or commentary, and in almost every case elucidated by appropriate tales and anecdotes. The high repute in which this volume stands is further indicated by the circumstance that the authorship has been in modern times attributed to Lao-tse himself, in his capacity of deified and 'venerable Prince' or incarnation of the *Tao.*[3] 'Every wise man,' writes a commentator,[4] 'ought to

---

[1] *Ibid.* p. 101.

[2] *Le Livre des Récompenses et des Peines,* ed. Julien, Paris, 1835.

[3] See above, p. 60. The *Livre des Récompenses* itself attributes the composition to *Thaï-Shang,* another name for Lao-tse. It is, however, in reality a compilation (how modern we cannot say) of sentences drawn or imitated from the *king* of the Confucianists, the *Tao-te-king* and other philosophical and moral treatises: cf. M. Julien's 'Avertissement,' p. x.

[4] *Livre des Récompenses,* &c. p. 519.

be full of respect for this book : he ought to believe
sincerely all the maxims it delivers, and ought to
practise them faithfully, regardless of all obstacles,
and without suffering the zeal he had evinced at the
commencement to diminish at the close of his career.
He ought every morning to read it aloud, and to
meditate on every phrase with serious attention. Let
him redouble his efforts to perform good works, and
his anxiety and ardour to correct past failings. Then
will happiness spring up within himself to recompense
his merits; and his end will be advancement to
the rank of the immortals.' While the general tone *Its eclectic*
of this production harmonises with the older treatise, *character.*
it bears frequent witness also to the presence of a
more eclectic and accommodating spirit. There was
no sympathy whatever between Confucius and the
founder of Tao-ism. The contemplative philosopher
was in the eyes of the more practical and bustling
sociologist a very ' dragon,' who rises high above the
clouds and floats in ether:' and Confucius had no
wish to understand him or to follow his example.
But this work of the disciples of Lao-tse, while it
condemned some other forms of misbelief and of mal-
practice, recognised as true the doctrine taught by all
the ' three religions,'[2]—that which had been long in
the ascendancy, and those which had been simply
tolerated at the date of its compilation. And in one
single passage a commentator actually makes the
author of Tao-ism add the worship of the god *Fo*
(or Buddha) to a list of other meritorious actions.[3]

---

[1] See the version of this well-
known story in the *Tao-te-king,*
'Introd.' p. xxix.

[2] *Livre des Récompenses,* p. 422.
[3] *Ibid.* p. 517.

The original conception of the *Tao* had now indeed been gradually obscured, and ran the risk of being quite obliterated. In this later treatise, the great business of man's life is not to master his affections and escape from everything that tends to agitate his soul, or bind his spirit to the earth, but rather, as we saw in Buddhism,[1] to accumulate the largest possible stock of merits. It is the duty of the 'three counsellors,'[2] or, elsewhere, of the 'god presiding over life,' 'the prince of spirits,'[3] to register the bad actions of all men; and according to the measure of their turpitude, as grave or venial, 'to cut off twelve years or else a hundred days from the duration of human life. When the allotted period is exhausted the man dies; but if, at the hour of death, a crime remains unexpiated (or, in other words, if no sufficient compensation has been made), it causes the transmission of unhappiness to his children and his grand-

Particular precepts.

children.'[4] Urged by this regard to the well-being of himself and his posterity, every genuine Tao-ist labours hard to regulate his wishes and to purify his intentions.[5] He must set his own heart right, and then attempt to influence others.[6] He must be humane, abstaining even from all cruelty to the minutest animals.[7] He must practise filial piety,

---

[1] Vol. I. p. 238.

[2] *Livre des Récompenses*, p. 13. 'These are names given by the Chinese to six stars, placed two and two, which correspond to $\iota\kappa$—$\lambda\mu$—$\nu\xi$ of the Great Bear.'

[3] *Ibid.* pp. 13, 502.

[4] *Ibid.* p. 502. The possibility of repentance and its efficacy, as here glanced at, are both recognised more fully in p. 514.

[5] *Ibid.* pp. 328, 512. 'Nous devenons coupables dès le moment que nous avons formé ce désir. Si l'homme peut rectifier son cœur lorsqu'il est seul et désœuvré, il pourra le conserver pur et intact au moment du danger.'

[6] *Ibid.* p. 65.

[7] *Ibid.* pp. 51, 73. In the latter passage, it is added: 'Si vous les blessez, vous n'imitez point la

must be affectionate as a brother, and respect his
seniors.[1] He must pity the orphan and the widow ;[2]
he must sympathise with the afflicted,[3] and rejoice
with all who prosper.[4] He must help the needy,
and take part in rescuing those who are in peril.[5]
He is not to boast of his superiority, nor divulge the
imperfections of other men.[6] He is to act from
kindly motives without waiting for a recompense;
and, finally, he must not murmur against Heaven :[7]
while they who fail to act according to these noble
principles, are said to 'violate the duties which
society imposes on them, dishonour their ancestors,
stifle the germs of virtue which Heaven has planted
in them, and corrupt public manners.'[8]

In the system of Confucius we are seldom able to *Moral
motives.*
detect the slightest reference to a pure and righteous
God whose moral law is broken by iniquity. The
same remark must be extended also to Tao-ism.
Once or twice indeed the doctors of the 'Way' incite
us to the imitation of Heaven and Earth, who manifest
their gentle nature in dispensing life to all the creatures ; but the check imposed on evil thoughts and
evil actions is more commonly the fear of giving
umbrage not to God, but to the spirits of earth or
heaven, who are affected, it is urged, by all the works
of men, and have the power to punish or reward according to their quality.[9] The good man's pathway
is encompassed by a host of these invisible agents,

bonté du Ciel et de la Terre, qui
aiment à donner la vie aux créa-
tures.'
  [1] *Ibid.* p. 56.
  [2] *Ibid.* p. 68.
  [3] *Ibid.* p. 74.

[4] *Ibid.* p. 77.
[5] *Ibid.* pp. 79, 83.
[6] *Ibid.* pp. 91, 93.
[7] *Ibid.* pp. 107, 372.
[8] *Ibid.* p. 328.
[9] *Ibid.* p. 1.

who are all continually engaged for his protection;[1] and in one remarkable passage, where a Chinese scholar had been strongly tempted to unchastity, the tempter fled confounded by his reference to the super-sensuous world, and the proximity of purer beings: ' the spirits of heaven and earth,' he argued, ' encircle us on every side; how then could one think of sinning in their presence ?'[2]

Degeneracy of Tao-ism. We have scarcely any means of ascertaining the amount of influence exercised by this religion in the centuries immediately succeeding the death of Lao-tse. In later ages many of his opinions were disseminated far and wide, not only in China proper, but in Cochin-China, in Tonquin, and in Japan.[3] As early, however, as the reign of Woo-te, the sixth of the Han dynasty who mounted the imperial throne, 140 B.C., a very large accession is recorded to the ranks of the Tao-ists.[4] The fear of death had fallen with unwonted power on many who were filling high positions in the Chinese empire, and unable to find peace or comfort in the tenets of Confucius, crowds of them resorted to the schools of his more spiritual opponent. But Tao-ism, as presented to us in this

---

[1] *Ibid.* p. 126. On the contrary the demons are said to stand aloof from him through terror and respect (p. 124).

[2] *Ibid.* p. 331: cf. pp. 489, 490.

[3] Julien's ' Avertiss ment' to the *Livre des Récompenses*, p. viii. The same writer in his ' Introduction' to the *Tao-te-king* (p. xi.) has pointed out a serious error in some current statements on this subject, according to which Tao-ism was said to have been once extensively propagated in Tibet and northern Hindústán. The

mistake arose from confounding *Tao-sse*, followers of Lao-tse, and *Tao-jin*, followers of Śákya-muni —a name given to the Chinese Buddhists before they were called *Seng* or ' Doctors.'

[4] Gutzlaff (I. 235) attributes this accession to the influence of the empress who was addicted to the creed of Lao-tse, ' and considered the heartless doctrines of the Chinese sage [Confucius], as the greatest enemy to the mystical system of her beloved master.'

later stage of its development, had passed into a very different phase. Proceeding, it appears, on the hypothesis that 'holy men' are so completely identified with the *Tao* as to have acquired a perfect mastery over natural forces, which are still, however, fettering ordinary mortals, the Tao-ists grew most ardent in their cultivation of theurgy and various forms of magic.[1] They became, in some degree, the Neoplatonists of China. Their talk was now of spells, of amulets, of gifts of second sight, of charms, of incantations, of specifics in the very handwriting of the prince of demons; and affecting most of all to tranquillise the apprehensions of their votaries, they sought to manufacture an elixir of such potency, that all who drank it would be rescued from the grasp of death himself.[2]

Henceforth the school of Lao-tse, in spite of all its early promise, occupied itself far too exclusively in the pursuit of these phantastic and debasing superstitions. To the Christian missionaries of the seventeenth century, the Tao-ists seemed the most 'abominable' sect of China, living only to corrupt and fascinate the populace by magical performances, in which

Actual condition of the sect.

---

[1] Thus in the *Livre des Récompenses*, &c., where magic is condemned whenever it is used for exciting social tumults (p. 422), there is no doubt expressed as to the 'supernatural powers' of some Tao-ists: see, for instance, the 'Histoire' in p. 423, where a magician of the sect was said to have brought down, for immoral purposes, 'toutes les déesses du Ciel et celles du mont Wouchan.'

[2] No traces of this 'elixir vitæ' are found in the *Tao-te-king.* It is said, however, that as early as

209 B.C. a Chinese expedition was sent across the Eastern sea into Japan to seek for such a medicine (Prichard, IV. 493). The idea may possibly have been derived from the *amrita* (=ambrosia) of ancient India (see Vol. I. p. 179, n. 1). From the East it travelled into Egypt, where Ptolemy Philadelphus, in possession of the secret, could declare ὅτι μόνος εὕροι τὴν ἀθανασίαν: Athenæus, Lib. XII. c. IX. (p. 536 F, ed. Casaubon).

they still are said to figure, at one time as mere
jugglers, at another as physicians, at a third as
fortune-tellers, at a fourth as gifted with the power
of drawing secrets from the world invisible, through
intercourse with those who are possessed by demons.
They are notwithstanding held in high repute by
nearly every class of the Chinese: the ordinary appellation of their chiefs is that of ' heavenly doctors,'
and the arch-chief of the sect, resembling in consideration and magnificence the Grand Lama of Tibet, is
commonly believed to exercise, as the incarnate *Tao*,
absolute dominion in the sphere of the invisible.
'He appoints and removes the deities of various
districts, just as the emperor does his officers; and no
tutelary divinity can be worshipped, or is supposed
capable of protecting his votaries, until the warrant
goes forth under the hand and seal of this demon-
ruler, authorising him to exercise his functions in
a given region."[1]

How remote are all such representations from the
glorious facts of Christianity, and from the cheering
visions of the Christian Apocalypse! 'Fear not:
I am the first and the last: I am He that liveth and
was dead, and, behold, I am alive for evermore,
Amen; and have the keys of hades and of death'
(Rev. i. 17, 18).

§ 3. *Fo-ism,*[2] *or Chinese Buddhism.*

The sad experience of five centuries had gradually
suggested to reflecting China-men, that neither of the
two religious systems heretofore espoused, could ex-

---

[1] Medhurst, pp. 200 sq.   of *Fŏ-t'a* or *Fu-t'a* = *Buddha*.
[2] *Fo* or *Foĕ* is the first syllable

tricate the human spirit from perplexities in which
she found herself involved, nor satisfy the wants and
longings of our moral nature. One of these religions
had succeeded doubtless in imparting form and animation to Chinese society, but meanwhile pushed
into the background every question which affected
our relationship to God and to the world invisible.
Its chief concern was with the present life. The
other, mystic and imaginative in its whole complexion, had run wild as it grew older; it was rapidly
transforming the ideas of Lao-tse into a system of
most abject demonology,—little if at all distinguishable from the ancient superstitions, whose main object
was the deprecation and disarming of malignant principles.

While brooding over these momentous topics, and, *Introduc-*
it may be, half despairing for himself as well as for *tion of*
Buddhism
his people, an intelligent emperor, Ming-te, about the *into China.*
sixtieth year of the Christian era, is reported to have
had a most remarkable vision. According to one
account[1] there stood before him a resplendent figure,
of gigantic size, and with a glorious nimbus round
the head; and when his ministers of state were all
consulted as to the most probable meaning of this
dream or apparition, one of them replied that the
description of it corresponded to a story he had heard
of some great genius in the western country, who
might therefore be intending to solicit the notice of
the emperor. Another version of the legend is, that
in the maxims of Confucius himself, was one affirming
that the 'Holy Man' is in the west,[2] or will hereafter

---

[1] Pauthier's *Chine*, p. 256.   early missionaries in China, who
[2] Gutzlaff, I. 250. Some of the   gave currency to this legend, (*e. g.*

issue from the west; and that impressions which this oft-repeated sentence left on the imperial mind could never be obliterated. In either case the sequel of the story is precisely the same. A deputation of mandarins proceed across the western mountains in the hope of learning fresh particulars respecting this mysterious personage; and on returning home they are accompanied by a Hindú teacher, bringing with him a large stock of books, and, as a present to the emperor himself, the portrait of Sákya-muni.

Its early fortunes. Thus the Buddhism of the Middle Kingdom rose at once into the rank of a 'religio licita;' its formal recognition occurring in the very year when the Apostle of the Gentiles passed in chains to the prætorium of the Cæsars, 'thanking God and taking courage' (Acts xxviii. 15). Buddhism, it is true, has never been allowed to interfere with the administration of the Chinese empire, nor been able to dethrone the old religion of the country. It was more or less contemned by the Confucianists, as foreign, inno-

---

Duhalde, *De la Chine*, &c. 1. 360 sq. Paris, 1735), were of opinion that Confucius actually intended to point out the birth of Christ, and that the Chinese envoys actually started on a journey into Palestine to hail the advent of the Great Redeemer. On their way they encountered certain Buddhist missionaries coming from India, whom mistaking for true disciples of Christ they carried back as teachers of their fellow-countrymen. 'Thus,' says the translator of Schlegel, *Philosophy of Religion*, p. 136, note, 'was this religion introduced into China, and thus did this phantasmagoria of hell intercept the light of the Gospel.'

No one has, however, been able to detect the saying here ascribed to Confucius in any of his extant writings. The passage most likely to have suggested the current story is one in the *Chung-Yung*, c. xxix. §§ 3, 4: yet there even no allusion whatever is made to a country *in the west*. It is only declared with reference to the true sage: 'Il conforme ses actions aux lois du Ciel et de la Terre, et il n'éprouve aucun trouble; il se règle sur les intelligences supérieures à l'homme, et son esprit n'éprouve aucun doute: *il est cent générations à attendre le saint homme*, et il ne se dément jamais.'

vating, and seditious. Patronised by one prince, it was sometimes roughly handled by another;[1] and in the century after that which witnessed the establishment of Christianity in the great metropolis of the west, the Chinese Buddhists, now attaining some numerical importance, were exposed to very bitter persecutions. Edicts from the prince of Wei not only authorised the demolition of their temples and the burning of their sacred books, but also instigated a general massacre of the Buddhist monks.[2] In the succeeding reign, however, dating from A.D. 452, the triumphs of their cause grew visible in almost every part of China. Cloisters rose again with marvellous facility, and multiplied so fast, that at the end of the next fifty years the total number of such buildings had been swollen, it is said, to thirteen thousand.[3] At the same time frequent intercourse with India, some account of which is happily preserved to us in records of the pilgrimages of Fa-hian[4] in the fourth, and of Hiuan-Thsang[5] in the seventh century after Christ,

---

[1] Pauthier, p. 257.

[2] Gutzlaff, I. 291 : Schott, *Über den Buddhaismus in Hochasien und in China*, p. 19, Berlin, 1846. Until this period it seems as if the new religion had made very little progress in China: cf. *Tao-te-king*, 'Introd.' p. x.

[3] Schott, as before, p. 20. The same kind of activity is just now visible in Birmah, where new temples and monasteries ('kyums') are daily springing up, even in the districts under British authority: Wilson, in *Journal of As. Soc.* XVI. 260.

[4] Translated by Abel-Rémusat, Paris, 1836.

[5] Translated by M. Jullien, Paris, 1853. This latter pilgrim

spent seventeen years (A.D. 629—A.D. 645) in countries situated to the west of China. In one passage (p. 26), he thus describes the object of his travels: 'J'étais vivement affligé de voir que les livres sacrés étaient incomplets, et que leur interprétation offrait de fâcheuses lacunes. Oubliant alors le soin de ma vie et bravant les obstacles et les dangers, j'ai fait serment d'aller chercher dans l'occident la *Loi* [Dharma] que le Bouddha a léguée au monde :' cf. p. 44, where he says that on his return to China he will translate and circulate the sacred books, and ' beat down the thick forest of errors.' ' Ensuite j' interrogerai la multitude des maitres, et

resulted in the importation into China of Buddhist pictures, books, and relics, and in the enlistment of a host of fresh auxiliaries, all burning to diffuse a knowledge of the law, or *Dharma ;* till, won over by the zeal of Hindú doctors (*Fan-seng*)[1] and ascetics (*shamans*),[2] a large portion of the Chinese populace were numbered with the followers of this foreign creed ; nay, emperors themselves, the sons of Heaven, were not unwilling to lay down their sceptres, if they might but pass the evening of their lives beneath the shadow of a Buddhist monastery.[3] The culminating point of these successes was the fall of the Mongol dynasty in 1368.

Varieties of Buddhism.   I may have hitherto appeared to speak of Buddhism as of one organic system, animated by a definite creed, directed by a common hope and purpose, and binding all its converts to one centre of administration. But such inference is unquestionably incorrect. What Buddhism was when it put forth its earliest aphorisms, the 'undeveloped' *sútras*, we have seen[4] already, while engaged in tracing the career of Gautama and analysing the first principles of his philosophy. Yet exactly in proportion to the wondrous elasticity of the system he had founded, and its marked superiority to those distinctions which had long been severing man from man and one people

---

de leur bouche je recevrai l' enseignment de la droite *Loi.* Une fois de retour (en Chine), je traduirai les livres, je répandrai au loin des vérités inconnues ; j' abattrai la forêt épaisse des erreurs, je détruirai les artifices des fausses doctrines, je réparerai les lacunes de *la doctrine de l' éléphant* [the translator (p. 467) corrects this into ' *la doctrine des images*'] (la doctrine bouddhique), et je fixerai la boussole de la *porte mystérieuse* (de l' enseignment religieux).'

[1] *Fan*-seng (= ' doctors out of India') has been represented in other languages under the form of *Bonzen* or *Bonzes.*

[2] See Vol. I. p. 239, n. 2.

[3] Schott, p. 20.

[4] Vol. I. p. 222.

from another, is the freedom and the ease with which Chap. I.
it commonly allied itself to pre-existing forms of
heathenism, until the thoughts and symbols proper
to it have been well-nigh buried in a motley crowd
of foreign and conflicting elements. Buddhism once
prevailed, or is prevailing, not only in Hindústán[1]
the birthplace, and Ceylon the sacred island of the
creed, but also in Tibet and Tatary, in China and
Japan, in Cochin-China and Tonquin, in Siam and
the Birman empire, to say nothing of its ancient rule
in Java, and the remnant of it now surviving in Bali,
an islet of the Indian archipelago, and possibly in
regions still more distant and diverse.[2] Of all these *General*
heterogeneous populations none so truly represent the *distinct-*
genuine forms of Buddhism, none so cordially agree *ions.*
together, as the natives of Ceylon, of Birmah,[3] and
Siam, whose sacred books almost entirely correspond,
because translated not as in the other cases from
Sanskrit, but from Páli. In those countries also
images are numerous, yet with the exception of sub-
sidiary figures, which are never worshipped, such as
dragons and lions, they are 'all of the same character,
representing Gautama or his disciples, generally in
a sitting posture with the legs crossed, and the hands

[1] Even after the general expulsion from India small bands of
Buddhists were still found in particular localities as late as the 12th
century: and Jainism, which may
be regarded as the surviving twin-
sister of Buddhism, continued to
produce effects at a far later date;
for instance, modifying the ethical
spirit of the Tamil literature: see
Caldwell, as above, pp. 86 sq.

[2] 'Ob noch weitere Verbreitung
des Buddhaismus nach *Polynesien*
oder gar nach *Süd-Amerika* hin
stattgefunden habe, wie man ver-
muthet hat, darüber fehlt vor der
Hand noch jeder sichere Anhalts-
punkt: jedenfalls hat sich da-
selbst nichts davon direkt erhalt-
en.'—Weber, as above, p. 66.

[3] In Sangermano's *Burmese
Empire*, ed. Tandy (Or. Tr. Fund,
1833), p. 83, it is stated that the
only Buddhists recognised as orthodox by the inhabitants of that
empire are the Buddhists of Ceylon.

CHAP. I. in the act of prayer or benediction."[1] On the contrary, as one result of the accommodating character of this creed, amalgamations are elsewhere so numerous that in spite of the original identity of the books disseminated, it requires no ordinary effort to understand wherein consists the family-likeness of the different sects.[2] They all, in general terms, are *Buddhist;* but the main conceptions of their votaries are divergent, nay, in many points are fundamentally opposed.

Fo-ism and Lama-ism. Perhaps there is no readier and more profitable way of representing this vast disparity than by contrasting some of the chief features of two neighbouring and related systems—the Fo-ism of China, and the Lama-ism of Tibet: for in so doing I may dissipate objections to the Gospel which have long been drawn from the alleged consistency of Buddhism, its compactness and numerical predominance. The new religion was extensively adopted in both those countries at nearly the same date; they both together inherited the sacred texts according to the same recension; yet so very inefficient was Buddhism in curbing and subduing the more wayward nationalities with which it came in contact, that, except in isolated

---

[1] Prof. Wilson, in *Journal of As. Soc.* XVI. 253.

[2] 'In its migrations to other countries, since its dispersion by the Bráhmans, Buddhism has assumed and exhibited itself in a variety of shapes. At the present day, its doctrines, as cherished among the Jainas of Guzerat and Rajpootana, differ widely from its mysteries as administered by the Lama of Tibet; and both are equally distinct from the metaphysical abstractions propounded by the monks of Nepál. Its observances in Japan have undergone a still more striking alteration from their vicinity to the Syntoos; and in China they have been similarly modified in their contact with the rationalism of Lao-tseu and the social demonology (?) of the Confucians. . .But in each and in all the distinction is rather in degree than in essence.' Tennent's *Christianity in Ceylon,* pp. 206, 207.

cases, the Chinese, who have adopted what they call
'the customs of India,'[1] are scarcely in their general
character to be distinguished from the vulgar followers
of Confucius and Lao-tse. The only genuine Buddhists[2] are the monks and mendicants. They only
can be said to recognise a common symbol, or con-
fession of faith; they only have initiatory rites; they
only form a separate and sacred corporation. Others
who are known as worshippers of Fo, and constitute
one half, or possibly two-thirds,[3] of the enormous
population of the Middle Kingdom, are rather tolerated
than approved by the authorities of the sect. They
are expected to confess the general excellence of their
religion, to confide in some particular Buddha, or
to worship one or other of the numerous Pusas
(*Bódhisatwas*); to abstain from all the grosser forms
of vice, to venerate the sacred writings of their predecessors, and the topes, or *sthúpas*, in which some
reliquiæ of a departed Buddha are interred; and
finally, to aid by contributions from their substance
in supporting the *shamans*, monks, ascetics, and
devotees.[4] The strict fulfilment of conditions such

---

[1] *Catechism of the Shamans*, ed. Neumann, p. 117.

[2] Gutzlaff, in *Journal of As. Soc.* XVI. 89.

[3] The same writer (*Ibid.*) con-jectures that two-thirds of all the religious edifices in China are nominally Buddhist: but as Schott observes (*Über den Buddhaismus*, &c. p. 23, and 'Zusätze,' p. 127), statements of this kind are only true in a certain sense, *viz.* as im-plying that the eclectic polytheism of the Chinese populace extends itself so far as to include Buddhas and Bódhisatwas among the ob-jects of common worship.

[4] Schott, *Ibid.* p. 17. The ex-treme laxity of Fo-ism is never shewn more vividly than in the fact, that the Chinese have little or no scruple on the subject of destroying animal life (cf. Vol. I. p. 227). They are said to be 'an omnivorous race; few living be-ings escape being made food for men, and are slaughtered and eaten without the least scruple. But to shew some regard for life, notwithstanding, they now and then dedicate some pigs to Bud-dha, which are permitted to live their natural space of life, and are never killed' (*Journal of As.*

as these entitles them, it is believed, to higher spheres of being after death, but does not raise them to the dignity of the 'enlightened,' nor facilitate their passage to *nirvána*, the goal of genuine Buddhism. In Tibet this utter laxity of principle has never been so fully and so openly avowed; yet even there the old divinities are not dethroned entirely, and the poorer classes make their offerings, with the public sanction of the Lamas, to genii of the hills, the woods, the rivers, and the valleys.[1]

Why the primitive Buddhism was unacceptable in China.

The difference in the measure of amalgamation which took place in these two countries, is attributable to the different tempers of the people, and the circumstances under which the new religion had been introduced. It is recorded[2] of Sákya-muni himself, that on observing no immediate prospect of success among a nation like the China-men, so long at least as the missionaries attempted to communicate his metaphysical doctrines, he suggested the employment of some other means more calculated to effect his purpose. The *Dharma* was to follow gradually upon the track of secular propagandists, who were smoothing the approaches to the Chinese mind, by giving lessons in arithmetic and astronomy. Others might be won by an appeal to the emotional province of

Soc. xvi. 84). The Shamans, on the contrary, (*Catechism*, as above, p. 124) are directed to be extremely careful in this matter: they are not even to use *dry* wood in cooking, lest they should destroy insects in it.

[1] Major Cunningham's *Ladák*, p. 366, Lond. 1854.

[2] Schott, p. 42. The parallel in modern times is unmistakeable: 'Es sind hier offenbar Arithmetik und Sternenkunde (nebst Sternendeutkunst) gemeint, also gerade diejenigen Zweige des Wissens, welche auch *den römischen Glaubensboten im* 17*ten und* 18*ten Jahrh. bis ins Innerste des kaiserlichen Palastes Eingang verschafften.*' Precisely the same course had been pursued in the 16th century, with a view to counteract the Reformation in Bohemia.

their nature; but the China-man by working on his reason and self-interest. Whatever degree of credit we assign to statements of this kind, they are most useful as implying the strong repugnance which the China-man would always feel to a religious system like that of unadulterated Buddhism. His social instincts were opposed to its monastic rigour, his active habits to the indolence in which it seemed to thrive and revel. More than other men, he proved himself a firm believer in the reality and permanence of the present universe. The Buddhist *sûtras*, on the contrary, proclaim[1] the absolute nothingness of all within us and around us: all is treated as an empty show: its origin is from nothing; its destination is to nothing; nay, the very core and essence of creation is declared to be non-being. Human life itself, so precious to the China-man, is in the creed of Gautama compared to single 'dew-drops, trembling on the leaf of the lotus.' Hence, indeed, arose the ardour of the primitive Buddhist in discoursing about the emptiness of human joys, and calling men to a complete renunciation of themselves and of the world. So far from meddling with the common business of society, they were each to seek a quiet refuge in the cloister, or attired in a peculiar dress, the cowl upon their head, the rosary suspended from their girdle,[2] to go forth and urge their fellow-men to bow before the majesty of the *Dharma*.

---

[1] Vol. I. pp. 229 sq.

[2] See Appendix II. at the end of Vol. I.; for in these and other points the monasticism of China resembles that of Tatary and Tibet. In the *Catechism of the Shamans,* as edited by Neumann, the second Part consists of the 'Regulations,' or directions touching the manners and customs of priests (or rather monks) after initiation. The editor remarks (p. 138): 'They so much resemble the monastic rules (Regula Monastica)

In Tibet, where Buddhism was appealing to an ignorant, a pastoral, a simple-hearted race, it seems to have at once produced a very deep impression. Its actual development is far more nearly that which might have been predicted from a knowledge of its general principles. Disgusted with the 'epicurean atheism'[1] which heretofore prevailed throughout the districts on the Indian frontier, the Tibetians of Ladák had eagerly embraced the offers of the Buddhist missionaries at an early period; and since the middle of the seventh century after Christ, with only one important interruption,[2] Buddhism under somewhat different aspects was enthroned as the religion of the whole country. Hence resulted the distinctive character of its dogmas, the apparent fervour of its moral tone, and the severity of its discipline. The mild Tibetians have for centuries been threatening to become a nation of religious mendicants. At the present day, the traveller is amazed by the ascendancy of the *lamas*,—monks, or literally 'superiors,' carrying each one in his hand the 'prayer-cylinder'[3] or 'precious and religious wheel,' a revolution of which is held to be equivalent to the recitation of a roll of prayers. In every family one at least of several children is devoted to the service of the

---

of the Middle Ages, that one might be supposed to be copied from the other:' cf. Medhurst, p. 217.

[1] This, according to Major Cunningham, *Ladák*, p. 357, was the religion of the 'Bons' or 'Pons,' connected with the Sanskrit *Punya* = 'pure.' Hence 'Pons' = Puritans, or Cathari.

[2] *Ibid.* p. 359.

[3] Major Cunningham has shewn

(*Ibid.* pp. 375 sq.) the very high antiquity of this device. So efficacious is it thought to be, that 'cylinders, about one foot in height, are placed in rows around the temples, and are turned by the votaries before entering. Larger ones are turned by water, which keeps them perpetually revolving day and night.'

cloister, so that the assemblages of monks and nuns, who flock to the *viháras* in hundreds and in thousands, constitute no inconsiderable part of the entire population. Owing probably to this enormous increase in the number of the *lamas*, the common law of Buddhism, by which mendicants are sternly interdicted from the exercise of all mechanical arts, is totally rescinded, and the *lamas* both of Tibet and of Tatary are permitted to support themselves by various handicrafts, while living in the convents.

But another point in which the Fo-ism of the *Fo-ism* Middle Kingdom has diverged still more consider- *without a regular* ably from the Lama-ism of the adjacent regions is *hierarchy.* the absence from it of a regular and graduated hierarchy. When the creed of Śákya-muni finally won its way into the palaces of China, it was only raised to the position of a secondary (non-official) creed. As such the advocates of Buddhism were content to see it left. They urged that it was merely the completion,[1] not the contradiction, of anterior systems. In their teaching, they adhered as closely as possible to the language of the sacred writings (*king*); they left the education of the masses in the hands of the imperial government; they recognised the excellence of the Confucian morality, although Confucius was himself esteemed inferior to Śákya-muni, and no fitting object of men's worship;[2] but in order most directly to secure their hold on the affections of the Chinese populace, they cordially accepted current maxims on the duty of sacrificing

[1] Schott, as before, p. 22.
[2] Thus, in the *Catechism of the Shamans,* it is directed (p. 92):
'You shall not stay in a temple of the followers of Confucius and Lao-tse.'

to departed ancestors,[1] nay, freely acquiesced in the established worship both of good and evil spirits.[2] Thus, the continuity of old traditions remaining undisturbed, the 'Son of Heaven' was under no immediate apprehension of losing his supremacy by the admission of the foreign creed. His vast authority, exceeding in religious matters the prerogatives enjoyed by many an autocratic emperor of Byzantium, enabled him to regulate and curb all classes of his subjects, the compliant Buddhists not excepted. The Grand Lamas *Hierarchy of Tibet.* of Tibet were, on the contrary, the sole depositaries both of temporal and spiritual power. Until comparatively recent times they were the masters of large tracts of country, which they governed in the spirit of the Roman Pontiff during the palmy days of Innocent III. They corresponded with the 'Sons of Heaven' on terms of brotherhood and of equality; and even now, when China has by force of arms obtained possession of Tibet, their claim to jurisdiction, as lords spiritual, continues to be freely recognised, as well in their own neighbourhood as in the hordes of barbarous Calmucks roving from the marshes of the Volga to the ruins of Samarcand. In some respects, indeed, these powerful Lamas and their agents are unlike the lordly pontiffs of western Christendom. Their theory of toleration[3] is most

---

[1] See above, p. 34.

[2] In the *Catechism*, as above, p. 102, the priest (or monk), taking the food at dinner in his left hand, is ordered to pray and say: 'O ye bad and good spirits, I now offer you this. May this meat be spread out for all bad and good spirits unto all the ten quarters [?] of the world.'

[3] When a Franciscan missionary of the xivth century was describing the state of religion in China, he adverted to this characteristic laxity in the following terms: 'In isto vasto imperio sunt gentes de omni natione quæ sub cœlo est, et de omni secta; et conceditur omnibus et singulis vivere secundum sectam suam.

comprehensive. As examples of a system of belief
which thrives wherever men are lapsing into pantheism or utter atheism, they hold that each religion
of the world has in it all the elements of necessary
truth, and consequently that every one ' shall be
saved by the law or sect which he professeth.'

Yet meanwhile outward forms of Lama-ism are *Lama-ism*
often strikingly akin to rites and customs of Mediæ- *and Mediæ-*
val Christ-
val Christianity. ' The use of the cross, the mitre, *ianity.*
the dalmatic, the hood, the office of two choirs, the
psalmody, the exorcisms, the censer of five chains,
the benediction of the lamas by placing the right
hand on the head of the faithful, the rosary, celibacy
of the clergy, spiritual retirement, the worship of
saints, fasts, processions, litanies, and holy water;"[1]
such are specimens of the minute coincidences still
adduced by Roman-catholic missionaries in proof of
the amalgamation which Buddhism had effected in
some districts with the ritual system of the Christian
Church.[2] In what way soever the liturgical affinities
in question are most satisfactorily explained; whether
we regard them as genuine imitations rising out of
some actual intercourse, or whether they exhibit no
more of real sympathy than is implied in the fortuitous

Est enim hæc opinio apud eos, seu
potius error, *quod unusquisque in
sua secta salvatur.'* Raynald. *An-
nal. Eccl.* ad an. 1326, § 31. Marco
Polo, in like manner, ascribes a
similar declaration to Kublai-
Khan (Bk. II. ch. II.): ' There are
four great Prophets, who are reverenced and worshipped by the
different classes of mankind. The
Christians regard Jesus Christ as
their divinity; the Saracens, Ma-
homet; the Jews, Moses; and the

idolaters, *Sogomom-bar-kan,* the
most eminent among their idols.
I do honour and shew respect to
all the four.' Instead of the corrupt expression here italicized,
read *Sâkya-muni Burchan* (' Burchan' being the Mongolian word
for ' Buddha').
[1] See *Journal of As. Soc.* XVI.
263.
[2] Cf. Vol. I. pp. 381 sq., where
this subject is considered in detail.

resemblance of the ape to man,[1]—it is remarkable that only a few of them exist beyond the confines of Tatary and Tibet; while in respect of general organisation, passing downwards step by step from the Grand Lama to inferior orders of the hierarchy, China can as yet present us with no parallels whatever. The communities of Fo-ists in that empire seem to be all virtually independent; they are barely held together by the recognition of common precepts, and the bond which keeps them all in due subordination to the officers of the state-religion.

Doctrine of hereditary incarnations: Again, the Lama-system differs fundamentally from that of Chinese Buddhism in the doctrine of hereditary incarnations. The great thought of some intelligence, issuing from the Buddha-world, assuming the conditions of our frail humanity, and for a time presiding over some one favoured group of Buddhist monasteries, had been long familiar to the natives of Tibet. The founder of the confraternity of *red* Lamas,[2] dating as far back as the eighth century after Christ, is said to be an instance of this self-humiliation. In the following centuries the practice was for

---

[1] 'The enemies of Christianity, since the time of Voltaire, have not failed, at the name of Bonzes, to throw out many malicious epigrams against religion. The similarity here observed is not real, but is that caricature resemblance the ape bears to man, and which has led many naturalists into error; for the ape has with man no real affinity, no true internal sympathy in his organic conformation, but merely the likeness of a spiteful parody....We may lay it down as a general principle that the greater the apparent resemblance which a false religion, utterly and fundamentally different in its spiritual character and moral tendency, externally bears to the true, the more reprehensible will it be in itself, and the greater its hostility to the truth.' F. von Schlegel, *Phil. of Hist.* p. 134.

[2] Cunningham's *Ladák*, p. 367. This Lama (Urgyan Rinpoche), who was invited into Tibet, is said to have been an incarnation of the Buddha Amitábha, the fourth of the celestial Buddhas of that region.

monks or mendicants of particular tribes to choose a kind of ' chief-abbot,'[1] in the hope of thus preserving the continuity of their order for successive generations. Of such distinguished potentates we have examples in men like Tsong Kaba,[2] who founded the great monastery of Khal-dan near Lhassa, in 1409, and by whose influence, it is said, a multitude of changes were effected both in the administration and the ritual system of Tibetian Buddhism. Still no progress seems to have been made, until the latter half of the same century, in ripening the idea of *perpetual* in-carnations. Then it was that one chief-abbot, the ' perfect Lama,' instead of passing, as he was entitled, to his ultimate condition, determined for the benefit of mankind to sojourn longer on the earth and be continuously new-born.[3] As soon as he was carried to his grave in 1473, a search was instituted for the personage who had been destined to succeed him. This was found to be an infant, who established its title to the honour by appearing to remember various articles which were the property of the Lama just deceased, or rather were the infant's own property in earlier stages of existence. When the proofs of such identity were deemed irrefragable, the new candidate was formally promoted to the vacant chair: and in the fifth abbot of this series originated the famous hierar-chy of the Dalai-Lamas (in 1640). So fascinating *why so prevalent.* grew the theory of perpetual incarnations, that a

---

[1] *Ibid.* p. 369.
[2] Also written Tsong Khapa. He is viewed as an incarnation either of Amitâbha or of Manju-sri. His tutor was the strange Lama ' from the far west,' who

may possibly have imported Christ-ian ideas: Vol. I. pp. 381, 382, and *Journal of As. Soc.* XVI. 263.
[3] Cunningham, as before, pp. 368, 369.

fresh succession of rival Lamas (also of the *yellow* order) afterwards took its rise at Teshu-lambu, while the Dalai-Lamas were enthroned in Lhassa; and at present[1] every convent of importance, not in Tibet only, but in distant parts of Tatary, is claiming for itself a like prerogative. Each confraternity believes that the departed abbot is still actually present with his subjects though enshrouded in a different body. Conscious of the dark malignity of demons, quivering at the thought of men who practise demoniacal arts and lead astray by their enchantments, these Tibetians are 'in bondage to fear;' their only refuge is the presence and superior holiness of one who, by his mastery over all the adverse forces[2] of creation, is believed to rescue his true followers from the rage of their oppressor. The religion of Tibet is thus from day to day assuming all the characteristics of man-worship.[3] Anxious cravings after some invincible protector there impel the human spirit to fashion for itself a novel theory of salvation; and the sight of one who styles himself incarnate deity excludes all living faith in God and in the things invisible.

From these remarks on characteristic differences

---

[1] *Journal of As. Soc.* XVI. 254.

[2] 'The Lamas in Tatary are constantly exorcists and magicians, sharing no doubt very often the credulity of the people, but frequently assisting faith in their superhuman faculties by jugglery and fraud:' *Ibid.* p. 264. This use of magic seems, however, disallowed in some other districts: for the *Catechism of the Shamans*, ed. Neumann, p. 111, prohibits the Buddhist monks from study-ing 'the works of Lao-tse' on demonolatry, &c.

[3] 'Durch diese vielen leibhaften Gegenstände der Andacht ist die buddhaistische Religion in Tibet *ein wahrer Menschen-Cultus* geworden, indem besonders ihre geistlichen Ober-häupter wahrhaft *göttlicher Verehrung* sich erfreuen. Auch werden die irdischen Überreste jedes Ober-Lama's als Reliquien aufbewahrt und angebetet:' Schott, as before, p. 33.

between the Fo-ism of China and the Lama-ism of
other regions, I pass forward to examine some fresh
points which serve no less directly to evince the
fluctuating and elastic genius of the creed we are
reviewing. Buddhism then, as extant both in China
and Tibet, is not the Buddhism of Śákya-muni, nor
the Buddhism of the earliest race of his disciples.
Primitive Buddhism, there is little or no cause for
doubting, was entirely atheistic.[1] As such its primary tenet led directly to the thought of ultimate
annihilation. There was nothing to receive the spirit
of man on her eventual extrication from *sansára*, the
world of appearance; and therefore instead of being
absorbed as in the old Bráhmanical theology, and so
escaping through absorption from the fatal liability
to repeated births, the elements of life were all declared
by early Buddhist doctors to be literally 'burnt out,'
—the spirit passed at length into extinction, or *nirvána*.[2] Atheism was thus attaining its most dismal
consummation in proclaiming an abyss of universal
void.

On the contrary, there often lingered in the mind
of northern Buddhists the idea of some great Being
separable from this frail and shadowy world, superior
also to the highest of created entities, and constituting
in himself the only source of ultimate felicity. The
very Buddha who persisted in ignoring the Creator
and the Judge of men was sometimes elevated to
this dignity; while the *nirvána* of his early followers,
far too cold, too dreary, and too abstract, was ere

---

[1] Cf. Vol. I. pp. 228 sq.
[2] This point has also been recently discussed by Mr. Max

Müller, *Buddhism and Buddhist
Pilgrims*, pp. 45 sq. Lond. 1857.
See above, Vol. I. p. 233, and n. 3.

in Nepál and Tibet;

long invested by the popular imagination with a different class of attributes, nay, changed into a paradise of inexhaustible enjoyment. In Nepál, and portions also of Tibet, we find the traces of a still more definite and systematic theology, yet there it had been borrowed, we have reason to believe, from the adjacent Bráhmanism.[1] By five spontaneous acts of wisdom and reflection, the self-existent Ádi-Buddha has projected from his own essence five intelligences of the first order ('The celestial Buddhas'); which in turn, by their exertion of corresponding energies, give birth to other five intelligences of the second order ('the Bódhisatwas').[2] These became creative agents in the hands of God, or serve as links uniting him with all the lower grades of creaturely existence.

how far operative.

But to other countries lying within the circle of Buddhist witchery this doctrine of spontaneous emanations is utterly unknown. The Buddhas are, in every case, 'enlightened' men, advancing upwards by the natural force of merit from one stage of greatness to another, till at last they are exempted altogether from the sad contingencies of human life. The Bódhisatwas (or, in Chinese, *Pusas*)[3] are, again, incipient Buddhas; they are all accredited competitors, approaching the possession of like immunities and like distinctions; they are rising by self-sacrifice

[1] Prof. Wilson, in *Journal of the Asiat. Soc.* (1856), XVI. 255, 256. The intermixture is still further illustrated in the numerous elements derived by Buddhists of Nepál and of Tibet from the mystical system of the Hindú Tantrists. Thence, for example, came the 'filthy theory of the Buddhist Sáktis,' or the female energies of the Dhyáni Buddhas: Cunningham's *Ladák*, pp. 366, 384.

[2] See Abel-Rémusat, *Mélanges Posthume* , p. 48, Paris, 1843.

[3] 'Bódhisatwas' = *Pu-ti-sa-ta*, then *Pu-ti-sa* and finally *Pu-sa*. In the estimation of the ordinary Fo-ist a *Pusa* is a god, one inmate in the crowded pantheon: Schott, p. 23.

and through the salutary influence they exert upon their fellow-men to that which forms the summit of all human efforts. Yet this very goal which Buddhas have attained, and Bódhisatwas are attaining, is to be the final destination of all sentient beings. Every age produces an array of Bódhisatwas, and hereafter at the winding up of universal nature, when its mighty revolutions are complete, *sansára* will have been utterly depopulated by the gradual drafting of its tenants to the Buddha-sphere, *i. e.* by their annihilation, in the language of philosophy, or by their deification, in the language of the simple and unlettered. In this system, therefore, it is plain that the idea of God, though not expressly and in terms excluded, has been robbed of all its force, its meaning, and its vitality ; and hence, in spite of rapturous invocations now and then addressed to a superior Buddha, as identical with a supreme Intelligence, the Fo-ists of the Middle Kingdom can be hardly said with any measure of propriety to know or fear, to love or worship God. Their ethical writings[1] are devoid of reference to His being: they contain no single precept on the duties which men owe to Him.

But is it then to be concluded that the Chinese Buddhists are without a definite object of religious worship? On the contrary, the empire is now *Fo-ist objects of worship.*

---

[1] *e. g.* the *Catechism of the Shamans,* passim. The Buddhist monk when called to his devotions by the sound of the wooden bell is to utter a wish that it may 'glorify the religion,' and that 'all living creatures may become enlightened' (p. 101): but there is no mention of any duty which men owe to God. The most that we can say of the 'God-like nature' is, that it dwells 'in an atmosphere of eternal complacency and repose; no greater sympathy [being shewn] with good than with evil, no displeasure against sin, no manifestation of approval of virtue.' Sir J. Bowring, *Kingdom and People of Siam,* I. 294. Lond. 1857.

thickly studded with their temples: 'they combine irreconcileable principles of atheism and polytheism,' insomuch that it is easier 'to find a god than a man in China.'[1] Towering high above the other images are three colossal forms which reappear in almost every temple. These are either representations[2] of a Buddha and two of his chief disciples; or else of three Buddhas, past, present, and future; or in other cases they are meant to symbolise the primitive Buddha, Sákya-muni, as allied with *Dharma*, the religion he had founded, and with *Sangga*, the community or confraternity of religious men. It is, however, most remarkable, as again exemplifying the multiformity of Buddhism, that the 'Three Precious Ones' of modern China are not identical with the 'Three Supremacies' of somewhat earlier generations. Sákya-muni has indeed his constant votaries not only as the Shakya-Thubba of Ladák, and as the Kodom or Gautama of other regions, but also as the She-kia and the Fo of Chinese Buddhism.

Sákya-muni supplanted. Yet his fame appears to have been long declining even where the solemn sacrifice of flowers and perfumes still continues to be offered; and hereafter, on the expiration of five-and-twenty centuries from the present time,[3] he is expected to be absolutely superseded by a fresh and more benignant Buddha, called *Maitréya* or *Mi-le*. It was probably a consequence

---

[1] Medhurst, p. 219.

[2] Wilson, as before, p. 253. Abel-Rémusat (*Mélanges Posthumes*, p. 26,) has cited a prayer where he thinks that worship is rendered to Buddha as *the first member of a triad.* The form is this: 'Adoration à *Bouddha*, adoration à *Dharma*, adoration à *Sangga*,' to which is annexed the Bráhmanical *Óm.* See Vol. 1. p. 277.

[3] Schott, p. 13; Bowring's *Siam*, 1. 305; Sangermano's *Burmese Empire*, p. 85.

of this foreboding as to his eventual deposition that
led in China and in some adjacent districts to the
worship of three other objects, scarcely inferior to
Gautama himself, yet all of them unknown to the
original Buddhists.[1] Such are Amitábha (O-me-to[2]),
Avalókitéswara (Kwan-shi-in[3] or Padma-páni), and
Manju-śrí[4] (Jámya or Jam-pal). The last, though *Manju-śrí.*
chiefly occupied, as men believe, in the diffusion of
religious truth, and in such office bearing in his hand
a naked sword, the symbol of his power and his
acumen, has not hitherto absorbed so large a share
of popular devotion[5] as the two with whom he is
immediately associated. His province is the world
of intellect; while Kwan-shi-in, the second of these *Kwan-shi-*
three divinities, is the author of all joy and happiness *in, or Padma-*
in the family-circle, and has even been deputed to *páni.*
administer the government of the whole earth. In
many districts of Tibet, which seems to claim his

[1] Wilson, as before, pp. 241,
242. Two out of the three are
first noticed in the account of the
pilgrimage of Fa-hian (at the
close of the 4th century): Cunningham's *Ladák*, pp. 362, 363.

[2] The Chinese modification of
the Sanskrit *Amitábha* (= 'unmeasured, infinite Light.')

[3] Kwan-shi-in = 'world-inspecting *Sound*,' a mistaken rendering of the Sanskrit *avalókita-
íswara* = 'world-inspecting *Lord*.'
The mistake arose from not perceiving the fusion of *a* + *i* into *é*,
and so reading *swara* 'sound' for
iswara 'lord.' The other title
Padma-páni is also pure Sanskrit
(= 'lotus in his hand,' or 'lotus-
bearer'), and is said to accord in
signification with the Tibetan
name *Chakna-padma*: Schott, p.

30, n. 1. Major Cunningham, on
the contrary, identifies *Avalókitéswara* with the Tibetian *Chan-
razik*, and regards Padma-páni as
a different and still later Bodhisatwa: *Ladák*, pp. 362, 363, 383.

[4] Another form, also of Sanskrit
origin, is *Manju-gósha*. The first
seems to indicate a being of 'mild
or gentle majesty;' the second a
being of 'mild or gentle voice':
Schott, p. 40, n. 1. The Chinese
corruption of *Manju-śrí* is *Wen-
choo;* while the Tibetian form is
Jam-pal. According to one version (Lassen, III. 777) *Manju-śrí*
was a veritable man, by whom
the conversion of Nepál to Buddhism had been originally attempted, in the tenth century after
Christ.

[5] Schott, p. 41.

more indulgent patronage, he is incarnate, under the name of Padma-páñi, in the person of the Dalai-Lama: and perhaps no cry so often strikes the ear of travellers in that country as *Om! Mani-padme! Húm*, 'Glory to the Lotus-bearer, Húm!'[1] Both there and in Mongolia, this far-stretching potentate is represented sometimes with innumerable eyes and hands, and sometimes with as many as ten heads, all bearing crowns and rising conically one above another:[2] but in every part of China the imagery employed is far less cumbrous and ornate; and what is more remarkable, this single tenant of the Buddha-world, in violation of a law by which distinctions as to sex are not perpetuated in the most exalted stage of being, is invested with a female figure, and with feminine decorations.[3]

Amitábha or O-me-to.

High above the head or heads of Padma-páñi, and so forming the very apex of that sacred cone or pyramid, is seen the visage of his great superior, Amitábha, who, radiant with the glories of a perfect Buddha,[4] is perhaps the most revered of all the

[1] *Mani-padme* is a misreading or corruption of the Sanskrit *Padma-páñi*. The whole of this invocation, alluding to the way in which Padma-páñi was first revealed, is said to have been suggested directly from heaven, as the bearer of innumerable blessings to the human family: Abel-Rémusat, *Mélanges Posthumes*, p. 403: 'Neubekehrte Fürsten der Mongolei lernten vor Allem diese Formel beten, vermuthlich damit der heilige Schauer, den sie ihnen einflössen sollte, das Feld ihres Glaubens desto fruchtbarer machte; und noch heutzutage ist sie in beiden Ländern [Tibet and Mongolia] dem Laien eben so geläufig als dem Geistlichen, und behauptet sich neben seinen anderen vorschriftsmässigen Gebeten.' Schott, p. 61.

[2] Schott, p. 45; Wilson, as before, p. 242.

[3] *Ibid*. Perhaps this notion may be borrowed from the theory of Buddha-śaktis, or female energies, which is, and has been for some ages, current both in Nepál and in Tibet: see Cunningham's *Ladák*, p. 364.

[4] 'Den Chinesen ist nun A-mita, (O-me-to) ein vollendeter Buddha, wie Śākjamuni, aber von diesem bestimmt geschieden:' Schott, p. 49.

objects worshipped in the Fo-ist temples. It is
probable that he was once regarded only as an image
of the absent Śākya-muni, who on finishing his
salutary work is thought to have retreated for a
while into some deep abstraction, without absolutely
ceasing to exist. Amitábha may thus have been to
the originator of the Buddhist creed exactly what his
offspring and co-regent, Padma-páni, will in course
of ages be to him. So great, however, is the present
dignity of Amitábha, that all the other gods of China
are apparently outstripped by him, and well-nigh
thrown into the shade.[1]

To him the Fo-ist looks for grace, for mercy, for *Supremacy*
deliverance from all kinds of evil. Starting like the *of O-mi-to.*
previous Buddhas from a low position, he has worked
his way, it is believed, through a succession of new
births into the loftiest sphere of the invisible regions.
There he sits enthroned for ever on a lotus, his
celestial court comprising an array of *Pusas* (or
advanced competitors for Buddha-ship), and closer
still in place and honour to his own unrivalled majesty, appearing his chief-minister and disciple, the
co-regent Padma-páni.[2]

The main features of this paradise of Amitábha *Paradise of*
are deserving of a more extended notice, partly on *O-mi-to.*
the ground that they are altogether irreconcileable
with the early creed of Buddhism,[3] and partly as

[1] 'Mit seinem *unendlichen Lichte* [the meaning of Amitábha] hat er Śákjamuni selber fast ganz ver- dunkelt.' *Ibid.*

[2] *Ibid.* p. 50.

[3] Schott, who has translated largely from a Chinese work in- tended to excite men's faith in the *Tsing-t'u* (or paradise of Ami- tábha), says with perfect truth that very much of the description, and the whole theory respecting this Buddha, is in direct contra- diction to the creed of Gautama. 'Amitábha soll ein vollendeter Buddha sein, obschon ein Solcher

suggesting a comparison with images that sometimes meet us on the page of sacred prophecy. 'This paradise includes within it every thing most noble and most sumptuous; and the city of the gods is all constructed of gold and precious stones, arranged with perfect art. The atmosphere is ever redolent of spices, and resounds with blissful harmonies. The streams again move forward like a tender strain of music. Round about are stately trees of silver with branches of pure gold, all covered by a rich variety of precious stones and the most gorgeous fruits. The spaces also are occupied by trees of eight different sorts, consisting each of two different jewels, on whose leaves and on the lotus-flowers there growing in the midst, innumerable seats have been provided for the Buddhas. A golden vault responding to the breath of every zephyr in celestial harmonies extends its shadow over all the trees, and at their feet flows forth in gentle murmurs many a copious stream of water, holy, living, wonder-working. The tenants of this paradise are all without distinction of rank or sex;[1] they all are equal, glorious in form and aspect, and exempted from the possibility of future births into a world of misery. In the centre of the

---

nicht einmal vom Himmel aus an dem Erlösungswerke ferneren Antheil nimmt. Er und die seligen Bewohner seines Reiches sollen *ewig leben*, obschon dies einem Axiome des Buddhaismus geradezu widerspricht. Die im Tsing-t'u Wiedergebornen leben dort. . .mit Pusa's zusammen, sind im Besitz derselben Gaben, im Genusse derselben Vortheile, und doch keine eigentlichen Pusa's.' (p. 57).

[1] In a different description of the paradise of *O-me-to* (Amitâbha) communicated in Medhurst's *China*, p. 207, it is said that 'there are no women; for the women who live in that country are first changed into men.' The legend then continues: 'The inhabitants are produced from the lotus-flower, and have pure and fragrant bodies, fair and well-formed countenances, with hearts full of wisdom, and without vexation,' &c.

region is a grove consisting of the goodliest trees; where peerless in his beauty and resplendent as the evening sky reposes the great Buddha Amitábha, a peacock and a lion forming the supporters of his throne. His right hand, the dispenser of his grace, is white, and rests upon his lap: while in his left hand, he is holding a dark vase of holy water. Round about him sit the Bódhisatwas, his elect, who offer up their prayers for the well-being and conversion of all creatures."[1]

The possession of this supreme felicity is said to *Salvation* have resulted in all cases, not as in the primitive *by O-me-to.* Buddhism[2] from ascetic habits painfully acquired by free submission to an almost endless series of new births, but simply from unbounded trust in Amitábha, and unceasing prayer to him in his capacity of champion and rewarder. He swore, it is believed in China, that 'if any being in all the ten worlds should, after repeating his name, fail to attain life in his kingdom, he would cease to be a god.'[3] The process of salvation was now represented, in accordance with the earth-ward tendency of men addressed, as something far more easy and indulgent than was commonly imagined. 'It requires no whole day, but only a few instants every morning. What it asks for is, one prayer [*O-me-to Foĕ*, or 'Amitábha Buddha'], ten times repeated. It is, therefore, burdensome to no man: it will interfere with no man's social duties,

---

[1] Translated from a Mongolian source in Schott, pp. 52, 53. The Chinese legends on the subject, which, as he observes, are very numerous, preserve the same general outlines, but, as might have been anticipated from the genius of the people, all the details are less florid and grotesque.

[2] Cf. Schott, pp. 57, 58.

[3] Medhurst. *Ibid.*

Faith in O-me-to.

nor his worldly business. . . . Yes! it is the work of an instant every morning, and nevertheless it brings advantages that are to last for all eternity."[1] Faith, however, is imperatively needed in the human subject ere this saving work can be achieved. Without it there ensues no movement in the right direction, just as when the will refuses to exert its force upon the bodily organism. 'A Buddha can deliver all creation, yet is powerless in respect of men, who have no faith.'[2] The vilest sinner, on the contrary, who is possessed of this most efficacious principle, will rise at once superior to the fear of death, and will be rescued from the pains of hell. If at the hour of dissolution he have strength enough to supplicate the mercy of *O-me-to*, and can repeat the supplication ten times, 'the images of hell are sure to be transformed into a lotus; and the sinner, snatched from ruin, will obtain admission into paradise. The Buddha,' it is added, 'can effect all this, because his mercy and his wonder-working power are both indefinitely great.'[3]

Apparent resemblance to Christianity.

The reader may be tempted to infer, on meeting with this very remarkable language, that the authors of the documents in question were not altogether strangers to Christianity itself, whose tenets they appear to be adopting and distorting. And in favour of such interpretation is the fact, that their idea of

---

[1] Translated by Schott from the *Tsing-t'u-uen*, as before, p. 65.

[2] *Ibid.* p. 81.

[3] *Ibid.* p. 94. A discussion follows as to whether the intercession of the living is available for the comfort or recovery of the dead. 'In den *Sûtras* steht geschrieben: "Die verdienstlichen Handlungen, welche Andere nach seinem Tode für den Menschen thun, erwerben nur eins von sieben [*i. e.* the harvest is disproportionate to the seed sown]; was aber der Mensch *für sich selbst bei seinen Lebzeiten thut*, das wird ihm tausendfältig vergolten." Warum also wartet man bis an seinen Tod, und bittet Andere, statt seiner zu beten ?'

absolute faith in one divinity as *the* condition of deliverance from all forms of evil, was unknown to every
other creed of heathendom, until, in times comparatively recent, it was also manifested in the Krishña
worship of the Bráhmans, and perverted by them
into pretexts for unbounded laxity and self-indul-
gence.[1] Every one, moreover, is disposed to grant
that the Chinese conception, as here indicated, is quite
foreign to the ethics and religion of Sákya-muni, and
in truth was a production of far later ages.[2]

Possibly, when some adventurous heralds of the *Intercourse of Christians and Fo-ists.*
Gospel, in the seventh and following centuries after
Christ, began ' to turn their faces towards heaven,
and, travelling with the Book of Truth,'[3] surmounted
the vast obstacles that severed China from the western
world, the influence they exerted in the presence of
a creed so flexible as Fo-ism, was more deep and
lasting than is generally believed. Or it may be
that in still later ages, when the courts of the Great
Khan were thronged by ardent representatives of all

---

[1] See Vol. I. pp. 257, 333, 334;
and the more recent consideration
of the subject in Weber's *Indische
Skizzen*, pp. 92 sq. He is now
even more persuaded that Christianity was at the bottom of those
thorough changes in the old beliefs of India (p. 94).

[2] Schott, p. 58, who refers these
modifications to a period, ' in
welcher man selbst den Geistlichen keine grossartige Selbst-
verläugnung und keine ange-
strengte Meditation mehr zutrauen
konnte.'

[3] This phrase occurs in the famous Syro-Chinese inscription,
the genuineness of which has
been disputed for more than two
centuries : see, on the one side,
Abel-Rémusat, *Nouveaux Mélanges Asiat.* II. 189 sq., and on the
other, Prof. Neumann, in the
*Jahrbücher für wissenschaft. Kri-
tik* (1829), pp. 592 sq. Mr. Kesson,
The Cross and the Dragon, pp. 16
sq. Lond. 1854, and (more in
detail) M. Huc, *Le Christianisme
en Chine*, I. 48—93, have reviewed
the whole question. But, however that particular controversy
may be settled, there is no doubt
that soon after A.D. 782 (the date
of the inscription) Christianity
did find its way as far as China
through the wide-spread influence
of ' Nestorian,' or Syrian, missionaries (Huc, I. 98 sq.).

known religions; when the Christian preachers in particular were 'commanded to attend him and bring with them their Book;'[1] and when, as the result of this indulgence, both the Latins and Nestorians dared to plant their missions even in Peking itself, the eastern capital of the empire, some of the vibrations thus excited in the Chinese mind had led to an occasional adoption of Christian phraseology, analogous to what is happening in the *Tae-ping* rebels of the present day.

Real antagonism between the two systems.

But whatever be the true account of the phenomena to which I have adverted, it is obvious that the actual changes in the Fo-ist system did not penetrate below the surface. Faith in Amitábha bears the slightest possible relation to faith in Christ the Righteous. The phantastic paradise of Amitábha has no common ground with that which Christians see prefigured on the glowing page of the Apocalypse. In both those heathen parallels the most essential element is one that has receded most of all into the background. Holiness of heart and life is not proclaimed in them as the concomitant of genuine faith, nor as the one condition of eventual blessedness; but, on the contrary, the novel tenet has been there adopted with the plain avowal that by it mankind will be exonerated altogether from the stern injunctions of the moral law. On sifting all such specious but entirely hollow approximations to the doctrine of our blessed Lord, one is continually reminded of the daring counterfeits disseminated far and wide by the abettors

---

[1] See the narrative in Marco Polo, Bk. II. ch. II (p. 167, ed. Wright) and Huc, I. 367 sq. The title of M. Huc's chapter is 'Le Catholicisme à Péking pendant le treizième siècle.'

of the earliest heresies. The solifidianism of Hindú- stán and China is the solifidianism dissected and denounced by the believing Irenæus.[1] It is alien from the spirit of pure and Catholic Christianity. Attempts to mix what is incapable of admixture, were accordingly resisted and defeated here and there upon the very threshold. Men discovered that they could not 'sew a piece of new cloth on an old garment:' concord or consistency was felt to be impossible: 'the new piece taketh away from the old, and the rent is made worse.'

It is, indeed, the clear opinion of those modern writers who have had the largest opportunity of tracing out the principles of Buddhism to their practical results, that while it has appeared to flourish most in Birmah and Siam, its course in China has for centuries been one of retrogression and decay. The very monks of Fo-ism, who are nominally bound by far more stringent regulations than the rest of the community, are said to go beyond their pupils in the puerility of their superstitions and the immorality of their lives. 'The ignorance, selfishness, chicanery, mendacity, mendicancy, and idleness of the bonzes cannot be exaggerated,'—such is the deliberate judgment of one[2] who spent his days in China, chiefly

Present decline of Fo-ism.

---

[1] 'Quapropter nec ulterius curarent eos [*i. e.* prophetas] hi, qui in eum [Simonem] et in Helenam ejus spem habeant, et ut liberos agere quæ velint : secundum enim ipsius gratiam salvari homines, sed non secundum operas justas.' Iren. *Contra Hæreses*, Lib. 1. c. XXIII. § 3 (ed. Stieren).

[2] See Gutzlaff's communication, which he sent to Europe not long before his death, in the *Journal of*

the *As. Soc.* XVI. 73 sq. His testimony is echoed on the whole by that of Sir John Bowring, who cannot be charged with disparaging Buddhism in order to exaggerate the importance of Christianity. He writes (*Kingdom and People of Siam*, 1. 297, Lond. 1857): 'The real and invincible objection to Buddhism is its selfishness. . . . A bonze seems to care nothing about the condition of those who

in the hope of elevating the moral and religious status of the Chinese people. And even if it be contended that the Christian zeal of men like Gutzlaff caused them here and there to overcolour their descriptions of the blindness and the inefficiency of Fo-ism, no one will deny that its material strength has long been rapidly declining, and the outward glory of the system vanishing from day to day. The Fo-ist temples 'are now mostly deserted, and in a state of ruins; the votaries fewer and fewer, and the offerings very sparing.'[1] What may be the future of this mighty empire, what the changes that may supervene hereafter on the agitation of the present times, it were not easy to conjecture. The Christian missionary may have still occasion to sit down and cry despairing on the frontier, 'O that the everlasting gates of rock would open!' but one fact appears to have been well established, that in this particular 'China during the last twenty or forty years has undergone a very great change, and is still verging to a more important crisis.'[2]

I am far, however, from contending, with some Christian writers, that the vast dissemination of Bud-

surround him: he makes no effort for their elevation or improvement. He scarcely reproves their sins, or encourages their virtues. He is self-satisfied with his own superior holiness, and would not move his finger to remove any mass of human misery.' Wuttke, by a different process, comes to a result substantially the same: 'Thatsächlich hat der Buddhismus in China allen Geist verloren, ist faul und dumpf geworden: ein ganz mechanisches Formel-wesen, dem Chinesen so natürlich, hat die Stelle der gewaltigen Ideen eingenommen.' (II. 84.)

[1] Gutzlaff, as above, p. 91.

[2] *Ibid.* How far the struggles now proceeding may affect the ultimate position of Chinese Buddhism is also matter of deep interest to those who watch the fortunes of the Middle Kingdom: for it is well known that the rebels have invariably betrayed a most decided hostility to Fo-ism, its doctors, and its images.

dhist tenets was in former days so utterly adverse to Chap. I.
the higher interests of humanity. To say of this *How far*
religion that its votaries are people 'whose business *primitive Buddhism*
is to do nothing, to think on nothing, and to live *was a*
as much as possible on nothing,'[1] is a representation *civilizing agent.*
meagre, hasty, and one-sided. When Buddhism
started on its northern missions, full of youthful hope
and unextinguishable ardour, we behold it shaping
many a savage horde into a peaceful confraternity;
it quenched the violence of domestic strife; it sheathed
the scimitars of the bloodthirsty Mongols, who were
bent on carrying desolation to the very heart of
Europe; it planted convents, and therewith conventual
schools and libraries in regions heretofore oppressed
by every kind of demonolatry and darkness; it carried
some imperfect elements of Hindú civilisation far
across the sandy wastes of Tatary, and shed some
glimmerings of a higher light within the borders of
Siberia; and even if the proselytes it made have
far too frequently relapsed into their old condition,
and so proved the utter impotence of Buddhism to
effect a permanent and radical change,[2] the partial
benefit resulting from its propagation ought on no
account to be forgotten. Buddhism should in fact be *Its ethical*
measured, not by Christian, but by heathen standards; *character.*
and when so regarded, it will, in its palmier days,
appear almost to justify the startling eulogy bestowed
upon it by a modern writer, when he speaks of
Buddhism as the 'Christianity of the East.'[3] The

[1] Neumann, *Pref.* to the *Catechism of the Shamans*, pp. xxiii, xxiv.

[2] See Vol. I. pp. 238, 356.

[3] 'On a désigné le bouddhisme par le nom de *Christianisme de l'Orient*, et, à la convenance près, cette exagération exprime assez bien l'importance des services qu'il a rendus à l'humanité': Abel-Rémusat, *Mélanges Posthumes*, p. 237.

stress which it originally placed on ethics in their social and political aspect; its contempt for principles which long created an impassable gulf between the different orders of Hindú society; its fuller recognition of the rights of woman; its mild and inoffensive spirit, its equanimity under suffering, its forgiveness of injuries, are some of the peculiar features which adorn its moral code. Instead of ministering[1] to all the grosser passions, like the theories of Islam, it carried its appeal directly to the intellectual and contemplative province of man's nature; instead of finding its chief stimulus in struggles after fame and in the offer of material prosperity, it preached the vanity of earthly goods, the hollowness of human approbation; instead of teaching man to hoard the produce of his industry, it not unfrequently suggested the devotion of superfluous treasure to the founding of a refuge for the blind, the destitute, the crippled, the diseased. Some kings are mentioned,[2] who, starting

---

[1] See the *Dharma* contrasted in this particular with the *Kurán* by Major Cunningham, *Bhilsa Topes*, pp. 53, 54.

[2] The following picture of a model Buddhist king is well worth transcription. It is taken from the *Vie et Voyages de Hiouen-Thsang*, ed. Julien, pp. 204, 205: 'Suivant la tradition, le trône était occupé, il y a soixante ans, par un roi nommé Kinaï-ji (*Ciláditya*): il était doué de grands talents et possédait de vastes connaissances. Il était humain, affectueux, bienfaisant et dévoué pour le bonheur du peuple. Il était plein de respect pour les Trois Précieux [the *Buddha*, the *Sangga*, or assembly of religious, and the *Dharma*, or Law]. De puis son avénement au trône jusqu'au moment de sa mort, nulle parole inconvenante ne s'échappa de sa bouche, et la colère ne rougit point son visage. Jamais il n'eut l'idée de faire du mal à ses sujets ni de tuer une mouche ou une fourmi. Dans la crainte de causer la mort aux insectes qui vivent dans l'eau, il ne permettait pas d'en donner à boire aux éléphants ou aux chevaux avant de l'avoir soigneusement filtrée. Quant aux hommes du royaume, il leur défendait sévèrement de tuer des animaux. De là vient que les bêtes féroces s'attachaient aux hommes, les loups oubliaient leur fureur; la paix régnait dans l'intérieur des frontières, et des présages de

from the worship of the 'Three Precious Ones,' had
carried their philanthropy and tenderness for every
kind of animal life to most absurd extremes, and
even were accustomed to dole out in alms not only
the immense accumulations in the royal coffers, but
the whole of their personal ornaments.

It would, perhaps, be difficult to single out a *The last hours of Hiuan-Thsang;* Buddhist of any period in the range of history who
manifested such a high and generous nature as the
pilgrim, Hiuan-Thsang, to whom I have before alluded.
The best portion of his life was all consumed in
perilous wanderings, undertaken with the aim of
rescuing the *Dharma* from the errors which had over-
grown it, and of recommending it on every side to
the affections of his fellow-men. In these researches
he was able to collect a multitude of sacred writings,
which on his return to China he translated, in concert
with a band of his disciples, into the language of his
native country. When the hour of death was fast
approaching, he commanded all his worldly goods to
be distributed among the poor ; he caused the votive
statues to be fashioned ; he required the brethren of
his convent to recite the usual prayers. At last his
friends are all invited to assemble round his couch
and take a joyous leave of his ' impure and despicable
body,' which, after having played its part, is lost to

bonheur éclataient chaque jour.' Another king of the same name, and contemporaneous with the traveller himself, was in the habit of convoking general as- semblies, and there distributing all his wealth among his subjects. On one occasion he gave away in alms the whole of his royal orna- ments. ' Maintenant que j' ai pu (par l'aumône) les déposer dans le *champ du bonheur*, je les regarde comme conservées à jamais. Je désire, dans toutes mes existences futures, amasser ainsi d'immenses richesses pour faire l'aumône aux hommes, et obtenir les dix facultés divines dans toute leur plénitude : (p. 256).

him for ever. 'I hope,' he adds, 'that all the merits I have gained by my good works may now accrue to the advantage of other people. My wish is to be born with them into the heaven of the *Touchitas* (the blessed), to be admitted into the family of *Mi-le* (Maitréya), and to serve this Buddha of the future, who is full of tenderness and of affection. When my fate is to descend afresh into the world, and undergo another series of existences, I hope at every new birth to do my duty towards the Buddha with un-wearying zeal, and ultimately to arrive in turn at the supreme Intelligence.' He then gave utterance to his deep regrets on feeling that the world was fast receding from his grasp; but at the very moment of dissolution, when his pupils asked him, 'Master, have you really obtained the right of being born into the assembly of *Mi-le?*' his quivering lips responded 'Yes;' and so he yielded up the ghost.[1]

[1] 'Puis il leur dit: "Le moment de ma mort approche; déjà mon esprit s'affaisse et semble me quitter. Il faut promptement distribuer en aumônes mes vêtements et mes richesses, faire fabriquer des statues et charger des religieux de réciter des prières." Le vingt-troisième jour, on donna un repas aux pauvres et l'on distribua des aumônes. Le même jour, il ordonna à un mouleur nommé *Song-kia-tchi* d'élever, dans le palais *Kia-chcou-tien*, une statue de l'*Intelligence* (Bôdhi); après quoi, il invita la multitude du couvent, les traducteurs adjoints et ses disciples "à dire joyeusement adieu à ce corps impur et méprisable de *Hiouen-Thsang* qui, ayant fini son rôle, ne méritait plus de subsister longtemps. Je désire, ajouta-t-il, voir reverser sur les autres hommes les mérites que j'ai acquis par mes bonnes œuvres; naître, avec eux, dans le ciel des *Touchi-tas;* être admis dans la famille de *Mi-le* (*Maitréya*) et servir ce *Bouddha* plein de tendresse et d'affection. Quand je redescendrai sur la terre pour parcourir d'autres existences, je désire, à chaque naissance nouvelle, remplir avec un zèle sans bornes mes devoirs envers le *Bouddha*, et arriver enfin à l'*Intelligence transcendante* (*Anouttara samyak sambôdhi*)." Après avoir fait ces adieux, il se tut et entra en méditation; puis, de sa langue mourante, il laissa échapper d'amers regrets, en sentant qu'il ne jouissait plus du *monde des yeux* (de la faculté de voir), du *monde de la pensée* (de la faculté de penser), du *monde de la connaissance qui naît de la vue* (de la con-

A spectacle resembling this in many of the outward circumstances, yet presenting also many a deep
and touching contrast, was beheld soon afterwards
within the walls of a secluded convent in our own
Northumbria. It was the death-scene of the Venerable Bede. He also was the brightest luminary of
the sphere in which he moved; for though his creed
may in some few particulars have been alloyed by
elements of thought and feeling at variance with the
genius of primitive Christianity, his heart was ever
true in its allegiance to our heavenly Father, and he
died receiving as the end of his faith the crown of
glory that fadeth not away. The days and years
of Bede, like those of Hiuan-Thsang, had been devoted mainly to the spread of sacred literature, and
when his strength was failing and his peaceable career
was gliding to its close, we see him in a crowded
circle of affectionate pupils, eager to imbibe the treasures that continued to pour forth from his capacious
memory. Among his brother-presbyters he also
parted the small remnant of his worldly substance,
'giving with much love and joy what he had previously received from God.' The tears of the by-
standers were at length beginning to flow fast; for
each of them perceived that Bede, the master-spirit
of their thriving confraternity, had girded up his

---

naissance des objets sensibles), du
monde de la connaissance qui naît
de l'esprit (de la perception des
choses spirituelles), et qu'il ne
possédait point la plénitude de l'
Intelligence.' The 'Master of the
Law' then uttered two *gáthás*, aspirations to *Maitréya tathágata.*
For some time he continued mo-
tionless and took no food. At

last, 'au milieu de la nuit, ses
disciples lui demandèrent : "Mai-
tre, avez vous enfin obtenu de
naître au milieu de l'assemblée
de Mâitrêya?" "Oui," répondit-
il, d'une voix défaillante. A ce
mot sa respiration s'affaiblit de
plus en plus, et, au bout de quelques instants, son âme s'évanuit.'
Ibid. pp. 344 sq.

loins to die; yet sorrow was in their case all transmuted into joy, when they remembered that the
spirits of the just are in the hands of the Omnipotent,
and Christ the risen Lord of dead as well as living.
'They rejoiced,' is the account of an eye-witness,
'when he said, "It is time that I returned to Him
who made me, who created me, and formed me out
of nothing. I have had a long life upon the earth;
the merciful Judge has also been pleased to order for
me a happy life. The time of my departure is at
hand, for I have a desire to depart and to be with
Christ." And with many such like remarks he
passed the day until eventide. Then the boy, whom
we have already mentioned, said to him, "Still one
sentence, dear master, remains unwritten." He replied, "Write quickly." After a little while, the
boy said, "Now the sentence is finished." He answered, "You have spoken the truth—it is indeed
finished. Raise my head in your hands, for it pleases
me much to recline opposite to that holy place of
mine, on which I used to pray, so that, while resting
there, I may call upon God my Father." And being
placed upon the pavement of his cell, he said, "Glory
be to the Father, and to the Son, and to the Holy
Ghost"—and as soon as he had named the name of
the Holy Spirit, he breathed out his own spirit, and
so departed to the kingdom of heaven."[1]

---

[1] Beda died A.D. 735, about seventy years later than Hiuan-Thsang. The most accurate version of this narrative of Cuthbert will be found in Mr. Stevenson's 'Preface to Beda,' pp. xv. sq. Lond. 1853.

CHAPTER II.

Religions of America, particularly the Mexican.

‘Darin besteht eben die Bedeutung der Amerikanischen Religionen,
  dass sie mehr als andere, wenigstens mehr als andere Religionen
  von Kulturvölkern, das primitive und unabgeschwächte Heidenthum darstellen.’

IT is now established that the eastern promontories
of the New World were sighted by the storm-tost
Greenlander, and trodden by the sturdy foot of the
adventurous Northman long before[1] the last ‘discovery’ of that continent in 1497. Yet little or no
definite information resulted from such voyages beyond the fact that certain media really existed for
connecting the barbarians of Labrador, of Nova
Scotia, and of Massachusetts, with the people on the
coasts of Scandinavia, and the consequent possibility
of transporting thither some vague knowledge of white
men and some few germs of Christianity.[2] Nor do

Vagueness of American traditions.

---

[1] See the interesting revelations
in Rafn's *Antiquitates Americanæ*,
Hafniæ, 1845. and Humboldt's
Cosmos, II. 234 sq. Sabine's ed.
The first recorded view of the
American coast was obtained in
986. In 1000, Leif actually landed
with thirty-five companions on a
point which he called Helluland,
identified with Labrador. From
thence one of the party penetrated
further south to what they called
Vinland (from the wild vines
growing there).

[2] Some white men appear to
have remained in America at an
early period, and in 1121 we find
a Greenland bishop making a
voyage to Vinland : cf. Münter,
Kirchengesch. von Dänemark, &c.
I. 561. Leipzig, 1833.

Chap. II. any of the frequent narratives sent home to Europe by the first 'Conquistadores' throw much light upon the primitive traditions of the various tribes whom they subdued. Intoxicated by their lust of gold, devoting all their wondrous energies to the extension and consolidation of their empire, many of them were deaf not only to the pleas put forward by the native in behalf of his hereditary freedom, but also to the war-songs and the legends that continued to give utterance to his baneful superstitions. Other Spaniards in a frenzy of fanaticism were instigated to destroy[1] the only archives, by the light of which we could have hoped to track with any certainty the course pursued in the migrations of the 'civilised' families of America; while in reference to the Indians proper, the historical materials then as now surviving are no better than a mass of wild hyperboles; they tell of 'nations creeping out of the ground—a world growing out of a tortoise's back—the globe reconstructed from the earth clutched in a muskrat's paw, after a deluge.'[2] Hence the difficult nature of the problems which confronted the ethnologist when he proceeded by more scientific methods to determine the mutual relations of the tribes and peoples of America, to penetrate still further into mysteries connected with their past condition, and educe some elements of light and order from the midst of that

---

[1] 'The strange, unknown characters inscribed on them [the picture manuscripts] excited suspicion. They were looked on as magic scrolls; and were regarded in the same light with the idols and temples, as the symbols of a pestilent superstition, that must be extirpated:' Prescott, *Conquest of Mexico*, p. 32, Lond. 1854.

[2] See *History, Condition, and Prospects of the Indian Tribes*, ed. Schoolcraft (recently compiled for the Government of the United States), Part I. p. 13.

far-spreading chaos, which had, in the judgment of Chap. II. the superficial writer, hopelessly enveloped the history of the New World.

The first great generalisation thus obtained had *Homogeneity of American tribes.* reference to the physical characteristics of the native population. It was found that, on eliminating a subordinate class of 'singular and inexplicable diversities,'[1] the people of that continent, in all their geographical distribution, from the Arctic Ocean to Cape Horn, may be described as homogeneous, or the scions of one parent stock. The squalid Esquimaux, at one extremity of the chain, the polished Aztec, or Peruvian, at the other; agriculturists, and hunters, and canoe-men; tribes frequenting the shores of the great northern lakes, or scattered in the dense savannahs of the South; the stunted Chayma, the athletic Caraib, and the half-clad native of the Land of Fire, exhibit the same general lineaments, and constitute together one distinct variety of the human species. They 'possess alike the long, lank, black hair, the brown or cinnamon-coloured skin, the heavy brow, the dull and sleepy eye, the full and compressed lips, and the salient and dilated nose.'[2] But in the *Linguistic difficulties.* course of wide and patient investigations which have issued in this grand result, another class of facts were sometimes felt to wear a very different aspect and to point in very different directions. So far was the explorer of American antiquities from meeting with a common language, or one group of kindred dialects,

---

[1] There is still some difference of opinion among ethnologists respecting the extent and value of these 'diversities'; see Prichard, v. 290 sq.

[2] Morton's *Crania Americana*, quoted with other testimonies to the same effect in Squier's *American Archæological Researches*, No. 1. pp. 23, 24, New York, 1851.

that varieties of human speech were found to be almost innumerable; each narrow tract of country being occupied by tribes continually at war with each other, esteeming every stranger an enemy, and possessing few, if any, of the ordinary means of intercommunication.

Peculiar characteristics of American languages.

Here again, however, science has contributed her timely aid in filling up the blanks of primitive history. It has been shewn, entirely to the satisfaction of all competent philologers, that if, as in the former case, we make a few exceptions, capable of being explained on the hypothesis of accidental or colonial intercourse with foreign countries, the discordant languages of America are all held together by common and peculiar principles of construction, pointing to a primitive centre, and acknowledging the plastic influence of one mother-tongue. These languages are neither monosyllabic, like the Chinese, the primitive Malay, and other kindred idioms; nor dissyllabic, like a second class of ancient languages related to the Hebrew; nor analytical, like the tongues of modern Europe, which are substituting, or have substituted, for the old inflections a vast number of auxiliary particles. The proper description of the American dialects, as spoken for the last three hundred and fifty years, is *polysynthetic*,[1] meaning that their organ-

---

[1] The credit of working out this idea belongs to Mr. du Ponceau: see Prichard, v. 305 sq., who has added (pp. 313 sq.) some judicious observations on the probable causes of the vast dissimilarity in the words themselves. This may be referred, partly to the isolation of the various tribes, partly to the wonderful richness of their first vocabulary, partly to the feverish activity of their imagination and rhetorical faculty, which are ever coining new expressions; but resemblance is perhaps most of all destroyed by certain current principles of truncation and agglutination, impelling the American Indians to cut off the beginning and the end of

isation is so flexible, so artificial, and so highly complex, as to make them far more capable than any
other dialects of combining a large assortment of
ideas and various shades of meaning into one poly-
syllabic term. In other words, however manifold
those languages may be as to their vocabulary, their
structure and grammatical forms are all peculiarly
related,—so peculiarly, that traits of family-likeness
and the same distinctive physiognomy are seen pervading the whole group.

But harder questions in the mean time have been
agitated by American archæologists, with reference
to the ultimate affinities of the native population;
and while one school are persuaded that nothing
whatever has transpired which can be fairly thought
to militate against received ideas of aboriginal unity;
a second, in proportion it would seem to their belief
in the specific oneness of the 'American race,' have
manifested a desire to disconnect the Old and New
Continents entirely. They assert not only that the
measure of civilisation attained by some of the
American tribes is altogether underived, but (which
is a distinct and totally independent theory) that the
race itself is strictly autochthonic, and is therefore
a new *species* of human beings.[1] As writers of the
last century were sometimes ready to contend that
every thing American had been imported from the
shores of the Old World, these champions of the

Origin of the Ameri- can people.

polysyllables almost without limit,
and to form other words by merely
aggregating a number of such
fragments into new compounds.

[1] Pott, who seems to be himself influenced more especially by
philological reasons, has collected
(in his *Die Ungleichheit menschlicher Rassen*, Lemgo, 1856, pp.
242 sq.) the main arguments of
those who are led by the perplex-
ing phenomena of the New World
to deny the derivation of the
human family from a single pair.

autochthonic theory must needs assume an attitude no less defiant, and a phraseology no less emphatic: they affirm accordingly that *nothing* has been so derived.

Are they a distinct species?

Now difficult, or even, with our extant means, impossible as it may be to single out the parent stock, in which the fathers of the New World had their origin, I hold the multiplication of productive centres, both in this and other cases, to be absolutely unnecessary, and, in the present state of ethnological science, to be utterly unjustifiable.[1] If no ray of light whatever could be thrown upon the questions which concern the primitive population of America; if no analogy to their case had existed in the spread of the Malayo-Polynesian tribes across the islands of the Eastern Archipelago and the Pacific Ocean; if the speech of the Americans had absolutely no affinities with any other human dialects; if their traditions, meagre as these are, had hinted nothing of a distant home and of a perilous migration; if insoluble enigmas were presented by the physical structure of Americans, or if their moral powers and mental capabilities were such as to exclude them from a place in the great brotherhood of men; if, lastly, no resemblances were found, I will not say, in primary articles of belief, but in the memory of specific incidents and in those minor forms of human thought and culture which will hardly bear to be explained on the hypothesis of ' natural evolution,' we might then, perhaps, have cause to hesitate in our decision, or to treat the peopling of America as

[1] See Part i. ch. ii. *On the* pp. 47 sq.
Unity of the Human Race, Vol. i.

something more exceptional than had been hitherto
supposed.

But no necessity whatever has been shewn for *Objections* the adoption of such theories. There is literally *answered.* nothing, say our ablest writers, either in the bodily structure or psychology of the American tribes to prove an independent origin, or even to beget suspicions touching a plurality of human ' races.'[1] In the limits of the American family, and notwithstanding the mutual resemblances which it unquestionably offers, we can find varieties of human beings, passing, there as elsewhere, one into another by graduated shades of difference; while the Esquimaux, who are as genuine members of that family as the Aztecs or Algonquins, link it on by speech as well as by traditions, to the natives of the sister-continent. Again, if the diversities of language could be fairly cited as conclusive of the absolute distinctness of the whole American people, they would prove with equal force that every single tribe is also autochthonic. The loss of primitive vocables in one case would remain as wondrous and inexplicable as in the other. The development of any primitive speech into the finished and elaborate forms presented by the living dialects of America is antecedently not less improbable than the first deflection of the polysynthetic family from one original type of language. Neither is the want of correspondency between the speech of the Old and New Continent so absolutely universal as had once been represented. Without affecting to pronounce a judgment on the merits of particular controversies,— as, for instance, that relating to the Othomi of Central

[1] Prichard, v. 541.

Positive proofs of foreign influences.

America, whose language[1] has been held to be mono-syllabic and akin to the Chinese,—I may remark that writers adverse to the theory of unity are sometimes driven to admit the known existence of as many as one hundred and eighty-seven words,[2] which are the common property of the Old World and the New. But more convincing proofs of some great exodus from Asia to America are furnished by the vague traditions of the early emigrants. The tide of popu-lation in the New Continent is always said to have been propagated from the west and north-west. If credit be conceded to the stories of the Mexicans and others, they all issued from that very region; in one case they had crossed the water, in a second they had marched along some frozen pathway. They were previously acquainted with white men; they were accustomed to the representations of animals familiar to Asiatics, but unheard of, during the historic period, in America itself.[3] The picture or mnemonic writing[4]

---

[1] Cf. Pott, as above, pp. 252 sq., and Ampère, in the *Revue des Deux Mondes*, 1853, Tome IV. pp. 93, 94.

[2] Squier, as above, p. 26. Of these words, it is remarked, 'one hundred and four coincide with words found in the languages of Asia and Australia, forty-three with those of Europe, and forty with those of Africa.'

[3] These and many other points are dwelt upon by Wuttke, whose chief conclusion is as follows (1. 346): 'Alle diese Erscheinungen lassen uns an der asiatischen Ab-stammung der halbgebildeten Völ-ker von West-Amerika nicht mehr zweifeln. Die bestimmten bei den verschiedenen Indianerstämmen sich wiederholenden Sagen von einer Einwanderung aus Westen über ein Meer oder eine Strasse, die nachher zugefroren,—Sagen, welche mit den erwähnten sibir-ischen von einer Auswanderung nach Osten übereinstimmen [p. 157], verstärken das Gewicht der mexikanischen Überlieferung noch mehr.'

[4] See above, Vol. 1. p. 70, n. 2. Niebuhr (*Lect. on Ancient Hist.* 1. 49, 50) points out the approxim-ation made in some districts of Central America to the 'hieratic' mode of writing practised by the Egyptians. The use of *Knoten-schnüre* (knot-strings) as an aid to the memory was common, both in America, and in almost every other part of the ancient world (Müller, p. 359), anterior to the introduction of the art of writing.

of the Old World reappears in different latitudes of
the New. The practice of erecting huge pyramidal
temples, corresponding not in general structure only,
but also in minute and arbitrary details, has been
common to the demi-civilised tribes alike of Asia and
America.[1]   Arguing therefore from coincidences such *By what*
as these, which are in every case more likely to have *channel*
these influ-
been the fruit of some external intercourse than of *ences were*
exerted.
mere accident or of spontaneous growth in discon-
nected regions, I incline to the opinion that the old
inhabitants of America had either crossed by Behring's
Strait, or else along the way of the Aleutian islands,
which in fact supply a bridge between the two continents.   Such primitive colonists might be an early
offshoot from the stock of nations which was rapidly
propelled across the steppes of central Asia, and who,
lapsing more and more completely into barbarism,
had finally escaped through various channels into
islands of the Eastern and Southern Seas.   Regarded
thus the primitive people of America belong to a
great section of the human family which is entitled
the 'Turanian': they are ultimately one with the
Malays; they are a part of that mighty stream of
population which under the name of Tshud and Turk
and Scythian was diffused throughout the whole of
upper Asia, was pushed forward by the growing
vigour of the Chinese empire, was displaced by

---

[1] Squier, as above, p. 83.
'What striking analogies exist,'
cries Humboldt (as there quoted),
'between the monuments of the
old continents and those of the
Toltecs, who, arriving on Mexican
soil, built several of these colossal
structures, truncated pyramids,
divided by layers, like the temple
of Belus at Babylon.   Whence
did they take the model of these
edifices?   Were they of the Mongol race?   Did they descend from
a common stock with the Chinese,
the Hiong-nu, and the Japanese?'

CHAP. II. the triumphant progress of the Áryans in the vast peninsula of Hindústán.   Or it may be, that the peopling of America resulted from a long succession of such movements, and that ruder tribes were subsequently intermixed with others[1] more advanced in civilisation and more capable of gaining that ascendancy which some of them had finally enjoyed.   Objections, I am quite aware, have been directed against both of these hypotheses, and in the present state of knowledge it may be impossible to give a satisfactory answer to every one of such objections.   Yet on looking at the problem as a whole, I am persuaded that the vast preponderance of testimony is favourable to the idea of Asiatic immigration, not only as accounting for the presence of materials out of which the 'civilised' communities were framed, but also as affording the best clue to many a mystery connected with the barbarous tribes themselves.

Distinction respecting the religions of America.   As soon as we approach the subject of American religions, it is most essential on the very threshold that we realise the force of a distinction here indicated between the 'civilised' and savage populations who occupied the New World when it was first explored

---

[1] This is the conclusion of Mr. Schoolcraft, who closes his careful summary of the ante-Columbian traditions (Part 1. pp. 19 sq.) in the following passage (p. 26): 'Thus we have traditionary gleams of a foreign origin of the race of the North American Indians, from separate stocks of nations, extending at intervals from the Arctic Circle to the Valley of Mexico. . . They point decidedly to a foreign, to an oriental, if not a Shemitic, origin.   Such an origin has from the first been inferred.   At whatever point the investigation has been made, the eastern hemisphere has been found to contain the physical and mental prototypes of the race.   Language, mythology, religious dogmas,—the very style of architecture, and their calendar, as far as it is developed, point to that fruitful and central source of human dispersion and nationality.'

by Europeans. The former class comprise[1] the Mexicans and Peruvians, together with the intermediate
families of Mayans, and Muyscas of Bogota, who,
planted on that side of the continent which looks
directly towards Asia, were each an independent
centre of civilisation in the midst of wild and barbarous hordes.[2] The second class may be distributed
into (1) the Red Indians of North America, (2) the
Indians of the Great Antilles, (3) the Caraibs or
Carribees, (4) the Indians on the Eastern coast of
South America. These two varieties of men, though
generally like each other in physical conformation,
and though speaking similar and cognate tongues,
were intellectually in almost opposite conditions.
The half-civilised American had even worked his
way above one group of tribes and nations on the
Old 'Continent; he was superior to the Finn, who
represented the best phase of culture in the ' Scythian'
family ; he took precedence also of the Mongol, who
at nearly the same period flashed from time to time
across the theatre of general history, and then relapsed into the darkness of his native steppes. The
barbarous American was, on the contrary, as destitute
of all the higher forms of culture as the wild man
of New Zealand or Kaffraria: his delight was to
retard the intellectual progress of his fellows, and

---

[1] In this distribution, I follow
Dr. J. G. Müller, whose *Geschichte
der Amerikanischen Urreligionen*
(Basel, 1855), though far from
satisfactory in some respects, has
the great merit of being well arranged.

[2] It should, however, be remembered that the area of North
American civilisation had once
been far more extensive than it
was in the age of Columbus ; as
may be inferred from the ruins
which are being constantly brought
to light, for instance, in the valley
of the Mississippi: *Ibid.* pp. 45
sq., Schoolcraft, Part II. pp. 84 sq.

intent on what is called 'a nameless principle of tribality,' to foster habits which could hardly fail to issue in the utter disintegration of society.

§ 1. *The wild Tribes of America.*

Uniformity of nature-religions in all continents.

My observations on this class of men will be restricted within very narrow limits, partly because the members of it are seldom or never likely to provoke comparison with Christians, and partly because the leading principles of their religion are the same as will be found in tribes of every age and climate, so long as they continue standing on the same moral level. In the old 'Turanian' creed of China we observed how prominent was the place awarded, first, to spirit-worship,—understanding by that term not only adoration or deprecation of local genii and demons, but commemorative offerings made in honour of departed ancestors; and secondly, to worship of the powers or laws of nature, and especially the element of light itself as centred in the host of heaven. Now both these forms of primitive heathenism recur at every turn among the Indians of North and South America. Their religion, speaking generally, consists of two great factors; spirit-worship, which is found to be more deeply rooted in the higher latitudes, and element-worship, which appears to have exerted a peculiar witchery in countries lying nearer the equator. In America, however, as in China, the two phases of belief are seen existing side by side, and not unfrequently are made to touch and interpenetrate each other.

Excepting the manes of departed ancestors,[1] which ought perhaps to constitute an independent class, the spirits worshipped by the heathen of America are not unfrequently embodied in specific forms or objects, corresponding to the *fetishes*[2] alike of Greenland, Africa, Australia, and Siberia. Some particles of true divinity are thus believed to tenant the thing worshipped, which accordingly ceases to be regarded as the beast or brute matter it really is, and rising far above the character of a type, or emblem, is identified completely with the thing it represents.[3] One object of this kind becomes *the* god, the patron-spirit of the fascinated savage : it he carries constantly about with him, or treasures as the glory and the safeguard of his wigwam ; so that, nothwithstanding the very partial exercise of the imagination and

[1] Compare the following account of Mr. Schoolcraft, Part 1. pp. 38, 39, with the remarks already made in chap. 1. pp. 32, 33 on the similar custom of the Chinese: 'The periodical offering of cakes, libations, flesh, or viands at the grave to ancestors. . . . .is seen to be an idea incorporated into the practice of the American, at least the Algonic Indians. These Indians, believing in the duality of the soul, and that the soul sensorial abides for a time with the body in the grave, requiring food for its ghostly existence and journeyings, deposit meats and other aliment, at and after the time of interment. *This custom is universal,* and was one of their earliest observed traits.' The same remark is applicable to the Caraibs and Brasilians: Müller, p. 73. The same superstitious ideas prevail through the whole of the country north of the Zambesi : see Livingstone's *Researches in South Africa,* p. 434.

[2] The word 'Fetishism' which has now obtained general currency as descriptive of one early stage in the religions of heathendom, is derived from the Portuguese *fetisso,* 'a magical charm' or 'spell.' It was adopted from thence by the Negroes of Western Africa : cf. the Chinese *joss* and the Portuguese *dios.*

[3] Müller, p. 52. The same writer says truly (p. 75): 'Das Thier, das als Fetisch verehrt wird, ist nicht Symbol dieser oder jener göttlichen Naturkraft, sondern überhaupt ein göttliches Wesen wie jedes andere.' Mr. Theodore Parker is, therefore, in error when he talks of the visible object being in Fetishism a *type* of the Infinite Spirit : *Discourse,* pp. 32 sq. Lond. 1850.

reflective faculty which seems to be implied in every form of spirit-worship, the worshipper is always under the necessity of localising the object of his special adoration and of bringing it directly under the cog-

Worship of the heavenly bodies. nisance of the senses. On the other hand, the more conspicuous and commanding objects of external nature, as the sun, the moon, the planets, are not worshipped barely as material and inanimate substances. The wild man of America, like other heathen, both of civilised and barbarous races, has been long accustomed to the thought that all the heavenly bodies are possessed of animation, and even gifted with some measure of intelligence. To each, accordingly, has been ascribed one independent, vitalising soul. The sun-god, for example, is the living sun itself, and worship is never paid to it symbolically, as though it were the representative of some invisible or absent spirit, but because it is an actual depository of the supersensuous, an embodiment of the Divine.

Primitive Pantheism. The two main lines of thought exemplified in spirit-worship, and in deification of the elements and heavenly bodies, may have thus been gradually blended into one. The subtle spirit is corporealised; the higher forms of matter are each tenanted and consecrated by the energy of some appropriate spirit. If the term 'God' be chosen to express the aggregate of all such spirits, it may be affirmed with equal truth that ultimately God is every thing, and every thing is ultimately God. The wild man of America is in fact a worshipper of all above him and around him. As the skies, the woods, the waters are his books, they also form his oracles and his divinities.

Pervaded by some spiritual essence, every leaf that
rustles in the forest, quite as much as the great orbs
that move in silent majesty across the firmament,
conveys to him a message from the unseen world.
The threatening cloud, the genial shower, the lightning, thunder, and *aurora borealis*, flowers of every
hue and animals of every shape and species are alike
regarded as instinct with supernatural virtue, and as
fitted to enkindle in the human heart the sentiments
of awe or love, of adoration or of deprecation.

In systems where it is admitted by all writers *The Ame-*
that principles like these are ever active and pre- *rican doc-*
trine of
dominant, we naturally fail in the attempt to vindi- *a Great*
cate a proper standing-ground for any doctrine bearing *Spirit.*
close resemblance to Christian theism. Passages
exist, indeed, in which the wild man of America
expresses a belief in some Great Spirit,[1] manifesting
itself not only as the root and basis of all being, but
at one time in the light of a beneficent Creator, at
a second as the sun-god, at a third as the great God
of heaven, and not unfrequently in more appalling
aspects as the god of battle and of death. At first
the European missionaries,[2] in their zeal to seize all

---

[1] Thus, Mr. Schoolcraft (*passim*) thinks this doctrine 'at the base of their theology,' although he argues that in practice they were polytheists to a man. Mr. Pres- cott (*Conquest of Peru*) begins his third chapter with a similar state- ment: 'It is a remarkable fact, that many, if not most, of the rude tribes inhabiting the vast American continent, however dis- figured their creeds may have been in other respects by a child- ish superstition, had attained to the sublime conception of one Great Spirit, the Creator of the universe,' &c. He also adds, however, that these elevated ideas 'do not seem to have led to the practical consequences that might have been expected.' On the ideas current in South Africa, respecting a Supreme Being, see Livingstone, pp. 641. 642.

[2] Müller, who adduces many proofs of this position (pp. 99 sq.), affirms: 'Diese Ansicht ist nicht bloss bei Englischen und Französ-

CHAP. II. possible points of contact with the old beliefs of those
whom they were seeking to recover, had unconsciously
diverged into the track of infidels, who represented
the natural religion of the wild man as almost on
a level with the highest truths of Christianity, and,
after labouring to explain away his human sacrifices,
anthropophagy and the like, waxed eloquent in prais-
ing the unrivalled purity and spirituality of his
worship. In the present day, however, when inquiries of this kind are prosecuted in a far more
critical temper, it is generally agreed that all approximations to monotheism observed among the tribes
of the New World are little more than verbal. Their
Great Spirit is at best the highest member of a
group,[1] the brightest inmate of a crowded pantheon;
as the sun-god of their system, quickening, gladdening, fructifying; a personification of the mightiest of
all natural energies, but not a personality distinct
from nature, and controlling all things by his sovereign will. The greatest Spirit of the Indian is
accordingly declared to be the offspring of an evil
mother,[2] subordinate to some inexorable Fate, the
victim of some will-less and unchanging Principle
by which his rule is ever liable to interruption and
reverse. But, what is more observable, that Spirit
is devoid of every thing which constitutes the glory
of the God of revelation. In spite of all his grandeur,
goodness, and ubiquity, he exercises no control upon

ischen Deisten und Populärphilo-
sophen, sondern auch bei Reisen-
den und Missionären sehr ver-
breitet.'
[1] Cf. Wuttke, 1. 91, 92, Müller,
p. 102, pp. 114 sq.

[2] Müller, p. 149. This writer
shews, in discussing the religion
of the Caraibs, the identity of
their supreme Mother with Fate
and the Principle of evil (p. 230).

the lives of individuals, or the government of the
world. 'There is no attempt by the hunter, priesthood, jugglers or powwows, which can be gathered
from their oral traditions, to impute to the great
merciful Spirit the attributes of justice, or to make
man accountable to him, here and hereafter, for aberrations from virtue, good-will, truth, or any form of
moral right.'[1]

The passing illustrations thus afforded of the old *Their sys-*
American theology enable us to understand some *tem really dualistic.*
other of its characteristic principles. With the idea
of one inscrutable necessity ever present in the background, the more prominent features of the system
were all rigorously *dualistic.*[2]

Minor gods, whose operation was regarded as *Good divin-*
beneficent, were ranked in one special series, with *ities sub-ordinate to*
the sun-god as their glorious chief. In him, the *the sun.*
great dispenser of all radiance and fertility, 'the
being by whose light and heat all living creatures
were generated and sustained,' the various tribes of
the New World had uniformly recognised the highest
pitch of excellence; and even where, transformed into
a god of battle, he was worshipped with horrid and
incongruous rites, or fed by human hecatombs,[3] the
sun-god never ceased to occupy the foremost rank
among the good divinities. His titles were the
'father,' the 'sustainer,' the 'revivifier;' and to be

[1] Schoolcraft, I. 35.
[2] 'Everywhere our Indians
have upheld this idea of a duality
of gods, giving one good, and the
other evil powers, with its ancient
developments of subordinate polytheisms.' *Ibid.* III. 60. The same
antagonism was even more strongly manifested among the Caraibs,
and on the eastern coast of South
America: Müller, pp. 260, 261.
[3] See Müller, pp. 141 sq., and
below, on the human sacrifices
offered to the great Mexican divinities.

CHAP. II.　at last translated to the sun, or his attendant stars,

Evil divinities subordinate to the moon.　was deemed the summit of felicity. On the other hand, the rude American was haunted by the thought of some coequal and coordinate array of hostile deities, who manifested their malignant nature by creating discord, sickness, death, and every possible form of evil. These were held in numerous cases to obey the leadership of the moon,[1] which, owing to its changeful aspects, had become identical with the capricious evil-minded Spirit of American Indians. It especially, as in their creed the parent of misfortune, many of them were ever anxious to propitiate and

Indian worship chiefly deprecative.　disarm. In it is found the chief divinity of all the warlike races, more especially the Caraibs;[2] and everywhere the worship of the Indian was mainly occupied in deprecating powerful and malevolent spirits, demons, spectres, fiends, hobgoblins, whose errand was to poison human joys and aggravate the load of human wretchedness. If only the American could turn away their anger, and evade or disappoint their malice, he had realised the principal aim of his religion. Hence his constant dread of some unearthly apparition. Hence the meaning of his fetishes, his amulets, his charms, his exorcisms, his trembling and convulsive efforts to explore the secrets of the past or future, his wild cries, and frantic dances. Hence again the vast ascendancy obtained by seers and witches, payés, jossakeeds, and medicine-men, with

---

[1] Müller, p. 53, p. 170, p. 272. Livingstone (p. 235) found moon-worship prevalent among some tribes of South-Central Africa.

[2] 'Während indessen anderswo gewöhnlich der Sonnendienst an der Spitze dieser höhern Naturverehrung steht, herrscht bei den Karaiben der Mond vor, ähnlich wie bei einzelnen nordischen Wilden und Grönländern,' etc. p. 218.

other dark and nameless instruments of heathen
sorcery.

It is true the wild man of America was not entirely *Gloomy as-*
lost to his original destination. He dreamed of *pects of the*
Indian
having once been master of some purer language, *creed.*
of a world divided from the present by some dire
catastrophe, of service rendered by his ancestors to
milder and more powerful chieftains.[1] Whether push-
ing his rude canoe across the waters, or chasing the
buffalo amid the depths of his primeval forests, he
would muse at times, as did the Aztec in his massive
temples, on the advent of a gracious Spirit, conde-
scending, under various shapes of man or animal,
to battle with a legion of hideous monsters,[2] who
were said to have delighted most in the enslaving
of the human species. Yet in spite of all such happy
memories, and such vague presentiments of something
higher and more satisfying, the wild tribes of America
were commonly overwhelmed by gloom, anxiety, and
terror. Their habitual 'notions of the spirit-world *Bondage*
exceed all belief; and the Indian mind is thus made *to fear.*
the victim of wild mystery, unending suspicion and
paralysing fear. . . . . . Not to be in misery from these
unnumbered hosts is to be blessed.'[3] The whole

---

[1] Schoolcraft, I. 16. The current story of some mighty deluge
will be considered in discussing
the religion of Mexico.

[2] The mythe or legend of Manabozho (Müller, pp. 126 sq.,
Schoolcraft, I. 317—319), as held
among the Algonquins, has its
parallel in many other tribes,
most of all, perhaps, in the Mexican account of Quetzalcoatl.

[3] Schoolcraft, I. 16. Compare
Livingstone's account of the Afri-

can tribes: 'Their religion, if
such it may be called, is one of
dread. Numbers of charms are
employed to avert the evils with
which they feel themselves to be
encompassed. Occasionally you
meet a man, more cautious or
more timid than the rest, with
twenty or thirty charms round
his neck:' p. 435. 'There is
nothing more heartrending than
their death wails. When the natives turn their eyes to the future

CHAP. II. religion, writes another high authority, 'is the religion of fear, which even among cultivated nations so predominates in the religious character of the heathen, that Lucretius (VI. 23) could describe Epicurus, the subverter of religion, as one who had also made an end of fear. Daring as the Indian is at other times, in facing visible dangers under the impulses of passion; firm and self-collected as he shews himself in bearing the most poignant tortures, he is notwithstanding always full of awe, of fear, of horror, at the thought of the invisible spirits who hold rule in nature; and as soon as he is once mastered by this feeling, he becomes the most timid creature upon earth.'[1]

Doctrine of Manitoes.

We seldom see the darker traits of his religion so distinctly, as when brought together in the doctrine of *Manitoes*, which constitutes, it has been thought, the nearest approximation he has ever made to some originality of conception.[2] The word *Manito*, or Manedo, itself appears to signify 'a spirit': hence the foremost member in the series of good divinities, the Great Spirit of the old American, is called in various tribes, Kitchi or Gezha Manito;[3] the name of the

world, they have a view cheerless enough of their own utter helplessness and hopelessness. They fancy themselves completely in the power of the disembodied spirits, and look upon the prospect of following them as the greatest of misfortunes. Hence they are constantly deprecating the wrath of departed souls, believing that, if they are appeased, there is no other cause of death but witchcraft, which may be averted by charms:' (p. 440).

[1] Müller, p. 83. The same conviction is repeated (p. 260) with reference to the Indians of *South*

America: 'Man sieht, dass auch hier das Schauerliche und Furchterregende vorherrscht; Furcht ist ja das Grundgefühl, das durch das Vernehmen des Göttlichen auch bei diesen Naturmenschen erregt wird; die ganze Natur ist von einer Unzahl von Geistern erfüllt, die bei Tag und bei Nacht, beim Schlafen und beim Wachen, Welt und Seele mit Angst und Schauder erfüllen.'

[2] Schoolcraft, I. 34, 35.

[3] These names vary considerably: see a collection of them, Müller, pp. 104 sq.

evil-minded Spirit being Matchi Manito. But, when employed without such epithets, this title is restricted to a minor emanation from the Great Spirit, which, revealing itself in dreams to the excited fancy of the youthful Indian, and inviting him to seek its efficacy in some well-known bird or beast, or other object, is selected by him for his guardian deity, his friend in council, and his champion in the hour of peril. He believes, however, that other Manitoes may prove far mightier and more terrible than his own, and consequently he is always full of apprehensions lest the influence granted preternaturally to his neighbour should issue in his own confusion. Add to this the prevalent idea, that Manitoes intrinsically evil are ever exercised in counterworking the beneficent, and that the actual administration of the world, abandoned to these great antagonistic powers, is the result of their interminable conflicts, and we cease to wonder at the moral perturbations which mark the character of the wild man. The fever of intense anxiety is never suffered to die out; until at length he either passes to another world, the simple reproduction of the present, or migrates into viler forms of animal existence, or, as in the case of the most highly favoured, is emancipated altogether from an earthly prison-house, and rescued from the malice of his demoniacal oppressors.

§ 2. *The demi-civilised Tribes, especially the Mexican.*

Although the barbarous population of the New World had always far outnumbered those who in the age preceding the discoveries of Columbus were struggling up the lower slopes of intellectual culture, it is rather in the creed of the minority, as indicating more of genius and reflection, that we seek for any definite resemblance to the facts and institutions of the Bible. There is reason to believe that some of these advances towards civilisation should be dated from a very high antiquity, especially in Yucatan and other parts of Central America, in which the Mayan family[1] had risen far above the intellectual level of their neighbours; but the Mexicans, who settled in a savage state upon their northern border, will at present be selected as the type of demi-civilised heathenism in the New World, partly because our fund of information respecting Mexico is comparatively copious and exact, and partly because, an opportunity is there presented of watching a late phase in 'the religion of humanity' associated in the end with no small progress in political organisation and in many of the higher arts of life. That Mexicans had borrowed largely from the Mayan builders, who, already in the dawn of history, erected towns and palaces and pyramid-temples, rivalling those of Egypt in area and magnificence, is now conceded both by European and American archæologists. That numerous elements of faith and worship had been also gradually derived from the more cultivated Mayans, whom they conquered or displaced, as well as from the Toltecs,[2] their own kinsmen and immediate pre-

[1] Prichard, v. 339 sq., Müller, pp. 452 sq., and Fancourt's *Hist. of Yucatan*, pp. 114 sq. Lond. 1854.

[2] It is in tracing the fortunes of the Toltecs that we first obtain a tolerably close approximation to historical exactness. The traditions of them handed down by the Aztecs, or Mexicans proper, inform us that ,they migrated from an unknown country called

decessors on the soil of Anahuac, is a statement likely to receive continuous illustration from researches of the present day. But much as Mexico might profit by the early dissemination of intelligence and the creations of artistic skill upon the confines of her empire, it is certain that when studied by the Spanish conquerors, the various factors in her social and religious life had all been moulded into one harmonious system : veils of allegory, woven partly if not altogether by her own imagination, were thrown over many a wild tradition of her simple ancestors; her creed, her laws, her ritual, and administrative principles, had all assumed a very definite and distinctive character. The Aztec, in his general policy, became the Roman of the New World; and, after crushing and absorbing minor states, in virtue of his martial prowess and fanaticism, had succeeded in building up an absolute monarchy upon the basis of a terrible superstition, which reminds us, in its dark and sanguinary spirit, of the Siva-ism of Hindústán, and of the Baal or the Moloch-worship of western Asia.

On proceeding to discuss the central tenets of the

---

the primitive Tlapallan about 544 of the Christian era, and, advancing southwards, settled in Mexico about 648 (see Prichard, v. 328; Prescott's *Conquest of Mexico*, ch. 1). It is also worthy of notice that the epoch 544 corresponds with the ruin of the Tsin dynasty in China, which occasioned many violent commotions beyond the limits of the Chinese empire, and may have been instrumental in propelling a new race of colonists as far as North America (cf. Wuttke, 1. 349). The Mexicans proper, issuing from the far north, did not reach the borders of Anahuac till the beginning of the 13th century, and only fixed their habitation near the principal lake in 1325. 'At the beginning of the sixteenth century, just before the arrival of the Spaniards, the Aztec dominion reached across the continent from the Atlantic to the Pacific; and under the bold and bloody Ahuitzotl, its arms had been carried far over the limits already noticed as defining its permanent territory, unto the farthest corners of Guatemala and Nicaragua.'

ancient Mexicans we are confronted by a question which deserves to rank the foremost in this species of investigation—'What were their ideas respecting a Supreme Intelligence, the one, true, living God?' In Mexico, as in most heathen countries, very different answers have been given to such inquiry; some writers declaring that the Mexicans, in spite of their two hundred objects of worship, were ultimately and in truth monotheists; while others, who regard the term monotheism as importing no less than Christian theism, have repudiated the interpretations put on Mexican phraseology, and ranked the ancient Aztec with the nature-worshippers of other parts of heathendom. It is worthy of notice that the Mexican name for god[1] is *teo-tl*, which, on separating the termination from the root, approaches nearly to θεός, *déva, deus, tius*, and other kindred forms, as well as to the *tao*[2] of China and the *tua*[3] of the South-sea islanders. It is deserving also of consideration that the term *teo-tl* was not inherited from the Toltecs, and was not imported into the land of Anahuac by the Mexicans themselves, but gradually adopted from the aboriginal population skirting them upon the southern frontier of their new dominions.[4]

[1] This word was accordingly employed by the early missionaries as the equivalent of *Dios*, not, however, without exciting disputes like those already noticed in reference to the Chinese *Shin* and *Shang-te*.

[2] See above, p. 64.

[3] Russell's *Polynesia*, p. 68, Lond. 1852. The fullest form of this Polynesian word is, however, not *tua*, but *atua*, the *a* being, it would seem, a component part of the title. (Shortland's *Traditions*,

&c. *of the New Zealanders*, p. 61, Lond. 1854). Other persons, on similar grounds, have maintained the original identity of *Votan*, the serpent-god of the Mayans, with the *Odin* and *Woden* of Teutonic heathenism, and even with the *Buddha* of eastern Asia. But all such attempts at identification are merely fanciful, or at the best exceedingly precarious.

[4] Müller, p. 472. In Nicaragua, which received the names of its divinities neither from the Toltecs

If it should eventually be established that the Mayan race who occupied this frontier were an Asiatic colony, forming the centre and the nucleus of American civilisation, the presence of a word like *teo-tl* will undoubtedly assume a higher importance than has hitherto belonged to it. But until historical media have been fully ascertained, it is presumptuous to advance a theory on the strength of merely verbal resemblances, which in some other cases can be shewn to have been altogether accidental.

The word *teo-tl* was, however, used with epithets and adjuncts that forbid us to dispute the grandeur of the object it was meant to designate. The Mexicans *Traces of a* beheld in him the being[1] 'by whom we live,' 'omni- *Supreme Spirit.* present, that knoweth all thoughts and giveth all gifts,' 'without whom man is as nothing,' 'invisible, incorporeal, one God, of perfect perfection and purity,' 'under whose wings we find repose and a sure defence.' This Being also had been worshipped by some elevated spirits, without image, sacrifice, or temple. He was called the 'Cause of causes,' and the 'Father of all things.' He was reverenced as the parent and productive principle in nature ; he was actually identified with the sun-god, which on this account was designated *the* Teo-tl. In proportion also as the Aztecs had invested the chief powers and spirits of their ruder ancestors with human shapes and attributes, the reigning tendency to anthropomorphism might have led them to ascribe a human will and personality to the supreme Spirit. On the

nor the Aztecs, the word *Teot* (pl. *Teotes*) was in common use, and was applied equally to the superior gods and to the Spaniards.
[1] Prescott, p. 19, Lond. 1854.

other hand, it is more probable that this only God of Central America was a conception far too vast and glorious for the ordinary intellect. To such he was a vague, impersonal abstraction: he was never worshipped by the many;[1] no attempt was made to circulate a knowledge either of his being or his character; and practically the administration of the world was not referred to Him, but to inferior spirits, good and evil, ruling each in his own single province, and presiding over this or that peculiar energy of physical creation. In effect, the only difference to be traced between the popular theology of wild and demi-civilised Americans, is that which we have traced already in describing the Áryan of the Véda and the Áryan of the second, or 'heroic,' period of Hindú history and religion. All the beings worshipped in the former case are spirits, demons, genii, with no definite shape in the imagination of the worshipper, haunting every form of nature, animate and inanimate; while in the second stage of natural religion, the divinities are far more generally humanised, assuming forms in which, amid a number of grotesque embellishments, the features of humanity are ever struggling to obtain expression and predominance. The amulets and fetishes of the American Indians are seldom, it is true, abandoned altogether, but are moulded into human effigies minute in form[2] and occupying the subordinate rank of *lares*

Actual development of religion among the demi-civilised tribes.

---

[1] 'The idea of unity—of a being, with whom volition is action, who has no need of inferior ministers to execute his purposes —was too simple, or too vast, for their understandings; and they sought relief, as usual, in the plurality of deities, who presided over the elements, the changes of the seasons, and the various occupations of man.' Prescott, *Ibid.;* cf. Müller, p. 474.

[2] Müller, p. 571. They are called the 'little ones' (*tepitoton*).

and *penates.* The sacred corner of the wigwam, where the ancient fetish was reposited, or the sacred mound on which the wild man, writhing under some calamity, offered his best victim to the sun-god, has been superseded by a group of splendid temples ('houses of God,' or *teo-calli*), crowning a gigantic pyramid, and glittering with the costliest decorations. Seers and medicine-men have given place to regular priests and priestesses, the fountains of all popular education; the frantic shrieks of former generations have been softened into measured chants, their lawless rites into a pompous and elaborate liturgy; while holidays, originally restricted for the most part to the annual commemoration of departed ancestors, have multiplied so fast that ' every week, nay almost every day, is set down in their calendar for some appropriate celebration.'[1]

Standing at the head of thirteen[2] chief divinities, *Tezcatlipoca;* whom ancient Mexico has learned to worship, either jointly or in rotation, is Tezcatlipoca, whose rank appears to be ' inferior only to that of the Supreme Being.' Several writers, who have earnestly endeavoured to make out affinities between the Old Testament religion and the creed of Mexico, and by this process to connect the Aztec tribes with the Semitic family of western Asia, go so far as to recognise the One God of the ancient Hebrews in Tezcatlipoca; and in aid of their conjectures they adduce a long

[1] Prescott, p. 24.

[2] The special number *thirteen,* in reference to the greater gods of Mexico, appears to be connected either with a monthly division of the calendar (cf. Müller, p. 94), or else with the very peculiar cycles of the Mexicans, which included fifty-two years (13 being a quarter), years of eighteen months, months of twenty days, half decades, and half lunations of thirteen days: see Prichard, v. 353, 355.

CHAP. II.
*attributes
ascribed to
him.*

*Different
character-
istics.*

array of epithets, investing him with every species
of divine perfection.   According to this view he was
represented as the 'merciful and long-suffering,' and
yet 'the stirrer-up of strife,' a god of vengeance and
of battles; the 'Creator of all things,' and the 'Giver
of life,' and yet requiring the blood of sacrifice to
flow for ever on his altars; pardoning the guilty only
in consideration of the blood of the innocent; supreme
and unapproachable, and yet enlisting numerous
fellow-workers in the government of the universe.
He was 'the Holder of all things in his hand,' 'the
Giver of inspiration, who laughs at human wisdom;'
'the Trier and Prover of hearts, who made man in
his own likeness,' 'the Acceptor of vows,' 'the For-
giver,' 'the Enjoiner of charity.'[1]   But the force of
such expressions is materially abated when we view
them in relation to others of no less authority.   These
latter seem to have connected, if not absolutely identified, Tezcatlipoca with the ancient sun-god of the
New World.   In the remarkable address, for instance,
of the Mexican high-priest, the language runs as
follows: 'We entreat that those who die in war may
be graciously received by thee, our Father, the Sun,
and our Mother, the Earth, for thou alone reignest;'[2]
and in a subsequent passage, the place of happiness,
reserved by him for warriors slain in battle, is declared
to be the sun itself.   The name Tezcatlipoca, being

---

[1] These and other like epithets
are collected and expounded in
Lord Kingsborough's *Antiq. of
Mexico,* IX. 179, who concludes
his summary by remarking, that
'all the attributes and powers
which were assigned to Jehovah
by the Hebrews, were also bestowed upon Tezcatlipoca by the
Mexicans.'

[2] Squier's *American Archæological Researches,* p. 162, New
York, 1851; Müller, p. 620. This
prayer contemplates him chiefly
in his character of 'god of death,
and of the dead.'

interpreted, is the 'Shining Mirror;' on the monuments and in the paintings he is often represented
as encircled by the disc of the sun.[1] His proper
home is in the heavens;[2] from thence he came,
descending on a spider's web, to persecute Quetzalcoatl, the benignant deity of the Toltecs; and in
strict accordance with such representation, his choicest
influence seems restricted to the world of the invisible;
his face is covered with a mask; he is declared to be
impalpable as 'night and air'; he has the power of
granting immortality, and reigns supreme in all the
regions of the dead.

Upon the whole, that view seems preferable which *Explana-*
makes Tezcatlipoca the deified impersonation of the *tion of these various*
generative powers of nature. As such he was united *titles.*
to the primitive goddess and first woman of the
Mexicans, Cihuacohuatl, the 'female serpent.'[3] As
such his highest type and aptest emblem was the
sun; as such he was occasionally entitled Tonaca-
teucli ('embodied lord sun').[4] As such, he bore the
semblance of a handsome man, endowed with inexhaustible vigour, and rejoicing in the periodic renewal

[1] Squier, p. 163.
[2] See Müller, p. 614.
[3] Much as Mr. Squier may
ridicule 'the error of the bigots,'
who discovered an allusion to Eve
and the Tempter of our first
parents in the representation of
the Great Mother, Cihuacohuatl,
always giving birth to twins,
'bequeathing the sufferings of
childbirth to women, as the tribute of death,' and uniformly accompanied by a snake, or feather-
headed serpent,—I would suggest that there is in such resemblances abundant matter for grave
philosophising. 'In all this,'
writes Mr. Prescott, 'we see much
to remind us of the mother of the
human family, the Eve of the
Hebrew and Syrian nations' (p.
464). Cf. Wuttke, 1. 263, Lüken,
Traditionen, &c., pp. 121, 122, the
latter of whom declares, after
comparing the legend with others:
'Auf die merkwürdige Uebercin-
stimmung der Sage in so vielen
Theilen mit der Bibel brauche ich
den aufmerksamen Leser wohl
nicht hinzuweisen.'
[4] Squier, p. 161. This etymology is not, however, absolutely
certain.

of his youth. As such, the costliest sacrifice of all was offered annually in his temple, during the arid month of May,[1] when vegetable nature seemed expiring, and when fears began to be expressed for the well-being of the harvest. Then it was that pontiffs singled out one human being, in the spring of life, and of unblemished beauty, to personate, and suffer for and with, the highest member of their pantheon. When the day of this great sacrifice arrived, and the career of mirth and revelry assigned to the unhappy victim was completed, his heart, still palpitating under the murderous knife, was lifted up towards the sun and cast before the image of Tezcatlipoca, while the crowd below were bending breathless in the act of adoration.

If ever this divinity could justly claim to be compared with the all-holy God of revelation, he had forfeited his primal glory and descended altogether to the heathen level, when Mexico was first explored by Europeans, and her baneful idols put to flight by the advance of Christianity.

Huitzilo-pochtli;

But Tezcatlipoca, though appearing to receive unbounded worship from the later Mexicans, was not their national divinity; recourse was never had to him as to the oracle, the leader, and the special patron of the Aztec tribes. That post from ages out of memory had been allotted to the still more terrible Huitzilopochtli,[2]—a name compounded, it is

[1] Cf. Müller, p. 618, Prescott, pp. 24, 25.

[2] From *Huitzilin*, 'a humming-bird,' and *opochtli*, 'on the left hand': cf. Müller, pp. 591, 592. He is also of opinion that in earlier ages before the growth of anthropomorphism, this same divinity was called *Huitziton*, 'a little humming-bird,' and worshipped under that simple form, as a god of the air and firmament (p. 596). Prichard seems to prefer a different etymology, treating

said, of two words, importing ' humming-bird,' and
' left,' and illustrated by the fact that his gigantic
image always bore some feathers of the humming-
bird on the left foot. The reason of this etymology *meaning of*
is found in certain peculiarities of the bird in ques- *the title.*
tion; its rich and brilliant plumage serving to dazzle
the imagination of the Aztecs, while its frantic courage, as compared with its minute proportions, rendered it a favourite symbol of their own warlike,
daring and indomitable temper. Accordingly, whatever may have been the primary idea suggested by
the name Huitzilopochtli, or whatever may turn out
to be the true interpretation of the marvellous story
of his birth,[1] it is indisputable that he grew ere long
into the Siva and the Mars of Central America.
Another of his titles (Mexitli) had been transferred
in early times to Mexico itself; and one of the first
structures raised by Aztec builders on the table-land
of Anahuac was the sanctuary of this, their guardian
deity. His image was of a colossal bulk, erected on *Symbolical*
a blue stone, quadrangular in form, and with a snake, *representa-*
or serpent, issuing from each corner: the chains or *tions.*
collars about the idol's neck were ten human hearts,
all made of gold; his girdle also consisted of a great
golden serpent. Some at least appear to have regarded this ferocious war-god as the brother of

Huitzilopochtli as an historical
personage (Huitziton), raised after
his death to the 'left hand' of the
god Tezcatlipoca (v. 365).

  [1] The story is as follows: ' The
mother of Huitzilopochtli was
a priestess of Tezcatlipoca (a
cleanser of the temple, says
Gama), named Coatlicue. She
was extremely devoted to the
gods, and one day, when walking

in the temple, she beheld descending in the air a ball, made of
variously coloured feathers. She
placed it in her girdle, became
at once pregnant, and afterwards
was delivered of Mexitli, or
Huitzilopochtli, full armed, with
a spear in one hand, a shield in
the other, and a crest of green
feathers on his head:' Squier,
p. 196, Müller, pp. 601, 608.

Tezcatlipoca;[1] the largest temple of the Mexican metropolis was their common property; and in the costly and grotesque embellishments of both we always find the symbol of the mystic serpent more or less conspicuous.

Various meanings of the serpent-symbol.

There is ample reason for believing that ideas embodied in this representation were substantially the same in Europe, Asia, Africa, and America.[2] Unable though we are to specify that one interpretation of the Ophite symbol which explains and harmonises all the rest, it is remarkable that many different views had coexisted in the same locality. The serpent was at one time treated merely as a type of primitive matter; at a second, it became the image of superior knowledge, cunning, and sagacity. The periodic casting of its skin suggested the adoption of this reptile as an emblem of returning life, of spring-tide, of fertility, of rejuvenescence; and, regarded in the same peculiar aspect, the 'great century' of the Aztec tribes was represented as encircled by a serpent grasping its own tail: while other facts appear to indicate no less distinctly that in both the Old World and the New, the serpent was employed to symbolise the highest forms of being, as the sun-god, the great mother of the human family, and even the First Principle of all things.[3]

---

[1] Müller, p. 615.

[2] *Ibid.* pp. 484 sq., 611 sq., and authorities cited above, Vol. 1. pp. 307 sq.

[3] 'This is the view adopted by the rationalistic Mr. Squier, one of the most recent inquirers, in his *Serpent Symbol* (American Archæol. Researches, Part 1.). He concludes (p. 243): 'Whether we accept the scriptural tradition of "the fall" in a literal sense, or as an allegory referring to man's departure from the original religion, under the seductions of an unholy superstition, of which the serpent was the emblem,—in either case the antiquity of the symbol is equally established.'

But though serpents were for reasons of this kind
exalted into objects of religious worship, and venerated both in heathen countries and by various sects
of Christian misbelievers as the primary source of
intellectual illumination, it is also true that many
primitive nations looked upon those reptiles with religious awe and horror, recognising in them a personification of the Evil Principle, or emblems of malignant
energies, in both the physical and moral world.[1] The
victory gained by Krishńa in his arduous struggle
with Kálíya was held to have been frequently repeated
in the wilder tribes of North America,—for instance,
where the arrow of the philanthropic Manabozho had
been guided to the heart of the Great Serpent,
Meshekenabek, at the same time striking terror into
an enormous brood of demons by which he was attended; and in Mexican paintings a huge serpent
is sometimes exhibited in the act of being cut in
pieces by the great divinity, Tezcatlipoca.

If I mistake not, the predominant idea connected
with the serpent-symbol, in the worship more especially paid by Aztecs to their national divinity, was
the idea of a terrific and destructive agent.   This at
least is certain, that the modern world is unacquainted
with a system of religious thought whose whole complexion was so dark, so ghastly, so funereal.   Everywhere it seemed to breathe of suffering and of death.
The numerous altars of Huitzilopochtli reeked continually with the blood of human hecatombs,[2] and
that in cities where, amid some cheering gleams of

---

[1] *Ibid.* pp. 227, 244.
[2] Prescott, p. 19.   Southey is
also quite correct when he speaks
of Mexican temples
'Whose black and putrid walls
    were scaled with blood.'

moral sensibility, the Conquerors found no lack of goodly structures and of graceful ornaments, to indicate the progress made by the ferocious Aztec in the arts of social life.   These desperate efforts to secure the favour of the gods by offering human victims were indeed by no means limited to ancient Mexico; for all the wild tribes of America[1] had been *Human sacrifices.* wont from ages immemorial to sacrifice both children of their own and prisoners taken in their savage conflicts with some neighbouring people.   Acting also on the rude belief, that such oblations would conduce to gratify the animal wants of their divinity, as well as to appease his wrath, they had contracted the vile habit of feasting on the remnant of these human sacrifices, and at other times proceeded to indulge in the most brutish forms of cannibalism.   But when the Aztec rule eventually prevailed in every part of Anahuac, the sacrificing of all foreign enemies became a still more solemn duty.   We are told that 'the amount of victims immolated on its accursed altars would stagger the faith of the least scrupulous believer;'[2] while cannibalism, that dark accompaniment of human sacrifice in almost every country, was in Mexico peculiarly rife, and from the partial efforts to disguise it, had become peculiarly revolting.[3]

The character of the national god, to whom each

---

[1] Müller, pp. 142 sq.

[2] *Ibid.* p. 502. The numbers vary considerably, and some accounts are doubtless much exaggerated (pp. 637, 638); but there is every reason to believe that not fewer than 2500 human beings were offered annually in the Aztec dominions.   As many as 136,000 human skulls were found by the companions of Cortés within the precincts of the temple of Huitzilopochtli (Prichard, v. 365; Prescott, p. 26).

[3] Prescott, pp. 27, 28, 49; Müller, pp. 628 sq.

Mexican had solemnly devoted all his strength, reflected, and in turn contributed to fix, the moral *Effect on* characteristics of the nation. Their ruling spirit was *the charac-* *ter of the* severe and sanguinary. Their familiarity with blood *people.* begat in them a brutal thirst for carnage. The great drum, composed of serpent-skins, was ever and anon emitting its disastrous challenge from the temples of Huitzilopochtli, and so calling men to arms. Their very wars were undertaken not so much from pride of conquest as in order to bring home fresh victims for the solemn festivals; and imitation of their bloody rites was always rigorously demanded as an indispensable condition of their friendship and alliance.

Of minor points connected with the worship of *Alleged re-* Huitzilopochtli one appears to be deserving of especial *semblance* *to Hebra-* notice. It is recorded how, in all the long migrations *ism.* of the Aztec tribes, four priests had been accustomed to bear aloft a wooden image of this great divinity;[1] the vehicle on which it rested being called the 'chair of god,' and serving like the sacred chest of other ancient nations to remind them of his special favour and his present personality. Some writers have moreover dwelt on these arrangements as supplying what they deem a close resemblance to the sacred chest, or ark, of Israel, which was carried by the Levites on their shoulders through the wilderness and even to the field of battle. But the fancied parallelism, like many others of the same description, will be found to vanish on a close analysis. Apart from contradictions which are everywhere discernible in the religious dogmas of the Hebrew and the Aztec, it is obvious that the purpose of the two sacred

[1] Müller, p. 594; Winer, *Realwörterbuch*, under 'Bundeslade.'

CHAP. II.

Ark of the covenant.

vehicles in question, and consequently all the main ideas thereby suggested to the people, were completely different.[1] The 'ark of the covenant' had always been the centre and palladium of the Hebrew system, not because it bore within it or without it a material representation of the Unapproachable and only God, or was contributing in any way to bring Him more directly under the cognizance of the senses, but because it was ordained at first as the repository of His holy Law. Its prominent position ever intimated to the Hebrew that the covenant in virtue of which he stood so very near to God was ultimately and entirely moral; that the term of his election depended altogether on his keeping of the commandments; that his mission to the world at large was to assert the unity and vindicate the holiness of God against the mass of errors and corruptions under which those precious truths were ever liable to be lost.

Had the Mexicans a sacred triad?

I am unable to discover any proof that Aztecs had arrived at the conception of a sacred trinity, or triad; though attempts have not been wanting[2] to establish such a theory in Mexico as well as in most other parts of ancient heathendom. The object commonly chosen to fill up the third place, thus uniting on a level with Tezcatlipoca and Huitzilopochtli, is the water-god of Central America, entitled Tlaloc.[3]

---

[1] Bähr, *Symbolik des Mosaischen Cultus*, 1, 399—407.

[2] *e. g.* in Lord Kingsborough's *Antiq. of Mexico*, VI. 410 sq., where Acosta declares that 'Satan, in order to increase the majesty of his own worship, has wished, by cunningly introducing the doctrine of the Holy Trinity among the Indians, to abuse it' (p. 411).

[3] Müller, pp. 500 sq. Children were among the victims offered at his altar; and it is worthy of remark that they were immolated during the dry season, in order, if possible, to draw down blessings from the angry water-god.

In accordance with this theory, he has been converted into the Preserver, while the gods already noticed were believed to act respectively as the Creator and Destroyer. The truth appears to be, that if the number *three* must be completed, the divinity whose character and influence best entitle him to rank with the chief tenants of the Aztec pantheon is Quetzalcoatl.

As the story of this god is in itself remarkable, *Quetzal-* and may be found hereafter to involve a series of *coatl.* important questions, bearing more or less directly on our general subject, I propose to give the chief particulars of it somewhat more in detail. Whether we regard the whole as purely mythical, or as belonging rather to the family of historic legends, it is probable that when the Toltecs entered Mexico[1] in the seventh century of the Christian era, Quetzalcoatl was enthroned already as their patron deity. From them it was that all the knowledge of him which is traceable in Anahuac had passed over to the Aztec tribes by whom they were succeeded. The current version of the story is as follows:

Quetzalcoatl (or the 'Feathered Serpent') had

His wife, or female counterpart, was called Chalchiucueje, and to her, the water-goddess, all infants immediately after birth were brought for purification; the rite then practised bearing some vague resemblance to Christian baptism. (*Ibid.* pp. 503, 652.) But, as Mr. Prescott well remarks, with reference both to this and many more affinities, the first race of missionaries 'fastened their eyes exclusively on the points of resemblance,' taking small account of other and essential contrarieties. 'In their amazement they not only magnified what they saw, but were perpetually cheated by the illusions of their own heated imaginations. In this they were admirably assisted by their Mexican converts, proud to establish—and half believing it themselves—a correspondence between their own faith and that of their conquerors' (p. 465).

[1] See above, p. 136, n. 2.

been destined to become the high-priest of Tula, the metropolis founded by the Toltecs on their immigration into Mexico. His birth, some writers have asserted, was miraculous;[1] and in proportion as he ripened into manhood it was obvious in how many points he differed from the multitude by whom he was surrounded. His complexion was not red, but fair, his eyes large, his forehead open, his beard thick and flowing. Raised ere long to the position which had been allotted to him by the gods, Quetzalcoatl underwent a course of voluntary penance;[2] substituting, it is said, for human sacrifices of the olden times the drawing forth of blood from his own body. He

[1] This view is strongly espoused by Mr. Squier, but I confess myself unable to verify some of his statements (pp. 185 sq.). His description of the birth of Quetzalcoatl is as follows: 'The god of the Milky Way, in other words, of Heaven, the principal deity of the Aztec pantheon, and the Great Father of gods and men, sent a message to a virgin of Tulan [Tula], telling her that it was the will of the gods that she should conceive a son, which she did without knowing any man' (cf. above, p. 60, n. 1). According to Mr. Squier, Quetzalcoatl was an intermediate demigod, or rather a reputed incarnation of the highest god, Tezcatlipoca, and was thus analogous (he thinks) to Buddha, Zoroaster, Osiris, Taut in Phœnicia, Hermes or Cadmus in Greece, Romulus in Rome, Odin in Scandinavia, Votan in Guatemala, Bochica among the Muyscas, &c. But how is such a theory to be reconciled with facts which Mr. Squier, in spite of all his archæological erudition, appears to have completely over-

looked? For instance, how would he explain the deadly feud between Tezcatlipoca and Quetzalcoatl, which led to the ejection of the latter and the absolute ruin of the principality?

[2] See Kingsborough's *Antiq. of Mexico*, vi. 177, where these penances are regarded as a species of 'self-sacrifice' (cf. Southey's *Madoc*, Part II. No. x.). Müller, on the other hand, maintains (p. 582) that the self-chastisements of Quetzalcoatl were not *penances*, properly so called,—arising neither from a consciousness of guilt nor from a mystic wish to extricate himself entirely from the fetters of the body,—but were partial oblations of human blood intended as substitutes for the human sacrifices of earlier times. The same writer has justly remarked (pp. 582, 590) that when the worship of Quetzalcoatl was adopted by the Aztecs, they forgot his own strong abhorrence of human sacrifices, and offered such to him as well as to the other gods.

then proceeded, with the help of Huemac,[1] the temporal prince of Tula, to instruct and civilise the people round about him. He compiled an equitable code of laws; he introduced a milder and a purer ritual; he arranged the calendar; he set his face against all forms of violence and bloodshed; he encouraged arts of peace, as agriculture, metallurgy, and the like. Beneath his genial influences, the Toltecs rose at once into a thriving principality. It was the golden age of Anahuac, when the corn sprang up with such luxuriance that one ear became a burden for a man; when cotton grew of all colours so as to supersede the art of dyeing; and when other products of the soil were so abundant that the life of the community might be described as one perpetual feast. The palaces of Quetzalcoatl were constructed of gold, of silver, and of precious stones; the air was laden with rich perfumes, while the birds in brilliant plumage gladdened every heart with their enchanting music.

But the reign of order and prosperity was not of long duration. The god Tezcatlipoca cast an envious eye upon this earthly paradise; and calling to his aid the powers of magic undertook in various garbs to mar and ruin the great work of Toltec civilisation. He seduced the daughter of king Huemac; from which event was dated the decline of moral purity and the diffusion of a lax and revolutionary spirit. The high-priest himself ere long succumbed beneath the same malignant opposition. He was tempted to purchase immortality by drinking a renowned elixir

CHAP. II.

His civilising labours.

How defeated.

---

[1] Müller, p. 587, who tries to make out that Huemac and Quetzalcoatl are really the same person, or at least are different names applied to the same personification in different stages of the mythe.

CHAP. II. which the chief divinity presented to him in the guise of an old man; but no sooner was the cup exhausted than Quetzalcoatl felt himself impelled to quit the scene of all his former labours and to visit Old Tlapallan, the great cradle of the Toltec race. Upon the eve of his departure he destroyed the costly palaces; the fruit-trees were all smitten with a curse of barrenness; the singing-birds were ordered to accompany him and entertain him on the journey. His *His second attempt:* path, of which the general tendency was eastward, brought him after some deflections to Cholula, where halting for a term of years he was permitted once again to carry out his great reformatory project, and even to diffuse a knowledge of his principles in countries lying farther to the south.[1] It was in Cholula that some of his enthusiastic followers first proceeded to invest him with divine prerogatives. A temple was there dedicated in his honour, and the ruins, bearing witness to its primitive grandeur, are still classed among the noblest monuments of Mexican *his disap-pearance:* heathenism. The final flight or disappearance of Quetzalcoatl is narrated differently in different versions of the story. All, however, represent it as both sudden and mysterious. The received account is, that on his last endeavour to reach Tlapallan he descended to the shores of the Mexican gulf; and as he entered the unearthly bark, composed of serpent-skins, that was to carry him across the ocean, he consoled his followers with the promise that he would

---

[1] 'Seine Herrschaft dehnte sich aber hier sehr aus, von Cholula aus sandte er Kolonien nach Huaxayacac, Tabasco und Campèche, spater rühmte sich der Adel in Yucatan von ihm abzustammen, und *in der neuesten Zeit fand man dort noch Leute seines Namens,* wie in Chiapas Nachkommen Votans:' *Ibid.* p. 579.

eventually return among them and establish his be- Chap. II.
nignant rule in every part of Anahuac. A belief *his expected return.*
in this return[1] was lingering in the heart of many a
Mexican as late as the arrival of the Spaniards.
Cortés was himself identified at first with the expected deity; his white and bearded followers were
esteemed the progeny of Quetzalcoatl, or revered as
'children of the sun'; and the locality from which
they sprang was still believed to be none other than
the fabled region of Tlapallan.

Now it is obvious that a narrative like this may *Is this story a mythe or a legend?*
be interpreted from very different points of view.
We may consider it, for instance, as a genuine mythe,
—embodying, under allegorical forms, the rude conceptions that prevailed respecting God and nature
at some early period in the annals of mankind; or,
secondly, it may be taken as a legend, more or less
historic in its subject-matter, setting forth in brilliant
colours the achievements of some true philanthropist,
whom love and gratitude at length exalted to a place
among the gods. According to one method of inter- *Was Quet- zalcoatl an ideal hero?*
pretation,[2] the Toltec tribes, long after they emerged
from barbarism, had formed the habit of ascribing
all their progress as a nation to the work of some
ideal hero, whom they designated Quetzalcoatl. He
was thus in their eyes a personification of the whole
community: its qualities had been transferred to him:
whatever it had done was said to have been done by

---

[1] On these and other strange
prognostics of the coming of the
Spaniards, see Prescott, pp. 104,
105, and Fancourt's *History of
Yucatan*, pp. 57—59.
[2] This is Müller's theory, who
remarks (p. 580): 'Eine genauere

Ansicht und Kritik dieser Erzäh-
lung, die sich auf die Analogie
mythologischer Gesetze gründet,
zeigt uns zunächst, dass Quetzalcoatl *die euhemerisirte Idee des
Toltekischen Kulturvolks in ihrer
religiösen Fassung ist.*'

him. For instance, as the principal seats of Toltec civilisation were Tula and Cholula, these were made the theatre on which he acted, and from which his principles had been transmitted to adjacent districts. As the Toltec tribes all vanished, or were driven onward to the south and east, in many cases owing to their dissolute habits, and in others to the violence of some encroaching and more warlike neighbour, the reverses of the nation are all vividly repeated in the life of Quetzalcoatl.

Was he originally a god of the air?

It is felt, however, by the authors of this quasi-mythic theory that the *deification* of the Toltec people, under the disguise of an ideal hero, is inadequately explained on their hypothesis as to the origin and import of the story. They accordingly attempt to trace it farther back into the region of pure mythus. They affirm that long before the age when Quetzalcoatl became the representative of Toltec nationality, a god with whom he was eventually confounded had been worshipped in the cycle of divinities who were supposed to tenant each one his own province in the realm of nature. Quetzalcoatl, as to the original conception, was, in other words, a nature-god, devoid of human form or human properties; and even after a prevailing tendency to anthropomorphism led men to devise for him a novel story, and invest him with exalted attributes befitting the ideal founder of Toltec civilisation, it is urged that frequent glimpses of his genuine character continue to be visible; they witness to the fact that even by the later votaries of Quetzalcoatl he was known to be a mere personification of natural energies. The sphere of action which, according to this view, the primitive world assigned to

him had always been the region of the air. The
symbols commonly connected with his worship were
the sparrow, the fire-stone, and the serpent; all
of which the author of the present theory does not
hesitate to claim as justifying his peculiar method
of interpretation.[1] The god who forms and regulates
the currents of the air is welcomed as the god of
health and joy, of affluence and fertility. The struggle waging between him and the divinity Tezcatlipoca is resolved into the action of conflicting elements :
the breeze of heaven, opposed and vanquished by the
fiery sun-god, is compelled to seek a refuge in some
distant clime to which the singing-birds all follow
him. The ultimate return of the benignant Quetzalcoatl from the east is similarly identified with the
recurrence of the trade-winds blowing from that
quarter ; the idea of him as the great national benefactor having been suggested by the plenteous showers
which then descend in periodic blessings on the table-
land of Anahuac.

Yet how plausible soever this interpretation of *Objections*
the story may seem at the first glance, it cannot *to this view.*
stand the test of thoughtful criticism. Its author
seems to have forgotten that Toltec civilisation, rising
as it does alone like some oasis in the desert, is a fact
demanding an historical explanation ; and we naturally ask what better explanation can be given than
that which traces known improvements to their

---

[1] *Ibid.* pp. 593 sq. The employment of a bird to symbolise
the air-god is all natural enough ;
but there is greater difficulty in
tracing the fitness of the two remaining symbols. The fire-stone
(sometimes black, sometimes
green) is supposed to have been
originally an aerolith ; while the
serpent is here viewed under its
benignant aspects, as an emblem
of rejuvenescence and fertility.

ordinary sources,—to the genial impulse first communicated to a multitude by some one master-spirit? He assumes that after a nation has grown weary and ashamed of its barbaric usages, there is a general disposition felt not only to pe sonify itself, but also to bow down and worship such personification, as though it were reality. He assumes still further that a nation at this period of its growth is likely to engraft the worship of ideal heroes on some primitive worship of the elements, thus combining in the process two incongruous mythes, entirely different in their texture, and resting on a different basis.

The legendary hypothesis.

On the other hand, if we approach the tale of Quetzalcoatl, unencumbered by mythic theories of our own, we cannot fail to be impressed by the remarkable semblance of reality pervading almost every part of it. Embellishments there doubtless are in that, as in most other stories, which have been transmitted through the same precarious media ; but the argument which prompts us to reject it as unworthy of all credit, on the ground that we can never wholly disentangle the historic from the non-historic elements in its composition, would require us also to resolve the brightest worthies of the Middle Age into a series of mythic beings, because some dreamers of the school of Simeon Metaphrastes have, in ministering to the unhealthy cravings of the period, garnished all their 'Lives of Saints' with fables and absurdities. Affected by considerations of this kind, the ablest writers on American heathenism contend for the reality of several of the leading acts ascribed to Quetzalcoatl. He is viewed as an *historic* personage : historic as Confucius, notwithstanding all the

myriad temples now devoted to his worship; historic
as the Rajah Brooke in Borneo, notwithstanding all
the wondrous tales which may, and probably will,
be circulated in the Eastern Archipelago by the
Dyaks of some future age.

One class of writers[1] have discovered in the Toltec *Was he*
worthy an illustrious priest or prince of Tula, who *a native Toltec?*
on the decline of power and civilisation in his own
locality had fled in search of his mysterious father-
land; but rallying his attendants for a while had
been intrusted with the government of Cholula, and
had planted there a sacerdotal principality which
long survived as the metropolis of some new system
of religion. This method of accounting for the story
fails, however, in what seems to me a most essential
point. No circumstance has been more uniformly *Or a phil-*
mentioned than the *foreign* air of Quetzalcoatl. He *anthropic foreigner?*
was a white man, wearing a long beard.[2] Such testi-
mony to his strange appearance is remarkably corroborated by the language of the Mexican king[3] as
handed down by Cortés. The story is there lifted
altogether from the region of pure mythus. Quetzalcoatl is an ordinary foreigner, retiring hostile and
indignant far across the waters and expected to return
and conquer Mexico in the most literal sense. Nor

---

[1] Prichard, for example, acquiesces in this view (v. 364, 365).

[2] Müller's only resource in get-
ting rid of these peculiarities is
to urge (1) that Quetzalcoatl was
said to be of fair complexion, because his *restments* were white,
and (2) that he was said to have
a thick and flowing beard, because
the Toltec priests were in the
habit of wearing their hair very
long! Wuttke, on the contrary,

is so influenced by these special
features in the narrative as to
pronounce absolutely on the
foreign extraction of Quetzalcoatl:
'Dass die bildende Wirksamkeit
eines Mannes von fremden und
weissem Stamme die Veranlassung
zu der Vorstellung dieses Gottes
wurde, ist nicht zu bezweifeln'
(I. 262).

[3] *Ibid.* p. 261.

CHAP. II.

Other traditions of white men.

is it unworthy of remark that stories of white men were current in some other districts of America. The arrival of mysterious strangers in the highlands of Peru[1] had given birth to all the civilisation which it finally attained; and this commencement, a great writer has suggested, coincides in point of time with the original 'discovery' of the middle and southern parts of the United States by mariners from the north of Europe.[2]

The symbol of the cross;

We are not, perhaps, at liberty to gather any definite inference, touching the origin of Quetzalcoatl, from the circular shape of temples dedicated to his worship: yet the presence of the symbol of the cross, embroidered on the long white mantle of his priest and planted here and there upon the shrines of Yucatan, has not unnaturally given rise to the idea that he possessed some meagre knowledge of the Christian faith. The Spaniards all grew confident[3] on witnessing these strange phenomena that the Gospel had been propagated in America long before their own arrival; some appealing for an explanation

how introduced.

---

[1] The two 'children of the sun' (brother and sister, husband and wife) to whom the Peruvians ascribed their knowledge of civilised life, were called Manco Capac, and Mama Oello (*Ibid.* p. 305; Prescott, *Conquest of Peru*, pp. 3 sq. Lond. 1854): cf. Squier, as above, pp. 187—192, on other parallels, real or imaginary.

[2] Humboldt, *Cosmos*, II. 298, Sabine's ed.

[3] See Kingsborough's *Antiq. of Mexico*, VI. 418. On the other hand it must be borne in mind that the Spanish conqueror occasionally taught the natives to engraft the symbol of the cross on their abominable ritual. Thus Peter Martyr (of Anghiera, living at the court of Madrid) declares in his *Decades of the Newe Worlde*, Lond. 1555 (Dec. III. fol. 157): 'Owre men gaue them a painted picture of the blessed vyrgine, which they placed reuerently in their temple, and aboue it a *crosse*, to be honoured in the remembrance of God and man, and the saluation of mankynde. They erected also an other great crosse of wood in the toppe of the temple, whyther they oftentymes resorte togither to honour the image of the vyrgine.'

to the labours of St. Thomas, others clinging to the
thought that they had been preceded by the Spanish
fugitives who left their country when King Roderic
was defeated by the Moors; but all agreeing that
the presence of their venerated symbol, in the midst
of a revolting form of paganism, arose from the unhallowed commerce of Americans with the prince of
darkness. It might far more plausibly have been
contended that this hollow approximation to the
ceremonies of the Latin Church, if not in every case
fortuitous, was due to some extrinsic influence which
is known to have been exercised by Quetzalcoatl.
We are told, indeed, that in the Toltec districts he
himself had introduced the symbol of the cross, and
also recommended the practice of adoring it.[1] We
learn again that his peculiar principles, whatever
these might be, were rapidly diffused beyond the
city of Cholula, and survived long after in the sacred
colonies which he had placed in Yucatan.[2] Yet, on *Was this*
the other hand, it should be stated that the use of *symbol ne-*
cessarily
crosses in religious worship might have been at first *Christian?*
entirely independent of Christian agencies.[3] The
passion for symbolic representations, deeply rooted
in the human breast, prepares us to expect that any
simple figure like the cross would almost certainly be
appropriated in one or other of the heathen rituals of

---

[1] Müller, pp. 499, 500.
[2] Above, p. 154, n. 1.
[3] So Mr. Prescott seems to
think (pp. 464, 465). In speaking of the early missionaries he
remarks: 'They could not suppress their wonder, as they beheld
the cross, the sacred emblem of
their own faith, raised as an object of worship in the temples of
Anahuac. They met with it in

various places; and the image of
a cross may be seen at this day,
sculptured in bas-relief, on the
walls of one of the buildings of
Palenque, while a figure bearing
some resemblance to that of a
child is held up to it, as if in
adoration.' The style in which
the whole of this work is executed
appears to leave no doubt as to
its heathen origin.

CHAP. II. antiquity; and with regard to many parts of Central America, there is reason for believing that this emblem was religiously employed from early and præ-Christian times. Its office there had been to symbolise the god of rain;[1] and, consequently, as a form embodying the ideas of health, of joy, of plenty, it had grown into a common object of popular adoration.

Mexican theory of chronological cycles.

But whatever be the real import of particular features in the legends of Quetzalcoatl, I am satisfied that he presents to us one clear example, shewing the existence of some intercourse in very distant ages between the Old and New continents. Nor is this the only kind of evidence adducible in proof of such connexion. Many a tenet in the general creed of Anahuac bears no small resemblance to the dreams of Eastern Asia, and the cosmogonic theories of other ancient nations. It was held, for instance, quite as firmly in the New World as the Old, that the material universe had passed through a limited number of chronological cycles, each concluded by a grand catastrophe, of which the agent was some one or other of the physical elements. To quote the language of a high authority, we shall find the same traditions in their substance 'reaching from Etruria to Tibet, and forward to the ridge of the Mexican Cordilleras.'[2] The system of the Aztecs and Tibe-

---

[1] Müller, pp. 496—500.

[2] A. von Humboldt, in Prichard, v. 360. See the whole discussion, pp. 357—361. The first age of the Mexicans (the Age of the Earth, or the Age of Giants), corresponding to the Krita or Satya-yuga of Hindústán, was held to be 5206 years in duration. The human race of this age was destroyed by famine. The second period was the Age of Fire, in which birds only escaped the final conflagration, except one man and one woman, who saved themselves in the recesses of a cavern. The third period was the Age of Wind or Tempests, which two men only had survived. The fourth period was the Age of Water, the dura-

tians is perhaps in one respect at variance with ideas
prevailing in the different branches of the Indo-European family ;[1] for it is said to recognise as many as
five such periods in the life-time of the universe,
while they give only *four:* yet even in the case of
Mexico, we are assured, there is some want of uniformity as to the number and the order of the different
ages.

What appears to be of most importance is the *Traditions of a Deluge*
fact, attested by the hieroglyphic paintings of the
Mexican as well as by the tales now current in all
quarters from the Arctic Ocean to Cape Horn,[2] that
one of these great periods called 'the Age of Water'
closed with a convulsion, the account of which, in all
its broader outlines, is remarkably akin to the Mosaic
record of the Deluge. It was not, of course, to be
expected that discoveries of this kind, eliciting, as
they did, from long-forgotten races of the human
family a corroboration of the truths of Holy Writ,
would be allowed to circulate without a challenge ;
and accordingly attempts were made in different
quarters, either to explain away American legends
of a deluge, or resolve them all into a series of
'cosmogonic mythes.'[3] They were considered at the

tion of which is said to have been 4008 years. The earth was in-habited by men, whose mother was the 'Female Serpent' (above, p. 143, n. 3). Then came the period in the midst of which the world now is: its human popula-tion being all descended from one man and one woman, who were rescued from the general calamity at the close of the Age of Water. Some reflections on these sub-jects, as regarded from a geolo-

gical point of view, will be found in Mr. Hugh Miller's *Testimony of the Rocks*, Lect. VII. VIII.
[1] See, for instance, Vol. I. pp. 304 sq.
[2] Lüken's *Traditionen, &c.* pp. 216—235 : Faber's *Origin of Idol-atry*, II. 141 sq.
[3] Müller, p. 112. On return-ing to the subject (pp. 515, 516) he pronounces even more dog-matically : 'In solchen Analogien mit der biblischen Fluthcrzählung

Chap. II.

not mythi-cal.

very most to indicate a popular belief in some 'creation out of the water and in spite of the water.' Yet so numerous, so minute, and so extremely arbitrary, are the points in which those legends are now found to have approached the sacred story, that some species of affinity between the two is far more generally recognised; excepting where an archæologist or schoolman is incorrigibly blinded by his love of system-building. Even the divines of Germany,[1] beneath whose shadow every kind of mythic theory has sprung up with rank luxuriance, seem to have been almost reconciled to a belief, that the traditions now and formerly current in America respecting some great deluge, must have all been carried over from the Old Continent.

Specimens of these traditions.

Instead of dwelling on this subject, I shall ask the reader to examine for himself the following specimens selected almost at random, partly from the wilder tribes, and partly from the more refined communities of North America. The first[2] is still in actual circulation among the Cherokees; yet so peculiar is its form, that efforts have been made in

ist weder eine historische Abhäng- igkeit der Urvölker von einander, noch ein christlicher Einfluss auf die amerikanischen Erzahlungen anzunehmen, sondern selbstständ- ige Gestaltungen.'

[1] Thus Ewald, in *Götting. Ge- lehr. Anzeigen,* 1855, No. 69, p. 688, shews a leaning in favour of the common view, which, on this ground especially, refers the peopling of America to immigra- tion from Eastern Asia. With regard to the minute coincidences between the Mexican and Hebrew versions of the Deluge, he de-

clares: 'In solchen wesentlichen Gleichheiten können wir kein zufälliges sich Begegnen finden.' One of the best-informed, and at the same time most dispassionate of American writers on these sub- jects (Mr. Gallatin) has, in like manner, come to the conclusion that the native legends originated 'in a real historical recollection of an universal deluge, which overwhelmed all mankind in early ages of the world' (Prichard, v. 361).

[2] Schoolcraft, *Notes on the Iro- quois,* pp. 358, 359, Albany, 1847.

vain to represent it as a recollection of some Christian
teaching. In the gifts of speech and prophecy there
attributed to the Dog, we are reminded rather of the
service rendered to Manu, according to the Áryan
legend,[1] by the mighty and mysterious Fish. The
story of the American Indians has been thus reported
from their own lips by an intelligent explorer of
every thing connected either with their present or
their past condition :

'The water once prevailed over the land, until every person
was drowned but a single family. The coming of this calamity
was revealed by a dog to his master. This dog was very per-
tinacious in visiting the banks of a river, for several days, where
he stood gazing at the water and howling piteously. Being
sharply spoken to, by his master, and ordered home, he revealed
to him the coming evil. He concluded his prediction by saying, that the escape of his master and family from drowning
depended upon their throwing *him* into the water; that to
escape drowning himself, he must make a boat, and put in it
all he wished to save; that it would then rain hard a long
time, and a great overflowing of the land would take place.

The dog then told his master to look for a sign of the truth
of what he had said, to the back of his neck. On turning round
and doing so, the dog's neck was raw and bare, the bone and
flesh appearing. By obeying this prediction, the man and his
family were saved, and from these rescued persons, the earth,
they believe, was again peopled.'

The other legends hereunto appended are both

[1] See Vol. i. p. 318. The
difference is, however, no less remarkable. In the Hindú story,
the Fish who acts as an incarnation of the Deity, is moving in
his own proper element, and
simply rescues the small remnant
he has taken under his especial
patronage; while in the case
before us, the Dog, according to
his true character, is made to die
for his master's family in the
deluge which he had predicted.
Müller, it may be noted, suggests
(p. 515) that Coxcox in the Mexican story of the deluge is himself
a humanized representation of
some ancient Fish-god, corresponding to the Dagon of Syria,
&c.

Chap. II. silent as to any warning which prepared the human race for the outbursting of the Deluge; but some of the minutiæ there preserved are most remarkable. The account is furnished by A. von Humboldt,[1] one of the chief authorities respecting the picture-writings of ancient Mexico.

'Of the different nations that inhabit Mexico, the following had paintings representing the deluge of Coxcox, *viz.* the Aztecs, the Mixtecs, the Zapotecs, the Tlascaltecs, and the Mechoacans. The Noah, Xisuthrus, or Manu of these nations, is termed Coxcox, Teo-Cipactli, or Tezpi. He saved himself, with his wife Xochiquetzatl, in a bark, or, according to other traditions, on a raft. The painting represents Coxcox in the midst of the water waiting for a bark. The mountain, the summit of which rises above the waters, is the peak of Colhuacan, the Ararat of the Mexicans. At the foot of the mountain are the heads of Coxcox and his wife. The latter is known by two tresses in the form of horns, denoting the female sex. The men born after the deluge are dumb. The dove from the top of a tree distributes among them tongues represented under the form of small commas.'

Again :

'The people of Mechoacan preserved a tradition that Coxcox, whom they called Tezpi, embarked in a spacious *acalli* with his wife, his children, several animals and grain. When the Great Spirit, Tezcatlipoca, ordered the waters to withdraw, Tezpi sent

---

[1] A. von Humboldt, *Vues des Cordillères et Monumens de l'Amérique*, pp. 226, 227. This great writer very justly asks : 'Ne doit on pas reconnoître les traces d'une origine commune partout où les idées cosmogoniques et les premières traditions des peuples offrent des analogies frappantes jusque dans les moindres circonstances ?' That the South Sea islands are no exception to this rule may be seen in Ellis, *Polynesian Researches*, I. 387 sq. A very striking instance has been brought to light in the *Mission Field* (July, 1859) : it is the Dyak version of the Deluge. 'They say that long ago there was a great overflow of the sea, which drowned the world, and that only one human pair of each of the four races, 'Orang Puteh', Malays, Chinese, and Dyaks, were saved from destruction, each in their prahus.'

out from his bark a vulture, the zopilote, or *vultur aura.*. This
bird did not return on account of the carcases with which the
earth was strewed. Tezpi sent out other birds, one of which,
the humming-bird, alone returned, holding in its beak a branch
clad with leaves. Tezpi, seeing that fresh verdure covered the
soil, quitted his bark near the mountain of Colhuacan.'

CHAPTER III.

Religions of Oceanica.

'I believe that the ignorance which has prevailed regarding the mythological systems of barbarous or semi-barbarous races has too generally led to their being considered far grander and more reasonable than they really were.'

CHAP. III.

Discovery of Oceanica.

THE name of 'Oceanica' is here employed in its extended signification, as embracing the whole group of human beings who are scattered through the myriad islands of the Eastern and Southern Seas, from Madagascar on the eastern coast of Africa to the western shores of the New World. It seems to have been ordered in the plans of the Almighty, that the natives of this Archipelago should remain almost entirely strangers to the other sections of the human family, until, upon the dawn of that eventful epoch which divides the Modern from the Mediæval life of Europe, all the bearings of the grand discovery could be adequately perceived. The Spaniard had secured his empire in America, and was introducing there some feeble germs of Christian civilisation, when the pride of conquest once again impelled him onward into other spheres of enterprise. A fleet, despatched from Mexico itself, in the third quarter of the sixteenth century, enabled him to plant the Spanish flag on many of the Philippines. The Portuguese, and

after them the Dutch, approaching from the opposite
side, extended the horizon of man's thoughts and
stimulated the new spirit of adventure; while Eng-
land, now advancing proudly to her place among the
maritime powers of Europe, was importing from the
Farther East not only the choice products of a tropical
soil, but stories tending to beget compassion for 'poor
infidels captived by the devil.' The first of her great
mariners returned in 1580 from his perilous voyage
round the globe.

Henceforward almost every year was serving to *General*
lift up the veil that covered some remoter province *character of the re-*
of the Eastern Archipelago. Another world, as new *gion.*
to Europe as the continent discovered by Columbus,
and affording not a few distinct analogies to that
remarkable region, was now gradually laid open to
the skilful navigator, and explored by men of science,
and by heralds of the Christian faith. It stretched
on every side in groups of islands, differing in soil
and structure, as in geographical distribution; here
presenting to the eye a mass of savage and volcanic
mountains, towering high into the clouds; there a
cluster of low coral reefs that scarcely peer above the
surface of the water; here abounding in luxuriant
pastures and sparkling like so many 'gems under the
sunny sky of the Great Ocean;' there a long succession of untrodden wilderness and sombre forest; here
suggesting the idea of an old continent dismembered
and in part submerged, and there of one that seems
at present only in course of formation.

The inhabitants of this region are at first sight no
less various in their aspect than the island-groups on
which they have been severally planted; and accord-

ingly the first impressions of the European mariner who touched at several of these groups in succession were commonly adverse to the thought of primitive unity.

Original unity of the population. He found the natives of different islands and different parts of the same island varying widely from each other in temperament, in physical structure, in habits, and in speech. Yet here, as we have seen already in America, it was rather to a superficial and unscientific gaze that local variations had presented insurmountable difficulties. Fresh inquiry brought to light fresh points of contact between tribes where such affinity was not at first suspected; and so numerous are the common elements of thought and feeling, language and mythology, which after a minute analysis are seen to underlie the startling discrepancies in physical organisation, that ethnologists on merely scientific grounds are more and more disposed to hesitate before pronouncing against the ultimate derivation of the Oceanic islanders from one parent stock. It is remarkable that within the last few years, the speech of the Malays, itself originally monosyllabic, has been grammatically connected[1] with idioms spoken as far northward as the confines of eastern India and western China; thus directing us again to the conclusion, that morally as well as geographically the Indian Archipelago is only a prolongation of the Indo-Chinese world, and Asia the great centre out of which the population of the whole had radiated long anterior to the birth of pagan history. This clear approximation in two languages,

---

[1] See Mr. Max Müller's 'Last searches,' in Bunsen's *Phil. of Results* of the Turanian Re- *Univ. Hist.* I. 403 sq.

of which the seat of one is on the mainland, of the Chap. III. other on the islands, furnishes a fresh and still more definite link of union between Asia and Polynesia,— a link, 'which, even by itself, is strong enough to hold two of the mightiest chains of languages together; the Nomads of the sea extending from the east coast of Africa to the west coast of America; the Nomads of the continent swarming from the south-east to the north-west of Asia.'

Neglecting, for the present, some few tribes of Oceanica,[1] whose ethnological affinities are still undetermined, we shall find that all the rest are capable of classification under two great varieties. *Two existing varieties.*

The members of the first, and probably the elder of the groups, have very much in common with the Khonds and other primitive people scattered in the mountains and forests of Central India,[2] and in some 1. *Papuans.*

---

[1] *e. g.* The people known by the various titles of 'Arafuras,' 'Alfoers' and 'Alforians' (? Arabic الْخَرَاج). 'Nothing,' says Prichard (v. 255), 'can be more puzzling than the contradictory accounts which are given of their physical characters and manners. The only point of agreement between different writers respecting them is, the circumstance that all represent them as very low in civilisation, and of fierce and sanguinary habits.' Yet even this representation is disputed by D. H. Kolff, *Voyages, &c.*, translated from the Dutch by Mr. Earl (Lond. 1840), pp. 156 sq. Mr. Earl's own account (*The Native Races of the Indian Archipelago, or, Papuans*, pp. 61 sq., Lond. 1853) is probably the most correct. He thinks that 'Alforias' is not a generic term for a particular race of people; 'but was generally applied to the inland inhabitants of these islands, to distinguish them from the coast tribes.' He derives the name from the Portuguese 'Alforias' = 'freedmen' or 'manumitted slaves;' but it would rather seem to have been imported directly from Arabia, and not through a European medium, so that its proper sense would be 'outsiders,' 'persons beyond the influence of the coast settlements.'

[2] See Vol. I. p. 370, where the earliest or præ-Aryan population of Hindústán are said to be 'very black, ill-shapen, and dwarfish, and to have countenances of *a very African character.*' The Papuans were certainly of the same race with the Semangs of the Malay Peninsula (Earl, as above, ch. IX.), and with the na-

Chap. III. adjacent regions; but they most of all resemble the African negroes in the sooty blackness of their skin, their crisped and woolly hair, their broad noses, thick and prominent lips, receding chins and foreheads, and even in their general build.[1] These Oceanic negroes, also termed Negritos, and more properly Papuans,[2] have now their stronghold in New Guinea, where indeed they are enabled to retain their old supremacy, as absolute masters of the sea-coast. In other islands, they are found at some distance only from the shore, among the woods and mountain-fastnesses, maintaining their unequal struggles with a different race of settlers, and in spite, as it would seem, of all their physical prowess, destined in the end to melt away. Their utter extirpation in particular islands is matter of authentic history.

2. Malayo-Polynesians. The second group of Oceanic tribes and nations, by which indeed those great displacements were effected, is best known as the Malayo-Polynesian family, the brown or copper-coloured race. It seems that long after the Papuans were diffused in nearly all the intertropical islands, a fresh current of emigration had begun to set in that direction from the eastern continent of Asia. Lively, graceful, and

---

tives of the Andaman islands in the Bay of Bengal (ch. x.). Other woolly-haired tribes are also said to exist at present in the mountain-range which traverses the eastern side of the Indo-Chinese Peninsula (*Ibid.* p. 158). To the early influence of this family may be perhaps attributed the fact that many of the ancient idols of the Hindús 'have negro characteristics' (p. 160).

[1] W. von Humboldt, *Über die Kawi-Sprache,* I. p. iv. Berlin, 1836. Some of the full-blooded Papuans have spiral and twisted hair growing in large tufts to a considerable length: others have hair growing in short and closely-frizzled curls: Prichard, v. 4.

[2] 'Pua-pua,' or 'Papua,' means 'crisped', and as referring to the quality of the hair, has come to be applied to the entire race: Earl, *Papuans,* p. 3.

in general structure not unfrequently reminding us of Arabs, these new settlers form a pointed contrast to their sullen, savage, and ill-favoured predecessors. Instead of shunning the society of white men, and thus resisting all endeavours to promote their intellectual and religious elevation, few of them have ever yet relapsed entirely to a state of barbarism. They constitute the demi-civilised population[1] of the Oceanic world. It seems most probable[2] that after *Probable course and stages of migration.* entering the Indian Archipelago, upon their work of conquest or extermination, they alighted first of all in Sumatra and next in Java; thence, like genuine Tatars of the Ocean, they roved onward in their swarming *prahus* to the different coasts of Borneo, to the Cœlebes, and northward to the Philippines,— a group of islands where the traces of them are especially manifested by the regularity and richness of the native speech.

Advancing now beyond the zone of what are termed the pure Malay dialects,[3] one section of this copper-coloured family appears to have wandered eastward in search of other territories, and, avoiding for a time all fresh collisions with the powerful

---

[1] 'Alle diese Völkerstämme nun besitzen solche gesellschaftlichen Einrichtungen, dass man sie mit Unrecht von dem Kreise civilisirter Nationen gänzlich ausschliessen würde. Sie haben eine fest gegründete, und gar nicht durchaus einfache, politische Verfassung, religiöse Satzungen und Gebräuche, zum Theil sogar eine Art geistlichen Regiments, zeigen Geschicklichkeit in mannigfaltigen Arbeiten, und sind kühne und gewandte Seefahrer': W. von Humboldt, as above, p.

iii. On the contrary, few, if any, instances exist in which the Papuans have been known to manifest like qualities: cf. Earl, pp. 94, 111.

[2] See Shortland's *Traditions, &c. of the New Zealanders,* pp. 30 sq., Lond. 1854, and Russell's *Polynesia,* pp. 37 sq., Lond. 1852: where objections on the score of distance and the difficulties of navigation are fully considered.

[3] W. von Humboldt, as above, p. ii.

CHAP. III. Papuans of New Guinea and the neighbouring groups, had found their way to the Ladrones, to the Carolines, and ultimately to the Sandwich Islands on the northern border of the Tropics. From this centre[1] it is not unusual to derive the kindred streams of population, which proceeding southward occupied the clustering islands commonly known as Polynesia Proper, and penetrated even to New Zealand: so that, in the widest meaning of the term, Malayo-Polynesian tribes have been diffused across the whole of Oceanica, and have now become the dominant race, excepting in one narrow circle, where the elder family, as we have seen, with more or less admixture, still continue to preserve their ancient independence.

Foreign influences in the Eastern Archipelago.   But before I enter on some points relating to the native creeds of Oceanica, as brought especially to light by recent missionary enterprise, it is important to observe, that in the northern territory, or the part approaching nearest to the ancient seats of Asiatic culture, there were islands which had been indebted largely for the rudiments of civilisation to other and non-Christian powers, in ancient times to Bráhmanism and Buddhism,[2] and in modern times to indefatigable preachers of Islám.[3]

---

[1] Shortland, as above, pp. 32, 33. The New Zealanders themselves have preserved traditions of the voyage of their ancestors from Hawaiki, which this writer identifies with the largest of the Sandwich Islands: cf. the full discussions respecting the original 'Migrations of the Oceanic tribes' in Mr. Hale's *Ethnography and Philology of the United States' Exploring Expedition*, pp. 117—196, Philadelphia, 1846.

[2] See above, p. 83. As modified into Fo-ism this religion is still being propagated here and there by Chinese traders and colonists, *e.g.* on the coast of New Guinea and in Borneo.

[3] The Muhammadans entered the Archipelago in the 13th century after Christ, when their creed was very generally accepted by the Malays. See, for instance, Mr. Horace St. John's *Indian Archipelago*, I. 42, 274, Lond.

The island first and principally affected by these Chap. III. foreign influences was Java, which in turn, as the *Hindúism in Java.* 'Phœnicia of the East,' became an ever-active agent for disseminating the new opinions through far wider circles,[1] among the Batta of Sumatra, in the Cœlebes, and even on the western coast of Borneo. It is more particularly worthy of remark, that not a few of the ideas thus propagated over so large an area had been first imported from Hindústán by peaceful colonies of priests and sages, who without material succours were permitted to fix their residence among the natives, and had gradually instilled the principles which they brought with them, till at length there rose in Java a Malay community so tinctured with the languages, the literature, the mythes and the philosophy of India, as to furnish a most faithful copy of Hindú civilisation. 'Perhaps,' says a great authority,[2] 'no second example is to be found of a nation undergoing such a complete infusion of the national spirit of another race, without losing its own independence.' If we fix our thoughts entirely on the province of religion, it appears that at some time

1853. At the present time this creed is again making considerable progress, as, for instance, in the Arru Islands, and even on the coast of New Guinea, with which it has been connected by means of some commercial intercourse between that island and the Moluccas.

[1] See W. von Humboldt's investigation of this point, as above, I. 238—254; and Lassen's *Ind. Alterth.* II. 1054.

[2] W. von Humboldt, p. viii. Elsewhere he writes (I. 4): 'Râma, Arjuna, die ganzen Geschlechter Pându's und Kuru's, und die übrigen Helden der Indischen Vorzeit leben nicht nur noch jetzt im täglichen Andenken des Volks, sondern mehrere von ihnen werden als einheimisch angesehen, und Java selbst gilt für den Schauplatz vieler ihrer oft besungenen Thaten.' Additional light has been thrown upon this very interesting subject by inquiries which have been since made into the literary remains of Bali; see Weber's *Ind. Studien,* II. 124 sq.

or other during the interval between the Christian era and the introduction of Islám in the 14th century, the Javanese had to a great extent appropriated one or more of the indigenous creeds of India. This may be collected, partly from the numerous literary relics of the island which are found to have been based on corresponding works of the Hindús, and partly from surviving images and inscriptions, or from actual ruins of magnificent temples dedicated to the Hindú *Specific* gods. It does not seem, however, that the new belief *character* of Java was in strict propriety of language either *of the new* Bráhmanism or Buddhism. The highest object of *creed.* men's worship was Batára Guru ('the Venerated Teacher'),[1] whom his followers had enthroned superior to all other members of their pantheon. The best supported of the theories respecting him affirms that he was originally a creation of Bráhmans,[2] at the crisis when they had been forced into collision with the Buddhists of their native province, and when consequently the necessity arose of putting forth a rival object, worthy to compete with Sákya- *Its wider* muni. The unwonted prominence ascribed to him in *diffusion.* Java led to the diffusion of his name in far more

[1] Some writers have connected *batára* with *avatára*, and so discovered an allusion to Vishñu; but the true etymology seems to be the Sanskrit *bhattára* = 'worthy of veneration:' Lassen, II. 1050, Weber, *Ind. Studien*, II. 126, note.

[2] Very different opinions are entertained on this subject, some writers labouring to identify Batára Guru with Gautama Buddha, others with a second Buddha or Bodhisatwa; but I think that

Lassen's arguments are fatal to this theory (*Ind. Altert.* II. 1049 sq.). His own view is that the first Bráhmans, who settled in Java long before the arrival of Buddhists, were of the Vaishñava party, *i. e.* members of the Hindú sect which had invested Vishñu in particular with the attributes of the Supreme Being, and had put him forward, in opposition to the Buddhists, as *the* object of men's worship.

distant regions. It is used, for instance, by the Batta of Sumatra to denote the first of three principal divinities,[1] and in the Cœlebes, Batára is said to mean the eldest son of the Supreme Being.[2] At the time when Hindú colonists and traders first arrived in Java, Buddhism, we have reason for believing, was totally unknown among the native population. It had certainly obtained no footing there as late as A.D. 414,—the year in which a Chinese pilgrim halted on the island for the purpose of investigating the religious state of the inhabitants.[3] Eventually, however, Buddhist doctrines seem to have been introduced in very many provinces, and, what is most remarkable, had flourished for a season side by side with one or more[4] varieties of Bráhmanism. To this harmonious coexistence may be traced the startling intermixture of religious dogmas in the extant literature of Java, the confusion of symbolic representations on so many of the works of art, and the uncertainty which now exists, and will most probably continue to exist, respecting all the details of her sacred history.

[1] These were Batára Guru, Seri Pada and Mangala Bulan; but if we may credit the account of some missionaries, there stood above them a Supreme Father and Creator, Debata Hasi Asi. According to a native composition, some of the chief divinities were named, with obvious reference to Hindúism, Mesewara (Maháśwara = Śiva), Bisnu, Brehma, Sri, Cala (W. von Humboldt, I. 238, 239).

[2] *Ibid.* p. 249. In Luzon, one of the Philippines, the name also recurs under the form *Bathala*, as denoting the Supreme God, or Godhead in the abstract (p. 251).

[3] See Lassen, II. 1041, 1042. Fahian remained in Java five months, and speaks both of unbelievers and of Bráhmans, but not a word of Buddhists.

[4] The worship of Śiva, in particular, seems to have been intimately associated with Buddhism (cf. Vol. I. p. 363, n. 1): W. von Humboldt, I. 280 sq. The effect of this unnatural union was to discountenance and displace the older worship of Vishńu (p. 288).

§ 1. *The Papuan Family.*

Low state of religious sensibility.

Our knowledge is more scanty still[1] as to the character and condition of the native races, anterior to the age when elements of culture were thus brought among them by the colonies from Hindústán. The absence of vernacular words,[2] expressing the idea of Godhead in the abstract, has been cited as a proof that the religion of the primitive masters of the Archipelago was mournfully corrupted and debased. This verdict is emphatically true, as it applies to the Papuan family,—a race which constituted the first layer of population in the islands of the Farther East. At no great distance from the tombs and other monuments that serve to illustrate the ancient rule of Hindú civilisation, there are remnants also of this older race of Oceanic negroes, who, retaining all their inextinguishable hatred of the foreigner, have handed down the rudest possible forms of unimaginative superstition. Such, for instance, are the scattered tribes of Semangs,[3] who still linger in the northern forests of the Malay Peninsula. They remind us not unfrequently of African negroes; but their creed has also much in common with that of wild Americans, as well as with the Shamanism that

---

[1] *Ibid.* I. 72.

[2] Even the Javanese *Yïeang*, which was ultimately used by itself to signify the Godhead, does not appear to have had this meaning in the first instance (*Ibid.* I. 102 sq.). The common term for 'god-like' was *batára*, and for 'Godhead' *dévatá*, both of Sanskrit origin. A similar remark, touching the absence of all words which designate the Deity, is also made with reference to the Marian Islanders: Prichard, v. 176. Among the Dyaks of Borneo there are two names for the Supreme God, '*Dewata*', and '*Tuppa*'; the latter is thought to be the true Dyak name.

[3] H. St. John's *Indian Archipelago*, I. 74.

now predominates in all the higher latitudes of Asia, and in many of the oldest tribes of Hindústán. In these remote localities, we can discern no more than feeble glimmerings of the true religion. The idea *Papuan* of God has well-nigh vanished from the human spirit; *idea of God.* for as often as attempts are made to hold communion with Him she is always under the necessity of local- ising, or dividing, the object of her thoughts, until the great mysterious Power, of which she stands in awe, has been degraded into one or other of the physical elements. A *moral* order and a *moral* Governor of the universe are both of them concep- tions too exalted for the dark and narrow faculties of the savage. Hence it is that few, if any, heathen of this class are ever known to pay their acts of adoration to the Being[1] whom in words they will acknowledge as their chief divinity: all worship is in their case nothing more than deprecation; it is ever tending to propitiate hosts of angry and malignant demons.

Other points in which a family-likeness may be *Worship of* traced between the creeds we are considering, are *the dead.* the periodical commemoration of the dead, and more especially the worship of departed ancestors. For instance, the Ajetas, a Papuan tribe surviving in the Philippines, are still accustomed to assemble annually at the tombs, in order to deposit there fresh offerings of betel and tobacco.[2] At the time

---

[1] See above, Vol. I. p. 376, and compare E. T. Turnerelli's *Kazan*, II. 133, respecting the religious ideas of the aboriginal tribes in that neighbourhood.

[2] Earl's *Papuans*, p. 132. To-

bacco was also offered up in sa- crifice by very many of the wild tribes of America (see Müller's *Amer. Urreligionen*, pp. 59, 86, 92, 130, and elsewhere).

of sepulture the favourite bow and arrows of the hunter are suspended over his grave, from a conviction that he still enjoys the privilege of issuing forth at night, and so reverting for a season to his former occupations. Crude and childish as this fancy is, we may discover in it germs of a belief in some futurity, or reproduction of the present life.[1]

Have the Papuans a religion? According to the testimony of recent travellers in Oceanica, the Papuans of New Guinea and elsewhere continue for the most part void, not only of poetic feeling and mythology, but also of those leading elements which enter into the received idea of a religion. 'We could not discover the slightest trace of religion among them,' such is the report of one intelligent writer,[2] in speaking of New Guinea. 'The Ajetas,' writes a second,[3] 'have no religion, and adore no star.' Yet, on the other hand, it is apparent from the context of these passages that the authors both intended by 'religion' a coherent system of belief and worship governed by a regular hierarchy. Of such there are no traces, either in the wild tribes of America or of the Eastern Archipelago. We ask in vain among those primitive

[1] See above, pp. 34, 35, p. 127, n. 1, on the analogous idea of the Chinese and the American Indians; and Livingstone, p. 319, of the negroes of South-Central Africa. The Alforias, on the contrary, appear, at least in some districts, to have no conception of the immortality of the soul (Kolff, *Voyages*, &c., translated by Earl, p. 159). When a man dies, it is related that his friends assemble and destroy all the goods he may have collected during his life :

even the gongs are broken to pieces and thrown away.
[2] Modera's *Reize naar de zuidwest Kust van Nieuw Guinea*, as quoted by Earl, *Papuans*, pp. 49, 50. It is worthy of remark that the same statement had been previously made by Kolff, *Voyages*, &c., p. 158, with reference to the 'Alforias' of the Arru islands.
[3] De la Gironière, *Souvenirs de Jala Jala*, quoted in Earl as above, p. 132.

people for the shrines and temples dedicated to the worship of particular deities.[1] We ask in vain for any sacerdotal family, or any institution bearing close resemblance to the Hindú law of caste.[2] The right of sacrificing is there held to be the common property of all, and that in cases where it may be practically restricted either to the head-man of some patriarchal group,[3] or else to seers and medicine-men and wizards, who establish their pretension to a mastery in the world of spirits by the frequent use of exorcisms, of incantations, and of magic spells. So far indeed are the Papuans from abjuring *all* *Their ideas* religion that we find them everywhere betraying *of the di-* *vinity.* a keen sense of their relation to invisible agents and led captive by a number of most abject superstitions. They believe that the mysterious Power above them is discerpted and diffused in almost every part of nature, animate and inanimate; and selecting some one form in which this power is thought to be especially active, they embrace it as their fetish and their guardian deity. Such fetish is at one time a rude piece of sculpture, as a snake, a lizard, or some other reptile; at a second time it is a bit of

[1] 'The want of any form of public worship, or of idols, or of formal prayers or sacrifice, makes both Caffres and Bechuanas appear as among the most godless races of mortals. . . . .Though they all possess a distinct knowledge of a deity and of a future state, they show so little reverence, and feel so little connexion with either, that it is not surprising that some have supposed them entirely ignorant on the subject:' Livingstone, pp. 158, 159. A Portuguese account, translated by Purchas, declares that the 'Caphar nation is the most brutal and barbarous in the world, neither worshipping God nor any idol, nor having image, church, or sacrifice,' &c.

[2] This is the more noticeable, because a species of caste-system does prevail in many parts of Polynesia proper.

[3] Earl, p. 85, speaking of the natives of Dory, in New Guinea: cf. above, Vol. I. p. 376.

bone or mineral; at a third it rises to the dignity of a human figure, small in size and absolutely hideous in expression. This third variety indeed, which in New Guinea is entitled *karwar* (a mean figure carved in wood and holding up a shield), may be regarded as their highest mode of representing or embodying the divine. It occupies a prominent place in every cottage, serving there the two-fold purpose of an oracle and an idol. The persons who consult it are said to 'squat before it, clasp the hands over the forehead, and bow repeatedly, at the same time stating their intentions. If they are seized with any nervous feeling during this process it is considered as a bad sign, and the project is abandoned for a time; if otherwise—that is to say, if they really wish to carry out the proposed object—the idol is supposed to approve. It is considered necessary that the *karwar* should be present on all important occasions, such as births, marriages, or deaths.'[1]

Veneration of the wa-ringin-tree. Among the few minute peculiarities, which recent enterprise has brought to light, in aid of the endeavour to connect religious thoughts and customs of Papuans with those of continental Asia, there is none perhaps more striking than the veneration paid to the waringin-tree,[2] a species of banyan or Indian fig. So strong is their devotion to it that the wilder tribes of Ceram lodge and almost live among its branches; and throughout the aboriginal family of the Archipelago,[3] this tree has been no less invested with sacred and mysterious characteristics. A similar

[1] *Ibid.* pp. 84, 85.
[2] *Ibid.* p. 116: cf. p. 160.
[3] *Ibid.* where Mr. Earl adds that the lower classes, at least, of China have imbibed precisely the same ideas, even where they are 'untainted with Buddhism.'

kind of veneration, we have seen,[1] prevailed in every part of India from a high antiquity. The *vata* was there absolutely worshipped by the superstitious multitude; beneath its sacred shadow the ascetic wasted his remaining strength in the attempt to consummate his reabsorption into Brahma; and thither, as their favourite haunt, resorted poets and philosophers, all eager to bestow on it their choicest appellations, and rejoicing to behold in its majestic form the 'tree of knowledge and intelligence.' If these coincidences do not actually warrant a belief that in the intertropical islands, as elsewhere, the veneration paid to the waringin-tree is a distorted reminiscence of events recorded in the opening chapters of Holy Writ, the general circulation of such a story both in Eastern Asia and in Oceanica will at least supply us with additional hints as to the ultimate and generic unity of the populations there located.

§ 2.   *The Malayo-Polynesian Family.*

In passing from the older to the younger family of *Ethnological affinities of the Vitians.* Oceanic islanders, attention is arrested by one special group, which either from a geographical or ethnological point of view may be regarded as transition-links between the black and copper-coloured races.[2]

[1] See Vol. I. p. 306, and the references there.

[2] M. Dumont d'Urville (quoted in Prichard, v. 243, 244) was the first to draw attention to this point, having observed that in many of their characteristic habits the Fijians resembled the Malayo-Polynesians more than the Papuans: 'La circoncision,' he continues, 'se pratique généralement parmi les peuples de Viti : le kava est usité chez eux, et le betel ne l'est point, bien que la noix d'arek se trouve sur leur sol. Ces îles sont donc la *limite com-*

CHAP. III. These are the Fijians or Vitians,[1] lying midway between the shores of India and America, and on the very confines of the zone of population where Papuans are still intermixed with Polynesians proper. To what extent such intermixture has actually taken place in the Viti islands, may be very difficult to determine, either from the physical structure of the people, or the genius of their native language: but all writers on the subject now agree, that notwithstanding their generally dark complexion, they exhibit much of the plasticity, the animation, and the intellectual power which characterise their graceful neighbours in the Tonga or Friendly islands.

*Their san-
guinary
spirit.*
With regard, however, to the spiritual condition of the former, the reports of recent missionaries and explorers are both absolutely appalling. Those Vitians who continue strangers to the Gospel, are the Aztecs of the Oceanic world. Their vigour is expended chiefly on the field of battle, and familiarity with bloodshed, while creating a fanatical depreciation of human life, appears in the majority of cases to be drying up the springs of natural affection. We behold in them, as in the Mexicans, a dark exemplification of the way in which some knowledge of the useful arts may co-exist with almost every species

---

mune de la race cuivrée ou Polynesienne, et de la race noire Océanienne ou Mélanésienne.' This intermediate character is said to find a parallel in the natives of Madagascar at the western extremity of Oceanica (*Ibid.* p. 253), who, although belonging to the Malayo-Polynesian family, have numerous points in common with Papuans.

[1] An interesting account of the present state of these people will be found in Dr. Berthold Seemann's *Viti: an Account of a Government Mission to the Vitian or Fijian Islands in the years* 1860—61: Cambridge, 1862. The natives term their islands collectively '*Viti*'; the common designation '*Fiji*', or '*Feejee*', comes from the Tonguese, who cannot pronounce the *v*: p. 404.

of atrocity,[1]—with infanticide, with human sacrifices, with the strangulation of whole families in honour of some fallen chief, with brutish feasts upon the bodies of their foes and even of their fellow-subjects. It may be that very many of these horrible usages were first of all adopted under the influence of the devil-worship, which prevailed, and is prevailing, in every part of heathendom; but the Vitians of the present day are instigated to commit such deeds of darkness, rather by a false idea of immortality than by eagerness to pacify a host of angry and vindictive spirits. Arguing, for example, that the state of man after death[2] will be at first identical in every way with that in which he died, they generally destroy a friend or relative, long before the natural close

---

[1] The best, and indeed the only full, authority respecting the savage customs of these islanders is Wilkes's *Narrative of the United States Exploring Expedition*, Vol. III. Lond. 1845. The practice of putting widows to death at the funerals of their husbands seemed to W. von Humboldt a proof of Indo-Malayan influence; and, he might have added, that in both cases the future happiness of the victim was thought to be involved in this act of devotion; but among the Vitians, widows are not the only persons so immolated; slaves and even children of the deceased sometimes sharing the same fate. Speaking of the negroes of South-Central Africa, Dr. Livingstone says, that 'when a chief dies, a number of servants are slaughtered with him to form his company in the other world' (p. 318). He then adds, 'As we go north, the people become more bloodily superstitious.' Captain Wilkes's description of the cannibalism of the Vitians is inexpressibly revolting (III. 97, 102): cf. Russell's *Polynesia*, pp. 265, 266; and Seemann's *Viti*, pp. 173 sq. The same horrid usages prevail as extensively among the savage natives of the New Hebrides and New Caledonia (Russell, p. 427).

[2] Wilkes, *Exploring Expedition*, III. 96. He had previously remarked (p. 94): 'This belief in a future state, guided by no just notions of religious or moral obligation, is the source of many abhorrent practices.' The report, however, of Mr. Hale, philologist to the United States Expedition (p. 54, Philadelphia, 1846), is, that according to the general belief of those islanders 'the soul passes through two states or conditions of future existence [the first, of happiness; the second, of misery] before it undergoes its final destiny—annihilation.'

Chap. III. of his existence. They are guilty also, here and there, of self-immolation; in the hope of thus securing an escape from misery and decrepitude in this life and from permanent dishonour in the next. So rife indeed has grown the practice of strangulation or of burying men alive, from one cause or other,[1] that only a single instance of natural death came under the observation of Europeans during a protracted stay in one of those islands.

Serpent-symbol.

If we now proceed to question the same authorities with reference to specific tenets there prevailing, we discover, as in Mexico and other regions, that the symbol of the mystic serpent has been always made to play a very prominent part. The highest member of the Viti pantheon, and the ruler (as men think) of all the island-world, is Ndengei,[2] who, though manifesting himself, it is believed, from age to age in a variety of human forms, is actually worshipped as a mighty serpent; the figure of that reptile being

---

[1] The cause may be, and often is, a real wish to benefit the person immolated; and it constantly happens therefore that a son strangles his parents at their own request. 'Mr. Hunt did all in his power to prevent so diabolical an act; but the only reply he received was, that she was their mother, and they were her children, and they ought to put her to death. On reaching the grave, the mother sat down, when they all, including children, grandchildren, relations, and friends, took an affectionate leave of her. A rope, made of twisted tapa, was then passed twice around her neck by her sons, who took hold of it, and strangled her; after which she was put into her grave, with the usual ceremonies. They returned to feast and mourn, after which she was entirely forgotten as though she had not existed' (p. 95). See also Seemann, *Viti*, pp. 192 sq.

[2] 'The word *Ndengei* is supposed by some to be a corruption of the first part of the name *Tanga-loa* (great Tanga), the chief divinity of Polynesia' (Hale, as above, p. 184); which seems to fall in with the received opinion that the Vitians, if not originally Polynesian, adopted some of the religious tenets, as well as some of the arts, of their Polynesian neighbours.

dominant in all the representations, even where it has
not been exclusively adopted. Some few glimmerings
of moral consciousness are visible in the wide-spread
notion that one class of disembodied spirits, who
would fain revert to the immediate presence of the
highest god, are constantly repulsed by an enormous
giant wielding a large axe.[1] 'With this weapon he
endeavours to wound all who pass him.' The ap- *Sons of*
proach to Ndengei is, however, much facilitated by *Ndengei.*
the mediation of two other Viti deities, the sons of
Ndengei, who connect the highest god with a descending series of minor spirits, each the tutelary genius
of a single island or a separate tribe.[2] But here,
as elsewhere, the benignant spirits are continually
thwarted by the arbitrary powers of mischief and
misrule, who constitute the gods of the infernal regions.[3] One of these, it is contended, sits upon the
brink of 'a huge fiery cavern, into which he precipi-
tates departed spirits.' Another ('the one-toothed
lord') is pictured to the warm imagination of the
trembling native as inhabiting the figure of a man,
with wings instead of arms, and claws to snatch his
victims. 'His tooth is large enough to reach above
the top of his head: it is alleged that he flies through

---

[1] Wilkes, III. 83. 'Those who
are wounded dare not present
themselves to Ndengei, and are
obliged to wander about in the
mountains.' But as Captain
Wilkes continues, 'whether the
spirit be wounded or not, *depends
not upon the conduct in life*, but
they ascribe an escape from the
blow wholly to good luck.' A
singular coincidence is found in
some districts between opinions
of the natives and those prophecies of Holy Writ which carry on
our thoughts to the great winding
up of all things. They hold,
'that all the souls of the departed
will remain in their appointed
place, until the world is destroyed
by fire, and a new one created'
(p. 94).
[2] *Ibid.* p. 84.
[3] *Ibid.* pp. 84, 85.

Bondage to fear.

the air emitting sparks of fire.' The dread of such malevolent beings far outbalances the hope inspired among these tribes by vague ideas respecting the beneficence of other spirits; and as happiness itself is seldom there associated with the presence of moral qualities, either in the judge or in the human subject, but is treated merely as the fruit of chance or of caprice,[1] the sentiment of fear is still more terribly awakened whensoever the Vitian, in the hours of silence or of sickness, listens to the beating of his inmost heart, and communes more directly with the world invisible. To the consternation thus excited we may trace the number of the *mbure* ('spirit-houses'), where he stops to deprecate the powers of darkness and present his horrible oblations. On this feeling had been grounded the despotic sway[2] long exercised by the *ambati*, or members of the sacerdotal order, each of whom was venerated as the mouthpiece of a spirit ruling in one single district, and as able by his frantic gestures to ward off impending evils, or extort a favourable answer to the cry of the oppressed.

Primeval traditions.

We may perhaps discover some faint echo of a primitive tradition in the story circulated far and wide among the Viti islands as to the extraction of all human beings from one single pair.[3] The first-

---

[1] 'At Rewa, it is believed that the spirits first repair to the residence of Ndengei, who allots some of them to the devils for food, and sends the rest away to Mukalou, a small island off Rewa, where they remain until an appointed day, after which they are all doomed to annihilation. The judgments thus passed by Ndengei seem to be ascribed rather to his caprice than to any desert of the departed soul:' p. 85.

[2] *Ibid.* pp. 87 sq.

[3] *Ibid.* p. 82 : cf. Hale's *Ethnography, &c. of the Exploring Expedition*, pp. 177, 178, where a similar tradition, long prevalent in the Tonga islands, is explained as 'an ancient mythos, under

born of mankind, according to this story, shewed himself unfaithful to his Maker and grew black.[1] The second-born, less biassed on the side of wickedness, was fairer and was better clad. The last in order of production, but the first in virtue and intelligence, were members of the white race. But a more remarkable coincidence is furnished by the legend of some mighty deluge, which, however startling from its close affinity to the sacred narrative, can hardly have been coloured in late years through intercourse with Europeans, since it is alleged that the precedence of one island (Mbenga) is derived entirely from the general currency which this tradition has obtained among the rest.

The story is thus reported to us by a recent hand :[2]

'After the islands had been peopled by the first man and woman, a great rain took place, by which they were finally submerged; but, before the highest places were covered by the waters, two large double canoes made their appearance. In one of these was Rokora, the god of carpenters; in the other, Rokola, his head workman, who picked up some of the people, and kept them on board until the waters had subsided; after which they were again landed on the island. It is reported that in former times canoes were always kept in readiness against another inundation. The persons thus saved, eight in number, were landed at Mbenga, where the highest of their gods is said to have made his first appearance. By virtue of this

which the early history of the islanders is veiled, though in the passage of centuries the real parts have been forgotten, and the story has received of late a new application,' owing to the intercourse with Europeans.

[1] Cf. Livingstone's *Travels*, p. 24.

[2] Wilkes, pp. 82, 83. Mr. Hale, as above (p. 55) confirms this statement, and conjectures (in a note) that the whole alluvial plain on the east side of the group of islands might be easily submerged by one of the immense waves that sweep across the Pacific. See also Seemann, *Viti*, pp. 395 sq.

tradition, the chiefs of Mbenga take rank before all others, and have always acted a conspicuous part among the Fijis. They style themselves *Ngali-duva-ki-langi* (subject to heaven alone).'

Conversion of the Viti-ans to Christian-ity.

It is refreshing to narrate that, in addition to such intimations of original oneness with the rest of men, a nobler proof of the humanity of the Vitian has been found, during the last twenty years, in his religious susceptibility. Those very islands, which were stained from age to age by every species of licence and atrocity, have now become the starting-point of vigorous efforts[1] to disseminate a knowledge of the Gospel on the farthest shores of Oceanica. The mariner who touches now at spots where until recently no symptom had been shewn of spiritual improvement, is amazed on finding how the fiercest wolves of heathendom are tamed by Christian agencies, how cannibals have lost their relish for the blood of others, and how brutal

---

[1] See Russell's *Polynesia*, pp. 264 sq. pp. 420—424; and *Events in Feejee, narrated in recent letters from several Wesleyan Missionaries,* Lond. 1855. Until 1841 the progress of the Gospel was very slow, but in 1846 nine of this group of islands were wholly or mainly Christian, and twenty-four, including the two large ones, were partially illuminated. The following extract from a letter printed in the *Wesleyan-Methodist Magazine* for 1856, p. 460, is a very remarkable testimony to the further progress of the same great undertaking. This letter is dated Viwa, Feejee, August 23, 1855: 'Thousands,' says the writer of it, 'have within the last few weeks abandoned heathenism, and made a profession of Christianity; and their conduct now presents a delightful contrast to their proceedings during the former part of this year. The first eight months of our residence in Feejee contributed some of the darkest records to the pages of Feejeean history; the most experienced missionaries confessing them to have no parallel. Now a glorious change is effected, by the power of the Spirit, in many towns which a few months ago a missionary or teacher durst not enter, the prevailing practice being war and cannibalism. The people then trusted to their gods and reverenced them, strictly prohibiting admission into their temples: now they crave teachers and books, and are endeavouring to sing the praise of God, and learning to read the Bible.'

and barbaric clans are being fast converted into peaceful confraternities. 'Violence shall no more be heard in thy land, wasting nor destruction within thy borders.'

But the Gospel has been also propagated in some other islands of the Archipelago, and has taken root especially in one distant group, of which the natives seem, with slight admixture, to be genuine Polynesians.[1] If the Viti islanders were made to furnish the best type of mixed or intermediate families, uniting the Papuan to the younger stock of Oceanic nations, an example of these latter, scarcely altered from their primitive condition, might be studied some few years ago among the people of New Zealand. 'The Maori of New Zealand,' we are told,[2] 'are one of the branches of the Polynesian family, who seem to have been preserved, to the greatest extent, unmixed with foreign alloy;' and as the principal superstitions, until lately dominant in those parts, are said to represent with singular fidelity the state of religious feeling which has long obtained 'throughout the great mass of the islands of the Pacific Ocean,'[3]

[1] Some writers have suspected (Prichard, v. 126 sq.) from the diversities of physical character that the Maori ought not to be considered one race of people, but are in reality a mixed nation, consisting (1) of the remains of an aboriginal population (Papuan), and (2) of a Polynesian race who conquered them, and became gradually blended with them by intermarriages. Yet similar varieties exist in all the other Polynesian islands, and as the natives of New Zealand are themselves unconscious of any radical distinction between the various classes of their own community, it is most probable that the existing variations of type result from certain differences of caste, which are extensively recognised among all the islands of the Great Ocean.

[2] Shortland, *Traditions, &c. of the New Zealanders*, pp. 79, 80.

[3] Sir G. Grey, *Polynesian Mythology*, p. xii. Lond. 1855; where the resemblance is thought to extend in some measure as far as the 'religious system of ancient Mexico.' It may be definitely asserted that the same general ideas, and very many of the same

the Maori have on this account been here selected for a more particular notice.

Original character of the Maori. It appears to be established that the colonisation of the group of islands called New Zealand is comparatively modern, stretching backwards at the furthest to a period of five or six hundred years.[1] When Cook approached that region in 1769, the natives had already earned a very bad pre-eminence; they were noted for their lack of conscientiousness, as well as for their gross and murderous ferocity; and the reception given to all succeeding visitors, of whom no small proportion fell into the snare of the infuriated savage, only added to the prevalent conviction that the people of New Zealand had become incorrigibly vile, and must in future be entirely abandoned.[2] The low tone, however, of the moral system there prevailing, the weakness of domestic instincts, the decay of parental authority, the desecration of the marriage-tie, the general disregard of human suffering, the perpetu-

Their religious sensibility. ation of a cannibalism, as rife and horrid as in other parts of heathendom,—these all were superadded to

minutiæ, are, or were till recently, extant in (1) the Navigator Islands, (2) the Friendly Islands, (3) the Society Islands, (4) the Hervey Islands, (5) the Austral Islands, (6) the Gambier Islands, (7) the Low or Dangerous Archipelago, (8) the Marquesas, (9) the Sandwich Islands, the most northerly group of Polynesia; together with a multitude of smaller clusters, and, as the most remote of all the Polynesian settlements, Easter Island, which is at no great distance from the coast of South America.

[1] Shortland, p. 19; Grey, pp. 132 sq. Hale, *Ethnography*, as

above, pp. 146 sq. This last writer, while agreeing that the New Zealanders are 'evidently of the pure Polynesian stock' (p. 11), cannot help noticing how, in complexion, form and profile they 'come very near to North American Indians.' Mr. Earl (*Eastern Seas*, p. 277) is similarly struck by 'the extraordinary and almost perfect resemblance' which the Dyaks (a variety of the copper-coloured race) bear to 'those aboriginal tribes of South America, which occupy a similar description of country.'

[2] Russell, *Polynesia*, p. 347.

an eminent measure of spiritual susceptibility. Like the men of Athens, whom St. Paul attempted to impress with the idea of one almighty and illimitable God, as well as of the common origin and consanguinity of the human species, it was found that Polynesians proper carried their habitual manifestations of religious feeling to a more than ordinary pitch (δεισιδαιμονέστεροι). 'When we compare them,' says an accurate writer,[1] 'with the natives of Australia, who, though not altogether without the idea of a God, hardly allow this idea to influence their conduct, we are especially struck with the earnest devotional tendencies of this people, among whom the whole system of public polity, and the regulation of their daily actions, have reference to the supposed sanction of a supernatural power; who not only have a pantheon, surpassing, in the number of divinities and the variety of their attributes, those of India and Greece, but to whom every striking natural phenomenon, every appearance calculated to inspire wonder and fear,—nay, often the most minute, harmless, and insignificant objects, seem invested with supernatural attributes, and worthy of adoration. It is not,' he continues, 'the mere grossness of idolatry, for many of them have no images, and those who have, look upon them simply as representations of their deities, but it is a constant, profound, absorbing sense of the ever-present activity of divine agency, which constitutes the peculiarity of this element in the moral organisation of this people.'

What, then, was the general state of feeling in the heathen of New Zealand, with respect to a most

The Maori ideas of God.

---

[1] Mr. Hale, as before, pp. 16, 17.

vital point of all religions,—that of one supreme Creator? The reply is, such conceptions of the Godhead were unknown to them, and when at first presented to their notice by the Christian missionary, were received with no small measure of repugnance and contempt.[1] According to the Maori creed the ultimate origin of all things, even of the higher gods themselves, is Night and Nothingness. The wild traditions of that people, dating as they constantly profess[2] from ages long anterior to their settlement in New Zealand, all 'begin with nothing, which produced something, and that brought forth something more, and generated a power of increasing.'[3] And as night, in their philosophy, preceded day, the oldest order of the Maori gods are also gods of darkness; one who has been deemed the prototype of all the rest is there entitled the ' Great daughter of Night,' the goddess of gloom, of solitude, of hades, and of death.[4] There seems, however, to have always lingered in the mind a glimmering of some purer and more noble class of verities; men felt that spirit in its essence is superior to all forms of matter, and that thought must therefore have been pre-existent, planning and directing the formation of the visible

---

[1] Thus Mr. Taylor, in his *Te Ika a Maui, or New Zealand and its Inhabitants* (p. 13, note; Lond. 1855), tells us that ' speaking to Te Heuheu, the powerful Chief of Taupo, of God, as being the Creator of all things, he ridiculed the idea, and said, Is there one maker of all things amongst you Europeans? is not one a carpenter, another a blacksmith, another a shipbuilder?' &c. ' And so was it in the beginning; one made this, another that: Tane made trees, Ru mountains, Tanga-roa fish,' &c.

[2] Shortland, p. 42.

[3] Taylor, p. 14, Shortland, p. 39.

[4] Her Maori name is *Hine-nui-a-te-po,* which under slight modifications is also found in other islands, as in Tonga, Tahiti, and Hawaii: Taylor, p. 41.

world.[1]   In this particular, indeed, we recognise a
faint approximation in New Zealand to the cosmogonic theories that long absorbed the interest of the
speculative China-man.   The Absolute of the one[2]
is only a more philosophic method of expressing the
First Thought of the other.   But resemblance is *Mythe of*
more clearly traceable in the texture of the ancient *Heaven and Earth.*
mythe, in which the moulding of the universe into
its present shape has been referred to an abrupt
division between Heaven and Earth,[3]—the two great
powers, or principles of nature, which heretofore were
blended into one, or held together by some potent
and indissoluble bond.   Their names, according to
the Maori creed, were Rangi (Heaven) and Papa
(Earth).[4]   Till this divulsion, says a native story,
the six children born to them were ever musing
within themselves as to the difference between light
and darkness.   Wearied by the long continuance of
impenetrable void, they rose eventually into an attitude of wild rebellion; and muttering to each other,
asked what should be done with Rangi and Papa.
'Shall we slay them, or shall we separate them?'
Tu-mata-uenga[5] said, 'Yes, let us kill them.'   Tane

---

[1] Taylor, p. 14, who styles the first period in their mythological system the 'epoch of thought,' and observes with reference to this branch of their traditions, that they 'mark a far more advanced state' of intelligence than is discernible among the heathen of the present day.

[2] See above, pp. 48, 49. Mr. Taylor, without making any allusion to these coincidences, points out some particulars of dress and manufacture which betoken, to his thinking, a Chinese or Japanese origin : pp. 184, 185.

[3] Above, p. 52.

[4] Grey, *Polynesian Mythology,* pp. 1 sq.; Taylor, pp. 19, 20.

[5] Sir G. Grey explains this word as meaning 'man,' or 'fierce man'; and Mr. Taylor identifies Tu-mata-uenga with Tute-nga-nahau, the third son of Rangi and Papa,, and the grand author of evil, who, according to the same story, 'cut the sinews' that united Heaven and Earth.

Mahuta[1] replied, 'No, by no means, rather let us

separate them; let one be placed above and let the other remain below; let the one be like a stranger far removed from us, let the other be near as a father or mother to us.' Five of their unnatural offspring hearkened to this counsel; one alone was strongly opposed to the idea of separation; five decided that their parents should be riven asunder; one only loved them. This affectionate son was Tawhiri-matea, the father of the winds, who, at the close of the catastrophe, determined to chastise his brothers for their foul impiety. Tane, who is viewed as the progenitor of trees, or rather as a tree himself, was shaken and uprooted; Tanga-roa, in like manner, the presiding spirit of the ocean, foamed and quivered under the avenging tempest; and accordingly the universe, as now existing, had been cradled in the midst of elemental wars, of furious conflicts and convulsions.

One result of the great severance between Earth and Heaven was the projection of a second order of divinities,—the rebel sons of Rangi and Papa,

---

[1] Tane is the first of living creatures or emanations, and to him has been assigned the work of 'propping up' the heavens. This was his first great duty; afterwards we hear of him giving birth to trees and every kind of birds. The other sons of Rangi and Papa, were Tiki or Tii, a (male?) divinity from whom proceeded man (cf. Taylor, p. 23; Hale, *Ethnography*, &c. pp. 23, 24); Tahu, the author of good, but never prominent in this system of mythology; and Tanga-roa, the father of all fish, and the great god of ocean. This last name varying in different parts of Oceanica (as *Tangaloa, Tanaloa, Taaroa*) is thought by some to indicate a self-existent God, 'the creator of the earth, or at least of the islands of the sea, and of the human race' (Hale, p. 22). 'At the little newly-discovered island of Fakaofo, the natives spoke of him with great awe as *Tangaloa i lunga i te langi* (Tangaloa above in the heavens):' *Ibid.*

who are thus distinguished from the members of the older series as the gods of light. They constitute at present the chief divinities of heathen Polynesia; their place is in the highest and most glorious of the ten heavens.[1] Conjectures have been made to the effect that long before the first migrations of the Polynesian tribes, they were accustomed, as a people, to adore one principal divinity,[2] who was, eventually, on the formation of the mythe respecting the divorce of Earth and Heaven, confounded with a son of Rangi and Papa, the marine god Tanga-roa. It has also been suggested, but with far less probability, that these islanders had originally confined their worship to three leading aspects in the character[3] of the Supreme Being, and had thus arrived at the conception of three grand personifications,—the Creator, the Sustainer, the Revealer. Still, whatever may *Maori polytheism.* be thought of these suggestions, it is clearly ascer-

---

[1] Taylor, p. 17.

[2] Hale, p. 22. In the mythology of the Tongans, this divinity (Tangaloa) is made to fish up their group of islands and to cover it with fruits and animals, like those of Bulotu (his own special paradise), but perishable and of inferior quality. 'He sent his two sons, Toobó and Váca-ácow-ooli, with their wives, to people it. Váca-ácow-ooli was wise and virtuous; Toobó idle and depraved. Envying the prosperity of his brother, Toobó at length killed him [? Cain and Abel]. Tangaloa, enraged at this, sent Váca-ácow-ooli and his family with prosperous gales to an eastern land, where they became ancestors of the Papalangi, or White People. The descendants of Toobó were condemned to be black, because

their hearts were bad [cf. the Vitian legend, above, p. 189]: they remained at Tonga, and are the present race of inhabitants:' Prichard, v. 107, 108. I am disposed to think that the Orongo, Orono, and Rono of the Sandwich Islanders are only debased forms of Tangaroa; and it is curious to remark, that traditions were there also prevalent respecting visits of White Men as somehow connected with this divinity, insomuch that Captain Cook, like Cortés in America, was actually taken for their favourite god, and reverenced on that account.

[3] e. g. Hale, as above, p. 24; who adds, however, that the meaning and application of the three names which he proposes, 'have been much confused.'

CHAP. III. tained that the New Zealander of modern times, in
common with all other natives of Oceanica, was in
principle as well as practice an avowed polytheist.
His pantheon, we have seen, outnumbered that of
India or of Hellas. Everything that came within the
cognizance of the senses was believed to be the organ
of one special god, the offspring of one present and
peculiar energy, which the Maori called its 'father.'[1]
This diffused, discerpted Power was sometimes represented as devoid of form or personality; its mode
of manifestation being absolutely identified with startling and mysterious processes of nature, as displayed
in meteors, rainbows, whirlwinds, and the like. At
other times, such manifestation was restricted to the
form of a particular beast, or bird, or reptile, as the
dog, the shark, the woodpecker, the rat, the ant, the
lizard. Or in cases when the gods[2] assumed distinctly
human shapes in the imagination of the Maori, and
were consciously invested with human attributes,
they always bore, as in the rest of heathendom, a
close resemblance to their ordinary worshippers; and
Character hence the brightest heaven of this mythology does
of the little more than reproduce the various ills and con-
humanized flicts of the present life. The history of a god, in
divinities.

[1] See Mr. Taylor's catalogue of some of these 'creative fathers,' pp. 32, 33, note.
[2] 'On nearly, if not quite, all the groups [of Polynesia] there have been, at a very late period, men who have been regarded by the natives as partaking of the divine nature,—in short, as earth-ly gods:' Hale, p. 20. At the Marquesas the common title of these persons is 'atua, or gods, who receive the same adoration, and are believed to possess the same powers as other deities' (p. 21). 'At Depeyster's Group, the westernmost cluster of Polynesia, we were visited by a chief, who announced himself as the *atua* or god of the islands, and was ac-knowledged as such by the other natives' (*Ibid.*). These remark-able phenomena remind us very forcibly of the modern man-wor-ship of Tibet (above, p. 94).

other words, is that of some great chief or warrior, frequently disfigured by the grossest of all human vices, and too seldom calculated to suggest one noble wish or stir one generous emotion. These gods ' were cannibals; they were influenced by like feelings and passions with men, and they were uniformly bad. To them were ascribed all the evils to which the human race is subject; each disease was supposed to be occasioned by a different god, who resided in the part affected.'[1]

The generic name of a divinity, in the language *Nature of worship in* of New Zealand, is *atua*,[2] varied in the other districts *New Zea-* of Polynesia to *hotua* and *etua;* but, as might have *land.* been anticipated from the character imputed to such beings, they are seldom or never made the objects of religious worship in the Christian meaning of the term. The constant purpose of their votaries was to pacify, to vanquish, to disarm them. In the vast majority of cases, the *atua* was a powerful adversary skilled in supernatural arts, and rendered proof against all ordinary weapons. Hence arose the multitude of charms and rites of divination (*karakias*[3]), forming the chief element in the Maori worship. Every act of grave importance, hunting, fishing, war, the planting or the reaping of the *kumara* (sweet potatoe), was preceded by a multitude of solemn incantations,

---

[1] Taylor, p. 34.
[2] Cf. above, p. 138: to which remarks it may be added, that *tua*, so far from being equivalent to *atua*, means in Polynesia 'back' or 'behind,' and hence a member of the lowest class, a peasant (Hale, pp. 31, 32, 335).
[3] 'They have spells suited for all circumstances—to conquer enemies, catch fish, trap rats, and snare birds, to make their kumara grow, and even to bind the obstinate will of woman; to find anything lost, to discover a strayed dog, a concealed enemy; in fact, for all their wants:' Taylor, p. 72.

uttered with the hope of throwing obstacles in the way of some antagonistic power, of binding him by potent and unearthly spells, and so constraining him to waver in his purpose or withdraw his opposition. The same feeling was again predominant whenever the Maori brought his scanty sacrifice to one or other of the gods: he laboured to avert by offerings the displeasure he had previously awakened by the repetition of some mystic formula.

Worship of departed ancestors. It seems, however, that a closer approximation to our ideas of worship was occasionally manifested in the tribute paid by Maori to the souls of their departed ancestors.[1] These, also, were included in the multitude of the *atuas ;* and on them, indeed, as genii intimately connected with the present race of men,[2] the hopes and fears of their posterity were principally fixed. Each tribe, and single family of a tribe, rejoiced in the protection, or was trembling under the disapprobation, of its own *atua.* To that narrow circle he became the chief of the divinities. He issued forth to battle with his kinsmen; he was hovering near them in the hours of gloom, of peril, of privation; and so long as they were true to their ancestral courage, he was ever struggling at their

---

[1] Hegel (*Phil. of History*, Lond. 1857. p. 99) seems to think this worship of the dead a special characteristic of the African negroes. 'Their idea in the matter is that these ancestors exercise vengeance, and inflict upon man various injuries—exactly in the sense in which this was supposed of witches in the Middle Ages.'

[2] Mr. Shortland (p. 61) seems to think that these were the only *atuas,* who produced any sensible effect on the religious character of the New Zealanders. Mr. Taylor writes in like manner: 'Their ancestors were addressed as powerful familiar friends; they gave them offerings, and i it can be said that any prayers were offered up, it was to them that they were made' (p. 72). The same has been already observed in speaking of the Chinese (above, pp. 34—36): cf. Russell's *Polynesia*, p. 69.

side against an army of invisible assailants. When
consulted by the Maori, on occasions of extraordinary
moment, the *atua* was believed to give his answer by
appearing personally in the sacred house to which
his presence was invited, and discoursing there in
a mysterious sound, 'half whistle, half whisper.'[1] *The* ariki.
At ordinary times a powerful link between the natural
and supernatural was furnished by the head-chief[2] of
the tribe (*ariki*, whether male or female),[3] who, as
standing in a blood-relation with their patron-deity,
was thought to be admitted more than others to
a secret knowledge of his will. But, in addition
to this higher class of mediators, very many of the
principal households of New Zealand had their own *The to-*
tohunga[4] (family-priest or 'speaker'), occupied in *hunga.*
uttering charms and offering sacrifice on their behalf.
Him also a divinity was in the habit of possessing,[5]
and arousing to so great a pitch of fury, that the
multitude who gathered awe-struck round about him
were all eager to detect the will of Heaven amid the
cries and horrible contortions of the seer.

In some few districts of New Zealand it was *Image-*
thought again that intercourse with the invisible *worship.*

---

[1] Shortland, p. 100, pp. 64 sq.
[2] In many of the tribes visited by Dr. Livingstone in South Africa, there was nothing like a priesthood. He remarks, however, on approaching the mouths of the Zambesi, 'The chiefs in these parts take upon themselves an office somewhat like the priesthood, and the people imagine that they can propitiate the Deity through them:' (p. 581).
[3] Shortland, p. 84, Taylor, pp. 42, 43. The *Ariki* of New Zea-land was identical with the *Aliki* and *Arii* of other islands.
[4] Mr. Hale, however (p. 20), is disposed to consider the *tufunga*, *tohunga*, *tahuna*, *tahua*, &c. 'merely as persons appointed by the real priests,—*i. e.* the *aliki*, or chiefs,—to go through the drudgeries of their office, with which they are unwilling to be troubled.'
[5] Taylor, p. 41. The same kind of frenzy has been noted in the wild tribes of America (above, p. 132).

world might be secured or furthered by the use of wooden images,[1] resembling the fetishes of the Papuan family. Here, however, the amount of reverence paid to the material object can scarcely be regarded as idolatrous, in the proper meaning of the phrase. 'The natives declare they did not worship the image itself, but only the *atua* it represented, and that the image was merely used as a way of approaching him.'

Maori form of baptism :

It is still more worthy of remark, as tending to elucidate our special subject of inquiry, that one sacred ordinance, which seems to have been practised by the Maori long before their intercourse with Europeans, bears at first sight a distinct analogy to Christian baptism.[2] Soon after the birth of a child, the custom was to carry it to the priest, who, at the

[1] *Ibid.* p. 73: cf. Hale, p. 26, Russell, p. 69, whose accounts are somewhat different; but these writers seem to agree that there was less image-worship in New Zealand than in most other districts of Polynesia. The absence of regular temples in New Zealand is equally remarkable, although the Maori have a singular tradition respecting some great Red House (*Whare-kura*), which they fancy had once existed among them, and which 'the Christian natives compare to Babel' (Taylor, p. 68).

[2] The practice of circumcision, in the Friendly, the Viti and the Society Islands, has also been adduced as furnishing some possible link of connexion with the Asiatic continent (*e.g.* Russell, *Polynesia*, p. 36): yet, as this writer observes, 'it is not regarded in the South Sea as a *religious ceremony*, but perpetuated merely as an ancient custom of which no account can be given, and for the use of which no reason is assigned.' Examples of the same, or of a similar, usage are recorded in the New World. Thus, the South Americans, in some districts, used to crop the ears of their children soon after birth (Müller, *Amer. Urrelig.* p. 285). Various parts of the body (the ears, the tongue, the breast, &c.) were circumcised among the natives of Central America (*Ibid.* pp. 479, 480), and still more among the Aztecs, where the ceremony was connected with some dedication to Huitzilopochtli (p. 640), and as such might be esteemed equivalent to an oblation of human blood. In the Friendly Islands it was not unusual for the natives to cut off a finger, in the hope of appeasing the gods.

close of some preliminary forms recited a long list of names belonging to the ancestors of the child, and ended by selecting one of them for it. As he pronounced this name he solemnly sprinkled the child with a small branch of the *karamu* (coprosma lucida): while in other districts of the island, where a somewhat different rite prevailed, the ceremony was always conducted near a running stream, in which the child, when it received its name, was not unfrequently immersed.[1] Yet, notwithstanding this apparent affinity *how different from the Christian rite.* between the heathen and the Christian ordinances, it is not difficult to trace in them a fundamental contradiction. The infant of the Maori was regarded from the moment of its birth as 'an exceedingly sacred object,'[2] and as such was to be handled in the first instance only by the sacred few. The Gospel, on the contrary, has taught with emphasis that every one 'naturally engendered of the offspring of Adam' brings into the world a tainted, vitiated, fallen nature, and that baptism was itself appointed by the New Man from heaven, with special reference to the counteraction of that taint and the removal of that moral disability. Hence, while there is not the slightest recognition in the Maori 'baptism' either of sin or guilt or the remissibility of guilt, the Christian sacrament derives its character entirely from the recognition of such doctrines. While the Maori charm was contemplating the dedication of the

---

[1] Taylor, pp. 74 sq.; cf. Shortland, p. 121. Sir G. Grey (*Polynesian Mythology*, p. 32) makes use of language calculated to suggest still closer affinities between the heathen and Christian rites;

e. g. 'hurriedly skipped over part of the prayers of the baptismal service.' On the Mexican custom of dedicating infants to the water-goddess, see above, p. 150, n. 3.

[2] Shortland, p. 122.

CHAP. III. boy to nothing higher than Tu,[1] the god of war, and
was invoking on him, as the greatest of all excellencies, that he might 'flame with anger,' and have
'strength to wield a weapon,' the young Christian,
on the contrary, has been enrolled under a very
different Captain; he is sworn as the soldier of the
Cross, to fight manfully against sin, the world, and
the devil, and daily to proceed 'in all virtue and
godliness of living.'

Institution
of tapu:
There is another usage common to the Maori, and
to all the Polynesian tribes,[2] however distant from
New Zealand, which is often thought to be among
their most essential peculiarities. This is the institution of *tapu* (taboo), a word employed like many
others of the Oceanic dialects, either as a noun, an
adjective, or a verb. According to one etymology,
it means no more than 'thoroughly marked,'[3] and
hence may have arisen its ordinary application to
sacred things and persons, and restrictive or prohibitory laws. *Tapus*, however, in this latter sense
must not be ranked with arbitrary regulations instituted by some ancient legislator for political or

---

[1] Taylor, p. 75, where the *kara-kia* is given at length. Tu is the god of war in the north of New Zealand; Maru, still more Satanic, fills that office in the south.

[2] Whatever may turn out to be the ethnological position of the Vitians, it is noticeable that they also have the usage of *tapu*, which they call *tambu* (Hale, p. 51). Perhaps they have adopted it from their Tonga neighbours, just as the Muslim was induced to borrow the Hindú theory of caste from the people he invaded. The name for *tapu* in the island of Mada-

gascar is *fady*, but the usage is there also substantially the same: Prichard, v. 208.

Shortland, p. 81, who says that it 'only came to signify sacred or prohibited in a secondary sense, because sacred things and places were commonly marked in a peculiar manner.' In Mr. Hale's *Polynesian Lexicon*, as before, p. 331, we have the following entry: '*Tapu*, *tabu*, ubiq., sacred, and hence, forbidden,' while *tapui*, in the Samoan, is 'to make sacred,' &c.

social objects. They were uniformly made to rest upon religious ideas; all their sanctions were derived immediately from precepts of religion, and in this respect we may compare them with enactments of the Jewish law,—for instance, that on clean and unclean meats, or that in virtue of which the Hebrew might contract uncleanness by touching a dead body, or most of all, perhaps, with the sabbatical institutions, which under pain of God's displeasure periodically rescued a space of time from secular and common purposes. One principle which forms a characteristic of the Maori system was, 'that if any thing *tapu* [sacred] is permitted to come in contact with food, or with any vessel or place, where food is ordinarily kept, such food must not afterwards be eaten by any one, and such vessel or place must no longer be devoted to its ordinary use.'[1] This law, pervading *its practical working.* though it did all classes of society, and modifying their most common thoughts and occupations,[2] was especially manifested in the case of the *ariki,* or head-chief, whose sacredness in their minds bordered very close on absolute divinity. His house, his garments, everything relating to him was *tapu.* The spot on which he trod, external to his own domain, was consecrated and appropriated by that act.[3] It was believed that persons who partook by accident of any food which had been cooked for the *ariki,* did so at the peril of their life;[4] and though a cere-

---

[1] Shortland, *Ibid.*

[2] Taylor, p. 57. In these cases the *tapu* was for a time thrown over workmen, employed in some task of great importance to the community at large: *e. g.* 'No one but the priest could pause in front of the party engaged in gathering the *kumara ;* those who presumed to do so, would be either killed or stripped for their temerity.'

[3] Shortland, p. 84.

[4] Taylor, p. 56.

monial was provided by means of which restrictions of this kind were softened or entirely taken off,[1] the Maori was perpetually haunted by the dread of violating the appointed ordinance, and trespassing on sacred ground.

Philosophy of the tapu-system.   I am disposed to think with one who has bestowed considerable pains on this investigation, that the tapu-system had arisen gradually in Polynesia, in proportion as the theory of religion there prevailing was more fully mastered and developed.[2] When the many were familiarized with the idea that an *atua*, or divinity, resided in some principal chief or priest, it followed that a portion of his spiritual essence was communicated of necessity to all the objects he might touch. It followed also, 'that the spiritual essence so communicated to any object was afterwards more or less retransmitted to any thing else brought into contact with it.' Hence accordingly arose the duty of protecting aught in which that spiritual essence was inherent, or over which its virtue had been temporarily diffused, from every risk of being polluted by contact with articles of food; since the act of eating what had touched a thing *tapu* must carry with it the necessity of eating particles of the sacred essence of the *atua*, from which its own sacredness was all derived.[3] In this way had been formed the mightiest of political engines for exalting the importance of the priest-king of New Zealand, for

---

[1] Shortland, p. 83. When the *tapu* was taken off, the object became *noa*, 'free,' or 'common'; *i. e.* was deprived of all the sacredness with which it was before invested.

[2] *Ibid.* p. 82, Hale, pp. 19, 20.

[3] Mr. Shortland adds (but less conclusively) : 'If to eat an enemy was the greatest insult to be offered him, how horrible to eat any thing containing a particle of the divine essence.'

strengthening his iron arm, and thus investing him with almost supernatural powers for good or for evil.

It were difficult to single out a legend that more fully serves to illustrate the modes of thought and feeling once predominant in Polynesia, than the cluster of wild fables which from time to time have gathered round the primitive story of Maui the Young (*potiki*). He has not unjustly been regarded as *the* mythic hero of the Maori; in some particulars he well deserves to be entitled the Oceanic Baldur; in others, the Prometheus of the Southern Seas. There is no group of islands where he was not held in constant reverence under one or other of his numerous appellations;[1] but New Zealand he was made to claim for his own property, the native title of that region importing 'The Fish of Maui,' and so bearing witness to the popular belief that all the island had emerged originally from the depths of ocean through the exercise of his transcendent power.

The stories tell that Maui was the last-born child of Tara-hunga or Taranga,[2] being descended also, after many generations, from Tu-mata-uenga, one of the unnatural sons of Heaven and Earth.[3] Though

---

[1] Perhaps the oldest, certainly the fullest, form which it assumes is *Mafui*, current in the Navigator (Samoan) Islands. This with a suffix becomes *Mafuike* (? a member of the Mafui family), by means of which we are enabled to arrive at the form *Mafui'e* or *Mafu'e*, and finally at *Maui*. It has been thought indeed that Maui is the primitive form, and was intended to describe the person who first sighted land (*Ma-u-i*; Taylor, p. 29); but, on this hypothesis, what explanation can be offered of *Mafui?* Besides, it must be borne in mind that Maui was in all probability the offspring of an age long anterior to the first discovery of New Zealand.

[2] See the legend in Sir G. Grey's *Polynesian Mythology*, pp. 31 sq., and in Mr. Taylor's *Te Ika a Maui*, pp. 23 sq. The New Zealand *Taranga* explains the *Ti'iti'i-a-talanga* of other islands, and the *Maui-a-talana* of Hawaii.

[3] Above, p. 195, n. 5.

CHAP. III. finally admitted to the number of the gods, and
though at times confounded even with the highest
members of the ancient pantheon,[1] he is not unfrequently declared to be of purely human origin. His
youthful pranks, betokening always an exuberance
of life and vigour, and occasionally intermingled with
proceedings of more than dubious morality, remind
us of the early feats ascribed to the heroic Krishṅa;[2]
while his struggles with a huge sea-monster (Tunurua)
furnish some additional points of contact or comparison with the Hercules alike of India and of Greece.
On this account it was that he acquired a lasting hold
on the affections of the ancient Maori, and was scrupulously invoked by them as their own tutelary genius
on many grand occasions, and especially when they
were setting out upon some fishing expedition.

Very many of the strange adventures which are
told of Maui indicate his vast superiority over his
five elder brothers in strength, in cunning, in good
fortune. To astonish or to overreach them he would
voluntarily assume the form and other qualities of
a bird; and once, in this disguise, appears to have
succeeded in gaining admittance to the subterranean
world, in which his parents were detained. Ere long,
however, it was found that the mysterious visitor was
a man, or rather was 'a god,' and when his mother
finally beheld in him her own little Maui ('Maui
possessed of the top-knot, or power, of Taranga' , her
delight at the discovery was rapturous and unbounded.

---

[1] *e. g.* in the Tonga islands, it
is he who supports the earth itself, and causes earthquakes
(Prichard, v. 105, 152), just as
Tane props up the heavens; and
in the same district Maui, and
not Tangaloa, was said to have
fished up those islands out of the
sea with a hook and line. (*Ibid.*
p. 106, note; cf. Hale, p. 23.)

[2] See above, Vol. I. pp. 282 sq.

'This,' she exclaimed, 'is indeed my child. By the winds and storms and wave-uplifting gales he was fashioned and became a human being. Welcome, O my child, welcome! by thee shall hereafter be climbed the threshold of the house of thy great ancestor, Hine-nui-te-po (the goddess of the world invisible), and death itself shall thenceforth have no power over man.' With the express intention of achieving the fulfilment of this hopeful prophecy, the hero of New Zealand entered on the last and greatest of his labours. He had noticed how the sun and moon, which he was instigated to extinguish, were immortalised, because it was their wont to bathe in some living fountain : ' he determined, therefore, to do the same, and to enter the womb of Hine-nui-te-po, that is, Hades, where the living water—the life-giving stream—was situated. Hine-nui-te-po draws all into her womb, but permits none to return. Maui determined to try, trusting to his great powers ; but before he made the attempt, he strictly charged the birds, his friends, not to laugh. He then allowed Great Mother Night to draw him into her womb. His head and shoulders had already entered, when that forgetful bird, the Piwaka-waka, began to laugh. Night closed her portals : Maui was cut in two, and died. Thus death came into the world, [or rather, in accordance with a second and more congruous version, kept its hold upon the world]. Had not the Piwaka-waka laughed, Maui would have drunk of the living stream, and man would never [more] have died. Such was the end of Maui !"

[1] Taylor, p. 31, Grey, p. 57. The versions of the story are con- siderably different in different writers. In one case Maui is

In the main complexion of this fable, notwith-standing all its wildness and monstrosity, is found the aptest illustration which the mythes of Oceanica will furnish of the spirit there and everywhere engendered by the loss of real faith in God. Religion was de-based into a hopeless, loveless dread of physical suffering and disaster. Old presentiments of some exalted Champion, who might silence or suppress the agencies of evil and so glorify together all the members of the Maori household, were eventually abandoned in despair as treacherous and illusive; death, they felt, had triumphed over Maui, and not Maui over death. How cheering, therefore, to a people, prostrate, powerless, terror-stricken, were the tidings of great joy which circulate in every land with the diffusion of the holy Gospel! Here had been revealed the one, all-glorious and all-merciful *Atua*, 'manifest in the flesh,' yea, wedded by the bands of an eternal love to the humanity which He adopted. Hence arose new principles of life and health and blessed-ness, which, permeating through the various members of the Christian organism, united each to each by reconciling all to Christ, the Head and Saviour of the Body. 'He tasted death for every man.' 'Foras-much as the children are partakers of flesh and blood, He also Himself took part of the same, that through death He might destroy him that had the power of death, that is, the devil; and deliver them who through fear of death were all their life-time subject to bondage.'

made the bringer-in of death, through his abortive attempt to deceive the great goddess of Night (Grey, p. 10); in the other, he is only unsuccessful in his vigorous struggle to subdue it.

And already there is cause enough for gratitude, CHAP. III.
as we count up those precious harvests which the *Progress*
messengers of Christ are reaping on the blood-stained *of the*
Gospel in
shores of Oceanica. The wizards of New Zealand *Polynesia.*
bow at length before the majesty of the Gospel; the
expiring voice of every oracle proclaims that Christ,
the Son of Mary, is verily Divine.[1] Of Polynesia,
as a whole, it may be urged with equal confidence,
that she is waking from the death of sin, and stretching out her hands to God, her Refuge and Redeemer.
Island after island has been touched, rebuked and
quickened by the ministrations of His grace; and
with a promptness and expansive ardour that shone
forth so brightly in our Anglo-Saxon forefathers, as
soon as ever they were folded in the Christian
Church, those Polynesians are in turn transmitting
onward all the blessings they receive from us. 'Now,'
exclaims a chief of Raratonga,[2] pleading with his
pagan neighbours and extolling the incalculable good
that has resulted to himself and to his tribe from
a sincere adoption of the Gospel, 'Now we enjoy
happiness, to which our ancestors were strangers;
our ferocious wars have ceased; our houses are the
abodes of comfort; we have European property; we
possess books in our own language; our children can
read; and, above all, we know the true God and the
way of salvation by His Son, Jesus Christ. This
alone can make you a peaceable and happy people.

[1] When the first missionaries preached the Gospel in New Zealand, the natives consulted their *atua*, as to whether the teaching of the Europeans was true or false. 'It is a remarkable fact,' adds Mr. Shortland (p. 100), 'that wherever the inquiry was made, the answer invariably given declared Jesus Christ to be the true God;'—an answer which in part accounts for the rapid growth of Christianity in those regions.

[2] Russell's *Polynesia*, p. 274.

I should have died a savage, had it not been for the Gospel.'

May the bright and blissful era be approaching, when all Christendom, incited by the proofs of fresh vitality and vigour which come back to us from the antipodes, shall count it her chief glory to assist in adding weight to these grand impulses, and forwarding the consummation of the Gospel-triumph; when the Church of God, no more restricted to particular tribes and nations, but embracing in her bosom all varieties of man,—the white, the red, the black, the copper-coloured,—shall be eager to advance into her ultimate condition, a thrice glorious Church, unblemished, indefectible; when island shall no longer cry to island, 'Come over and help us,' but, 'all shall know the Lord, from the least unto the greatest.'

I conclude this portion of my present task in words more forcible than any of my own, because they are the words of one now toiling at his post amid the far-off isles of Oceanica, and there exhibiting from day to day how zeal and prudence, faith and charity, tenderness and manly vigour may exist in graceful combination, and contribute now, as in the age of Apostolic missions, to enlighten and evangelise the world: 'It is indeed,' writes Bishop Selwyn, 'a great and glorious work, appalling in its vastness, and yet sustained by the fulness of the promise that the prayers of the Son of God will never fail, till the Father has given to Him the heathen for his inheritance, and the utmost parts of the earth for His possession.'

PART IV.

RELIGIONS OF EGYPT AND MEDO-PERSIA.

RELIGIONS OF EGYPT AND MEDO-PERSIA.

CHAPTER I.

Characteristics of Egyptian Heathenism.

Οὐ μόνον δὲ τούτου ['Οσίριδος] οἱ ἱερεῖς λέγουσιν, ἀλλὰ καὶ τῶν
ἄλλων θεῶν, ὅσοι μὴ ἀγέννητοι, μηδ' ἄφθαρτοι, τὰ μὲν σώματα
παρ' αὐτοῖς κεῖσθαι καμόντα καὶ θεραπεύεσθαι, τὰς δὲ ψυχὰς ἐν
οὐρανῷ λάμπειν ἄστρα, καὶ καλεῖσθαι κύνα μὲν τὴν Ἴσιδος ὑφ'
Ἑλλήνων, ὑπ' Αἰγυπτίων δὲ Σῶθιν, Ὠρίωνα δὲ τὴν Ὥρου, τὴν
δὲ Τυφῶνος, ἄρκτον. εἰς δὲ τὰς τροφὰς τῶν τιμωμένων ζώων,
τοὺς μὲν ἄλλους συντεταγμένα τελεῖν, μόνους δὲ μὴ διδόναι τοὺς
Θηβαΐδα κατοικοῦντας, ὡς θνητὸν θεὸν οὐδένα νομίζοντας, ἀλλὰ
ὃν καλοῦσιν αὐτοὶ Κνῆφ, ἀγέννητον ὄντα καὶ ἀθάνατον.

EUDOXUS in Plutarch. *De Iside et Osiride*, c. XXI.

ON resuming this investigation into the distinctive phases of religious thought among the dominant nations of antiquity, the reader will be next invited to a sphere whose influence on the early march of civilisation it were difficult to overstate. The Valley of the Nile had ever since the oldest Pharaohs been the border-land, or point of confluence, where the African was brought into direct communication with his Asiatic brother, and the East was intermingling with the West. As one of the succession of luminous centres, which, emerging here and there amid the dimness of primeval history, are traceable from the

Mediterranean to the utmost bounds of Eastern Asia, Egypt, in some branches of her sacred institutions, will be found to have remarkable traits in common with the Aryan conquerors[1] of the Panjáb; while her monuments, alike in area and in massive grandeur, will remind us also of those primitive ages when the Mayan architect was rearing kindred structures[2] near the rivers of the New World.

Its connex-ion with the neighbour-ing coun-tries. But full as such analogies may be of interesting speculation, in reference to the ultimate extraction of the human family from one common stock, our present business is to mark the place and character of Egypt during the historic period, and as standing in more intimate relations to the people of her own immediate neighbourhood. The reputation for superior knowledge once enjoyed by all 'the children of the East country' was believed to be the special heritage of the Egyptian priests (cf. 1 Kings, iv. 30). Their cloisters were the recognised abode of art, of science, of religious mystery. Assyrian sculptors learned at Memphis what with greater or with less precision they have reproduced at Nineveh. The sons of Abraham, who like himself went down in search of shelter from a grievous famine, were constrained by closer contact with Egyptian modes of

---

[1] See Mr. Kenrick's *Ancient Egypt,* 1. 105 sq., Lond. 1850, where, after handling the subject very fairly, he concludes 'that there has been some connexion between the civilisation of Egypt and India, while the nations themselves have as much claim to be considered distinct as any others of antiquity:' cf. Sir J. G. Wilkinson's last publication, *The Egyptians,* Pref. pp. IX. x. Lond. 1857. Baron Bunsen, *Phil. of Univ. Hist.* I. 191, is far less guarded in his phraseology: 'The exploded notion as to an original connexion between India (the youngest child of Asia) and Egypt (the deposit of primitive undivided Asia) is as groundless as it is absurd.'

[2] Above, p. 136.

life to throw aside their old nomadic habits; and at length when they returned victorious to the land of promise, the great host was marshalled by a captain, who had grown to manhood in the court of Pharaoh, and was 'learned in all the wisdom of the Egyptians' (Acts vii. 22). Thither also in the dawn of western civilisation came the young philosophers of Hellas,[1] panting for some deep and transcendental lore, or listening with the eagerness and awe of children to the stories which had long been whispered in the learned circles of On, of Thebes, of Memphis; so that he who is desirous of understanding the precise development of human thought, alike in Western Asia and in Europe, in Athens, Rome, or even (some would tell us) in Jerusalem itself, must take up his position at this fountain-head of wisdom, and from thence survey the parting of the mighty stream as it flows forth into contiguous regions.[2]

Now the scholar of the present age has many fresh facilities[3] for the successful carrying out of such investigations. The recovery of the hieroglyphic character has given, and is still giving every year, a new complexion to the ancient history of the Valley of the Nile. We can no longer speak of

Advantages enjoyed by the inquirer of the present day.

[1] The evidence on this point is all collected in Lepsius, *Chronol. der Aegypter*, 'Einl.' pp. 41 sq.

[2] Uhlemann scarcely overrates the influence of Egypt, when, after sketching its position in the ancient world, and its relation both to Greeks and Hebrews, he adds (*Thoth, oder die Wissenschaften der alten Aegypter*, p. 6, Göttingen, 1855): '.Aegypten muss als ursprüngliche Quelle alles dessen betrachtet werden, was in

spaterer Zeit an diesen beiden und anderen von denselben abhängigen Völkern bewundert und angestaunt wird; ohne eine gründliche Kenntniss dieses Urquells kann Keins von beiden richtig erkannt, beurtheilt und gewürdigt werden.'

[3] 'Egyptian archæology and history have undergone a complete revolution since the commencement of the present century.' Kenrick's *Preface*.

Egypt barely as the 'land of ruins,' or the birthplace of insoluble enigmas; her true title is the land of sculptured monuments,—of monuments again made vocal to the ear of science, and from which their secret must ere long be wrested more completely by the ardent pupils of Champollion. Favoured by the excellence of the material, and the singular purity and dryness of the climate, the colossal tombs and temples, to say nothing of those minor works of art dug out of the sepulchral chambers, have preserved a rich variety of inscriptions, more or less decypher-

Variety of monuments. able, and more or less conducing to an accurate knowledge of the past. 'There was not a wall, a platform, a pillar, an architrave, a frieze, or even a doorpost, in an Egyptian temple, which was not covered within, without, and on every available surface, with pictures in relief, and with hieroglyphic texts explaining those reliefs. There is not one of these reliefs that is not history: some of them actually representing the conquests of foreign nations; others, the offerings and devotional exercises of the monarch by whom the temple or the portion of the temple on which the relief stood, had been constructed. ...There was no colossus too great, and no amulet too small, to be inscribed with the name of its owner, and some account of the occasion on

Sanguine hopes of Egypt- ology. which it was executed." We can easily understand that when the power of reading these inscriptions began to be recovered, men would turn with fresh enthusiasm to the study of Egyptian antiquities. Here, at least, they seemed to argue, we are building

---

[1] Osburn, *Monumental History* from Lepsius, as above, pp. 36, 37.
of *Egypt,* I. 195, substantially

on a definite and stable basis.   Our materials are
no more of doubtful age and questionable reputation.
The mind and spirit of that ancient world, with
which we long to hold communion, left its impress
deeply graven on the face of pyramids which tower,
as they have towered for ages, high above the sandy
flats of the adjoining desert.   There, accordingly, if
ever, we may hope to find the master-clue which is
to guide us through the intricacies of primeval
history, reveal afresh the hopes and fears which then
were struggling in the human bosom, and resolve for
us, it may be, many an arduous problem which con-
cerns the origin, the early wanderings, and the final
destiny of man.

Nor can we say that expectations of this kind have *Actual dis-*
been entirely disappointed.   Very large accessions to *coveries.*
our knowledge of the ancient East have flowed, and
are still flowing, from investigations of the learned
Egyptologer.   As we gaze for instance on the long
array of monumental paintings in our great Museums;
as we listen to interpretations of the hieroglyphic
texts by which those paintings are accompanied; the
daily life of men who were perhaps contemporary
with Moses has again been vividly depicted on the
dullest imagination.   We behold as well the toils,
the sufferings, and the pastimes of the many, as the
power and luxury of the few.   The peasant labours
at the plough or tends his cattle, while the lordly
owner of the soil is near him in a two-horse chariot.
The goldsmith and the scribe, the potter and the
glass-blower, the boat-builder, the weaver, and the
dyer, each is occupied in his appropriate calling.
Here we see a group of idlers watching the caprices

CHAP. I. of a game of ball, or listening in the midst of flowers and perfumes to the music of the seven-stringed harp: while there a countless multitude are shaping the materials of some stately edifice, or pressing a beleagured town, or marching home victorious with a lengthened train of captives.

Small assistance rendered to the theological student.

It seems to be confessed, however, by the great majority of Egyptologers, that notwithstanding the number and minuteness of these revelations, our familiarity with monuments of ancient Egypt has contributed in no proportionate degree to our acquaintance with the inner being of the people. The manners of the Old Egyptian we may thoroughly appreciate : his mental and moral life is still obscurely apprehended. Means are now at hand for studying the grotesque configuration of his gods, and tracing out the smallest details in his pompous ritual; yet the thoughts which underlay those symbols, and found utterance in those sacrifices,[1] must be learned, if ever, from a different source and by a different process.

Scope and spirit of the present inquiry.

If I venture, therefore, on a fresh discussion of such problems, it is not from any wish to speak with confidence where confidence is really unattainable. I do not purpose to invade the province of the Egyptologer, whose main conclusions are no longer open to dispute; but rather, taking those conclusions for a guide, wherever they are held in common by the learned in each special study, my aim will be to estimate the leading characteristics of Egyptian hea-

---

[1] 'When we endeavour to penetrate into the conceptions which this splendid ritual expressed, we encounter insuperable difficulties: Kenrick, I. 349 : cf. I. 437.

thenism, as one of many forms in which the moral wants and instincts of our nature found expression during the first ages of the world. In doing this, however, exception will be freely taken to the crude and arbitrary theories of some modern writers,[1] who, not content with 'reconstructing' almost every text which militates against their favourite dream of a society 'existing many thousand years before the date usually assigned to the Creation,' are further bent on sacrificing to a spirit of conjectural criticism the highest of all Christian teachings and the best convictions of the human heart.

The great antiquity which is now commonly attributed to Egyptian culture has in several cases been connected with the thought, that in the Valley of the Nile, the prominent forms of social and religious life had been completely stereotyped at once, and so distinguished in all future ages by an air of absolute immobility.

Was Egyptian civilisation always the same?

Now the same conclusion, we must bear in mind, was formerly adopted with respect to India and the regions of the Further East. So meagre was our knowledge of the subject, when presented to us by the earliest race of Oriental scholars, that the Védas

Parallel case of India and China.

---

[1] That English critics are not alone in their misgivings with respect to some of Baron Bunsen's generalisations may be gathered from an extract like the following. The author, Dr. Max Uhlemann, is also an Egyptologer of no mean reputation (*Aegyptisch. Alterthumskunde*, III. 12, Leipzig, 1858): 'Bunsen's Untersuchungen sind unbezweifelt und unbestritten ein geistreiches Werk, ... aber in der Chronologie enthalten auch sie, wie die aller übrigen Forscher, nur Muthmaassungen und unerweisbare Annahmen, die jedoch durch die Zuversichtlichkeit, mit der sie auftreten, dem *unaufmerksamen* Leser als unzweifelhaft erscheinen dürften, da durch Zahlenveränderungen, durch willkürliche Textverbesserungen, durch Hinzuthun oder Hinwegnehmen von Jahresangaben der Alten schliesslich Alles auf wunderbare Weise vortrefflich zu stimmen und sich wechselseitig zu bestätigen scheint.'

and Puránas, for example, were regarded as not only products of the same age, but also as reflecting the same modes of thought, the same archaic aspects of Hindú society. There, however, the unanimous verdict of a riper criticism, while fatal to pretensions of unfathomable antiquity, has certified us that the national spirit both of India and of China had been subject, in the lapse of ages, to extensive fluctuations.[1]

Mobility of Egyptian art, language, and religion.

And a like remark is equally true of Egypt, even while she bowed beneath the sceptre of the Pharaohs. Her supposed exemption from the law of human mutability is vanishing with every fresh accession to our knowledge. The minute inspection and decyphering of her monumental archives have disclosed to us a series of important transformations, have established the existence of successive strata of development, and thus contributed to make us conscious of distinctive epochs in the life-time of the whole community.[2] It may be, indeed, that all the principal characteristics of Egyptian culture, had, as in the case of China, been projected with so much rapidity at first, that we can never hope to understand the origin and real infancy of the people.[3] It may

---

[1] Above, Vol. i. pp. 188 sq., Vol. ii. pp. 23 sq.

[2] 'Avant que les dernières découvertes des égyptologues eussent jeté un jour précieux sur la chronologie des premières dynasties, sur les transformations et les altérations qui se sont opérées dans la langue, dans les institutions, dans le culte et les arts des Egyptiens, on se figurait que tout avait été immuable parmi eux. On prenait la vieille Égypte en bloc comme un monolithe historique qu'il fallait tirer du sable dans lequel il était enfoui, et l'on ne distinguait ni les localités ni les époques.' Maury, in the *Revue des Deux Mondes* (1855), Tom. xi. p. 1053.

[3] Wilkinson, *The Egyptians* (Lond. 1857), Pref. p. vii. who adds (p. viii.) that 'the *general character* of the people, as of their architecture, had been long established when we first become acquainted with them from their monuments, and continued to be the same till the decline of Egyptian power.'

further be contended, that the nationality of Egypt, or the genius which distinguished her from African and Asiatic neighbours, was 'very much the same' in earlier and in later times. All statements of this kind if not unduly pressed convey a large amount of truth; they serve to represent the *general* fixity of corporate as of personal idiosyncrasies; and yet we can no longer doubt that after Egypt had begun to print her records on the pyramids of Ghizeh and Sakkarah, she passed through numerous and important changes,—changes which affected not only her political institutions, but the character of art, of language, of religion.

The second province, that of language, where *The character of art* some modifying agency had been at work, I leave *at different* for the discussion of the competent Egyptologer.[1] *periods.* The third will come more properly before us at a future stage of our inquiry; but the point relating to the gradual changes in the quality of Egyptian art it is expedient to consider now, because the epochs thus obtained are thought by some who are most eminently learned in such matters, to agree with main divisions of Egyptian history in the Pharaonic era.

It is commonly admitted that the finest specimens *Early* of Egyptian art[2] are those which have the fairest *period.*

---

[1] See the *Revue des Deux Mondes,* as above, pp. 1055 sq. on the recent labours of M. de Rougé in this special province.

[2] See *The British Museum* (Egyptian Antiquities), two volumes in the 'Library of Entertaining Knowledge.' Mr. Osburn, *Monumental History of Egypt,* 1.

260 sq. (Lond. 1854), infers from the absence of all crude and 'imperfect' works of art in Egypt that the skill of the primitive artists was a 'portion of that civilisation which its first settlers brought with them when they located themselves in the valley of the Nile.'

claims to be regarded as the oldest,—those which fall within the period of the 'first twelve dynasties.' The bloom of youth is ever traceable on the productions of the early race of artists; all the statues and bas-reliefs are executed with surprising truthfulness and vigour; and although we must allow that both in purity and finish several works belonging to the close of this great period indicate considerable progress, it is no less certain that the character of the whole is so distinctive as to mark it off completely from the period next ensuing.

Middle period.   In the second stage of art, embracing monuments of 'the eighteenth and nineteenth dynasties,' the fervour and simplicity of earlier times have been succeeded by a large amount of stiffness and conventionality. It is the Middle Age of Egypt; during which the symptoms of deterioration are constantly apparent, even where the vast proportions of the works constructed must excite our deepest admiration of the power and energy of the builders.

Period of renaissance.   With the 'twentieth dynasty' commences a fresh era, the age of revival, when the artists of the Valley of the Nile, reverting to the ancient models, executed their works with far greater freedom; yet this period also was of short duration, and when Egypt was absorbed into the empire of the Ptolemies, and finally of the Cæsars, she retained but little of the old artistic spirit: all attempts to mingle Greek with native methods issued in comparative failure, and hastened the extinction of her pristine glory.

Length of intervals.   If, however, it be now established to the satisfaction of most writers that transitions of this kind are really visible on Egyptian monuments, far less has

been effected in determining the point of primary
departure, or the *length of time* to be assigned to each
successive period of Egyptian history. I shrink from
a minute investigation of the chronological difficulties
by which the present subject is confessedly embar-
rassed. While discussing the religions of ancient
India, it appeared to be sufficient for my purpose
if I pointed out the general *order* of the changes
which had supervened upon the old mythology and
habits of the people; and a similar course would be
adopted now, if statements were not hazarded in
various quarters with the object of discrediting the
Bible[1] as a whole, by ridiculing what is called the
'Mosaic chronology.'

How far, indeed, the Books of Moses, in their
present state, supply materials for constructing any
definite system of chronology has long been questioned by the ablest and most reverential of our
sacred critics. The important variations of the
Hebrew and Samaritan texts on one side, and the

Difficulties connected with the biblical chronology.

---

[1] See above, Vol. I. pp. 64, 66,
where two American champions
of human inequality adopt this
line of argument. In like manner,
the account of the Deluge, which
was prevalent both in the Old and
New World, is said by M. Bunsen
and others to have left no echo
whatever in the hieroglyphic legends of Egypt. Their avowed
object in reiterating this statement is to shew that the emigration of the Old Egyptians must
have been 'ante-Noachian,'and indeed many thousand years before
the date ascribed by them to the
'Caucasian' deluge. But the silence which has been alleged in
justification of their statement is
apparently a mere invention of

determined theorizers. Osburn,
for example (I. 239, 240), says
with reference to objections on
this very subject: 'We have no
hesitation whatever in stating our
conviction, that Lepsius is mistaken;' and accordingly proceeds
to demolish the 'stupendous pile
of inferences which are built on
this single assumption.' And
Uhlemann, in like manner, is
completely at variance on this
point with Lepsius and Bunsen.
He declares (*Aegypt. Altert.* III.
10): 'Die ägyptischen Priester
wussten sehr wohl von einer Zeit,
in welcher nach göttlichen Rath-
schlusse das sündige Menschen-
geschlecht vernichtet wurde,' &c.

Septuagint and certain passages of Josephus on the other, have involved the period reaching from the Deluge to the seventieth year of Terah in comparative obscurity. The whole duration of that period in the Hebrew is no more than 352 years; while in the Vatican manuscript of the Seventy it extends as far as 1172 years.[1]

Untrust-worthy character of some Egyptian traditions.

But the indefiniteness arising from this cause will never justify the random guesses of some modern Egyptologers, who, dazzled it would seem by the occasional brilliance of their own discoveries, are carrying back the civilisation of the Valley of the Nile to ages long anterior to the earliest glimpse of history in other regions of the world. Those writers should remember, while demanding our entire belief in catalogues of kings and 'palace-registers,' that in the North of India, where the course of civilisation was most parallel to that of Egypt, we have means of proving the untruthfulness of similar documents, and are able to convict their authors of antedating one event of great importance by as many as twelve hundred years.[2] Those writers should again remember, that the testimony of Egyptian priests is not above suspicion; that Herodotus and Diodorus both derived their information from the same authorities, and yet that while Herodotus extends the number of obscure descendants of Menes to 330, Diodorus limits them to 52; and while the former makes the native monarchy of Egypt to have lasted in all 11,340 years, the calculation of the latter stops short

---

[1] The sum total for this period, according to the various authorities, is *Heb.* 352; *Samar.* 942; *Septuag.* (Vat.) 1172; *Septuag.* (Alexand.) 1072; *Josephus*, 1002.

[2] Lassen, *Ind. Alterth.* I. 501.

at 4,700.[1] These, and other discrepancies, are so 'enormous and so fundamental as to preclude the idea that they can have been superinduced by lapse of time, and a variety of narrators, on a history originally authentic.'

And on turning to the works of Manetho, the *Manetho's* earliest[2] of native historians, who died in the third *lists of kings.* century before the Christian era, we find that such of his remains as have descended to us must be taken at third·hand. His famous lists of kings commence with gods, with manes and with heroes, who are said to have held sway in Egypt for a period of more than thirty thousand years; and even if it were conceded that a writer of his age, the first Egyptian priest who had been gifted with 'historic conscious-ness,' was equal to the task of carrying back the annals of his country for three or five thousand years, an obstacle was lying in his way which must have stubbornly resisted all real progress. Vast as may *Want of an* have been the astronomical knowledge of the Old *initial epoch.* Egyptians, great as was their aptitude in framing chronological cycles,[3] they 'do not appear at any

---

[1] Kenrick, *Ancient Egypt*, II. 84, 85.

[2] 'We hear of no *historical* work of that people before Ma-netho:' Bunsen, *Egypt's Place*, I. 23. Yet the *History* of this native writer, as distinguished from his *Dynasties*, is now lost: while the latter work (edited afresh in Bunsen, I. 605 sq.) is known to us only through Julius Africanus, and Eusebius, and from them through George the Syn-cellus, a Byzantine monk of the ninth century; of whom it should be added that he places the Crea-tion 5500 B.C. and arranges all his dates accordingly.

[3] Cf. Uhlemann, *Aegypt. Alt.* III. 2, 9. Both he and Lepsius are of opinion that the Sothis-period conducts us back to at least 2782 B.C. Mr. Browne, the learned and laborious author of the *Ordo Sæclorum*, has, however, called in question almost every one of the results obtained by German Egyptologers (see his able papers in Arnold's *Theological Critic*, I. 529 sq., II. 125 sq.). Mr. Browne contends that all the native lists of kings are based on

time to have reckoned in their public monuments by an *era*, like that of the Olympiads, but only to have dated events, as we date acts of parliament, by the years of the king's reign."[1] If Egypt, therefore, was in early times divided into several petty kingdoms; or if the names of co-regents, of pretenders, of provincial governors, assuming to themselves the royal style, were entered on the lists of dynasties, the sum of all the regnal years obtained by this process would very far exceed the true number. A large exaggeration is, indeed, acknowledged now by all our Egyptologers. It is believed that rulers in the primitive nomes, or cantons, may at first have been entitled kings, and also that the starting-point of calculation coincided in particular cases not with the accession to an undivided sovereignty, but with the time at which some ruler was admitted to the rank of a co-regent: for although the sum of regnal years, commencing from the earliest of the human rulers, and ending with the last of Manetho's dynasties, amounted to at least 5000, the number actually assigned upon the same authority as the duration of the *whole* period was not more than 3555 years.[2]

cyclical relations, the different cycles being referred to different epochs. According to his view, the *regular* chronology of ancient Egypt is reducible to one cycle, dating from 1805 B.C. (the reign of Joseph's Pharaoh). The 'reduced chronology' has also found another learned advocate in Mr. Nolan, *The Egyptian Chronology Analysed*, Lond. 1848.

[1] Kenrick, II. 95.

[2] Lepsius is disposed to take his stand on this number, which comes down to us through George the Syncellus (cf. *Kritik der Quellen*, p. 499). See, however, *Quarterly Review*, No. 210 (April, 1859), pp. 396 sq., where it is pointed out that this number 3555 may have come from the 'Old Chronicle' merely, and not from the genuine Manetho. The Egyptian years being reduced would give 3553 Julian years for the duration of the thirty dynasties of Manetho; and this, added to 339 (the year B.C. when the last dynasty expired) would also give 3892 B.C. for the foundation of the

But if despairing[1] of results which rest on this
precarious basis, we commence our exploration from
the age when Egypt is first drawn distinctly into the
general history of the world, and so endeavour to
trace out her course in the reverse order, we arrive
at early points of synchronism about 972 B.C., when
Shishak[2] (Sesonch) of the '22nd dynasty' invaded
Palestine, and in the fifth year of Rehoboam 'took
away the treasures of the house of the Lord, and the
treasures of the king's house' (1 Kings xiv. 25). And
as Shishak was the first member of a new dynasty,
it follows that a Pharaoh of the previous series was
father-in-law of Solomon (1 Kings ix. 16), and that
Tahpenes, the sister of the Egyptian queen, had been
espoused to Hadad, the Idumæan, as early as the
reign of David (1 Kings xi. 19 sq.). On these points,
indeed, there is no longer any difference of opinion;
but the placing of the Exodus itself, the next event
where contact with the annals of the Hebrew nation
is undoubted, still continues to present some formid-
able difficulties; inasmuch as it is found to be en-
tangled[3] with a further question touching the expul-

monarchy. Uhlemann, on the
contrary, persists in dating the
reign of Menes, the first king of
Egypt, 2782 B.C.

[1] 'The recovery of Egyptian
chronology, except by slow de-
grees, and with intervals of unknown lengths between the reigns
that are known, is hopeless.'
Engl. Review, (1846), p. 114; an
article on *The Pyramids and their
Builders*, attributed to Dr. Hincks.

[2] Browne, *Ordo Sæclorum*, §513.

[3] See one of the best discussions
of this point in Kurtz, *Gesch. des
Alten Bundes*, II. 173-203, Berlin,
1855. He advocates the old and

very plausible theory that the
'Phœnician' shepherds had invaded Lower Egypt in the period
between Abraham and Joseph;
and that the new dynasty (corresponding to the 18th of Manetho),
who persecuted and enslaved the
Israelites, were princes of Egyptian blood who had eventually re-
gained the sovereign power. The
only serious objection to this view
arises from the thoroughly *Egyptian* aspect of the court in the time
of Joseph; but Dr. Kurtz has
also done very much towards the
removal of this difficulty (pp.
199, 200).

sion of the Shepherd-Kings, or Hyk-sos, and their previous rule in Lower Egypt.

The Middle Kingdom.

Nor in passing upwards, from the origin of what is called the New Kingdom, or the first reign of the '18th dynasty,' has greater concord been established among writers who profess to be our guides through the confusion of the period next preceding.

Its existence problematical.

The duration of the three dynasties ascribed to it by Manetho is found to vary in the different systems of Egyptian chronology from 511 to 953 years; while other writers, arguing from the total want of monuments which bear the dates of kings later than the 12th dynasty, and earlier than the 18th, have begun to ask with some show of reason, 'Is the Middle Monarchy a real thing or not?'[1] Whatever be the true answer to this question, it is plain that till far more is known with certainty respecting such important intervals, we have but little hope of framing any rational hypothesis, or of inditing a coherent narrative.

The Old Kingdom.

And the same perplexity must haunt us on ascending to the 'Old' division of the Pharaonic monarchy. The names of kings belonging to that era are now

---

[1] Dr. Hincks in *Engl. Review*, as above, p. 117. Mr. Kenrick also admits the fact that 'not a single contemporaneous work of art has been found, from the 13th to the 18th dynasty.' He adds, however, (ii. 194) : 'These things are not sufficient to make us doubt the fact of the invasion and expulsion of the Hyk-sos; but they may excite a suspicion that the chronology of this period of oppression and confusion is not to be relied on, and that as usual it has been unduly extended.' I ought also to remind the reader at this point that M. de Rougé thinks he has at last discovered an allusion to the Hyk-sos rule on a papyrus relating to a war undertaken by a king of the Thebaid against the shepherd-king Apepi (Aphobis). The shepherds are there treated as enemies of the *gods* of Egypt. *Revue des Deux Mondes*, as before, p. 1063. cf. Brugsch, *Die Geographie des alten Aegyptens*, i. 50 sq. Leipzig, 1857.

extant, it is true, in very great profusion.[1] Monuments commencing with the time of Chufu (Suphis, Cheops),[2] the builder of the Great Pyramid, continue to bear witness to the fact that even at the opening of the '4th dynasty' the lower valley of the Nile was tenanted by an ambitious and accomplished people, organised into a regular community, as in the age of Abraham and Joseph, and already in possession of the hieroglyphic character, as well as of the reed-pen and the ink-stand.

Yet in spite of all these interesting revelations, Egyptology contributes very little towards the unriddling of the old question, namely, as to which of the primeval dynasties were contemporaneous, and which of them successive. One distinguished writer (as Bunsen) searches for the missing key among the chronological fragments of Eratosthenes, corrected, however, by his own hand; a second (as Lepsius) manifests no confidence in this auxiliary, and gropes his way alone to very different results; a third (as Mr. Browne, or Mr. Nolan, or Mr. Osburn) would curtail the length of early dynasties far more than either of the previous explorers; so that on arriving at the first event distinctly traceable in the archives of the infant colony,—the founding of Memphis, by

The chronological problem still unsolved.

---

[1] Especially in the famous Turin papyrus, which before mutilation must have contained 3 or 400 royal names (cf. Herod. II. 142), with the precise lengths of reign attached to each: see Sir J. G. Wilkinson's *Fragments of the Hieratic Papyrus at Turin* (privately printed, 1851). The same author in his last work *The Egyptians*, &c. (1857), while granting that the high antiquity once assigned to some of the monuments is now 'brought within more reasonable limits' is clearly of opinion that those of the fourth dynasty (the earliest of all) were executed not less than 2400 years B.C. (p. 3).

[2] Kenrick, II. 133. On the identification of the names, see Dr. Hincks, as above, p. 102.

the oldest of their mortal kings,[1] the 'Romulus of Egypt,'—nearly all our certain knowledge of the epoch when some mighty change was supervening on the population of the Nile-valley, may be gathered up into the vague conclusion of Josephus; who informs us that 'Menes, who built Memphis, preceded Abraham by many years.'[2]

Primitive state of Egypt :

But what, in such a case, may be conjectured of the primitive or pre-historic age anterior to the reign of Menes, and the first migrations of the tribe from which he was descended?

why of importance in this inquiry.

This inquiry is again of vast importance to the proper conduct of the enterprise immediately before us; since the ethnological affinities of heathen nations may justly be expected to throw light on the formation of their mythology.

Connexion with sacred history.

Some Christian writers have attempted to identify the founder of Egyptian civilisation with Ham (or Cham), the son of Noah; others with Mizraim, one of Ham's descendants: and although the efforts of those writers seem to me extremely infelicitous, the words on which their arguments are principally based will prove, I think, suggestive of more tenable conclusions.

Chami.

One native name of Egypt is *Chami*[3] (χημι),

---

[1] The author of the article *Ægyptus* in Smith's *Dict. of Greek and Roman Geography*, thinks that the word *Menes* is itself suspicious: it 'too nearly resembles *Manu*, the *Minyas* and *Minos* of the Greeks, the *Menerfa* of the Etruseans, and the *Mannus* of the Germans [cf. Sansk. *man* "to think"] to be accepted implicitly as a personal designation.' Eratosthenes, however, explains Μήνης as equivalent to Αἰώνιος, which is said to be justified by the Old Egyptian and Coptic use of *men* (μην) in the sense of 'to persevere': Uhlemann, *Aegypt. Alt.* III. 82. On the occurrence of the name upon Egyptian monuments, see Osburn, I. 226 sq.

[2] *Antiq.* VIII. 6, 2, ed. Havercamp.

[3] See Vol. I. p. 67, n. I. Plutarch, *De Iside et Osiride*, c. XXXIII.

connected with the Coptic χαμε 'black'; while the
appellation almost universally current in Semitic
countries is *Mizraim,*' *Misr,* or *Mezrén,* the fullest
of these forms, we should remember, being itself a
Hebrew dual noun. And on reverting to the genealogical table transmitted in the family of Abraham
(Gen. x. 16), it will appear that in the series of
Ham's descendants the first place is there allotted to
Cush (a common name for 'Ethiopians'); and the
second place to *Mizraim* (or the Old Egyptians,
occupying the two divisions of the Nile-valley).
Attention seems to have been thus directed to the
fact that all the earliest layers of population, as well
below the frontier-island of Elephantine as throughout the present Nubia and Ethiopia, were originally
homogeneous,—a result which is corroborated by
Egyptian history and in no wise inconsistent with
modern discoveries.

Yet some of these discoveries have, I think, ne- *Who were*
cessitated a fresh hypothesis with reference to the *the primitive civil-*
dominant race of Egypt in the period of the early *isers of*
Pharaohs. Like the Áryan conquerors of the Panjáb, *Egypt ?*

gives the following account of the
word: ἔτι τὴν Αἴγυπτον ἐν τοῖς
μάλιστα μελάγγειον οὖσαν, ὥσπερ
τὸ μέλαν τοῦ ὀφθαλμοῦ, Χημίαν
λαλοῦσι.
  ¹ Knobel (*Die Völkertafel der
Genesis,* p. 273) is disposed to
question the ordinary derivation
of this term מִצְרַיִם from the
bipartite character of Ancient
Egypt (Upper and Lower). He
urges that Isaiah (xi. 11) distinguishes Pathros, or Upper
Egypt, from Mizraim, the remainder of the country, which could
hardly have been the case, if the

Hebrews used Mizraim as equivalent to *both* divisions. Knobel
has accordingly suggested a fresh
origin for the term: 'Dieser Dual
gehört zu einem nicht vorkom-
menden Singular מָצֹר...er be-
deutet also eine doppelte oder
zweiseitige Einschliessung und
bezeichnet Aegypten ganz passend
als ein von 2 Seiten eingesch-
lossenes Land' (p. 274). But the
analogy of other duals (such as
Jerusalem = ἡ κάτω + ἡ καθύ-
περθεν, Joseph. *Ant.* v. 2, 2) is
in favour of the ordinary derivation.

they do not appear to be the primitive masters of the soil, but rather a deposit of new-comers, dating from some later epoch. The numerous paintings on the monuments, as well as osteological investigations in the tombs, will hardly suffer us to doubt that the Egyptians proper, even of the earlier dynasties, exhibit few decided characteristics of the woolly-haired or negro race, but constitute in some respects an independent people,[1]—of a type which, ethnologically speaking, is described as intermediate between *Earliest seat of civilisation.* the Syro-Arabian and the Ethiopic. There is very great uncertainty[2] again as to the point at which the leaders of the second colony effected their original

[1] Uhlemann (*Aegypt. Alt.* III. 57) is very emphatic on this point: 'Nicht von der Geschichte dieses dunklen Stammes hängt die Geschichte der politischen Entwickelung und Cultur der alten Aegypter ab, sondern vielmehr, wie alle noch erhaltenen Denkmäler beweisen, von einem Stamme ganz anderer Abkunft und Farbe...' Cf. Prichard, III. 227 sq., who infers that notwithstanding considerable diversity in figure and complexion, the Old Egyptians as a body 'had something in their physical character approximating to that of the negro' (p. 230).

[2] This uncertainty is connected with the vexed question as to the course pursued by the early civilisers of the Nile-valley. Did they advance northwards from the Thebaid to Lower Egypt? Such is said to be the general verdict of antiquity (Knobel, as above, p. 275); and Ezekiel in particular (xxix. 14), seems to speak of Pathros (Upper Egypt) as 'the land of their *birth*' (מְכוּרָתָם), the cradle of the whole Egyptian people. Thebes was in like manner taken for the oldest of Egyptian cities: whereas it seems to be the general opinion of living Egyptologers that the southern *monuments* at least (whatever may be said of the people) are far more modern than those of Lower Egypt (Osburn, *Mon. Hist.* I. 211); and that Thebes was really the metropolis of the first dynasties, not of the Old but of the *New* kingdom. Other accounts, however, tend to reconcile these two conflicting theories by pointing out that although historical Thebes is younger than Memphis, the course of civilisation did at first flow northwards; Memphis being itself built by an accomplished prince of Abydos in Upper Egypt. In connexion with this point arises the old inquiry respecting the possible influence of Hindús in shaping the original institutions of Egypt (above, p. 216, n. 1); and also the tradition respecting sacerdotal colonies from Meroë in Ethiopia (Diodor. I. 33: III. 3—6).

settlement in the Valley of the Nile. If we might argue from the fact that monuments adjudged the very oldest are all found in Lower Egypt, not far from On (or Heliopolis), the city which became in after-times one special centre of religious worship, it would seem most probable that the new race of immigrants crossed over by the isthmus of Suez, or the natural bridge connecting Africa with Asia; yet a contrary hypothesis, which represents the civilisers of the Nile-valley as a band of priests descending from the Ethiopian frontier, has been also able to attract a number of influential supporters.

Whatever be the ultimate decision of that controversy, a belief in some great secondary immigration, such as I have just indicated, is now current in all schools of Egyptology,[1] not excepting writers who are driven to ascribe the act itself to an unfathomable antiquity. At first, it may be, while the powerful chieftains, such as Menes, were all struggling to consolidate the primitive tribes or cantons[2] into a regular monarchy, the old inhabitants continued to preponderate as largely as the Gauls in France, who, though succumbing everywhere beneath the arms of Clovis, had been able to preserve the language[3] of

Fusion of the conquerors and the conquered.

---

[1] *e.g.* Bunsen declares, *Egypt's Place,* I. 443, that the facts established by modern researches into language and mythology give us precisely the same result. 'Both carry us historically back to Asia.'

[2] These νομοί (thirty-six in number?) into which the valley of the Nile was parcelled out are carried back by Diodorus (I. 54) to the time of Sesostris or Sesöosis (Ramses II.?): yet, as is well remarked, 'they did not originate with that monarch, but emanated probably from the distinctions of animal worship; and the extent of the local worship probably determined the boundary of the nome:' cf. Herod. II. 42.

[3] The most opposite views are still entertained respecting the affinities of the Coptic, or, with slight corrections, of the *Old Egyptian* language. On the one side, it is argued that the syntax of that language, and not a little

their former masters and communicate both it and their religion to the great majority of the Franks. A like amalgamation may have followed in the early centuries of the Pharaonic empire; and subsequently when the Hyk-sos gained possession of all Lower Egypt, and the seat of native power had been transferred to Thebes and to a neighbourhood in which the Cushite spirit still predominated, the great fusion may have been again more rapidly promoted, till at length historians had to deal with a community, consisting, as before, of diverse elements, imperfectly attempered to each other, yet so mixed as to produce what we entitle the specific nationality of Egypt.

Why no regular account is here taken of the oldest Egyptian mythology.

Now of these two factors, one, as in the somewhat parallel case of India, will be here comparatively disregarded. I am not attempting to investigate the characteristics of *primeval* heathenism in the Nile-valley, except so far as it has left its impress on ideas

of the vocabulary also, are related closely to the Hebrew and other members of the great Semitic family. A second class of writers look upon the Old Egyptians as intermediate between the Semitic and Indo-European families. ('The roots of the Egyptian language are, in the majority of cases, monosyllabic, and, on the whole, identical with the corresponding roots in Sanskrit and Hebrew. This is said advisedly:' Bunsen, *Phil. of Hist.* I. 185). A third class utterly deny the alleged connexion between Coptic and Hebrew: *e.g.* "Auch die älteste Sprache der alten Aegypter stand mit den sogenannten semitischen *in gar keiner Verbindung;* erst spätere Verkehrsberührungen haben einige Ausdrücke, besonders von Kleidern, Gefässen, Maassen und Gewichten, aus der ägyptischen Sprache in die orientalischen oder umgekehrt übergehen lassen:' Uhlemann, *Aegypt. Alt.* III. 58. In this opinion of an eminent Coptic scholar acquiesces the present Regius Professor of Hebrew, at Cambridge, who has kindly aided me in the examination of the string of words adduced as parallel by Mr. Birch *Egyptian Hieroglyphics* (appended to Sir J. G. Wilkinson's *Ancient Egyptians*), p. 251. Professor Jarrett is of opinion that it is impossible to establish any relationship between the Coptic and the Hebrew of a closer kind than that which, ethnologically speaking, may be said to exist between 'a Greek and a Negro.' See Appendix I.

and institutions which belong as properly to the
historic period. The remarks already made in sketching the religions of barbaric tribes, wherever scattered
on the surface of Asia, of America, of Oceanica, would
frequently apply with equal justice to the continent
whose people we are now considering,—not to provinces alone in which the black or negro type of
man evinced his true humanity by emerging here
and there into historical importance, but also in that
vast expanse of moral barrenness, which stretches
southward from the Mediterranean to the Cape, and
eastward from the burning cliffs of Guinea to the
pestilent mouths of the Zambesi.[1]

Yet even when the sphere of study is thus definitely narrowed, it becomes important to discriminate
afresh between the earlier and the later periods of
Egyptian history. Our judgment, with respect to
the development of religion in that country, should
be formed apart from clashing theories which come
down to us through Greek writers; for although
Herodotus, in spite of the absurd misrepresentations
of his dragoman, has furnished a large mass of information which is proved to be trustworthy by
according in the main with extant monuments, the
other tourists and philosophers who handled the same
topics, when the Delta was in part Hellenised, and
society most deeply tinctured by the foreign modes
of thought, can seldom challenge our assent in the
same proportion. The Thebaid, it is true, was still
comparatively isolated, and as such continued firm
in its profession of the hereditary faith, until the
sweeping edict of Theodosius, in A.D. 379; but on

Further discrimina- tion of the early from the Hel en- ised Egypt- ians.

[1] See Appendix II.

the founding of the Hellenic capital of Egypt by Alexander the Great, the country as a whole had witnessed the commencement of a new era, in philosophy as well as in political relations. The adornment of the great Museum of Alexandria with the obelisks and sphinxes of the Pharaonic cities, was itself an emblem of the fresh eclectic spirit, then and there imported into all discussions of the old mythology.[1]

Neo-Platonist theories respecting the mythology of Egypt.

One result of such eclecticism has been, that writers (native and Hellenic) of this later period, and especially the Neo-Platonist champions of expiring heathenism, as Porphyry, or Iamblichus, or Proclus, have at times so spiritualized or sublimated the religion of the Old Egyptian, and assigned such arbitrary meaning to the symbols of his ritual, that the primary ideas which it embodied will as seldom be derivable from their writings, as the first mythology of India can be ascertained from speculations of the school of Kapila, or from the aphorisms of the Védánta. Each of the opposing theories started long ago by this class of writers is reflected in the kindred contradictions of modern philosophers. One, for instance, may be heard contending that the basis of Egyptian mythology was altogether materialistic;[2]

[1] 'Alexandrie et la cour des Ptolémées étaient surtout le théâtre de ce mouvement syncrétique qui rapprochait la théogonie pharaonique du polythéisme grec systématisé par les philosophes.' *Revue des Deux Mondes*, as before, p. 1072.

[2] This was the position actually maintained by Chæremon, the Stoic ἱερογραμματεύς who was chief librarian of the Serapeum in the former half of the first century after Christ. According to his view the chief divinities of ancient Egypt were the seven planets and the twelve signs of the zodiac (cf. Uhlemann's *Thoth*, p. 250). In their mythology he recognises no incorporeal Principle, or unseen Intelligence. Prichard's general leaning is in the

another, on the contrary, that it was always an exalted system of pure idealism,[1] which taught men to enshrine the highest and most abstract truths beneath the guise of earthly symbols, and to recognise a master-spirit guiding the whole mechanism of physical creation. But there is reason to believe, as we shall see hereafter, that neither of these theories have done justice to the rude conceptions of the old mythographer.[2] He looked at nature with a deep but thoroughly childlike interest, seldom conscious of the metaphysical antitheses which enter into all our modern speculations; and accordingly his power of separating between the natural and the spiritual was very different from our own, or even from the corresponding faculty of his descendant, who might strive to systematise his notions, when the mythic age of heathendom was drawing to a close.

In seeking therefore to unite ourselves afresh with that remoter period in the history of Egyptian thought, the natural course is to inquire if any

Egyptian sacred books.

---

same direction (*Egyptian Mythology*, Lond. 1819); for, following in the steps of Eusebius (*Evangel. Præparat.* lib. III. c. 4), he concludes that the 'worship of the Old Egyptians was directed towards physical objects; or the departments and powers of nature' (p. 34).

[1] Thus Porphyry addressing a priest named Anebo inquires as to what the Egyptians really held to be the First Cause,—whether an intelligent principle (νοῦν) or something ὑπὲρ νοῦν (cf. a criticism of this passage in Creuzer, *Symbolik*, II. 269); and is answered by Iamblichus who assumes the name of an Egyptian priest, Abammon (*De Mysteriis*, VIII. 4, ed. Gale, 1678). His solution is that the Egyptians by no means affirm the physical origin of all things; but 'distinguish both the animal life and principle of intelligence from nature itself, not only in the universe but also in man' (cf. Creuzer, as above, p. 270).

[2] This judgment which accords substantially with Creuzer's (p. 276) will be also found in Hegel's *Lectures on the Philosophy of History*, p. 217 (Lond 1857). He argues that in 'Egypt natural and spiritual powers were regarded as most intimately united.'

written monuments are extant corresponding to the Hindú Védas and the 'sacred' books of the Chinese. Now Egypt also had a class of writings which may fairly be regarded in this very light. The ancient melodies, which Plato tells us were preserved from age to age as the productions of the goddess Isis,[1] point to the existence and diffusion of a 'sacred' literature. The common name applied to all such writings by the Greeks was 'Books of Hermes' (their reputed author being scribe of the gods, or the 'Mercurius' of the old mythology). From Clement of Alexandria[2] we can also ascertain the general character of these Hermetic books; for when he wrote the custom was to have them carried in procession through the temple of Isis by the heathen priests of the metropolis. The whole number (two and forty), comprehending various treatises on secular subjects, as on medicine, astronomy, and the chorography of Egypt, consisted of extensive disquisitions on religion and philosophy,[3] and also of minute directions for the 'sealing of victims,' the due oblation of the appointed sacrifices, the observance of solemn feasts, the training of the young, and more especially of members of the sacerdotal class, together

---

[1] *De Legibus*, II. 4 (*Opp.* VII. 516, Bekk.): cf. Diodor. I. 53, 72; XVII. 50.

[2] *Strom.* lib. VI. c. 4 (*Opp.* II. 756, ed. Potter): cf. Lepsius, *Chron.* Einleitung, pp. 45 sq., and Mr. Birch, *Egypt. Hieroglyph.* (as before), p. 186, where several titles of Hermetic Books are brought together. Bunsen, who considers the 36 books (excluding the last six on medicine) in five classes (1) Two Books of the Chanter, (2) Four Astronomical Books of the Horoscopus, (3) Ten Books of the Hiero-Grammatist, (4) Ten Ceremonial Books of the Stolistes, (5) Ten Books of the Prophets (Priests),—has summed up his inquiry by admitting that they 'contained no single section of pure history' (I. 23).

[3] ὧν τὰς μὲν λϚʹ τὴν πᾶσαν Αἰγυπτίων περιεχούσας φιλοσοφίαν οἱ προειρημένοι ἐκμανθάνουσι. *Ibid.*

with the full routine of duties daily claimed from the Chap. I. Egyptian either by the laws of his country, or by gods whom he believed to exercise especial sway in his own neighbourhood.

These works, however, with perhaps one sole exception, have been long unknown to Egyptologers, and are probably beyond the reach of modern exploration. The exception, which there seems at least some valid reason for acknowledging, is the famous *Book of the Dead*, or *Ritual;*[1] portions of it dating backwards, we are told, as far as the ' 12th dynasty,' and thus preserving to us a considerable fragment of the older Pharaonic times. In one department of our subject,—the supposed condition of the human soul after death, and the religious service rendered by her in the world invisible,—I hope to profit largely by suggestions borrowed from this quarter. With regard, however, to the leading characteristics of the old mythology, all other data now accessible to ordinary scholars are less copious and explicit. They consist of hieroglyphic names, or titles, or genealogies of gods, surviving with appropriate emblems on the various tablets, tombs, and obelisks; of colloquies between the gods and kings; of sacred formulæ, as chants in honour of some divinity, or prayers for the deceased, or exhortations to survivors, each transmitted to us on rolls of papyri, and most of them

Extant sources of information.

---

[1] Edited, in hieroglyphs, by Lepsius, with the title *Todtenbuch der Aegypter* (Leipzig, 1842). Mr. Birch, who is at present engaged upon an English translation of the whole, has given a short epitome of this curious volume in *Egypt. Hierogl.* pp. 271 sq. Portions of the work *in extenso* have moreover seen the light through other channels. I may also remark that the followers of the Seyffarth (anti-Champollion) school of interpretation have already access to a German version of the *Todtenbuch* in Seyffarth's *Theolog. Schriften der alt. Aegypter.*

CHAP. I. deriving fresh elucidation from reports of Herodotus, or else from statements drawn by Plutarch out of theological works of Manetho.

How far the older heathenism of Egypt was mono- theistic.

The question which, as heretofore, excites our special interest at the very outset of our task has reference to the old Egyptian theories on the central truth of all religion,—the being and attributes of God. Now in replying to this question it is commonly admitted that Egyptians had no single word in use by which to indicate the grand idea of a Supreme Intelligence. It may be that such term had never been unknown to the initiated few, though treated as unutterable in all ordinary circles;[1] yet the statement thus suggested carries with it also the admission that belief in one only God was far from being the established creed of the Egyptian people. And in strict accordance with this fact is the exceed- ing paucity[2] of statements and allusions which imply exclusive worship in one district of one sole divinity.[3]

Parallel case of India.

The aptest parallel is found, if I mistake not, in the history of Hindú religions. With a vague idea of unity which lingered in the background of his meta- physical system ages after it exerted any practical

---

[1] Wilkinson, who leans to the idea of some original monotheism, has suggested this account of the matter. The points, however, which Herodotus declines to pub- lish (e. g. II. 62) were of a some- what different kind. On the re- puted ἀπόῤῥητα of the 'greater mysteries' in Egypt and else- where, see Warburton, *Div. Leg.* Bk. II. sect. 4.

[2] 'It is worthy of remark that the worship of the supreme God is scarcely mentioned in the his- tory of the Egyptians.' Prichard,

E. Mythol. p. 292.

[3] See the motto at the head of this chapter, which is the passage generally adduced as evidence of a belief in one supreme God, *Kneph*, the ram-headed god of the Thebaid, 'unbegotten and im- mortal.' The assertion of Plu- tarch was not true, however, of any early period known to his- tory; and subsequently *Ammon* or *Ammon-Ra* was far more gene- rally worshipped in that region, if we except the island of Elephan- tine : see below, p. 253.

effect, the Old Egyptian had been fascinated more and more by the mysterious powers and processes of nature, till abandoning the ancient faith in God, he bowed in adoration of the world above, beneath, around him. He was still indeed possessed of phraseology which betokened some original conception of a Power superior to the physical elements, and even was accustomed to transfer to it the properties of spirit, as volition and intelligence, which in himself he felt to be inseparable from the true idea of power. He spoke at times of 'a great builder,' 'a creator of the universe,' 'a creator self-created,' 'a soul of the sun,' 'a lord of the two horizons,' a chief 'father of the gods,' 'a mother' also 'of the gods,' a god who was 'the husband of his mother,' 'a goddess-mother of the highest god,' whose glory was that she 'proceeded from herself'; nay, so completely had these forms of speech been tinctured with monotheism as to lead in many writers to a firm belief that all the various gods and goddesses of ancient Egypt are personifications only of Divine omnipotence, or rather are the issue of an intellectual struggle, which was bent on forming the most worthy thoughts of God, and paying homage in the vast profusion of its titles to one personal Deity.

But strict analysis[1] of all such titles, when con-

[1] 'We can find no sufficient evidence for the opinion that the various gods of Egypt are but symbols and personifications of the attributes and powers of one Being, whom the priests, if not the people, recognised as the only true God:' Kenrick, I. 437. The great Cudworth, who took his ideas of Egyptian theology from Iamblichus and other writers of that school, contended, not unnaturally, that the invisible gods of the pagans are the Divine attributes deified (*Intel. Syst.* II. 237 sq. Lond. 1845). He then proceeds as follows (p. 245): 'The pagan theology went sometimes yet a strain higher, they not only thus supposing God to pervade

Chap. I.
Practical polytheism of the system.
ducted in the light which we derive from a comparison of other ancient systems,[1] will be sure to make us hesitate before subscribing to this grand conclusion. Here, as there, it is discovered that so far from such personifications carrying up the mind to a transcendent unity, in which 'all the gods of the Egyptian mythology met and became one,' the opposite result has been more generally apparent. The bright memory of one only God has faded from the human spirit; His functions have been all assigned to a succession of subordinate divinities, who constitute *the* objects of Egyptian worship; and the want of fixity or depth in man's religious conceptions is again betrayed at every turn, by the facility with which he can attribute the same glorious titles to different divinities.

Its pantheistic basis.
The simplest key to all this vagueness and apparent vacillation is contained in the hypothesis, now frequently adopted, that the primitive form of paganism in Egypt was really pantheistic. Till the process, by which single powers of nature were gradually personified, had issued there as elsewhere, in the *humanising* of the earlier race of elemental gods, it was impossible to fix the line of demarcation by which one was distinguished from the other. The attributes were interchanged, the powers themselves were seemingly confounded, because they all at first were viewed as finite emanations of some all-pervading energy. 'Nature' thus became the highest god of the Egyptian

the whole world, and to be diffused through all things. . . . .but also Himself to be in a manner all things. That the ancient Egyptian theology, from whence the theologies of other nations were derived, ran so high as this, is evident from that excellent monument of Egyptian antiquity, the Saïtic inscription often mentioned: " I am all that was, is, and shall be":' see below, p. 250.

[1] Cf. above, Vol. I. pp. 179 sq.; Vol. II. pp. 31 sq.

priesthood; while the people brought their offerings to some one or other of the manifold powers of nature. Their divinities in general corresponded to the functions of the different sexes; they were either paternal or maternal, active or passive, generative or productive; now believed to be exerting their specific influence from the loftiest spheres of being; now in beasts that minister to our convenience, or in hideous reptiles that are crawling at our feet; at one time challenging the homage of the Old Egyptian in their simplest form of light or fire, of earth or water; at a second stooping down from his unclouded sky on gracious or malignant missions; at a third descending more completely to the region of the senses, or identified with local objects, and especially with that phenomenon which was and is the crowning wonder of his native valley,—the rise, the overflow, the retrogression of the waters of the Nile.

This rapid survey of the old Egyptian theology receives, indeed, most ample illustration as a fuller insight is obtained into the meaning of the ancient monuments. As early as the visit of Herodotus,[1] and probably for ages long anterior, the Egyptians were accustomed to distribute all their chief divinities into three special classes, the first consisting of eight, the second of twelve members, and the third, perhaps, of an indefinite number, all of whom were said to have been generated by gods of the previous class, as these

Different orders of Egyptian divinities.

---

[1] II. 145. He is pointing out in this passage that the order of the gods, according to the Egyptians, was very different from the Hellenic view: Ἐν Ἕλλησι μέν νυν νεώτατοι τῶν θεῶν νομίζονται εἶναι Ἡρακλῆς τε καὶ Διόνυσος καὶ Πάν· παρ' Αἰγυπτίοισι δὲ Πὰν μὲν ἀρχαιότατος, καὶ τῶν ὀκτὼ τῶν πρώτων λεγομένων θεῶν· Ἡρακλῆς δὲ τῶν δευτέρων, τῶν δυώδεκα λεγομένων εἶναι· Διόνυσος δὲ, τῶν τρίτων, οἱ ἐκ τῶν δυώδεκα θεῶν ἐγένοντο.

CHAP. I. owed their existence to the first. Some difficulty, it is true, has been experienced in determining which gods should be admitted to a place in the first of the three orders; and it seems most likely that Egyptians of different provinces[1] would, even in the age of Herodotus, have stated their belief respecting this great ogdoad with considerable variation.

Ptah, the chief elemental god of Lower Egypt.

Still if we may argue from the order in the list where Manetho professes to arrange the several gods,[2] who were believed to have held sway in Egypt, long before all human dynasties, the foremost rank should be assigned to *Ptah*, the Vulcan of the Latins,[3] and Hephæstus of the Greeks. If not the God of all Egypt, he was certainly regarded as supreme within the cycle of divinities who were especially adored at Memphis. One designation of the whole country had moreover been derived in early times from this alleged supremacy: for *Egypt* (Αἴγυπτος) seems to be not only identical with *Kopt*, but also a Greek form of *Kah-Ptah*[4] 'land of Ptah,' the land which recognised in Ptah her chief divinity. The special functions of this god are indicated by his title of 'creator of the

---

[1] Cf. Lepsius, *Chronol.* Einl. p. 253. note.

[2] 'Primus Ægyptiorum deus *Vulcanus* fuit, qui etiam ignis repertor apud eos celebratur. Ex eo *Sol* etc. Manethon. *Dynast.* (printed in Bunsen's 'Appendix of Authorities,' No. II.).

[3] He is Cicero's second Vulcanus (*De Nat. Deorum*, III. 55) 'in Nilo natus, *Phthas*, ut Ægyptii appellant, quem *custodem* esse Ægypti volunt.'

[4] Uhlemann, *Aegypt. Alt.* II. 11, 12, who instances the similar word Ἡφαιστία, which Greek writers applied to Egypt, and also mentions that the Ethiopic name of the country is *Gobzo*. The prefix *ai* may perhaps be illustrated by such forms as αἰγυπιός which was used by Homer for γύψ. Bunsen finds the derivation, or at least the sister-form, of *Ptah* itself in פתח 'to open' (*Egypt's Place*, I. 383, n. 252), so that *Ptah* (he thinks) was primarily the 'great Revealer.' Mr. Osburn, again (*Mon. Hist.* I. 263), discovers *Ptah* in *Phut*, the fourth son of Ham.

sun and moon.' He is not only, like the Greek Hephæstus, eminent for plastic skill, but also is the proper *demiurgus* of the universe, the shaper of primeval matter, the 'leader of the mundane artisans,'[1] or, in the highest and most abstract form of the conception, Ptah is the original force of nature and the world-begetting fire.[2]

The oldest representation of him was a child or bandy-legged dwarf, reminding us at once of pigmy statues sacred to Hephæstus, and also of the idols (the *Pataïkoi*)[3] carried by Phœnician mariners on the prows of their triremes. But in other, and it seems more recent, representations, Ptah is worshipped under a more perfectly human form. He is entitled 'lord of the gracious countenance' and also 'lord of truth.' As such he is accompanied by a female figure (Truth or Justice) with the ostrich feather on her head.[4] He holds before him in both hands an emblem of stability or duration, the so-called Nilometer,[5] which is combined with the symbols of life and the kukufa-sceptre. On his head he wears a skull-cap like the pilos of Vulcan; while the body is completely swathed, in mummy-fashion, so that the hands alone are seen protruding outside the envelope. 'Perhaps the swathed body and protruded hands may symbolise the first putting forth of a creative power in action,

---

[1] This is the expression of Iamblichus; cf. Wilkinson, *Anc. Egypt*, 2nd ser. i. 249 sq.

[2] 'Die erste als Urfeuer gedachte zeugende Kraft:' Döllinger, *Heidenthum und Judenthum*, p. 412, Regensburg, 1857. Similarly Eckermann, *Mythologie*, i. 74, Halle, 1848: 'Er ist das Lebensprincip im Universum, die zeugende Urkraft.'

[3] Herod. iii. 37: see Mr. Blakesley's note. The derivation which he seeks is probably to be found in the Egyptian *Ptah*: whence Παταϊκοί.

[4] Wilkinson, as above, p. 250; Bunsen, *Egypt's Place*, i. 382.

[5] Bunsen, *Ibid.*

CHAP. I. which had been previously hidden and quiescent."[1] The same functions are suggested more distinctly by a living emblem, which was specially sacred to the great Egyptian *demiurgus,* viz. the beetle of the Nile (or *scarabæus*). Some indeed have traced the ground of this connexion to different causes;[2] but the instinct which directs the beetle to deposit her egg on the soft wet mud of the Nile, and the astonishing skill with which she frames and finally rolls away 'the ball which is the nidus of her future offspring,'[3] are such vivid images of functions everywhere ascribed to Ptah, that I prefer this exposition of the symbol to all others which have been suggested.

Neith, the primitive goddess.

It is one of the prerogatives of Ptah in the Memphitic system of mythology, that he combines within himself the properties of both the sexes. He is one of two androgynal divinities. The second member of this class is *Neith,*[4] the Greek Athene;

---

[1] Kenrick, I. 380.

[2] *e.g.* It was believed that the Nile-beetles were all males, or else were altogether without distinction of sex, and therefore fit emblems of creative power, 'self-acting and self-sufficient.' M. de Rougé (*Revue Archéologique,* VIII° année, p. 53) has given his sanction to this view of the scarabæus-symbol. He also adds (p. 54) that the idea of divine generation as dwelt upon by Iamblichus 'n'est pas un produit de l'esprit philosophique des derniers temps, mais qu'elle appartient à la portion antique et traditionelle des mystères.'

[3] See Mr. Osburn's minute description, *Monum. Hist.* I. 204, 205.

[4] In Plato's time Neith (whom he identifies with 'Αθήνη) was specially worshipped at Sais in the Delta; and Cicero (*De Nat. Deor.* III. 59) speaking of his second Minerva adds : 'orta Nilo, quam Ægyptii Saitæ colunt;' but, as Mr. Kenrick remarks, it is plain from Herod. II. 59, that her worship also extended through the whole country. Mr. Blakesley, on Herod. II. 100, argues in favour of the old notion respecting the verbal identity of Neith and Athene. Improbable as this may be (Kenrick, I. 387, n. 1), there is no doubt that we discover an early trace of the Egyptian name in queen Nitocris (Neitokr = 'Αθήνη Νίκη). It is also interesting to remark that even Cambyses, who is commonly represented as waging a quasi-religious war in Egypt, was nevertheless extremely scrupulous in making the due offerings 'to Neith, the divine

Ptah in his exalted rank becoming to the male what Neith is to the female deities: and yet so closely are the functions of the two commingled or confounded in some representations that Neith is really the female counterpart of the great *demiurgus*. He is the primary paternal element in nature, she the primary conceptive element. He is the father of the sun, she is the mother of the same luminary ('the great cow, engenderer of the sun').[1] He is the primordial fire, while she is the primordial space or chaos, self-producing,[2] coeternal with him, and coequal, or in other words the 'feminine ether' everywhere diffused as the material basis of all forms of created being.[3]

In proportion, however, as the old Egyptians learned to *humanise* their chief divinity, they seem to have assigned him a more human consort. The 'beloved of Ptah' was Pasht (Bubastis, or 'Diana'), commonly depicted as the lioness- or rather the cat-headed goddess. Like Neith she was occasionally styled the Great Mother, and as such was represented carrying the emblems of life in her hands. She also was esteemed a great fire-goddess,[4] which explains the real ground of her alliance with Ptah; but, not-

---

mother of the principal gods of Sais:' see M. de Rougé's paper in the *Revue Archéologique*, VIIIe année, p. 40.

[1] Bunsen, I. 386: Kenrick, I. 390.

[2] Plutarch found this property in her very name, which he interpreted, rightly or wrongly, ʾΗλθον ἀπ' ἐμαυτῆς.

[3] Cf. the following language of De Rougé, as above, p. 59: 'Dans la génération des dieux célestes ou secondaires, identifiés avec les astres, je comprends encore le rôle maternel du ciel comme espace, χώρα, et même comme matière, ὕλη, *fournissant une portion de l'éther céleste au démiurge pour nourrir ses germes divins.*'

[4] See the passage from Brugsch's *Travels*, quoted by Döllinger, p. 412. That eminent Egyptologer is of opinion that Pasht was again superseded in later times by Neith.

withstanding, her precise relation to the older series of Memphitic gods is very difficult to determine.

Ra, or Phra, the sun-god. The next divinity, whose claims to be connected with that series are indisputable, is the sun-god of Lower Egypt, *Ra*[1] (or with the definite article *Phra*); the centre of whose worship was at On (the Heliopolis of the Greeks). By some he is promoted to the foremost place[2] in the Egyptian pantheon. He alone in the succession of the highest gods is not accompanied by a female counterpart. He only is invested with a plenary jurisdiction. To his honour it was chanted that, while he, and he alone, is the chief 'source of life in heaven and on the earth, he is himself the unbegotten.'[3] We have seen, however, that the luminary thus adored by the Egyptians, is described in other places as the offspring of Ptah; whom he succeeds accordingly in the administration of the world. We also heard him called the offspring of the goddess Neith, of her who, notwithstanding, had been made to publish almost in the same breath: 'I am the things that have been, that are, and that will be; no one has uncovered my skirts.'[4]

---

[1] Copt. ⲣⲏ 'sun'; ⲫⲣⲏ 'the sun.'

[2] Lepsius has of late years warmly advocated this hypothesis in a paper *Ueber den ersten Aegyptischen Götterkreis* &c. read before the *Akademie der Wissenschaften* (1851), and published among their Transactions. His main principle is thus stated (p. 193): 'Es bleibt folglich nur die umgekehrte Annahme übrig, und diese bestätigt sich meiner Meinung nach auf das Bestimmteste von allen Seiten, dass der *Sonnenkult* selbst der früheste Kern und das allgemeinste Princip des ägyptischen Götterglaubens war, welcher vor allen Lokalkulten vorhanden, in allen einen wesentlichen Theil bildete, und überhaupt nie, bis in die spätesten Zeiten, aufhörte als die äusserliche Spitze des gesammten Religionssystems angesehen zu werden.'

[3] See various passages to this effect excerpted by De Rougé, as before, pp. 54, 55.

[4] Mr. Kenrick is undoubtedly correct (I. 389, n. 5) in referring to Deut. xxii. 30 for the explanation of this language. It does not imply the mystery of Neith's

A simple key to all such enigmatical language will be found, if we remember only that Ptah and Neith are the two great parent principles of the universe, and therefore the creation of the sun, the disentangling of primordial light from darkness, would be naturally regarded as the work of one or both of them, according to the fancy of the different worshippers. The sun, it was concluded, like the other objects of external nature, had begun to be, and therefore owed his being to the Ultimate Principles of all things. This consideration will again enable us to understand the mythological language of some ancient hymns,[1] in which the worshipper, excluding from his view the functions of the *demiurgus*, and no longer dwelling on the old relation between Neith and Ra, has pictured the diurnal motion of the sun-god, as a species of relapse into his native element. 'Thou sheddest thy beams upon the back of thy mother.' 'Thy mother, the sky, is stretching out her arms for thee.' 'O father of the gods, thou reunitest thyself with thy mother on the western mountain. She receives thee daily into her arms.' 'When thou shinest in the dwelling of Night, thou revisitest the sky, thy Mother.'

It is not indeed unlikely that in very primitive times as well as through the period when such hymns as these were graven on the tombs of Lower Egypt, Ra had been exalted to the highest place in the affections both of king and people. Ramses the Great already sacrificed to him as to 'the lord of the two worlds, who is enthroned on the sun's disk, who

being (as De Rougé even seems to think, *Ibid.* p. 59), but the fact of her virginity.

[1] De Rougé, as before, p. 56.

moves his egg, who appears in the abyss of heaven."
Ra was thus emphatically *king*[2] of the gods: and
mortals who had been entrusted with the government
of Egypt were esteemed in some mysterious way his
progeny, his favourites, his vicegerents. His own
title (Ra or Phra) has reappeared in the official name
of *Pharaoh*.[3] None of the Egyptian kings,[4] indeed,
could be admitted to his office till instructed in the
secret learning of the priests, and, where such transfer
might be necessary, incorporated with the sacerdotal
order: yet as soon as his initiation was completed
he assumed a power analogous to that enjoyed of old
time by the Incas of Peru and now by Emperors
of the Middle Kingdom; he was 'president of the
assemblies;' he regulated the whole cycle of religious
worship as well as the machinery of the Egyptian
state; he was himself the object of one kind of
adoration;[5] for in him the gods, or more especially
the kings of gods and highest of all potentates, had
condescended to exert a more than human energy.

The Pharaohs children of the sun.

But on passing to the upper province of the Old
Mizraim, there is far less certainty respecting the true
character of her chief divinities. *Kneph*, or Chnubis,
who was once regarded as the master-spirit of the
system, as in some degree the fountain of vitality

Kneph :

---

[1] Bunsen, I. 387.
[2] Lepsius, as before, p. 194.
[3] Dr. Hincks (*Engl. Rev.* as before, p. 101) has also pointed out that the names of the earlier Egyptian kings consisted in almost every instance of the name of the sun, and a simple or compound epithet or qualification: cf. Müller, *Amerik. Urrelig.* p. 305. Similarly Potipherah, priest of Helio-

polis, (Gen. xli. 45) has been explained by Phont-Phra, 'priest of the Sun.'
[4] Wilkinson, 1st ser. I. 245, 246, 2nd ed.
[5] Diodorus (I. 90) speaks even more strongly: Διὰ δὲ τὰς αὐτὰς αἰτίας δοκοῦσιν Αἰγύπτιοι τοὺς ἑαυτῶν βασιλεῖς προσκυνεῖν τε καὶ τιμᾷν, ὡς πρὸς ἀλήθειαν ὄντας θεούς.

for Ptah himself, and *the* immortal, self-begotten
deity of the Thebaid,[1] is adjudged by Lepsius to
be one of the most modern products of the Græco-
Egyptian theorising.[2] Only as conjoined with Ra
could Kneph be styled 'the highest god,' and worshipped as the formative or spiritual principle. The
glorious Ammon, also, who had been invested with
a like pre-eminence, inasmuch as the Hellenic writers
were accustomed to entitle him the 'Zeus of Egypt,'
has been similarly disparaged and dethroned by
modern criticism.[3] It is contended that until the
seat of native empire was transferred to Thebes, and
some amalgamation of the pantheons of Upper and
Lower Egypt had resulted there in the projection
of a great compound divinity, who bore the title
Ammon-Ra, the primitive god of Thebes was strictly

---

[1] See the motto prefixed to this chapter. The story of Ptah springing from an egg, which issued out of the mouth of Kneph (? Copt. *nef*, 'to blow or breathe'), is no older than Porphyry; and although we may allow that the peculiar symbol of the mundane egg is very ancient, the use made of it by the Neo-Platonists, in its relation to Kneph, was obviously directed to the establishment of their favourite theory as to the priority of some Intellectual Principle in the old Egyptian system: see above, p. 238. Döllinger says of him with apparent justice: 'Seine Auffassung als göttlicher Lebensgeist oder Weltseele scheint erst der spätesten Zeit kurz vor oder nach Christus anzugehören:' p. 411.

[2] As before, p. 164, n. 1.

[3] *Ibid.* p. 173: ... 'war bis zur Erhebung Thebens wo er als Lo-kalgott verehrt wurde, ein unter-geordneter wenig genannter Gott.' Bunsen on the contrary maintains that 'he stands incontestably at the head of a great cosmogonic development.' (I. 371.) How-ever this may be, it is now gener-ally conceded that many of the earliest attributes of Ammon were identical with those of Khem, the ithyphallic god, or Pan of Herod-otus (cf. *Revue Archéol.* xive an-née, p. 211). Both have the title 'husband of his mother': both wear the same badge, or head-dress, of long straight feathers; and both are viewed as more es-pecially gifted with generative and productive power. Mr. Os-burn, in accordance with his the-ory, finds the son of Noah Cham (Ham) in the Egyptian Ammon (Amun); and Noah himself in Kneph.

local in his character, and so upon a level with the vast majority of deities.

Other phases of the sun-god.

The greater gods of Upper Egypt whom Lepsius places at the head of his new series, immediately after Ammon-Ra, are *Mentu* (Month) and *Atmu* (Tum).[1] Yet these again, he thinks, are both to be regarded as derivatives from the sun-god: they conjointly fill the place ascribed to Ra in the mythology of Lower Egypt; they are 'children of Ra,' the one an emblem of his superterranean, and the other of his subterranean power; the one associated with the rising, and the other with the setting or nocturnal sun.[2] In this connexion only is it true that Mentu-Ra became the 'god of both the Egypts'; or that Atmu could be called 'the author of all fecundity.' Another of the Theban gods was *Mue* (or Light), who is depicted here and there not only as a son of Ra, but also as the offspring of the solar deities, whose lineage we have just considered. In like manner *Tefnet*, the companion or feminine counterpart of Mue, whom Lepsius wishes to include among the greater gods of the Thebaid, is entitled with a similar import, 'daughter of the Sun.'

Probable course of amalgamation in the mythology of Egypt.

It must, however, be acknowledged by all candid minds that no small measure of uncertainty continues to hang over this attempted distribution of the primitive gods of Egypt. We are barely able to discern the outlines of a systematic classification. The fabric of the old theology, if such it may be termed, was

---

[1] Cf. Döllinger, p. 410. A learned friend suggests the Copt. ατ-μου = 'immortal' as explanatory of *Atmu*. In Copt. μου signifies 'death'; μουε 'light.'

[2] Lepsius, as before, p. 187. On this principle he explains the name 'Sun of Night' applied to Atmu.

built up gradually into a whole by 'the agglutination of parts having a separate origin.'[1] At first, as men relinquished the idea of one great Personal Spirit, ruling all things by His sovereign will, they yielded to the witchery of external nature and bowed down before a concourse of provincial deities: the varying phases of religious thought gave birth to corresponding variations of this first mythology; yet everywhere the felt necessity of relying on a god superior to the many, led afresh to the investment of some member of the pantheon with a relative supremacy; until, upon the union of the several nomes, the greater gods were all more fully merged in two large classes, corresponding to political divisions of the Nile-valley. Such a fusion had moreover been promoted from within by the existence of religious sympathy. A link connecting the mythologies of Upper and Lower Egypt was supplied in all the early stages of their formation by the glorious sun-god, Ra,—the offspring of the oldest gods of Memphis, and identified, as we have seen, with one or more divinities whose native sphere is the Thebaid. Ra was, in like manner, the chief medium for advancing that more perfect amalgamation, which begins to be distinctly visible at a later period: for how grave soever be the faults committed by Herodotus in classifying the old mythology of Egypt, the account is unimpeachable where he tells us, that in spite of all existing variations, the common worship of two deities prevailed in every canton of the great community.[2]

---

[1] Kenrick, I. 363; Döllinger, p. 407.

[2] θεοὺς γὰρ δὴ οὐ τοὺς αὐτοὺς ἅπαντες ὁμοίως Αἰγύπτιοι σέβον- ται, πλὴν Ἴσιός τε καὶ Ὀσίριος, τὸν δὴ Διόνυσον εἶναι λέγουσι. II. 42.

These potentates were Isis and Osiris, who, as overlying or eclipsing all the rest, stand forth conspicuous, from the mouths of the Nile to Elephantine, and supply a centre both of worship for the multitude and speculation for the priestly order. It is probable that certain compound names, like Ptah-Sokari-Osiris,[1] will turn out to be examples of transition from an earlier to a later way of thinking. They may also have borne witness to religious struggles[2] and to compromises effected in particular districts. But the fact itself remains indisputable, that in the whole of what is properly entitled the historic period, Isis and Osiris, with a family-circle of inferior deities, are made to play the principal part in the mythology of ancient Egypt.

What, then, is the true relation of these deities to gods who were confessedly members of the 'first order'? Did they constitute an independent and contemporaneous group? Or did they actually succeed the others in the manner intimated by Herodotus, and so commence, by their ascendancy alike in Thebes and Memphis, a new period of Egyptian history? Now in answering such inquiries it is most important to remember that the name, the emblems, and a few at least of the specific functions of Osiris, have been actually traced on monuments of high antiquity; for instance, on the coffin of Menkeres (or Mycerinus) belonging to the '4th dynasty.' Com-

---

[1] Wilkinson, 2nd ser. I. 253.

[2] It is well to keep in mind this possible source of change in the religious symbolism of Egypt. Lepsius, as before, pp. 196 sq., has given a detailed account of one struggle between pure sun-worship and Ammon-worship in the reign of Amenophis IV. of the 18th dynasty. The 'reformatory' labours of that monarch were, however, all undone by the reaction 'of the old national hierarchy.'

mencing therefore from such facts as this we soon arrive Chap. I.
at the conclusion that Osiris had for ages coexisted[1] *Worship of*
with Ptah himself in some departments of the Delta; *Osiris at first local.*
as Brahmá, the younger god of Hindústán, eventually
supplanted Indra, the most prominent of Vaidic deities.
The solemn worship of Osiris was at first, however,
circumscribed in somewhat narrow limits. In allusion
to that fact he is entitled 'lord of This' and 'lord
of Abydos'[2] in Upper Egypt; though for centuries
anterior[3] to the visits of Hellenic tourists, it is plain
that he was raised to a position of unrivalled majesty,
approaching far more nearly than the other members
of the pantheon to the rank of one almighty and
illimitable God. He gathers up into himself the *Final de-*
choicer and more god-like attributes of all the male *velopment.*
divinities; while Isis may be taken as the general
representative of functions belonging to the opposite
sex. The two together form a dyad. Osiris is the
active, plastic, generative principle; and as such he
is most naturally connected with a female counterpart, who, contemplated under different aspects, will
be found to have assumed to him the manifold relations of sister and of spouse, of daughter and of
mother.[4]

There is also reason for concluding that Osiris of *How far*
Abydos had been gradually identified with Ra, the *Osiris was identified*
sun-god of Heliopolis; for such amalgamation is not *with Ra.*

---

[1] Such is also Mr. Kenrick's conclusion, I. 358, 359.

[2] Lepsius, as before, pp. 190, 191.

[3] The same writer has offered a very probable explanation of the mistake of Herodotus in placing Osiris among the tertiary, instead of primary, gods of Egypt.

(*Chronol.* p. 253). Wilkinson had long before observed: 'If Osiris was not nominally one of the eight great gods, he in reality held a rank equal to any:' 2nd ser. I. 158, note.

[4] Döllinger, p. 413.

only implied in the new formula *Osiris-Ra,* but is expressly mentioned in the works of Egyptologers both ancient and modern.[1]　Like Ra, Osiris, though occasionally described as 'self-begotten,' had a mythological pedigree assigned to him: he was the eldest son of Seb (Κρόνος) and of Nut or Nutpe ('Ρέα),[2] to both of whom he is declared superior ('greater than his father and more powerful than his mother').　In one respect alone he differs widely from the older sun-god,—in requiring for the exercise of his specific powers the aid of some divinity like Isis, who inherits therefore the peculiar properties of the Great Mother, Neith, while he in virtue of some corresponding interchange with the old fire-god of Memphis reappears on more than one inscription as *Osiris-Ptah.*

Hymns in honour of Osiris.

　　Combining thus the several functions of creator, of enlightener, of fructifier, Osiris, in that ancient system of mythology, attracted to himself the homage, love, and adoration of the whole community.[3]

[1] Lepsius, *Ueber den ersten Aegypt. Götterk.* p. 194. This writer denies, however, very positively that there was any *genealogical* connexion between the Osiris-group and other old divinities, either in the Memphitic or the Theban series: cf. Diod. I. 11, where Osiris and Isis are plainly identified with the sun and moon respectively. Plutarch (*De Isid. et Osirid.* c. LII.) has given us substantially the same account; and in the monuments we have a further confirmation of this theory: 'ils nous apprennent en effet que la divinité qui remplit le premier rôle est le Soleil, et qu'Osiris, comme la plupart des personnages divins dont l'Olympe égyptien est si malheureusement encombré, n'est qu'une forme particulière de cette divinité:' *Revue Archéol.* XIVᵉ année, p. 193.

[2] This filiation is authorised in the *Book of the Dead* itself (*Rev. Arch.* as before, p. 202): yet the Copt. ⲛⲟⲩⲧⲉ seems to mean 'god,' and ⲛⲟⲩⲧⲉ-ⲡⲉ 'god of heaven.'

[3] Cf. Uhlemann, *Thoth,* pp. 27 sq., who remarks with more especial reference to his view of the Egyptian cosmogony which he elicits from the *Book of the Dead,* that it has 'viele Aehnlichkeit mit der mosaischen, die *ohne Zweifel* [!] aus ihr hervorgegangen; es findet sich in derselben Nichts von einem ungeordneten Chaos wie bei Griechen und Römern; auch bei Aegyptern ist die Welt aus Nichts geschaffen, Alles Vor-

Osirian hymns which are at length accessible to *Chap. I.* almost every student, will bear ample witness to this fact; for most of them are outbursts of religious feeling, stimulated by the thought of his transcendent quali-ties. Osiris is the 'lord of life,' 'the king of heaven,' 'the prince of gods,' 'the lord of ages,' 'the light of the world,' 'the dispenser of nutrition,' 'the quickener of the dead,' 'the guide,' 'the judge,' 'the leveller,' and 'the avenger.'

But instead of swelling this long catalogue of *One com-*names, which separately taken have an obvious ten-*plete speci-men of*dency to misinform the reader by suggesting paral-*such hymns.*lels that have no true foundation, I prefer to give one single hymn, as nearly as I may, in its original completeness. It will further serve to introduce us to some other members of the great Osiris-family, and acquaint us with some other aspects of their mythological character. The text of this remarkable hymn is found inscribed upon a *stele,* which the French translator[1] places in the seventeenth century before the Christian era.

HYMN TO OSIRIS.

"Hail, Osiris! lord of the length of times, king of the gods, of names exceeding many,[2] conspicuous for thy holy transforma-

handene aus der allmächtigen Hand der schaffenden Gottheit Osiris hervorgegangen.' But how, on this hypothesis, can we explain the co-existence of *two* cosmogonic principles, Ptah and Neith, Osiris and Isis? see above, 248, 257. It is surely far more probable that the dualistic cosmogony of the Greeks to which Uhlemann here refers was itself of Egyptian origin. Such a supposition, I may add, is entirely borne out by the narrative of Diodorus (i. 7), who speaks of the sun as being itself a product of the element of fire (τὸ πυρῶδες): just as the Memphitic Ra was the child of the fire-god Ptah.

[1] M. Chabas, in the *Revue Archéologique*, 14. année (1857), pp. 65 sq., pp. 193 sq.

[2] As the translator remarks (p. 195), one chapter of the *Ritual*

CHAP. I. tions and mysterious emblems in the temples: exalted dweller in Tattu;[1] chief inclosed in Sokhem; master of invocations in Oer-ti; enjoying happiness in Hon; whose right it is to rule in the place of double justice; mysterious soul of him, who is the lord of the sphere; the holy one of the White Wall; soul of the sun; his body itself reposing in Sûten-si-nen; author of invocations in the region of the tree Ner; whose soul is made for watching; lord of the vast abode in Sesennû; greatest of the beings in Shas-hotep; lord in Abydos of the length of times. The way of his dwelling is in the To-sar;[2] his name is constant in the mouth of mortals. He is a god of the earth, an Atûm[3] who in the midst of gods is showering happiness on the creatures; a beneficent spirit in the place of spirits.

"From him descend the waters of the heavenly Nile. From him proceeds the wind. The air we breathe is (also) in his nostrils for his own contentment and the gladdening of his heart: he airs (or purifies) the realms of space, which taste of his felicity, because the stars that move therein obey him in the height of heaven.

"He opens the grand doors; he is the master of invocations in the southern sky and adorations in the northern; the constellations which move onward are all under his immediate gaze; they form his dwelling-place, as well as constellations which remain at rest.[4] To him, by the command of Seb [his father] sacrifice is offered: gods in the firmament adore him with respect, divine chiefs with reverence, all with supplications. Those who rank among the venerable ones all recognise his high authority; the whole earth gives glory to him, when his holiness engages in a conflict: he is an illustrious Sahû among Sahûs, exalted in position, permanent in empire. He is the

---

(or *Book of the Dead*) enumerates as many as a hundred appellations under which Osiris was adored.

[1] This and the following proper names appear to denote localities especially connected with Osiris-worship.

[2] 'Un lieu que les mânes devaient traverser avant d'arriver à la demeure d'Osiris, l'Hadès égyptien.' Chabas, p. 70, n. 1.

[3] *i.e.* like *Atmu*, the solar deity; see above, p. 254.

[4] 'Nous voyons par notre texte que les Egyptiens se figuraient les *khimou* placés en face du Soleil, qui y faisait ses résidences, c'est-à-dire qui y stationnait tour à tour.' p. 71, n. 1.

excellent master of the gods, beautiful and lovely. All who see him of whatever country respect and love him. All who have enjoyed his condescension exalt his name to the highest rank. He has the power of command alike in heaven and earth. Abundant acclamations are addressed to him on the festival of Uk; consentient acclamations from the two worlds.

"He is the elder, the first-born of his brothers, the chief of the gods. He it is that executes justice in the two worlds, and plants the son upon the father's seat. He is the praise of his father Seb, the darling of his mother Nû [Nut]. Of mighty arm, he overthrows the impure; invincible, he crushes every foe; he strikes terror into all that hate him; he breaks down the barriers of the wicked; ever fearless, he is ever on the alert; he is the son of Seb, commanding both the worlds. He (Seb) has seen his virtues and directed him to guide the nations by the hand to larger measures of prosperity. He (Osiris) fabricated this world with his hand, the waters and the air, the vegetables, all fowls and winged creatures, all fish, all reptiles and four-footed beasts. The earth pays rightful homage to the son of Nû [Nut]; the world rejoices once again, when like the Sun he mounts upon his father's seat; he shines on the horizon, he diffuses dawn upon the face of darkness; he irradiates the light by his double plume; he inundates the world, like the Sun (which shines) from the highest empyrean. His diadem is conspicuous in the summit of the heavens; and is allied (united) with the stars: he is the leader of all gods. In will and word he is benignant, the praise of the greater gods and the delight of the less.

"His sister [Isis] has taken care of him in driving away her enemies by a triple rout; she sends forth her voice in the brilliance of her mouth;[1] wise of tongue, her word is sure to prosper. In will and word she (also) is benignant. Isis is her name, the illustrious, the avenger of her brother's wrong. She sought him without resting; she walked the circuit of this world, lamenting him; she rested not until she found him; light was given out from her;[2] a wind was produced by [the

---

[1] 'Le sens est que la déesse avait le don de l'éloquence.' *Ibid.* p. 75, n. 4.

[2] The meaning of this clause is said to be doubtful. M. Chabas renders: 'elle a fait de la lumière avec ses plumes.'

Chap. I. motion of] her wings: she made the invocation at the funeral of her brother: she carried off the elements [elementary particles] of the god of the tranquil heart: she extracted his essence: she made a child [of it]: she gave the foster-child her arm to suck.[1] The place where that occurred is unknown [to mortals].

"His arm (the child's arm) is become strong in the great dwellingplace of Seb. The gods are overjoyed on the arrival of Osiris, son of Horus, fearless, justified, son of Isis, son of Osiris. The divine chiefs collect around him: the gods recognise in him the universal lord. The lords of justice who are met together to correct iniquity are delighted to pay their homage in the great dwellingplace of Seb to the lord of justice. The reign of justice in that region appertains to him. Horus has found his justification (word of justice): he comes forward crowned with the royal wreath by order of Seb. He has received the royalty of the two worlds: the crown of the upper region is planted on his head. By him the world is judged in that which it contains: heaven and earth are under his immediate presence ('le lieu de sa face'). He rules all human beings, the pure, the race of the inhabitants of Egypt and the foreign (barbarous) people. The sun goes round according to his purpose, who also directs the wind, the river, the fluids, the wood of living plants and all vegetable nature. As the god of seeds, he is the giver of all vegetation, and of the precious *kufi:* he brings forth abundance and dispenses it to all the earth. Mankind are all in raptures, their feelings (bowels) are delighted, their hearts are full of joy, because of the lord of supplications. Every one adores his bounty: sweet is his love in us; his tenderness surrounds the heart; great is his love in all the feelings (bowels).

"We render justice to the son of Isis: his enemy falls beneath his fury, and the fautor of iniquity at the sound of his voice: the violent is hastening to his end: the son of Isis, the avenger of his father, is close by him.

"Sacred and beneficent are his titles: fear (or veneration) finds his place: his laws command immutable respect: the way is open: the footpaths are open: the worlds are both contented:

---

[1] See Plutarch, *De Isid. et Osirid.* c. XVI.

evil flies before him : and with him as her lord the peaceful earth is waxing fruitful. Justice is established by its lord, who menaces iniquity.

" Delicious is thy heart, O Únnefer (revealer of good), son of Isis! He has assumed the crown of the upper region : the title of his father is recognised for him in the great dwelling-place of Seb. He is Phra when he speaks, he is Thoth in his writings. The divine chiefs are satisfied.

" That which thy father Seb ordained for thee, let it be done according to his word."

Reserving the more ethical aspects both of this and other kindred hymns for independent consideration, it is first of some importance to remark, that the Osiris-group, as here depicted, consisting of Seb and Nut, of Isis and Osiris, together with the offspring of the latter pair, ('Horus, the child'), can scarcely have originated in the deification of purely Egyptian nature. In the present stage of the great mythe, there is no disposition, for example, to identify Osiris with the river Nile. His throne is still exalted high above the heavens : the sun itself is the majestic symbol of his universal sovereignty ; from thence he looks resplendent and complacent like the monarch of this sublunary world. He dies indeed, as in the later version of the story, and Isis,[1] sorrowing and indignant, searches for him in the double character

---

[1] ' Demeter was naturally identified with the Egyptian goddess [Isis]. As Isis bewailed the lost Osiris, so Demeter bewailed the lost Persephone. The sorrows of the bereaved mother and the widowed wife are, of all human sorrows, the deepest and the most hopeless. Unable to find consolation on earth, the sufferer yearns after heavenly sympathy, seeks and surely finds, among the objects of her worship, one who has borne the like afflictions, and is prompt to pity and to redress. Thus, if the comparison may be made without irreverence and without offence, the Isis and Demeter of Paganism were shadows which suffering humanity created for its comfort, in anticipation of the perfect type which it afterwards found in the Mater Dolorosa.' Clark's *Peloponnesus*, p. 37.

CHAP. I. of spouse and sister, and on finding him conducts his funeral obsequies. Here also he comes forth resuscitated on the mundane theatre of being, in the person of his royal son and representative, who therefore bears the sacred name Osiris. Yet in all such highly coloured pictures there are wanting not a few of those distinctive touches, which had afterwards, as we shall see, connected the Osirian mythus with the empire of the Pharaohs and localised it more completely in the Valley of the Nile.

Main ideas embodied in Osiris-worship.

The primitive worship of all objects like Osiris may be contemplated under two aspects, differing somewhat from each other, but incapable of any rigorous or formal separation. That worship seems to be in some localities directly *solar*. Fortunes of Osiris have been interwoven or identified with those of the great orb of day. His votaries have an eye exclusively to periodic motions of the sun and the vicissitudes of the seasons; not so much in reference to the increase or the decrease of his luminous functions, as to seeming changes in his fructifying, fertilising power. In winter he appears to the imagination of the worshipper as languishing and dying; and all nature, ceasing to put forth her buds and blossoms, is believed to suffer with him: while at other seasons of the year the majesty of this great king of heaven is reasserted in the vivifying of creation and the gladdening of the human heart. There is an annual resurrection of all nature; for the sun-god is himself returning from the under-world,— the region of the dead. Or if we study the same representation in its more *telluric* aspect, what is there depicted as a mourning for Osiris is no longer emblematic merely of prostration in the sun-god: it imports more frequently the loss of vital forces in the vegetable kingdom, as the consequence of the solstitial heat. The earth herself becomes the principal sufferer; and the cause of all her passionate and despairing lamentations is the influence that dries up the fountains of her own vitality.

Now which ever be adjudged the primitive form, or the correct interpretation, of this old Osirian mythe, we must remember that, historically speaking, the substance of the mythe itself is not by any means peculiar to the Valley of the Nile. It recurs in nearly all countries bordering on the Mediterranean. It can often be directly traced to Asia, and as often to the agency of those Phœnician colonists, who, scattered thickly in the islands to the west of Syria, were importing to far distant havens, not their amber only but their civilisation and religious knowledge.[1] In the mother-country of Phœnicia,[2] the Osirian worship had its ancient counterpart in mysteries of Adonis[3] and the annual ' weeping for Tammuz,'

Parallel in the Adonis-worship of Phœnicia.

---

[1] Movers, *Die Religion und die Gottheiten der Phönizier*, pp. 12, sq. Bonn. 1841.

[2] See especially Lucian, *De Dea Syria*, c. 6 sqq. Among other curious particulars he informs us that some of the people of Byblus, at the foot of Lebanon, where the mysteries of Adonis were celebrated every year, and into which Lucian was himself initiated, were of opinion that those ceremonies had been really instituted for *Osiris*, and that he was buried in their country not in Egypt: cf. Photius, *Biblioth.* cod. 242, p. 343, ed. Bekker. In the hymn to Osiris given above, the translator has conjectured independently of all discussions like the present, that Byblus was 'the region of the tree Ner,' there mentioned (p. 260) as one residence of Osiris. Since the above was written, I find that Brugsch, in his interesting paper *Die Adonisklage und das Linoslied* (Berlin, 1852), agrees in tracing the Adonis-mythe to Asia (p. 27), and in identifying Adonis and Osiris (p. 31).

[3] *Adonis*, there can be no doubt, is identical with אֲדֹנִי 'my lord': and also equivalent to *Tammuz*, Ezek. viii. 14, in which passage

(Ezek. viii. 14). There, again, the fate of the divinity was rigorously identified with periodic changes in the aspect of external nature. The idea of an Adonis in the prime of life was the most vivid image which the Syrian mind could fashion of all fertilising and benignant powers. At length, however, the divinity sinks down oppressed and overwhelmed; his heart is pierced by some mysterious arrow: he dies, and in the sacred month, 'the month of Tammuz,' when the scorching blasts of summer are well-nigh exhausted, a large crowd of Syrian maids and matrons flock together from all quarters; they bemoan the loss of Tammuz; but their vehement ejaculations are all quickly followed by a series of impure and diabolic orgies: symptoms of returning life in nature are to them a signal for festivity as frantic as their former grief. Vitality is coming back to earth: and in its advent they perceive another 'finding' of their lost Adonis (εὕρεσις Ἀδώνιδος).

Other proofs of connexion with Phœnicia.

Nor is this the only instance of some close affinity between the old mythographers of Egypt and Phœnicia. Mingling with the other progeny of Ptah, or the Egyptian Vulcan, stand the great Cabeirian brothers,[1] whose repute and worship were extensively diffused in various provinces of the west. The word *Cabeiri* is itself immediately explainable, if we resort to the Semitic languages: for there it means the

The Cabeiri:

---

the Vulg. renders 'ecce ibi mulieres sedebant plangentes *Adonidem:*' see Gesen. *Monum. Phœn.* II. 400. Among the Greeks the close connexion with Aphrodite-worship was still more apparent.

[1] Herod. II. 51, III. 37, and above, p. 247. Their father was also called *Sadyk* or *Sydyk*, which is possibly akin to צדיק. Movers (as before, p. 652) has very naturally expressed his wonder that any one should have doubted the identity of κάβειροι and כבירים (= θεοὶ μέγαλοι): for this identity was well known to the ancients.

'Great' or 'Mighty Ones'; and thus is pointing in the same direction as the ancient dwarf-gods, which were also sacred images of Cabeiri and were venerated with a kindred fervour by the rude Phœnician pilot and the polished priest of Memphis. The Cabeiri seem to have been eight in number; or, excluding *Esmûn* ('literally eight'), that one of the fraternity who was regarded as the chief or aggregate expression for the whole, we limit them to seven; which strongly indicates, in the opinion of some writers, an original identity of the Cabeiri with the more conspicuous of the heavenly bodies.[1] In the sacred books of China the 'seven brilliant ones,' deemed worthy of peculiar homage, are the sun, the moon, and the five planets; while the planets, when regarded singly, have been made to bear the corresponding title of the 'five heavenly chiefs.'[2] The Greek had similarly his seven θεοὶ μέγαλοι, and the Persian his 'seven ministers of the highest:' examples, which appear to be suggestive of the early spread of planet-worship, if they do not absolutely prove that astronomical principles had entered largely into the construction of all mythic systems,—that of Egypt not excepted.[3]

an example of planet-worship.

---

[1] Thus Xenocrates, a Carthaginian writer (quoted by Clemens Alexand. *Cohortat. ad Gentes*, c. v. § 66), declares expressly ἑπτὰ μὲν θεοὺς εἶναι τοὺς πλανήτας; and then adds in reference to *Esmûn* (the 'eighth' of the Cabeiri, Movers, p. 651) ὄγδοον δὲ τὸν ἐξ αὐτῶν συνεστῶτα κόσμον: cf. Cicero, *De Natura Deorum*, lib. I. § 34, who also quotes Xenocrates, to the same general effect.

[2] See above, p. 42, and n. 2.

[3] Uhlemann (*Aegypt. Alter.* II. 162 sq, *Thoth*, pp. 33 sq.) is a strong supporter of the 'astronomical principle' as applied to the unriddling of Egyptian mythology: but now and then his arguments appear to me unconvincing. He finds an astronomical reason for fixing the number of the primary gods at eight and of the secondary gods at twelve. Mr. Kenrick. (I. 367, 368), with less desire of systematizing, con-

CHAP. I.

*General re-
semblances
between the
religions of
Egypt and
Phœnicia.*

Be this however as it may, there is no longer any doubt that in Phœnicia, more than the adjoining nations, we discover proofs of correspondency and contact with the Egypt of the Pharaohs. In both countries[1] the foundation of mythology is completely *ditheistic.* The superior gods are ranked in pairs according to the functions of the different sexes: while the votaries of both those systems were familiar with the notion of androgynal, or compound, deities. The Baal of the Old Phœnician found the highest symbol of his vitalising power in the great monarch of the heavenly bodies; and corresponding with this fact, the sun-god, born of chaos and elemental fire, was the most glorious deity of the Old Egyptian. Both had also kept their hold with equal firmness on a mythe in which the changing aspects of the vegetable kingdom were set forth as periodic deaths and resurrections of the highest member of their pantheon. In both countries the ascription of benignant or of other properties to stars and planets, issued first of all in the idea of some inflexible Fate, some necessary Order, and then was culminating in the theory of a *magnus annus,* at the close of which it was expected that the whole creation would be re-absorbed, or would revert at least to its original elements.

These points of contact are indeed so many and so obvious, that explorers, setting out with different objects and as different preconceptions, can hardly

---

cedes the general truth of this theory, but adds that 'it is not likely that the whole system originated in any *one* principle.'

[1] On this characteristic of the Phœnician theology, see Vol. I. pp. 94 sq.

fail to meet together in the same conclusion,—a belief that the mythologies of Egypt and Phœnicia were pervaded by the same ideas and radiated from a common centre. Which of them was actually the older system; what had been the links of intercourse by which the two were held together, we are still unable to affirm with absolute certainty or precision. If, for instance, the historical character of the 'Old Monarchy' of Egypt have been fully vindicated by recent explorations, it will follow of necessity that interchanges of religious thought were long anterior[1] to the earliest inroads of the Hyk-sos or Phœnician shepherds; and the meeting-place will consequently have to be determined by following two great lines of civilisation farther backward, to that cradle of all art and language, of all science, letters and mythology,—'the primitive land of Aram and the primitive empire in Babel.'[2]

But before I pass to a minute consideration of the *Animal-worship of Egypt :* latest phase assumed in Egypt by the mythe of Isis and Osiris, or in other words the fullest evolution of the national belief in what may fairly be entitled the historic period, it is most important to recal attention to the creed of other and still earlier settlers in the Nile-valley. When the secondary race of colonists from Asia found their way to Egypt, they encountered there a form of superstition so thoroughly rooted in the heart of the people, that in spite of the political and social changes which passed over them, it always held its ground and went on flourishing until the

---

[1] Movers, as before, p. 41, is in favour of this hypothesis, considering that the solar and stellar worship was engrafted by the influence of the Hyk-sos on the old animal-worship of the Egyptians.

[2] Bunsen, *Egypt's Place*, I. 444.

overthrow of paganism in Egypt. I am adverting to the *animal-worship* of that country; which deserves to be regarded as at once the most repulsive and most universal of its manifold superstitions. We must not suppose indeed that this idolatrous devotion to brute animals had always been unknown in other countries.

its parallels in other regions. Traces of it are detected in the primitive paganism of the Hellenic and Germanic tribes: it seems to have prevailed in every district of America,[1] where gods and other spirits were believed on some occasions to 'possess' not only all varieties of living creatures, but the very plants and stones; it had existed, and exists at present, in all negro races, and indeed wherever man continues to be awed by a belief that the divinity he worships is impersonal Power, diffused throughout the universe, and manifested in all possible types of creaturely existence.

Why so startling and extraordinary in Egypt. Yet in Egypt this zoolatry appears in such exaggerated shapes and with such monstrous adjuncts, that to trace at length the stages of its progress and the secret of its perpetuity would fill a most remarkable chapter in the history of civilisation. The contemptuous exclamations of the later Greeks and Romans, on witnessing the coexistence of abstruse philosophy and artistic beauty with the worship of brute creatures, are familiar to all persons interested in this study. An admirer and apologist of the Egyptian creed was fully conscious of the reasons which had given birth to such opprobrious criticisms; for he confesses plainly that the multitude did not stop short at merely relative worship, but adored the

[1] See for instance, Müller's *Amerik. Urrelig.* pp. 60 sq., 256 sq., 420.

animals themselves[1] (αὐτὰ τὰ ζῶα). I must not,
however, leave unquoted the remarkable passage of
Clement of Alexandria, with reference to this question, because it shews as well the sanctity with which
the animals were all invested by Egyptians, as the
feelings which zoolatry was then exciting in the
minds of most spectators whether Christian or heathen.
After dwelling on the costliness and splendour of
Egyptian temples and directing our attention to the
veil inwrought with gold by which the adytum was
curtained off from the rest of the building, he continues:[2] 'But if you pass beyond into the remotest
part of the inclosure, hastening to behold something
more worthy of your search, and seek for the image
which dwells in the temple, a *pastophorus* [shrine-
bearer], or some one else of those who minister in
sacred things, with a grave air singing a Pæan in
the Egyptian tongue, draws aside a small portion
of the veil, as if about to show us the god; and
makes us burst into a loud laugh. For the god you
sought is not there, but a cat, or a crocodile, or a
serpent sprung from the soil, or some such brute
animal, which is more suited to a cave than a temple.
The Egyptian deity appears,—a beast rolling himself on a purple coverlet!'

We might deduce the very high antiquity of this *Sacred*
practice from the fact that many of the animals so *animals:*
worshipped had been always sacred only in particular
nomes;[3] and though the final consolidation of the

---

[1] Plutarch. *De Is. et Osir.* c.
LXXI. As contrasted with the
Egyptian notions he considered
the Greeks entirely orthodox
(λέγουσιν ὀρθῶς) in their dedication of particular birds and reptiles to particular divinities.
[2] *Pædagog.* lib. III. c. 2: cf.
Juvenal. *Sat.* XV. 7.
[3] Cf. above, p. 235, n. 2.

monarchy and the comparative fusion of religious tenets which resulted from it, had secured a universal reverence for the ox, the dog, the cat, the hawk, the ibis and two kinds of fish, there was no period when, with these exceptions, sacred animals of one nome were not treated as a common article of food in others, and not liable, on every outburst of fanaticism, to be assailed with open violence or contempt.[1]

Apis.

Conspicuous at the head of the zoolatry of Egypt stands the worship of the great Memphitic bull, Apis (Hapi),[2] which is carried back, in its more elementary condition, as far as the ' 2nd dynasty.'[3] In the reign of Ramses II., the great bull is made to bear the title 'second life of Ptah,'[4]—a fact which intimates that he was then regarded as the living shrine, or incarnation, of the chief god of Memphis, and a similar exaltation is suggested in the title ' image of the soul of Osiris,'[5] which has elsewhere been awarded to him. Viewed in this light Apis was to the Egyptian worshipper a present or incarnate deity. The luxuries deemed appropriate to the highest earthly monarch were all lavished on his service. He was fed with a religious scrupulosity. He was anointed with the choicest unguents. Mates of spotless beauty were

[1] On the various theories respecting the rationale of this kind of worship, see Kenrick, II. 2 sq., Uhlemann, *Aegypt. Alt.* III. 210 sq.

[2] According to Uhlemann (p. 208), the Coptic *hap* means 'the judge' [or rather, 'judgment']; perhaps with reference to the functions of Osiris in the underworld. Of three other bulls admitted to the foremost rank of animal-worship one was Mnevis of Heliopolis, who bore the title 'the resuscitated sun.' The worship both of Apis and Mnevis extended far beyond the cities where they were especially honoured.

[3] Osburn, *Mon. Hist* I. 247.

[4] *Revue des Deux Mondes,* as before, p. 1074. On the alleged preternaturalness of the birth of Apis, through the agency of a generific beam of light, see Herod. III. 28, and Mr. Blakesley's note.

[5] Plut. *De Is. et Osir.* c. xx.

provided for him.[1]   At death he was embalmed and
swathed : his funeral was performed with a magnificence unrivalled in the case of men : a sumptuous
monument which still attracts the admiration of all
artists was erected in his honour.   And since mortals
after death were thought to be in some mysterious
way united with Osiris, the dead Apis also was
entitled for this cause *Osiris-Apis* ('Οσοράπις), or
Serapis;[2] and as such was worshipped with supreme
devotion in the interval which elapsed before the
birth or 'manifestation' of a new calf,—the vehicle
to which the soul of the departed Apis was believed
to be immediately transferred.

While animal-worship had been thus amalgamated
more and more with adoration of the elements and of
spirits ruling in the heavenly bodies, the important
change to which I have before alluded had been also
passing over the complexion of the mythe which
centred in the greatest pair of national divinities.
There might indeed be no express intention either
on the part of priest or people to relinquish the conclusions of the old mythology.   In Osiris they might
recognise, as heretofore, the ultimate source of all
vitality, and as such might find the highest and most

[1] Wilkinson and others have
denied that still worse abominations were connected with the
animal-worship of the Egyptians
(see Diod. I. 85 ; Herod. II. 46) ;
but allusions like that in Lev.
xviii. 23 agree too closely with
the statements of the Greek historians : cf. Döllinger, pp. 226, 227.

[2] That this is the true account
of Serapis has been lately proved
by M. Mariette, *Mémoire sur le
Sérapéum,* to whose labours Lep-

sius was looking hopefully when
he wrote his own Appendix on
' Serapis' in the *Götterkreis* &c.
p. 213.   Respecting the Greek
version of the fetching of the god
Serapis from Sinope by order of
Ptolemy Soter, and the consequence of identifying Serapis with
the Greek Dionysus, see Bunsen,
Egypt's Place, I. 431, and Maury,
Revue des Deux Mondes, as before,
p. 1073.

adequate symbol of his functions in the great orb of day. They might continue also to associate Isis with him as the counterpart of his productive powers, and discerning an appropriate emblem of that goddess in the moon or in the earth, might still, in words, attribute all the higher phenomena of life to the harmonious action of these two divinities. But such is far from being a true account of the religion of the many, or the popular theology[1] of Egypt, in the later Pharaonic period. Owing to a general want of fixity in men's religious tenets, the ingredients of the mythe had been so altered, its area so contracted, its connexion with the world at large so broken and obscured as to have rendered it an almost novel version of the primitive story. The Egyptian mind is seen descending more and more entirely from the worship of the heavenly bodies to the contemplation of the marvellous agencies at work in its immediate neighbourhood. In earlier times Osiris was enthroned upon the sun; but now the Nile itself is substituted for that glorious luminary. Then the spouse of the great sun-god was the mother and the nurse of universal vegetation; now she is the single land of Egypt fructified and gladdened by the Nile. Then Osiris was a nature-god, a verbal representative of forces active in the varied processes of nature: now he has been moulded into the great civilising hero of Mizraim, binding men together in a fixed society, teaching agriculture, and subduing nations not by

---

[1] Thus Plutarch (*De Is. et Osir.* c. xxxiii) carefully distinguishes between the people and the more enlightened of the priests: Οἱ δὲ σοφώτεροι τῶν ἱερέων, οὐ μόνον τὸν Νεῖλον Ὄσιριν καλοῦσιν . . . ἀλλὰ Ὄσιριν μὲν ἁπλῶς ἅπασαν τὴν ὑγροποιὸν ἀρχὴν καὶ δύναμιν, αἰτίαν γενέσεως καὶ σπέρματος οὐσίαν νομίζοντες.

force alone but by the charms of eloquence and music.
Then his death was the suspension of all vital power
without the least distinction of locality; now it coincides precisely with that season of the year in Egypt
when decay and barrenness are everywhere ascendant
through the Valley of the Nile.

The reason of this gradual localising of the story, *Reason of*
—this confusion, one might call it, of the sun with *these modi-*
fications.
the Egyptian river,—is hardly to be sought in the
prevailing fancy that the Nile and sun were wont
to meet together at the western horizon, and after
plunging down into the under-world came forth again
together from the caverns of the east.[1] An explanation, simple in itself and serving also to account for
other kindred stories, is suggested by the fact that
the Egyptian had been gradually tempted to associate
every genial, fertilising power in nature with the
annual overflow of his great river. In one meaning
of the phrase Herodotus was right, when he declared
that Egypt is 'the gift of the Nile.'[2] 'My river is
mine own' was the ungodly boast ascribed to Egypt
in the vision of the Hebrew prophet (Ezek. xxix.
3, 9,) 'my river is mine own, and I have made it for
myself.' 'Turn the course of the Nile,' it has been
said, 'and not one blade of vegetation would ever
arise in Egypt.' And the more intelligent of modern
travellers, no longer open to the potent witcheries
which nature once exerted on mankind, but recognising the almighty hand of God Himself throughout
this 'annual miracle of mercy,' are still awestruck
by the grand phenomena presented to them as the
river bursts afresh into its ancient channels. 'All

---

[1] Osburn, I. 420.   [2] Herod. II. 5.

nature shouts for joy. The men, the children, the buffaloes, gambol in its refreshing waters; the broad waves sparkle with shoals of fish, and fowl of every wing flutter over them in clouds. Nor is this jubilee of nature confined to the higher orders of creation. The moment the sand becomes moistened by the approach of the fertilising waters, it is literally alive with insects innumerable."[1]

Other members introduced into the Osiris-group. Nor are these the only changes introduced into the primitive mythe of Isis and Osiris. Though the mother of both is still Rhea (Nut or Nutpe), doubts have been suggested touching the true name of their father; while the chief progenitors of the gods are now distinctly represented as giving birth to a second pair, which rank in some respects upon a level with the former. Set, or Typhon, is the brother of Osiris;[2] and, accompanied by his spouse and sister Nephthys, he is placed in a position of direct antagonism to the benevolent divinities, to Isis and Osiris, and especially to the younger Horus, their child and champion; while a definite character has also been attributed to Thoth,[3] the ibis-headed Hermes of Egyptian worship, the inventor of letters,

[1] Osburn, I. 13.

[2] Preternaturally born, however, Plutarch says (c. XII); μὴ καιρῷ, μηδὲ κατὰ χώραν, ἀλλ' ἀναρρήξαντα πληγῇ διὰ τῆς πλευρᾶς ἐξαλλέσθαι: cf. above, p. 60, n. 1.

[3] The place of this ibis-headed god, 'lord of Shmun' (Hermopolis), appears to be in what is called the secondary series of Egyptian divinities. Bunsen styles him (I. 393) the 'most important of all the Cabeiri' (corresponding to *Esmûn*, above, p. 267. As connected with the Osiris-group he is sometimes entitled 'begotten of Osiris' himself; but the relation indicated in the text is that which he sustains far more frequently. Mr. Kenrick observes of Thoth (*Anc. Egypt,* I. 428), that 'with a name nearly similar, *Taut,* he appears also in the Phœnician history, and in the same character of the inventor of letters.'

the depository of primeval wisdom, 'the president of the reasoning faculty,' the teacher, counsellor, and secretary of Osiris himself.

The greatest of the difficulties experienced as we analyse these fresh developments of the Egyptian mythology is connected with the origin and import of the evil-minded Typhon.   Some of the chief names by which he was at first distinguished are *Set, Seti, Sutech;* but in the course of modern explorations, it has come to light that he was also identified[1] at least on one inscription with the great Phœnician Bel or Baal: and in confirmation of this interesting fact we are enabled to establish that when the Hyk-sos made their grand descent on Egypt, they had recognised in Typhon their own national divinity, had chosen him for their sole leader, and had fought and conquered always under his immediate patronage.[2]   With their ascendancy in Egypt, Typhon also had become supreme.

Particular inquiry respecting Set or Typhon.

It is quite possible, indeed, that in far earlier times[3] he held a high position in some districts as the

Gradual modification of his character.

[1] See Lepsius, *Götterkreis* (as before), p. 206, who adds: 'Dieser Begriff des *Set* oder *Sutech* als des ausserägyptischen Gottes dürfte überhaupt den Schlüssel zu der räthselhaften Natur desselben und seiner zu verschiedenen Zeiten verschiedenen Auffassung darbieten.' This inquiry has since been ably followed out in the *Revue Archéologique*, XIIe année, pp. 257 sq. The original connexion between Baal and Typhon may, I think, be also traceable in the compound Baal-Zephon (צְפֹן בַּעַל) of Exod. xiv. 2, 9, Numb. xxxiii. 7 ; which may again have been identical with the Ἄϐαρις or Ἄϐαρις

of Manetho and Josephus; for this border-city of the Hyk-sos, identified by Lepsius with Pelusium (? *Pelishtim*, city of the Philistines), is described by them as πόλις κατὰ τὴν θεολογίαν ἄνωθεν Τυφώνιος. There is, however, some difficulty in ascertaining the original relation of Typhon to the hideous monsters of the primitive world, whom Greek writers, from Homer downwards, designated Τυφάων, Τυφωεύς, Τυφώς.

[2] Brugsch, quoted by Döllinger, pp. 421, 422.

[3] Lepsius, p. 204, Bunsen, I. 426.

elemental god who struggled periodically with the elder Horus, in the conflict ever waged by different atmospheric agencies, as light and darkness, rain and drought, production and decomposition.[1]　Studied under this peculiar aspect, Typhon may have seemed to the Egyptian of the older period a terrific but not always a malevolent divinity; just as Nephthys, 'mistress of the house,' and female counterpart of Typhon, was at first almost identical with Isis, and to some extent associated with kindly and maternal properties.　But after the expulsion of the hated Hyk-sos, Typhon was no longer tolerated in a single canton of the Nile-valley: his name was chiselled out of all the monuments,[2] where it had previously been ranked with those of kings and of superior gods: and in the future period of Egyptian history, Typhon was the synonym for 'evil genius'; he became the great personification of corrupting and disorganising forces, the author of disease, of impotence, of death itself.　His symbol was a human form, surmounted by the head of some fabulous animals; while the brutes especially 'possessed' by him were those which the Egyptian either feared or hated, as the incarnations of stupidity, of malice, or of violence—the ass, the crocodile, the hippopotamus, and the bear.

Explanation of the ultimate form assumed by him.　I think, however, that the latest form assumed by this Typhonic mythe admits of easy explanation, as soon as we have learned to see distinctly imaged forth in it the main peculiarities of Egyptian nature. While Osiris was the fertilising river, the fruitful land of Egypt was his spouse.　But Typhon his

---

[1] *Revue Archéol.* as before.
[2] *Ibid.* pp. 267, 268: cf. above,

p. 256, n. 2, for a similar attempt to suppress Ammon-worship.

malignant brother, born like him of Rhea, was the Chap. I.
enemy of Egypt, and as such allied with its mischances whether physical or political.[1] At one time
he is nothing but the sea, which swallows up the
waters of the Nile and circumscribes the empire of
the Pharaohs; but more commonly the Typhon whom
they dreaded was the glowing, scorching, and mephitic
blast, the south-wind from the desert. For this
reason Nephthys, who had once been merely a personification of the world unseen, as Isis of the visible
hemisphere, is now transmuted into the desert itself,
the birthplace of all joylessness and utter destitution;
thus completing the dark series of antagonisms which
parted Egypt from surrounding nations, and which
formed the very essence of the popular theology.

The reader will be now in a position to appreciate *Latest form*
the full-blown story of Osiris, which I give with *of the Osiris-*
some occasional condensation in the words of Plu- *myth.*
tarch's treatise;[2] written, it should be remembered,
to the chief of the Thyades at Delphi, who herself
had been initiated by her parents into the Egyptian
mysteries:

"Rhea [Nut] having secretly united herself with Cronos
[Seb], the Sun, who was indignant, laid upon her a curse, that
she should not bring forth in any year or month. Hermes
[Thoth], however, who was also a lover of Rhea, playing at
dice with the moon, took away the seventieth[3] part of each

---

[1] In this connexion it is worth
remarking that Typhon when ex-
pelled from Egypt was believed
to have fled on the back of an ass
for seven days. καὶ σωθέντα γεν-
νῆσαι παῖδας Ἱεροσόλυμον καὶ
Ἰουδαῖον (Plutarch, *De Is. et
Osir.* c. XXXI): cf. Lepsius, as

before, p. 210.

[2] *De Iside et Osiride,* c. XII—
c. XIX.

[3] A round number for 72, the
fifth part of 360 : cf. LXX as applied to the Seventy-Two trans-
lators of the Hebrew Bible.

CHAP. I. period of daylight, and from these made five new days, which are the ἐπαγόμεναι, or intercalary days. On each of these five days Rhea bore a child. On the first was born Osiris, the son of the Sun, at whose birth a voice was heard proclaiming that the Lord of all was coming to light: or, according to another version, a certain Pamyles drawing water, at Thebes, heard a voice from the temple of Jupiter, which charged him to proclaim that a great and beneficent king Osiris was born. On this account Pamyles was intrusted by Cronos with the nursing of Osiris, and hence the festival of the Pamylia, and a kind of *phallephoria* [as in the Bacchic orgies]. On the second day was born Arueris, son of the Sun, whom they call Apollo and the Elder Horus. On the third was born Typhon, not in the usual course, but bursting out with a sudden stroke from the side of Rhea. On the fourth day was born Isis ;[1] on the fifth Nephthys, who was called Teleute and Aphrodite,[2] and according to some, Nike. Osiris and Arueris were sprung from the Sun, but Isis from Hermes, and Typhon and Nephthys from Cronos......This last pair were married to each other. Isis and Osiris united themselves even before their birth, and their son was called, according to some,[3] Arueris, the Elder Horus, and the Apollo of the Greeks.

"Osiris being king at once proceeded to civilise the Egyptians; he taught them agriculture; he enacted laws for them; he taught them to worship the gods, and afterwards traversed the world on the same civilising errand, subduing the nations not by force but by persuasion, and especially the charms of music and poetry: on which account the Greeks concluded that he was identical with Dionysus.[4] In his absence Isis adminis-

---

[1] The text of Plutarch adds ἐν πανύγροις ('in very damp places'); but the reading is doubtful.

[2] This title brings Nephthys into parallelism with Astarte, the female counterpart of Baal, and the Aphrodite of Semitic tribes: see Vol. I. p. 98.

[3] The common story was, however, that the child of Isis and Osiris was the Younger Horus, or else Harpocrates.

[4] The conception of Osiris has probably an historical basis in the conquests ascribed to Sesostris; just as the Mexican mythe of Quetzalcoatl (above, pp. 151 sq.) had embodied the traditions of the populace respecting the labours of some true philanthropist. In Diodor. I. 19, it is affirmed that the civilising expeditions of Osiris extended ἕως Ἰνδῶν καὶ τοῦ πέρατος τῆς οἰκουμένης: and it is

tered the regency so wisely, that Typhon was unable to create any disturbance; but on his return he conspired against Osiris with seventy-two men and the Ethiopian queen Aso;[1] and having secretly obtained the measure of Osiris, caused a coffer splendidly adorned to be brought into the banqueting-room, promising to give it to the guest whom it should fit. Osiris put himself into it to make the trial; and Typhon and his associates immediately pegged and soldered down the case, and set it afloat on the river. It floated into the sea through the Tanitic mouth, which on that account Egyptians of later days regarded with abhorrence. These things were done on the seventeenth of the month Athyr, in which the Sun enters Scorpion,[2] and in the twenty-eighth year of the reign, or as some said of the age, of Osiris. The Pans and Satyrs who lived about Chemmis hearing of this tragedy and being agitated by it, sudden terrors of the multitude acquired the name of *panics;* while Isis cut off one lock of her hair and put on mourning, at the place where she first heard the news, which accordingly obtained the name *Coptos*[3]......Wandering to and fro disconsolate she finally met with some children who told her whither the coffin had floated, and hence the Egyptians deem the words of children to carry with them a prophetic power......She also learned that Osiris had inadvertently united himself with her sister Nephthys......and went in search of the child which had

---

[1] 'The co-operation of a queen of Ethiopia in the plot against his life is significant of the national hostility of that people against the Egyptians, and the prevalence of female dominion:' Kenrick, I. 413.

[2] The 17th of Athyr would correspond with the middle of November (1st Athyr = Oct. 28); and therefore the disappearance of Osiris took place in autumn, just before the sowing-season of the Egyptians, and at the time when darkness was proceeding on its triumph through the months of winter.

further worthy of remark as intimating a certain affinity between the mythe of Osiris and the history of Sesostris, that the latter on his return from his foreign conquests narrowly escaped death by fire at the hands of his brother. (Herod. II. 107).

[3] The modern *Keft*, the principal city of the nome Coptites in the Upper Thebaid. It is noticeable that the same Greek word κόπτεσθαι 'to lament for the dead,' was of such ill omen in the mind of a Greek, that Herodotus (II. 132, 171) shrank from naming Osiris, a deity analogous to the Apollo of his own traditions and a deity of the upper regions, in connexion with it or with a ceremony that indicated woe.

been put away as soon as it was born through fear of Typhon. This she found after great trouble by the guidance of a dog, who afterwards became her champion and attendant, with the name Anubis......

"She now ascertained that the chest had been floated as far as Byblus [in Phœnicia] and cast ashore, and that the plant *erica* had grown up about it and entirely enclosed it in the trunk, so that the king of the country, amazed at the vast proportions of the tree, gave orders for it to be cut down, and made of it a pillar[1] to support the roof of his palace. Isis guided, as they say, by a divine monitor came to Byblus,[2] and sitting down at a well, wretched and in tears, was there accosted by the queen's maidens, and on giving proofs of supernatural virtue, was entrusted with the nursing of the infant prince. She fed this child by giving it her finger to suck : she likewise put him every night into the fire to consume those portions of him which were mortal, and transforming herself into a swallow, hovered round the pillar and bemoaned her widowhood. At length, on making herself known, she was allowed to carry off the pillar, and taking out the enclosed sarcophagus of Osiris, she set sail for Egypt. Arriving at a desert place she opened the coffin and embraced the corpse of her husband with bitter tears......She brought it now to Egypt, and while going on a visit to her son Horus, who was being nursed at Butos, she deposited the corpse in secrecy. But Typhon, hunting by moonlight, happened to meet with it, and recognising the body of Osiris, he divided it into fourteen pieces, which he scattered about the country.[3] Isis, on learning this set out in quest of the remains, sailing over the marshy districts in a *baris*, made of papyrus, and as soon as she found one of the members she buried it there. All were ultimately recovered but one (τὸ αἰδοῖον); for it had been thrown into the river and devoured by the fishes, *lepidotus, phagrus,* and *oxyrhynchus;* which were

---

[1] Here again, as Mr. Kenrick observes (I. 413) we have an historical allusion, *viz.* to the use of Osiride pillars in Egyptian architecture.

[2] On the mythological affinities here implied, see above, p. 265,

n. 2.

[3] This story of the discerption of the body was meant to explain the circumstance 'that the honour of his interment was claimed by so many different places.' Kenrick, I. 413).

afterwards held in abomination. In the room of it, she made an emblem, to which the Egyptians still pay honour (in the φαλληφόρια[1]). Osiris afterwards came back from the under-world, and Horus, aided by the presence of his father, carried out the plan for vanquishing Typhon, and after a fight of many days took him prisoner. Isis, however, loosed his fetters and let him go; at which Horus was so enraged that he tore off his mother's diadem; but Hermes [Thoth] supplied its place by a helmet in the shape of a cow's head......In two more battles Typhon was completely mastered. Harpocrates, being sprung from the union of Isis and Osiris after the death of the latter, his birth was untimely and he had a weakness in his lower limbs."[2]

We should form however an imperfect judgment of the Old Egyptian theory of religion, if we failed to contemplate it also from a different point of view. As hitherto regarded, the chief god Osiris was either confounded with the elemental processes of nature, or, according to the best appreciation of him, was engaged in regulating natural agencies for the pecu-liar benefit of the land of Egypt. But existing side by side with this conception of Osiris was another, more exalted and more ethical; implying in its turn a larger measure of religious sensibility. The fore-most member of the pantheon was to many of the

Ethical aspects of the religion of Egypt.

Osiris, as moral go-vernor.

---

[1] In this feature of the mythe we easily discover the same desire to give a quasi-historical account of an existing usage. Phallic em-blems are very common in the earlier mythology of Egypt, as in the later Siva-worship of Hindú-stán: the object being in both cases to symbolise the generative and reproductive power of nature. This tendency in Egypt was per-haps most fully manifested in *Khem* (the Pan of Herodotus,

ii. 46), who became a kind of Priapeian Osiris.

[2] Plutarch's observation at the end of the mythe implies that a kind of reverence for the great Egyptian divinities induced him to suppress other particulars still more revolting : Ταῦτα σχεδόν ἐστι τοῦ μύθου τὰ κεφάλαια τῶν δυσφημοτάτων ἐξαιρεθέντων· οἷόν ἐστι τὸ περὶ τὸν Ὥρου διαμελισ-μὸν καὶ τὸν Ἴσιδος ἀποκεφαλισμόν. (c. xx).

Egyptians a personification of the good principle. As such, in his own person, or by means of the invincible spear of Horus, he had pierced and crushed the serpent Apap.[1] He was worshipped, therefore, as the friend of right, the enemy and vanquisher of wrong, the author of the blessings which now circulate among the living, and the judge and sovereign of the dead. Osiris was the 'sun-god' in the very loftiest meaning of such phraseology. Exalted far above this sublunary sphere, his piercing vision, as he rode majestic through the heavens, had made him cognisant of human actions; and returning to the under-world in which he was believed to join his mother, and to reign supreme, the Pluto of Mizraim, with no further dread[2] of the malignant breath of Typhon, he presided over a judicial process which should fix the lot of all Egyptians in the world beyond the grave.

It is desirable to consider this more ethical aspect of the creed of Egypt in two separate divisions, as affecting human conduct, (1) in the present, and (2) in the future lifetime of each individual member.

1. Now it is certain that in spite of the monstrosity pervading the whole structure of his mytho-

---

[1] See *Revue Archéol.* xive année, p. 194; Kenrick, I. 421. The letting loose of Typhon by the woman, Isis (Plutarch, c. xix. where also it is noticeable that an ὄφις appears), might not unnaturally be construed as giving free scope to the powers of evil, and might so have a remote relation to the sacred narrative of the Fall. Movers (pp. 522 sq.) distinctly connects the Typhon both of Phœnicia and Egypt with the Hebrew צִפְעוֹנִי, 'a basilisk,' or 'viper,'

e. g. Is. xi. 8; lix. 5; Jerem. viii. 17: and although in the Egyptian mythology the ill effects produced by Typhon were mainly viewed as *physical*, there was certainly no absolute limitation to that class of evils, (cf. Plutarch, c. L.).

[2] 'In dem Todtenkulte trat *Set* erklärlicher Weise mehr zurück. Daher fehlt er in den Götterlisten der Königsgräber; *im Reiche des unteren Osiris hatte er keine Macht.*' Lepsius, *Götterkreis,* &c. p. 207.

logical system, the Egyptian, as compared with some
of his more western neighbours, was preeminently
religious. He had ever borne the yoke of a most
irksome superstition with alacrity befitting a far
worthier cause. The time, the zeal, the treasure he
would lavish on the building of his multitudinous
temples, or the sustentation and the sepulture of
sacred animals, was constant proof of his intense
devotion to the service of his gods ; nay, rather than
devour or damage one such animal he was content
to suffer all the worst extremities of destitution or
disgrace. He seemed again to be continually oppressed by a conviction that divine or supernatural
powers were everywhere diffused around him. Nothing is more clearly traceable on papyri which accompany the mummies of the Old Egyptian than his
firm belief in the reality of the world invisible,—belief
which generating awe and dread became in him the
ruling sentiment that hourly cast its shadow on his
pathway and that haunted him at every turn.[1] The

---

[1] Osburn. *Mon. Hist.* I. 411.
Herodotus (II. 37) begins his description of the ritual observances
with the statement : Θεοσεβέες
δὲ περισσῶς ἐόντες μάλιστα πάντων ἀνθρώπων : cf. Döllinger (p.
406), who affirms 'Ihre religiösen
Gefühle waren wärmer, zäher
zugleich und leidenschaftlicher
als die der Griechen und Römer.'
On this question as to the general
temperament of the Egyptians, it
is curious to observe that modern
writers differ from each other *toto
cœlo*. Thus, the author of the
article *Ægyptus* in Smith's *Dic-
tionary* considers the old Egyptians a serious people, of a gloomy,
meditative genius : and finds in
this circumstance an explanation
of the fact that the whole of
Egypt, after the introduction of
the Gospel, was dotted over with
convents which gave birth to the
wildest Lives of Saints. Whereas
Sir J. G. Wilkinson in his last
work (*Ancient Egyptians*, pp. 7
sq. p. 13) affirms the very contrary : 'They were the reverse of
a serious people ; and while their
philosophers gave their attention
to grave abstruse studies, the rest
of the community appreciated a
merry life, and were remarkable
for a love of excitement, quite
consistent with the scenes of buf-
foonery and the talent for caricature so often displayed in the
paintings.'

warmth of his religious feelings was betrayed, and may have also been augmented and embittered, by diversities of worship in the different nomes and by collisions more or less fanatic,[1] which arose from such diversities. It has been urged indeed that the Egyptian was not always of a temper so morose and gloomy as some writers had formerly imputed to him; and perhaps there is sufficient ground for this correction; but in reference to the dominant genius of the popular religion, nothing in the ancient world can be regarded as more sombre and dejected. The one national air of Egypt was the Maneros,[2]—a threnody upon the death of Osiris. While the tourist could remark that the Hellenic gods were fond of gaiety and dances, those of Egypt were most gratified by demonstrations of an opposite kind, by dirges and a flood of tears. At banquets even it was not unusual to send round a small model of a mummy, to remind the guest in his more joyous moments that his tenure of the present life was fleeting and precarious.[3]

Ignorance and abject superstitions of the many. Whether this peculiar state of feeling was a product of peculiar ignorance on sacred subjects we may still be unable to determine with absolute precision; but there seems good reason for concluding that in no country of the ancient world, with the exception of India,[4] were the chasms so numerous and so wide between the different orders of society. Egypt was the land of esoteric dogmas and exclusive institutions. Egypt was the home and nursery of that spirit of

---

[1] Kenrick, ii. 26.

[2] Explained by Brugsch (*Die Adonisklage*, p. 24) as = *mââ-ne-hra*, 'come to the house,' 'come home again,'—the passionate cry of the 'sister,' 'spouse,' and 'mother' of Osiris.

[3] See other examples collected in Döllinger, p. 444.

[4] See Vol. I. pp. 204 sq.

eclecticism which had promoted the formation of the early 'Gnostic sects; and Egypt was accordingly a stronghold of the stoutest opposition which was offered to the primitive heralds of the Gospel by the cold and haughty advocates of human inequality. The natural consequence had been that in no country were the masses kept in greater darkness or more intellectually degraded.[1] Much as Plutarch wished to prove that the original aim of their mythology was high and elevating,[2] he was driven to acknowledge the failure of the system when his eye was fixed on some of its more popular developments. 'The Egyptians,' he wrote,[3] 'at least, the greater part of them, by adoring the animals themselves, and caring for them as for gods, have crammed their ritual full with subjects of laughter and opprobrium. Nor is this the least evil which results from their stupidity. A dangerous notion is implanted, which drives the weak and simple-minded into the worst forms of superstition, and the shrewder and more daring into atheism and beast-like speculations.'

So exclusively was any higher knowledge which they might possess confined to one special order, that the Pharaoh, as we saw already, was esteemed but little more than a divine administrator of the kingdom in the service of the other priests.[4] He ruled as the chief member of the sacerdotal college;

Power and privileges of the sacerdotal order.

---

[1] Wilkinson, who may be fairly reckoned among the numerous apologists of Egyptian heathenism, avows, notwithstanding, that 'the people were left in utter ignorance of the fundamental doctrines of their religion,' (2nd ser. i. 164); and that 'every one was not only permitted, but encouraged, to believe the real sanctity of the idol, and the actual existence of the god whose figure he beheld,' (p. 175).

[2] *De Isid. et Osir.* c. VIII.

[3] *Ibid.* c. LXXI.

[4] Cf. Uhlemann, *Thoth*, p. 11.

Chap. I. while to them had been committed not a few of the most onerous functions of the state. They were the legislators, and the judges, as well as the physicians, the astronomers, the architects, and the instructors of the youth ; and only through their instrumentality as organs of the gods, or as exponents of the will of holy animals, could secrets be extracted from the world invisible, or answers be returned to the inquiries of the doubting and desponding.

Existence of a regular cultus. We are no longer, it is true, at liberty to urge, like many of our predecessors, that Egyptians were all rigorously distributed into a series of hereditary classes,[1] corresponding to the permanent castes of India after she had been completely Bráhmanised. No *absolute* division of this kind appears to have been taught in reference even to the present life; while in the future it was held that all, on passing to the grand tribunal of Osiris would be placed in a position of complete equality. The fact, however, still remains indisputable that class-distinctions did exist with more than usual tenacity, and that the power of the Egyptian priest had always been enor-

Priesthood. mous. There was no period in the history of Egypt, as inscribed upon her monumental records, when such priesthood was not duly organised,[2] and when the hopes and fears of the remaining classes were not vitally connected with its absolute ascendency.

[1] Wilkinson has abandoned his former views on this subject (see *Ancient Egyptians*, p. 129), chiefly, it would seem, in consequence of M. Ampère's paper in the *Revue Archéologique*, v année, pp. 405 sq., where the monuments are shewn to indicate that there was no invariable custom nor any rigorous law, prescribing that the religious, military, or civil functions should in Egypt always be assumed as the result of family-inheritance.

[2] See Uhlemann, *Ægypt. Alt.* II. 182 sq. ; *Thoth*, pp. 89 sq.

The system thus compacted and administered was full of gorgeous and punctilious rites; the temples, *Temples.* glittering with a vast profusion of gold and foreign marbles and distributed into holy and more holy places (as the πρόναος, the σηκός, and the ἄδυτον), were thickly planted[1] in all cantons of the Nile-valley; festivals,[2] arranged throughout the year ac- *Festivals.* cording to a systematic calendar, gave rise to frequent pilgrimages and processions; while the oracles[3] *Oracles.* of Egypt long enjoyed the highest reputation, and, like 'mysteries' of which she was acknowledged the inventor, furnished models to the imitative genius of her western neighbours.

It is always in the sacrificial rites of a religious *Doctrine of* system that we trace the consciousness in man of *sacrifice.*

---

[1] *Ibid.* II. 188 sq., where attention is drawn to some resemblances between the arrangements of Egyptian temples and the Hebrew tabernacle: but see Bahr, *Symbolik*, I. 218. The magnificence of the Egyptian temples is explained at once by the enormous gifts and revenues conferred upon them by some of the more powerful monarchs. Thus the *Annals of Thothmes* III. (of the 18th dynasty) translated by Mr. Birch, in the *Archæologia* (1853), Vol. XXXV. pp. 116 sq., are full of instances in which the bounty of the prince was lavished on the great temple of Ammon-Ra, at Thebes, as the result of aid afforded to him by his tutelar deity during a successful attack on certain places in Palestine. 'Slaves, probably negroes, to open the doors; three fortresses of the Ruten [the Canaanitish enemy],—just as the Lake Mœris and the town of Anthylla supplied the pin-money of the queens of Egypt; linen of various sorts, gold, silver, lapis lazuli, copper, brass, iron, lead, colours for the monuments, bread, loaves of various kinds of food, cattle, geese, gazelles of different kinds, incense, wine, frankincense, offerings to the statues, to the obelisks; fields, meadows, and ponds, stocked with cattle, water-fowl, and pigeons, complete the long list of donations' (p. 154). Many of these provisions went for the daily banquet of the god and of his priests, which took place at sunset.

[2] Herodotus, who thinks that all religious pilgrimages and processions were devised in Egypt, describes six of the principal feasts (II. 59 sq.); but these were a small portion only of such public celebrations: see Uhlemann, *Aegypt. Alt.* II. 200 sq.

[3] *Ibid.* pp. 216 sq. From Herodotus (II. 57, 58) we also learn that the method of divining from victims (τῶν ἱρῶν ἡ μαντική) was of Egyptian origin.

Christ and other Masters.

his dependence on the powers above him, or of his estrangement from the source of life and blessedness. And Egypt, as we might anticipate, is no exception to this universal law. There, also, to omit the merely eucharistic[1] class of sacrifices, man had ever indicated his persuasion that he was no longer what he ought to be, nor what he knew he might eventually become. He felt that one or all the gods were standing to him in the posture of hostility, and therefore trusted by piacular offerings to avert the outburst of their indignation and alleviate the burden of his sin. With this conception, animal sacrifices seem to have been offered on Egyptian altars during the whole of the historic period. 'Without shedding of blood there is no remission.' Here had culminated the idea of heathen as of other sacrifices:[2] and in the case of Egypt it was put on record that the offerer sometimes manifested more than common sensibility as to the thoughts which underlie this branch of his symbolic ritual. He was accustomed to bewail the sufferings of the victim he had stretched upon the altar; and when it sank beneath the sacrificial knife he turned and smote himself.[3] A prayer[4] was also offered on more critical occasions that 'if any calamity were about to befall either the sacrificer or the land

---

[1] Cf. above, Vol. I. pp. 322 sq. Such offerings as wine, oil, or other liquid, or any single gift, as a necklace, a bouquet of flowers, a bunch of vegetables, and the like (Wilkinson, 2nd ser. II. 338) come under this description. They were generally the expressions of gratitude for benefits received, or, as in India, may have sometimes been connected with a fancy that the minor gods at least were actually delighted by human articles of food and dress.

[2] Wilkinson, 2nd ser. I. 146, 147.

[3] Lucian, *De Sacrificiis* (Opp. p. 187, n, Paris, 1615): αἱ δὲ θυσίαι καὶ παρ' ἐκείνοις αἱ αὐταί· πλὴν ὅτι πενθοῦσι τὸ ἱερεῖον, καὶ κόπτονται περιστάντες ἤδη πεφονευμένον.

[4] Herod. II. 39.

of Egypt, it might all be concentrated on the victim's head;' which was accordingly not eaten by the worshipper but thrown as a devoted thing into the Nile, or else was sold to foreign traders.

The oblation of such sacrifices was the more remarkable in Egypt, owing to the number of the sacred animals there worshipped and the depth of the reluctance which was felt to the effusion of their blood. It must indeed have been the memory of some older teaching, and the force of irresistible impulse thus communicated, which constrained the worshipper to sacrifice not merely geese and other birds, but also his choice oxen and the male calves of the herd. We trace, again, the consequence of struggles which had long been waged between the obligation to offer animal victims, and the obligation to preserve those brutes which he had deemed especially sacred, in the fact that cows and heifers were at length excluded altogether from the list of offerings, and that consequently to offer them was 'to sacrifice the abomination of the Egyptians.'[1] It is further noticeable, as supporting this conjecture, that a large proportion of Egyptian sacrifices were selected from the class of animals, which men had learned to call *Typhonic*, so that the thing offered was no more the choicest property of the sacrificer, but a creature hostile both to him and all the tutelar gods of Egypt.[2] An exemplification of such offering is presented in the custom of choosing *red*[3] oxen for

How connected with the worship of sacred animals.

Typhonic victims,

---

[1] See Exod. viii. 26, 27, and Wilkinson, 2nd ser. II. 347, 348.

[2] Plutarch, *De Is. et Os.* c. XXXI.: θύσιμον γὰρ οὐ φίλον εἶναι θεοῖς, ἀλλὰ τοὐναντίον, ὅσα ψυχὰς ἀνοσίων ἀνθρώπων καὶ ἀδίκων εἰς ἕτερα μεταμορφουμένων σωμάτων συνείληφε.

[3] Herod. II. 38; Diodor. I. 18. If a single black hair was found on the ox, it was sacred to Epaphus (Apis), and as such was accounted 'unclean,' or no proper subject for sacrifice.

oblations, on the ground that Typhon was himself entirely of that colour. And the same idea is also still more closely intimated in the ancient practice of sacrificing what were called Typhonic men,' or red-haired strangers,[1] at the tomb of Osiris. Attempts, indeed, are made continually by some writers to discredit the account, which comes to us from Manetho, in reference to this horrible distortion of the rite of sacrifice; but the existence of such usages appears to be unquestionable, attested as it is distinctly by a native priest, and illustrated by the constant practice of most other demi-civilised communities in both the Old World and the New. The very seal made use of in historic ages to denote the fitness of a given victim bore the figure of a man kneeling, with his hands bound behind him, and a sword pointed at his throat.[2] In this unnatural act of bringing to the altar of the gods a victim capable of perfect sympathy with the sacrificer, there is always visible, amid the glare of selfish and vindictive passions, the stern truth that nothing short of human blood was deemed an adequate offering to the highest gods of Egypt, or sufficient for the liquidation of the penalty entailed from time to time by human disobedience.

But the sacrifice which the Egyptian offered to his gods was followed, as in other parts of heathen-

---

[1] Diodor. I. 88. Porphyry, *De Abstinentia*, II. 55, and Plutarch, *De Is. et. Os.* c. LXXIII., both quote Manetho as the authority for this inhuman practice, which, he says, was abandoned by a king named Amosis, who substituted a waxen image for the live victim. Herodotus, however, denies (II. 45) that this practice, which had been abolished long before his time, had ever existed; asking, if the Egyptians were so scrupulous about offering animals, κῶς ἂν οὗτοι ἀνθρώπους θύοιεν;

[2] Kenrick, I. 442; Döllinger, p. 442; Uhlemann, II. 191. This scene, however, may possibly allude to the *vicarious* nature of the sacrifice.

dom,[1] by sacrifices for and to the spirits of departed ancestors. His dedication of himself to Ptah, to Ammon-Ra, or to Osiris, was the first and principal act of homage; but the next[2] consisted in the dedication of his own heart to his buried mother, and included a long series of funereal rites by means of which he strove to pay due honour to the 'authors of his body.' Offerings of this class appear to have especially evoked the better feelings of the Old Egyptian; and the prayers which he addressed to his departed ancestors, as well as to Osiris in their favour, prove, if not the moral elevation of his creed, at least the freshness and the strength of his domestic instincts.

2. It is, however, in the views presented of the Old Egyptian in the world beyond the grave that we discover the foundation of his ethical system. Principles of action which had guided him in this life are reflected with peculiar vividness and fulness in the judgment-scenes belonging to the next. The chief authorities for statements on the fortunes of the soul in hades are derived from extant Rituals of the Dead, rolled up in a cylindrical form and not unfrequently discovered in sarcophagi of different periods. As this class of documents, in one shape or other, may be carried back into the earlier dynasties,—supplying to the disembodied soul of every age a kind of guide-book for her pilgrimages in the train of Osiris through the regions of the under-world,—it is indisputable that the Old Egyptian was no stranger

Egyptian doctrine of a future life:

---

[1] See, for example, above, pp. 34, 127, 179, 200, and Appendix II. at the end of this Part.

[2] *Revue Archéol.* xiv° année, p. 194.

to the cardinal truths connected with the prolongation of man's being after death, his conscious and unwearying exercise of functions proper to humanity, and his exposure to the scrutiny of supernatural agents on account of ' things done in the body.'[1] Of the hundred and sixty-five chapters which fill up the most remarkable of these Rituals, one is entitled, ' On the life after death'; and the volume, notwithstanding all its mystic names and undecypherable images, is found to be pervaded by the same idea of indi-

its peculiar characteristics. vidual immortality. The vividness of such conceptions is particularly manifested in the fact that nearly all conditions of the present life, in their most earthy and unspiritual shape, had been transferred into man's theory of the life which is to come. At an Egyptian funeral, common articles of food and dress, and certain implements of war, of business and of pleasure, were deposited with or near the corpse: the scenes of daily life were pictured on the mummy-cases, not so much in order to express the piety of survivors, as to gratify and stimulate the dead: a string of prayers and other formulæ were also buried with him for his constant admonition, and as passports through the unknown world to which he had been destined; and at length, when he was entering the ' dark place' itself, the popular belief assigned him ' bread and drink, and slices of flesh off the table of the Sun; when he peregrinates the fields of the blessed, corn and barley are given to him, for he is as provided as he was upon earth.'[2]

---

[1] Mr. Osburn is at one with all Egyptologers when he says (*Mon. Hist.* I. 424): 'The truth that man will be judged after death was brought into Egypt by the first settlers, and universally received by their posterity.'

[2] *Todtenbuch* in Birch's *Egypt.*

It has been held indeed, on the authority of Herodotus, that the Egyptians were the *first* people of the ancient world to inculcate this doctrine of the immortality of the human soul; and doubtless the habitual and unfaltering affirmation of it was to some extent *Egyptian*, and was that which gave their highest charm to the Osirian tenets in the eye of other nations: but the language of the Greek historian, properly expounded, means[1] no more than that Egyptians were the first people, who, cherishing the thought of some ulterior existence, had imparted to it novel characteristics by presenting it in the form of a theory of transmigration. In thus embracing the idea of changes from the human to the bestial and the meanest even of all reptile forms, the Old Egyptians occupied the same position as Hindús throughout the second, or Bráhmanic, period of their history. In both those countries we have seen how the religion of the choicer few, as well as of the populace itself, was ultimately pantheistic; and in both accordingly the dogma of transmigration had been strengthened, if not first of all suggested, by the reverence men

Chap. I.

Antiquity of this doctrine in Egypt.

Hindú and Egyptian theories of transmigration.

Hierog. p. 272 : cf. Döllinger, p. 432, who traces the origin of this kind of phraseology to a principle which recurs in almost every heathen system, *viz.* a belief in the quasi-materiality of the human soul. It was not regarded as a purely spiritual essence, ' sondern als eine körperliche, nur feinere Substanz, welche im jenseitigen Leben durch mancherlei Wanderungen hindurchgehe, bis sie geläutert—als solche dargestellt in der Form eines Sperbers mit Menschenkopf zur vollen Anschauung des göttlichen Sonnenlichts sich emporschwingt.'

[1] After telling us (II. 123) that the Egyptians look upon Dionysus and Demeter (Osiris and Isis) as the rulers of hades, he continues: Πρῶτοι δὲ καὶ τόνδε τὸν λόγον Αἰγύπτιοί εἰσι οἱ εἰπόντες· ὡς ἀνθρώπου ψυχὴ ἀθάνατός ἐστι, τοῦ σώματος δὲ καταφθίνοντος ἐς ἄλλο ζῶον αἰεὶ γινόμενον ἐσδύεται· ἐπεὰν δὲ περιέλθῃ πάντα τὰ χερσαῖα καὶ τὰ θαλάσσια καὶ τὰ πετεινά, αὖτις ἐς ἀνθρώπου σῶμα γινόμενον ἐσδύνειν: the term of these transmigrations being 3000 years, *i. e.* one Sothis-period.

were taught to feel for each of the innumerable varieties of animated nature. Transmigration was, however, viewed in both these systems as a dire calamity; and therefore to obtain exemption from its fatal law became in both the foremost duty of their genuine votaries. Each pursued this object in a different spirit and by methods of his own devising. The Hindús of every school, the Bráhman and the Buddhist also, shrinking as far as possible from contact with material forms, and casting off as evil all that ministered to the idea of personal immortality, contended that emancipation could be only found amid the loftiest peaks of human knowledge; and accordingly pushed forward, in the one case to complete identification with Divinity itself, and in the other, to the dismal void of utter non-existence.

Egyptian interest in the fortunes of the body.

The Egyptian, on the contrary, had no such fundamental dread of matter and experienced no temptation to accept a theory fatal to the prolongation of his individual being. He was rather prone to speculations which distrusted or depressed the spiritual part of man. The conservation of the body, he imagined, was essential to the vigour and felicity of the soul. Attempts were, therefore, made in Egypt from an early period to exalt, and in one sense immortalise,[1] the body by the well-known

[1] This interpretation of the custom of embalming has come down to us through Servius (*ad Æneid.* III. 67); and has certainly the advantage of accounting for many practices connected with the burial of the dead. But we have now abundant reason for concluding that the *perfect purification* of the body, and not its conservation merely, was at the root of the ideas expressed in every act of mummification. Thus in Brugsch's edition of the *Saï An Sinsin* (p. 25), it is said, 'Dein Leib ist nun rein durch Wasser und Laugensalz, kein Glied an dir ist unrein; geläutert von allem Uebel und allem Schmutz kommst du zum Richterstuhle...dein Herz ist nun

system of embalming. Let the bodily organs, it was felt, be saved from putrefaction, and the spirit also will have something left on which to lean for help as her companion and receptacle. In virtue of the strength afforded to her by this union with the former cause of her vitality, she will continue to subsist in some analogous condition; disembodied, it is true, but still associating with her previous tenement, and still in some mysterious fashion living by its life.

The vast importance of such interaction had impelled the Old Egyptian worthy to lavish his chief skill and treasure on the building and adornment of his tomb. He made it capable of defying the malignity of Typhon and the wildest fury of the elements: he covered it with pleasant pictures, the mementos of a happy life on earth; he called the sepulchre itself, his dwelling-place and 'everlasting home.'[1] His mummy, in like manner, was entitled 'habitation of Osiris';[2] on the type supplied by the arch-mummy of that god, all others had from age to age been scrupulously moulded; prayers were also offered to Osiris for the purpose of securing their incorruptibility;[3] and as the principal organs of the body were all deemed essential to the rightful actings of the spirit, every limb was now consigned to the

Mummification.

das Herz des Ra, deine Glieder sind die Glieder des grossen Horus.'

[1] Diodor. I. 51: ἀϊδίους οἴκους προσαγορεύουσιν, ὡς ἐν ᾅδου διατελούντων τὸν ἄπειρον αἰῶνα. Wilkinson (2nd ser. II. 445) seems to think that this care of the dead body intimated a belief in its eventual resuscitation; but, as Prichard long ago remarked (*E.*

Mythol. p. 198), if this doctrine 'was really prevalent among the Egyptians, we must suppose that they took extraordinary care to conceal it, since not the slightest hint respecting it has reached our times:' cf. Müller, *Amerikan. Urrelig.* p. 402.

[2] Osburn, I. 427.

[3] See examples in Döllinger, p. 432.

protection of one single deity ; while Seb, the father of Osiris, was himself entrusted with the guardianship of edifices where the mummy was enshrined.

Judgment after death. But while conceding that some minor difficulties continue to embarrass the solution of this problem with respect to the precise intention of embalming, as well as to the limits placed by the Egyptian creed upon the metensomatosis of one class of disembodied spirits and their wanderings through 'the cycle of necessity,' it is impossible to doubt that, in the later periods of Egyptian independence, every spirit was believed to pass at once from this life to *Amenthe,* the dim region of the under-world, in which account was solemnly taken by Osiris of its actions and its words. In this belief, so universally diffused, we see the clearest and most urgent motive to a course of upright living which the Old Egyptian had been made to feel. The duties which he recognised as proper to the gods, his neighbour and himself, may all be gathered from the judgment-scenes enacted at the great tribunal of Osiris.

Light reflected on the nature of Egyptian ethics. On examining the pictures thus transmitted to us, we discover that not a few of the more heinous sins remaining to be expiated in a future life consisted of deflections from a long array of merely ceremonial precepts. Every thing in ancient Egypt, not excluding the most ordinary avocations and most trivial pastimes of the people, had been thrust beneath the iron yoke of arbitrary legislation. As the Nile, for instance, was a sacred river, and as such invoked in the Egyptian hymns[1] among the foremost of the

---

[1] A stanza of one such hymn is given by Mr. Birch, as before, p. 268.

national gods, whatever bore directly on the culture
of the soil and the succession of the crops in every
district of the Nile-valley was enforced among the
duties claimed from husbandmen by that divinity.
'To brush its sacred surface with the balance-bucket
at a forbidden time was a crime equal in atrocity to
that of reviling the face of a king or of a father.'[1]
The spirit, therefore, which presided over all the
social institutions of the Pharaonic empire was akin
to that which we have watched already shaping the
national character of the Chinese; it was exclusive,[2]
cramping, isolating, stern, prohibitive, despotic. And
corresponding to this general estimate is the discovery
that the virtues there imputed to the Old Egyptians
are nearly always of a negative kind. The spirit
at the bar of judgment ever struggles to evince her
own integrity,—'to justify herself'—and is accordingly most earnest in proclaiming her habitual ab-
stinence from open vice and from all possible breaches
of the ceremonial institute. She can declare, indeed,
on some occasions, that she has 'given bread to the
hungry, water to the thirsty, garments to the naked,
and asylum to the wretched outcast,'[3] as well as
proper victims to the gods and the funereal offerings
to the manes; but her language in the great majority
of recorded judgment-scenes is rather that of confident
disavowal; while confessions of innate depravity, or

[1] Osburn, I. 435.

[2] Thus in the deprecations of a
spirit on approaching the judicial
balance, she is made to protest 'I
have not changed the customs,
neither have I enacted foreign
abominations.' (*Ibid.* p. 432).
Hence the violent hatred of all
strangers which was highly characteristic of the Old Egyptians:
see Hengstenberg, *Dissertations on
the Pentateuch,* II. 458, Edinb.
1847.

[3] *Revue Archéol.* xiv⁰ année, p.
194.

appeals to the forgiving mercy of the judge, appear to find no echo in Egyptian Rituals.

Progress of the deceased in the under-world. The deceased is, in those Rituals, pictured, first of all, as undergoing a long series of preliminary transformations in order to evade the malice of infernal demons, and 'obtain his heart.' He enters the bark of the Egyptian Charon,[1] and crosses over to the 'Hall of the Two Truths'; the title of which is borrowed from the goddesses of Truth and Justice, who assist in all determinations of Osiris. Ever since the mythic death ascribed to this divinity, it is believed that he has sat in judgment on the souls of men; and every spirit on admission finds him ready at his post, attended by Anubis, 'the director of the balance,' by Horus waiting to conduct acquitted mortals to the nearer presence of Osiris, and by Thoth, the great recorder, with a tablet in his hand. The heart of the deceased, which after various struggles has been rescued from the demons of the under-world, is now submitted to the fatal balance. Formulæ of exculpation[2] are presented to him; and although he is supposed to meet the reckoning solely in his own strength and to escape the crisis only when assured of personal innocence, some friendly guidance is upon his own petition administered by Thoth, the Mercury of the Egyptian hades. Of the formulæ[3] here mentioned one consists of deprecatory

---

[1] According to Diodor. I. 96, the word *Charon* is itself Egyptian (χαρω = 'silence'): cf. Uhlemann, *Thoth*, p. 62. Rhadamanthus, in like manner, is by some connected with the Egyptian *Amenthe*.

[2] It is worth while to compare the protests of the Old Egyptian

as recorded in his *Ritual* with those contained in the 31st chapter of the Book of Job. The points of similarity and of contrast are equally instructive.

[3] They are translated from the *Todtenbuch* by Mr. Osburn, I. 430 sq.

addresses to the gods of the Hall of Judgment, the
divine assessors of Osiris. In the second a long
catalogue of sins are, one by one, denied or dis-
avowed, before the 'two-and-forty avengers,' who
as the personifications of the sins themselves are
represented waiting for the adverse inclination of the
balance, in order to inflict their torments on the soul
of the condemned.

I give the former series at full length, because *Formula of*
it tends far more than any others to exhibit the *self-exculp-*
ation.
religion of the Old Egyptians in a favourable light,
and il'ustrates the nature of that secret and self-
judging law, which everywhere in spite of intellectual
aberrations is still active, in the cause of truth and
righteousness, among the inmost fibres of the human
heart:

1. I have neither done any sin, nor omitted any duty to
   any man.
2. I have committed no uncleanness.
3. I have not prevaricated at the seat of justice.
4. I have not spoken lightly.
5. I have done no shameful thing.
6. I have not · mitted [certain] ceremonies.
7. I have not blasphemed with my mouth.
8. I have not perverted justice.
9. I have not acted perversely.
10. I have not shortened the cubit.
11. I have not done that which is abominable to the gods.
12. I have not sullied my own purity.
13. I have not made men to hunger.
14. I have not made men to weep.
15. I have done no act of rapine.[1]

---

[1] The besetting sin of the Old Egyptian appears to have been *theft*, for which he had obtained a special notoriety, as well as, it would seem, a kind of legal indulgence (Herod. II. 121; Aulus Gellius, xi. 18; Diodor. I. 80).

16. I have not accused of rapine falsely.
17. I have not revived an ancient falsehood before the face of man.
18. I have not forged the deeds of sluices, houses, or lands.
19. I have not forged any of the divine images.
20. I have not withheld the seven linen garments due to the priests.
21. I have not committed adultery.
22. I have not polluted the purity of my divine land (*i. e.* my tomb).
23. I have not been avaricious.
24. I have not forged signet-rings.
25. I have not cut down on my mother's land (*i. e.* my maternal inheritance) the timber that grows thereon.
26. I have not falsified the weights of the balance.
27. I have not withheld milk from the mouths of the infants.
28. I have not driven away the flocks from their pasturage.
29. I have not netted [the] ducks [of the Nile] illegally.
30. I have not caught [the] fishes [of the Nile] illegally.
31. I have not [unlawfully] pierced the bank of the river when it was increasing.
32. I have not separated for myself [clandestinely] a channel (*lit.* arm) from the river when it was subsiding.
33. I have not extinguished the perpetual lamp (*lit.* hourly lamp).
34. I have not added anything to any of the sacred books.
35. I have not driven off any of the sacred cattle.
36. I have not stabbed the god (*i. e.* sacred animal), when he comes forth [from his shrine].

Fate of the condemned. Wherever the Egyptian failed to pass this ordeal, and the second not unlike it, he incurred a dark succession of tremendous penalties. The hapless spirit, banished from the presence of Osiris, who inclines his sceptre in token of disapprobation, is now hurried back to earth by ministers of vengeance in the hideous form of apes. She migrates from the human to the bestial sphere of being, and commencing with some animal shape[1] to which indeed she had contracted an affinity by former habits, she proceeds from year to year, from century to century, now rising and now sinking in the scale of creaturely existence, till at last the destined cycle is completed by the winding up of all things. The most abject stage in this rotation seems to be the lowest region of *Kar-Neter*, the Phlegethon of the Greeks. 'None of the dead can endure it; the waters being of flame and waves of fire of the most intense and unconquerable heat; while the thirst of the dead in it is unquenchable; and they have no peace in it, because it is filled with weeds and filth.'[2]

But on the contrary the human spirit who has stood the various tests applied to her at the tribunal of Osiris, passes on with the permission of the demons, and moves freely through the joyous halls of *Aahlu* (Elysium). Her body also purified at length, by its evisceration,[3] from all properties which rendered it

Privileges of the acquitted.

---

[1] Wilkinson, as above, p. 447. It is rarely, however, as Mr. Kenrick remarks (I. 480), that we find 'among the funereal monuments of Egypt anything which relates to the metempsychosis;' the reason, perhaps, being that every embalmed corpse, duly interred, was *presumed* by the survivors to have passed the scrutiny of the infernal judge, and so was in a state of permanent felicity.

[2] Birch, as above, p. 275.

[3] See the remarkable passage in Porphyry (*De Abstinentia*, IV. 10), where is preserved the invocation addressed by the embalmers to the sun in the name of the deceased; at the end of which he is made to say, 'If I have committed any other fault during my life, either in eating or drinking, it has not been done on my own account, but on account of these'; pointing to the chest containing the viscera. Such passages (cf. Vol. I. p. 201) remind one of St. Augustine's statement respecting himself while he continued a Manichæan : 'Adhuc enim mihi videbatur, non esse nos qui peccamus, sed nescio quam aliam in nobis peccare naturam,' (*Confess.* v. 10). It is also worthy of remark that while expressions such as those just cited have a *Manichæan* aspect, overlooking or denying the freedom of the creature, the general

offensive to the gods has been assimilated by the mummifying process to the actual form of Osiris. The whole man, according to the later representations, has became *Osirianised;* the name of the great sun-god is combined, without distinction of age or calling, with the name of the departed mortal; he attains to a subordinate stage of deification; he acquires a faculty of self-translation and self-transformation,[1] just as the condemned are driven onward by some irresistible fate into the forms of animal life; he issues forth at will into the upper regions; he soars high above the earth with the alertness of the hawk or ibis; he revisits the sepulchre in which his body is preserved, and thence derives a fresh accession to his vital powers. He inherits the two-fold life of the divine Osiris; all his happiness consists in tracking that illustrious sun-god, in addressing adorations to him, and in sailing with him through his daily circuits, in the barge employed by him to circumnavigate the firmament, or 'waters of the heavenly Nile.'

In other words, the Sun which to Egyptians had for ages been the grandest symbol of their deities, and not unfrequently the glorious home or vehicle of Deity itself, was also the most lofty image they could form of pure and ultimate enjoyment. The reward of all acquitted spirits was translation from the sacred Valley of the Nile, its joys and sorrows

tendency of the religions of Egypt, of Phœnicia and of Babylonia, was rather towards a *Pelagian* estimate of human sinfulness.

[1] Döllinger, p. 434: cf. Vol. 1.

p. 304, n. 2; where a similar faculty is said to have entered into the Hindú conception of original 'perfectness.'

and mutations, to the one unchanging source of brilliance and fertility. 'This great god speaks to them
and they speak to him; his glory illuminates them
in the splendour of his disc, while he is shining
in their sphere."[1]

[1] Rosellini, in Kenrick, i. 487.

CHAPTER II.

Alleged Affinities between the Hebrew and Egyptian Systems.

Κατὰ τὰ ἐπιτηδεύματα Αἰγύπτου, ἐν ᾗ κατῳκήσατε ἐπ' αὐτῇ, οὐ ποιήσετε, καὶ κατὰ τὰ ἐπιτηδεύματα γῆς Χαναάν, εἰς ἣν ἐγὼ εἰσάγω ὑμᾶς ἐκεῖ, οὐ ποιήσετε, καὶ τοῖς νομίμοις αὐτῶν οὐ πορεύσεσθε. τὰ κρίματά μου ποιήσετε, καὶ τὰ προστάγματά μου φυλάξεσθε, καὶ πορεύεσθε ἐν αὐτοῖς. ΕΓΩ ΚΥΡΙΟΣ Ο ΘΕΟΣ ΥΜΩΝ. Levit. xviii. 3, 4. (LXX).

THAT some examples of external correspondency, more marked and less fortuitous than any we have hitherto detected, can be traced between the ritual codes of the Egyptian and the Hebrew, is no longer questioned even by the warmest advocate of supernatural religion.[1] These affinities, however, as we might at once anticipate from the absorbing interest of the points involved, give birth to a variety of conflicting interpretations. Some, for instance, have contended

---

[1] Thus Witsius, in his *Ægyptiaca*, p. 4, Basil, 1739, declares expressly 'magnam atque mirandam plane convenientiam in religionis negotio veteres inter Ægyptios atque Hebræos esse,' and adds : 'Quæ cum fortuita esse non possit, necesse est ut vel Ægyptii sua ab Hebræis, vel ex adverso Hebræi sua ab Ægyptiis habeant.' And Hengstenberg, in our own day, makes a similar admission : 'He [Spencer] sets out with an assertion—in the main correct, but pushed by him to an extreme—that many parts of the Mosaic ceremonial law present a striking agreement with the religious usages of heathen nations, particularly of the Egyptians.' *Dissertations on the Genuineness of the Pentateuch*, i. 4, Edinb. 1847.

that as early as the age of Abraham, the priests of Lower Egypt were induced to borrow from him certain portions of the patriarchal creed, as well as to accept instruction at his hands in secular and useful learning. Others, on the contrary, affirm that Abraham himself and his descendants in the time of Moses had not scrupled in particular cases to incorporate the riper wisdom of the land of Egypt with their own hereditary laws and their most cherished institutions. While a third class, arguing from the fact that both these peoples radiated from a common centre, would refer the numerous points of similarity which they exhibit to the influence of a purer and more primitive generation, when the fathers of the Hebrew race still[1] recognised the sacred character of worthies like Melchisedek, and communed with them as with 'priests of the most high God.'

The feelings also which suggest the different theories on this subject are as widely different as the theories themselves. On the one side stand the writers both of earlier and later ages, who are actuated by a strong conviction that we had almost 'as well not worship God at all as worship Him by rites which have been employed in paganism.'[2] The presence in the Bible of some element of faith or worship, known to have been actually borrowed from the primitive faith or worship of the cir-

Different motives of the theorisers.

---

[1] See Vol. I. p 97, n. 1.

[2] This is Warburton's characteristic way of putting the case of his opponents: cf. *Div. Leg.* II. 312 sq. Lond. 1846. A similar class of scruples have occasionally peeped out in discussions of the post-Reformation period on the subject of ecclesiastical vestments and other ceremonies: *e. g.* at the Hampton Court Conference, where objections were urged against the surplice, on the ground that such a dress was worn of old time by priests of Isis.

cumjacent heathen would in their view silence or invalidate all arguments in favour of a special Revelation; and accordingly they feel concerned to demonstrate that 'images of truth,' wherever such exist in Gentilism, were merely due to the refracted rays of supernatural light whose proper sphere was in the bosom of the sacred family. Others, unrestrained by feelings of this kind, nay, anxious even, it would seem, at all hazards to multiply the points of sympathy between the Hebrew and the heathen systems, find their only possible justification of the ceremonial law of Moses in assuming its profound dependence on the institutes of the Egyptian lawgivers. While particular branches of that ritual were (say they) intended to condemn or counteract the grosser vices of polytheism, the general object was to gratify a multitude of childish prejudices,[1] which the Hebrew had contracted in the course of his long residence in Egypt. Customs and ideas of heathenish extraction were engrafted on the Law, and that by

---

[1] Spencer's work, *De Legibus Hebræorum ritualibus*, is pervaded by this strange idea. As Bahr expresses it (*Symbolik des Mosaischen Cultus*, I. 41, Heidelberg, 1837), God appears in his theory 'as a Jesuit who makes use of bad means [Spencer himself says *ineptiæ tolerabiles*] to bring about a good result.' In some respects the legal institute might justly be regarded by the Christian Fathers as a kind of *condescension* to the wants and weaknesses of man, and consequently as a συγκατάβασις or *accommodation* to the actual status of its Jewish subjects (cf. Acts xiii. 18); but Spencer's theory is a coarse and violent perversion of this philosophic principle. Instead of looking on the law of Moses as a lower and symbolic form of true religion, possessing therefore an internal fitness, and a definite place in the grand scheme of man's redemption, he could see in it nothing more than a huge 'apparatus of ceremonies,' having 'no agreement with the nature of God.' Perhaps the closest of patristic approximations to his standing-ground occurs in one of the letters of Gregory the Great (Bed. *Hist. Eccl.* I. 30): with which may be compared the startling assertions of Mr. D. I. Heath, *Exodus Papyri*, pp. 103 sq. Lond. 1855.

the express authority of God Himself, in order to amuse the fancy, and preoccupy the spirit of the Israelitish people, who might else, through their incorrigible love of superstitious imagery and impatience of all purely spiritual truth, have been seduced into apostasy. One school of modern writers has, however, accepted this position so far only as to grant that several usages commanded in the Law of Moses were in fact adapted from the ritual code of the Egyptians; but instead of finding in that circumstance a reason for disparaging the ceremonial system of the Hebrews, they proceed to build on their admission a fresh argument in favour of the early date and high authority of the Pentateuch.[1]

Now, if we try to disembarrass our minds as far *Real influence exerted* as possible from any mere presumptions, it is evident *by Egypt on* that contradictory theories in vogue with reference to *the minds* alleged resemblances between the Hebrew and Egypt- *of the Hebrews.* ian systems are in almost every case extravagant or superficial or one-sided. We are bound, for instance, to acknowledge on the threshold, that some very deep impressions had been made upon the sons of Abraham by their continued sojourn in the empire of the Pharaohs. From the nature of the case the Hebrews must have been disciples and not doctors. Going down a handful of mere nomades to that country of the ancient world whose institutions had been longest

---

[1] This, for example, appears to be the moving principle of Dr. Hengstenberg in his *Die Bücher Mosi's und Aegypten,* Berlin, 1841, where the points of outward similarity are unduly multiplied. His own avowal is: 'Je ursprünglicher, selbständiger und einzigartiger die Israelitische Religion in Bezug auf den Geist war, desto weniger hatte sie es nöthig, mit scheuer Aengstlichkeit jede äussere Berührung mit den Religionen anderer Völker zu vermeiden,' (p. 153).

CHAP. II. organised, they could not fail to have experienced the transforming influence everywhere implied in such an altered mode of life. We know, indeed, for certain that the land of Goshen proved the nursery of their national spirit, and the training-school in which they gradually imbibed some elements of art, of agriculture, and of civil polity. We know, again, that during their abode in Egypt, the majority of Hebrews proper,—to say nothing of the 'great mixed multitude,' who having learned to share their fortunes were blended with them at the Exodus,—contracted more and more a fondness for Egyptian thoughts and customs, utterly at variance with the creed inherited from their fathers.[1] The same vicious predilection had moreover gained such stubborn hold upon them that in after-ages it was constantly evincing its importance, and could scarcely ever be eradicated.

Further speculations on this point. Nor have these considerations been sufficiently answered by the plea that all the popular bias on the side of Egypt, active as it was before the promulgation of the Law, had constituted an additional reason why the Lawgiver should abstain from every thing which countenanced or confirmed it: since, according to the framers of the theory of accommodation, it was politic in Moses to recognise and so to consecrate, as far as might be, what the present temper of the Hebrew people rendered him unable to displace. Nay, ask these writers, might not Moses be induced to grant some measure of indulgence to his weak and sense-bound followers by his own experience of the real strength of their temptations, or the real good

---

[1] On their religious condition while in Egypt, see Kurtz, *Gesch.* II. 38—42.

which might have been deducible from heathen customs? Educated from his earliest childhood in the court of the Egyptian monarch, and, it may be, actually initiated[1] into the sacred circles of the priesthood, was he not (say they) both skilled in the symbolic ordinances of Egyptian worship and enabled to discern the hidden truths which lay enveloped in the midst of it? If many of the oldest Greek philosophers, as Thales or Pythagoras[2] or Plato, who had sojourned there a shorter period, could return exulting from the land of Egypt laden with a rich variety of intellectual spoils; if through their visits many a germ of mathematical science and the outlines of a purer system of ethics and theology were rescued from comparative oblivion; if the principle of distributing their pupils into outer and inner classes, an enlarged conception of the grandeur of the universe, or a more fascinating list of dogmas, such as that of transmigration and the like, had all been widely spread along the shores of the Mediterranean, why should not the foster-child of Pharaoh's daughter have been equally imbued with reverence for ideas and institutions of his adopted country,[3] or at least

---

[1] Cf. Uhlemann's *Thoth*, p. 6.

[2] The prohibition by Pythagoras of *all* animal food and *all* animal sacrifices (adduced by Uhlemann, *Thoth*, p. 12, as an illustration of his Egyptising) has rather a Hindú aspect; and of later years, indeed, it has grown fashionable to speak of the founder of Pythagoreanism as a kind of Buddhist missionary; his name or title (Pythagoras = 'Buddha-guru') being quoted as confirmatory of such hypotheses. Others, however, dwell upon his supposed *Phœnician* origin, and so make him the depository of Semitic, if not Biblical, traditions; while many of his ascetic principles are clearly traceable among the Palestinian Essenes.

[3] Miss Martineau, *Eastern Life*, p. 104, tells us that Plato came to Egypt, 'and sat, where Moses had sat, at the feet of the priests, gaining, as Moses had gained, an immortal wisdom from their lips:' but when she adds that Moses learned to become 'a redeem-legis-

inclined to tolerate in others what to lofty spirits like
his own may have been radiant with the light of true
philosophy?

Antecedent improbability that heathenish ideas were adopted in Hebraism.   Now let it be conceded, in reply to these surmises,
that the 'human learning' of the Hebrew legislator
was from first to last *Egyptian.*   Let it also be conceded that the fondness of his subjects for Egyptian
ritualism was such as to have baffled all the wisest
schemes designed to counteract it; and enough will
yet remain to make us hesitate before subscribing
to this novel phase of the accommodation-theory.   If
the Books of Moses be accepted as our guide (and
other guidance in this region we have none), is it
consistent either with their letter or their spirit that
the Law, as authorised at such a crisis by God Himself, could carry with it any sanction of things *purely
heathenish* in their nature?   Was it not pervaded
by indignant protests against heathenism as such?
The call of Moses, the appointed legislator, was as
critical and peremptory as the call of the Apostle
of the Gentiles: it was also followed by a like in-
version and revulsion in the spirit of the 'chosen
vessel.'   He too had been sent to 'bear the name of
God before the Gentiles and kings and the children
of Israel,' and to suffer for that Name's sake (cf. Acts
ix. 15, 16).   He learned at starting on his mission,
and he kept engraven ever on his mind a clear idea
of the 'complete and absolute distinction of the Jewish
faith from that of any other ancient nation.'[1]   This
distinctness of position and belief, proclaimed no more

lator,' as Plato a 'spiritual philo-   [1] Cf. Dr. Donaldson's *Christian
sopher,' I confess my utter inabi-   Orthodoxy,* p. 117, Lond. 1857.
lity to understand her meaning.

through hieroglyphs intelligible only to the few, but in the ordinary writing of the Hebrew people, was exactly in accordance with the destiny marked out for them as conservators of the true religion. The whole genius therefore of their institutions was distinctive, separative, incapable of compromise, impatient of amalgamation; so distinctive, so peculiar, that the wonderful vitality of Hebraism in after-times can only be explained on the hypothesis that men's devotion to it had been supernaturally produced, and ever since the childhood of the nation had been growing upward with their growth. Or if advancing from these general probabilities we study some of the first chapters in the national records of the Israelites, we shall again perceive at every turn the traces of antagonism between their own and the Egyptian system. In the Exodus itself, which led the way to the formation of the legal institute, we have to witness no mere secular emancipation from the yoke of a new line of Pharaohs, but the mightiest of religious victories which the ancient world had seen. Designed to vindicate the personality and holiness of God, as well as the distinctness of His chosen people, it was ushered in by a succession of stupendous acts which tended to rebuke and stultify the nature-worship of Mizraim: it was consummated in that moment, when the Hebrews, flushed with hope and exultation, were all forward in responding to the grateful anthem of their leader: 'I will sing unto the Lord, for he hath triumphed gloriously. . . .The Lord is my strength and song, and He is become my salvation' (Ex. xv. 1, 2). As, therefore, in the parallel case where Christianity is struggling hand to hand with some bewitching or besotting form of heathenism, it is most needful to protect her neophyte against all risk of fresh contamination by decrying or discountenancing customs which may serve, remotely even, to perpetuate modes of thought and feeling adverse to the rightful exercise of her transforming influence; so the Pentateuch evinces a continual jealousy lest peradventure the old thirst for heathenish vices should be stimulated through the medium of unhallowed associations. Intermarriage, for example, with the neighbouring heathen is most sternly interdicted both by Moses and by Joshua whenever it is likely to involve among its fruits the imitation or adoption of heathen customs. The redeemed community have ample warrant for believing that they are no more a friendless band of foreign shepherds, mingled and well-nigh confounded with the meanest subjects of the Pharaohs, but 'a kingdom of priests, a holy nation, a peculiar treasure unto God above all people' (Ex. xix. 5, 6); and because the ground of such election, owing to the nature of God Himself, is ultimately and entirely moral, the elected race is under a proportionate obligation to exhibit in the sight of the surrounding world its moral superiority: 'After the doings of the land of Egypt, wherein ye dwelt, shall ye not do: and after the doings of the land of Canaan, whither I bring you, shall ye not do; neither shall ye walk in their ordinances. Ye shall do My judgments, and keep Mine ordinances, to walk therein: I am the Lord your God.' (Lev. xviii. 3, 4.)

Mode of investigation here followed. The question, therefore, as to the transmission of religious thoughts and usages from the Egyptian to the Hebrew is discovered to be far more complicated than at first sight may appear. It is a question little likely to be solved, as many writers have of late attempted, by adducing an array of bare presumptions on the one side or the other. To discuss it we must enter on a rigorous examination of the facts themselves; and with a view to such investigation, I shall here arrange all possible affinities in two separate classes:[1] (1) the minor points of ritualism which may have been inherited in common, or externally derived from one system to the other, without implying any true internal sympathy; and (2) the cardinal points of doctrine which must ever have determined the character of those systems, and have proved the real secret of their weakness or their strength.

§ 1. *Ritual Resemblances.*

Before entering on the criticism of any particular instances, it is important to recall attention to remarks already[2] made in reference to the offices discharged by symbolism in the religions of antiquity. The lack of any clear ideas on this point has tended more than other causes to becloud the whole of the discussions opened in the present chapter. I have urged that since the ancient Hebrew was in temperament, as also in the measure of his intellectual training, not unlike the native of surrounding countries, symbolism of some kind or other was most needful in that early period to the planting of religious truth and its development within him. He was far less capable than

General nature of ancient symbolism.

---

[1] All inquiries into merely civil and political arrangements are passed over as not directly bearing on the present subject.

[2] Vol. I. pp. 104 sq.

his remote descendants of all abstract and unearthly contemplation; he was living more than they in the impressions made upon the eyesight; and accordingly it was the part of wisdom in obtaining from him the acceptance of a supersensuous truth to represent, or, one might say, embody it in concrete shapes, to clothe it in more visible and sensuous drapery, and enforce it by suggestive actions and symbolical institutions. Here, as in the case of teaching by parable or allegory, a pure thought has been invested in expressive forms which bring it more directly under the cognisance of every human mind endowed with the *Character of the Mosaic institute.* most elementary of religious intuitions. Symbol was, in other words, a species of primeval language: the symbolic institutions were the illustrated and illuminated books, in which the early generations of the human family might learn the rudiments of true religion: and, aided as it was among the Hebrews by a series of collateral expositions ever guarding it from misconstruction and reverting to the spiritual principles on which it had been framed, the ritual law was one of God's chief agents in the education of the elder Church. It deepened in man's heart the consciousness of his dependence and degeneracy; it taught the need of a redemption and foreshadowed the Redeemer; while by it the grand conception of one holy God had been associated with the homeliest of man's actions, and diffused 'into the very midst of the popular life.' Compared with Christianity, indeed, that ritual system of the Hebrew was unripe and rudimentary; it was made up of 'weak and beggarly elements'; it proved itself a Pædagogue and not *the* Teacher; the result to which it ever pointed

the aspirations of its worthier subjects was not actually achieved until 'the fulness of the times had
come,' until the Incarnation of the Son of God and
the effusion of the quickening Spirit: yet in reference
to the stage of progress then attainable by man, it
offered an effectual apparatus for evoking and con-
serving the religious principle; and when at last the
sentence of abrogation was pronounced, the law of
ordinances fell, as scaffolding falls off, because the
edifice it served to rear had reached the full proportions, and because a system not inglorious in itself
has 'no glory in this respect by reason of the glory
that excelleth.'

If, then, sacred emblems of the ancient world
were thus peculiarly significant; if symbolic institutions were a species of necessity arising out of the
capacities and condition of the human mind, and so
were common to the rituals both of Jew and heathen,
all objections to the Bible which depend upon the
mere existence of resemblances between these rituals,
irrespectively, that is, of the ideas therein embodied,
fall entirely to the ground. It would be equally presumptuous to disparage or reject the doctrines of the
Gospel, prior to all scrutiny of its contents, because
these doctrines are transmitted to us in the ordinary
characters made use of in the printing of the other
writings of antiquity, or else because particular forms
of speech are found to be employed alike by the
Apostle of the Gentiles, and the orators, the poets
or the moralists of ancient Greece. The same outward act or emblem might continue to embody the
same primitive truth and so be equally innocuous
in both systems, which are made the subjects of

Under what conditions the symbolism of Hebrew and hea-then sys-tems might correspond.

Chap. II. comparison. Or, upon the other hand, it might be gradually connected in the lapse of ages with divergent if not opposite and contradictory ideas.[1] But wherever any emblem had been consciously transferred from one ancient people to another, care would doubtless be employed to rescue it from all supposed perversions then attaching to it, so that in its fresh position it might harmonise instead of jarring with the other members of the ritual system. Let this only be effected, and a symbol used extensively in heathen countries for the representation of a thing reputed holy might be also chosen as an apt exponent of a thing more lofty and more holy still; the freedom of the symbol from profane associations facilitating the adoption of it, and imparting to it an especial fitness for its new office.

Probable course pursued by Moses.

It is, therefore, highly probable that if the Hebrew legislator, acting here as always under the supreme direction of Jehovah, were induced to sanction rites and ceremonies current in the land of Egypt, or in other nations of antiquity, he was influenced by no

---

[1] The following observations of Kurtz (*Gesch. des Alten Bundes*, I. 310), though not expressing the exact view here advocated, are well worthy of attention · ‘In der hohen Blüthe ägyptischer Weisheit, Cultur und Industrie hatte Israel die beste Schule menschlicher Bildung, deren es für seine künftige Bestimmung bedürfte; durch die Bekanntschaft mit der tiefen Anschauung der Aegypter, die das ganze Leben mit allen seinen Aeusserungen und Verzweigungen unter religiösen Gesichtspunkt stellte, konnte selbst Israels *religiöse* An-schauung mehrfach bereichert werden, und in der Symbolik des ägyptischen Cultus fand es schon eine völlig ausgebildete *Form* des religiösen Lebens vor, die, weil *aus nothwendigen und allgemein gültigen Anschauungs- und Denkgesetzen des menschlichen Geistes hervorgegangen*, nicht ausschliesslich nur zum Träger des ägyptischen Pantheismus anwendbar war, sondern, von dem specifisch-israelitischen Princip beseelt, verklärt und umgestaltet, auch dem Cultus des israelitischen Theismus zum willkommnen Träger dienen konnte.’

wish to gratify the merely 'puerile superstitions' of Chap. II. his followers, but by reasons more exalted in themselves and more befitting his exalted character. He engrafted them into the legal institutions either because they were the uncorrupted heirloom of the patriarchal age, or else because, from their inherent fitness and expressiveness, they were commended to him as at once convertible in aid of the great project he was called to carry out.

The number of these ritual correspondencies is *Examples here chosen.* stated with considerable variety by different writers. Some,[1] however, I shall scarcely glance at; first, because the facts on which it is attempted to support them are extremely vague and problematical, and, secondly, because those facts, when fully ascertained, admit of a more simple and more rational explanation. In selecting the examples here subjoined for more minute analysis, I take the points which have been universally esteemed the most important of the series, and which century after century have furnished his

---

[1] Thus, the division of the Hebrews into twelve tribes, alleged by some writers as analogous to the territorial divisions of Egypt, naturally resulted from the number of Jacob's children. The distinction between clean and unclean meats, was pre-Mosaic and patriarchal, reaching backward to the Deluge. Hence may also be explained the strong repugnance felt to *swine* among the Israelites as well as the Egyptians, and the feeling of contempt with which they both regarded swineherds. The Levitical hierarchy had, moreover, several points of close resemblance to the various orders of Egyptian priests; yet most important differences are also traceable; for instance, in the perpetual exclusion of the Hebrew priesthood from all grants of territory. (Cf. Prichard, *Egypt. Mythol.* pp. 409 sq.). In this class of merely accidental correspondencies I am inclined to place the 'holy women' of the Israelites, a kind of nuns or female Nazarites, distinct from priestesses, but nevertheless devoted to ascetic modes of life (Ex. xxxviii. 8; 1 Sam. ii. 22): with whom may be compared the holy women of Egypt and Phœnicia (Herod. II. 54, 56).

main arguments to the impugner of the Books of Moses.

CIRCUMCISION.

Was circumcision exclusively Hebrew?

(1) The rite of circumcision, though practised by the Hebrews from an earlier epoch, was perpetuated in the ritual system of their legislator, and, as raised by him into a national institution, takes its place among the subjects handled in this chapter. Now that some such rite was also common in the land of Egypt, where Abraham himself had sojourned prior to its introduction into his own family, is definitely stated in a well-known passage of Herodotus.[1] He there informs us that the custom was native with Egyptians and Ethiopians, as also with the Colchians, who, according to his version of the matter, were an old deposit of Egyptians reaching backward to the conquests of Sesostris. He then adds that circumcision was derived from Egypt by the Syrians of Palestine and the Phœnicians. In the absence of all mention of the Jews, as well as of the Ishmaelites who, Abrahamic also in their origin, had practised the same rite, we may conjecture[2] that the information of Herodotus, which may have been derived exclu-

---

[1] II. 104; see Diodor. I. 28, and the abundant literature on the whole subject in Winer, *Realwört.* s. v. 'Beschneidung.' Sir G. Wilkinson affirms (Rawlinson's *Herod.* Vol. II. p. 171) that the rite was common in Egypt itself 'at least as early as the 4th dynasty, and probably earlier, long before the birth of Abraham.'

[2] See Mr. Blakesley's note on Herodotus, as above. The diffi-culty connected with 1 Sam. xviii. 25, 2 Sam. i. 20, etc., where 'Philistines' are distinguished as the 'uncircumcised,' Mr. Blakesley meets by remarking that 'subsequently to the time of Saul a great change took place in the population of the Philistine cities, and that a considerable Egyptian element [practising circumcision] had probably been introduced.'

sively from traders, was restricted to the *coast* of Chap. II.
Syria. Still there is no reason for suspecting the
general truth of the account, that centuries before the
date of his travels some conformity in this respect
existed between the Hebrews and Egyptians. The
'reproach of Egypt,' as adverted to by Joshua (v. 9),
is capable of two or more interpretations; but if taken
to mean 'that which Egypt would herself have stig-
matised,'[1] the phrase will intimate that as early as the
period of the Exodus the lack of circumcision[2] had
been held disreputable in Egypt; and although it may
be now successfully contended, more especially from
a profusion of extant mummies,[3] that the practice
had been far from universal, its prevalence in the age
of Moses may be urged with some show of reason.

The remote antiquity of the practice is again *Its exist-*
suggested strongly, if not absolutely proved, by its *ence in*
far-distant
existence far beyond the area both of Hebrew and *countries.*

[1] See Rosenmüller, *in loc.*, who refers to Ezek. xvi. 57; xxxvi. 15; Ps. xxxix. 9, in illustration of the Hebrew phraseology. Yet other texts appear to justify the passive rendering, 'that which exposes Egypt to reproach;' viz. uncir- cumcision (cf. 1 Sam. xvii. 26), or else idolatry (cf. Ezek. xx. 7), with which the Hebrews had been previously infected. New difficulties arise from the exami- nation of Jer. ix. 25, 26, where both the Hebrew and Vulgate (as expounded by St. Jerome, *in loc.*) are quoted to prove that many persons in Egypt and Edom, as well as Ammonites and Moabites, *did* practise circumcision, though strangers to the true faith: cf. Ezek. xxxi. 18; xxxii. 32, 29, 24, 30.

[2] Cf. Ex. iv. 24 sq., which im-

plies that, for some cause or other, the rite had been at first omitted, even in the household of Moses, although the obligation to ad- minister it was known to Zipporah, his wife. Its subsequent suspen- sion in the wilderness appears to have rested altogether upon *moral* grounds; the people 'who obeyed not the voice of the Lord' were for a season placed in the condition of the excommunicated, and there- fore were thrust back into the standing-ground of the unclean (cf. Josh. v. 5—7).

[3] 'From the examination of the mummies it appears that the prac- tice was very limited, not extend- ing to one in fifty; but it must be remembered that a large pro- portion of these are not of very high antiquity.' Kenrick, I. 450.

Egyptian influence. Traces of it have been found not only in the Cushite race of Ethiopians proper, and in Troglodytes[1] whose haunts were chiefly on the confines of the Red Sea, but far away at the extremity of the African continent,[2] among the distant isles of Oceanica,[3] and even, there is reason for supposing, in the very heart of the New World.[4] Yet if phenomena like these transport us backward to a period long before the call of Abraham or the adoption of the usage in his household, there is nothing in the language of the sacred penman which can fairly be regarded as at variance with such a supposition. The peculiar terms, indeed, in which the ordinance of circumcision was prescribed to him at first (Gen. xvii. 10) would rather indicate that the idea itself was older and was not unknown to him. The elevation of an ancient symbol to the rank of a Divine ordinance exactly corresponded to the change effected in a second ancient rite,—the practice of lustration, where the element of water, naturally associable with ideas of purity, was chosen by our

How related to the Abrahamic institution.

---

[1] Diodor. III. 32, who remarks that they acted παραπλησίως τοῖς Αἰγυπτίοις, though it is not altogether improbable that the Troglodytes were of Arabian lineage, and might thus derive the practice from Ishmael. It is still not uncommon in Abyssinia (cf. Uhlemann, *Aegypt. Alt.* II. 257), but whether adopted from the heathen natives or the Judaizers of the Early Church is matter of dispute.

[2] *e.g.* Dr. Livingstone writes (pp. 146, 147): 'All the Bechuana and Caffre tribes south of the Zambesi practise circumcision (*boguera*), but the rites observed are

carefully concealed.' He thinks, as there practised, it was 'only a sanitary and political measure,' and further suggests that, owing to the want of 'a continuous chain of tribes practising the rite,' it 'can scarcely be traced, as is often done, to a Mahometan source' (p. 149). Prichard (*Researches*, III. 287) believes it 'a relic of ancient African customs, of which the Egyptians, as it is well known, partook in remote ages.' The practice is still common in Æthiopia.

[3] Above, p. 202, n. 2.

[4] *Ibid.*

blessed Lord in His initiatory sacrament, to symbolise,
and by the working of His Spirit to convey, the
highest form of purification,—the remission of sins.

What then may be said to constitute the special *Specific*
and distinctive differences between the heathen and *differences between the*
the Hebrew rite of circumcision? It is not, I think, *Hebrew*
unlikely that this usage was connected first of all *and all other rites.*
with the idea of generative purity, and so of a transcendent fitness for religious service, and the higher
culture of the intellect. As such it had continued to
be prized in Egypt by the members of the hierarchy,[1]
even though neglected or disparaged by the bulk of
the people; among whom, indeed, on losing its original significance, it came to be regarded merely as an
ancient custom or a sanitary and prudential regulation.[2] It might also in some districts be corrupted,
with corruptions of religious thought, into a species
of bloody offering,[3] or might even as a substitute for
human sacrifices be administered in every case with
the intention of propitiating an angry god, like Moloch
or Huitzilopochtli. But whatever had become the
heathen version of this symbol, no one will deny that
when the Hebrew father circumcised the members of
his household, he both acted with a definite purpose

[1] Origen distinctly affirms this (*in Ep. ad Roman.* lib. II. c. 13; Opp. v. 138, 139, ed. Lommatzsch), adding that men of science were subjected to the rite of circum-cision, and that no persons un-circumcised were allowed to study the sacerdotal or hieroglyphic characters.

[2] Cf. Herod. II. 37, and above, p. 322, n. 2.

[3] Above, p. 202, n. 2. Döllin-ger *Heidenthum und Judenthum,* p. 790) appears to have adopted this theory: 'Erinnert man sich, dass auch in Rom und bei den Galliern frühere Menschenopfer durch eine leichte Wunde, ein Ritzen der Haut und Vergiessen einiger Blutstropfen ersetzt wur-den, so ist es wohl denkbar, dass auch die Beschneidung ein solcher stellvertretender Opfer-Ritus ge-wesen sei:' cf. Kurtz, *Gesch. des Alt. Bund.* I. 185.

and was animated by a spirit thoroughly religious. There the rite was not to be administered, as once it was in Egypt, at the age of fourteen and upwards 'when reasons of health or purity might prompt it,' but as soon almost as the recipient of it was a sharer in the blessings of existence,—on the eighth day after birth. As such it formed a strictly *national* solemnity, embracing not the favoured classes of society to whom it gave admission to the higher forms of intellectual greatness, but extending always to the lowliest member of the Hebrew commonwealth. And corresponding to the freedom of its spirit and its equal operation was the grandeur of the end for which it was appointed. Like the rest of the Mosaic institute, that symbol was profoundly ethical. Translated into words, the meaning of it was 'Be ye holy, for I am holy.' 'The Lord appeared to Abram, and said unto him, I am the Almighty God; walk before Me, and be thou perfect; and I will make my covenant between Me and thee, and will multiply thee exceedingly' (Gen. xvii. 1, 2). The rite of circumcision, as the narrative proceeds to tell us, was the seal and 'token' of this covenant (ver. 11). Outward in the flesh, and so according with the sterner genius of the old œconomy, it imprinted on the mind of every Hebrew the peculiar closeness of his own relations to the pure and perfect God, and the necessity therein implied of fearing and of loving Him, and circumcising more and more 'the foreskin of the heart' (Deut. x. 12—16).

CHERUBIM.

Egyptian sphinxes.   (2) Another instance where it is imagined that the symbolism of heathen countries has been reproduced among the legal institutions is the figure of the cherubim, compared with the Egyptian sphinxes of the Pharaonic times. No question of this kind has been more frequently discussed, and few, it might be added, to so little profit. There is now indeed far less uncertainty than heretofore about the shape and meaning of the ancient sphinx. It was in Egypt of three kinds: 'the *andro-sphinx*, with the head of a man and the body of a lion; the *crio-sphinx*, with the head of a ram and the body of a lion; and the *hieraco-sphinx*, with the same body and the head of a hawk.'[1] The first of these, which from the nature of its composition is most capable of being brought into comparison with the Hebrew cherub, is now regarded as a symbol of the union, in a fabulous shape, of mental and of physical energy;[2] the wisdom and intelligence of the man, combining with the courage and the brute force of the lion. Where a sphinx was planted by the Old Egyptian in the neighbourhood of the throne, the special properties which it was meant to symbolise were all attributed to the king himself; but where, as still more frequently happened, the position was in front of some Egyptian temple, it was rather meant to celebrate a union, in the deity[3] there worshipped, of the same exalted and commanding powers.

[1] Wilkinson, 2nd ser. II. 200. This writer justly observes that the head of the human being in the first division is never feminine, much less virginal, as Bahr (*Symbolik*, I. 358) has incorrectly reasserted.

[2] Wilkinson, *Ibid*. Hengstenberg, *Die Bücher Mose's und Aegypten*, p. 159.

[3] This reference to a deity is denied by Wilkinson, who thinks that all sphinxes, wherever placed, were 'types or representatives of the king': but the theological import of such at least as were placed before temples was known to Plutarch (*De Is. et Osir.* c. IX.), and is maintainable on other grounds: cf. Rawlinson's *Herodo-*

Chap. II.

Compound symbols in other countries.

The cherub not related to the griffin.

When we turn, however, to the Hebrew symbols which are often deemed in close analogy to this, and strive to ascertain their real form and meaning, it is most important to observe that such compounded representations had never during the historic period been exclusively Egyptian.[1] On the contrary, they seem to have abounded in all regions of the ancient world, in which the monuments of sacred art have been transmitted to our times. It has been stated, for example, that 'in the earliest Assyrian monuments, one of the most frequently met with is the eagle-headed human figure. Not only is it found in colossal proportions as sculptured upon the walls or guarding the portals of the chambers, but it is also constantly represented among the groups on the embroidered robes. In other cases, the head of the bird occurs united with the body of a lion, under which form it is the same as the Egyptian hieraco-sphinx.'[2]

One definite parallel to representations of this kind has been suggested in the griffin of the Greek mythographers, which was avowedly an importation from some eastern system; but the specious theory, framed by Herder[3] for connecting griffins by a second

---

tus, Vol. i. p. 633, on the Man-Lion and the Man-Bull, as symbols of two Babylonian divinities.

[1] See the numerous examples of the contrary collected in Bahr, i. 357, 358, who declares with reference to the compound figures of ancient Egypt, that he cannot find a single instance possessing any true affinity to the Hebrew cherubs. The nearest approach to any actual resemblance, viz. a combination consisting of the heads of *four* creatures (a lion, a man, an ox, and an eagle) seems

to be among the emblems of Hindúism (p. 352). Wilkinson, 2nd ser. ii. 275, was most reminded of the Hebrew cherubs and their position in the tabernacle, by two figures of the goddess *Thmei* (or Truth) overshadowing by their wings the sacred beetle of the Sun.

[2] Vaux, *Nineveh and Persepolis,* p. 32. Lond. 1850: cf. pp. 293, 294.

[3] See the ample refutation of it in Bahr, i. 350 sq. Dr. Donaldson, *Christian Orthodoxy,* p. 354, has somewhat extended the di-

link with cherubim of Holy Scripture, though revived
from time to time by the more daring of philologers,
is destitute of all internal probability as well as of
historic basis. Cherubim, as they occur in representations of the Bible from its earliest chapters to
the closing visions of St. John, are *not* mere guards,
or watchers, blocking the approach to some forbidden
object. In the text (Gen. iii. 24), which more than *Functions*
others will at first sight favour such interpretation *of the two dissimilar.*
of their functions, it is not asserted that the cherubim
were placed *outside* the garden; neither is it said
that they were planted on that sacred soil to 'watch'
it merely; for if 'watching' was in any sense ascribed
to them, as well as to the sword-like flame, the word
employed will shew that they were watchers only as
the first man was a watcher; they were doing there
what he had signally failed to do (ii. 15). And in
like manner the position of those emblems in the
Hebrew tabernacle had never been upon the threshold
of the holiest place, nor even before the mercy-seat,
but in immediate contact and connexion with the
throne of God Himself (Exod. xxv. 18). A careful
survey of these facts will be sufficient to repel the
notion that the cherubim were emblems only of ex-

mensions of this theory by connecting the Greek *harp-ies*, 'which
Homer designates as stormy
winds,' and the Greek *Kerb-erus*,
'which barred the entrance to
Hades,' with the sphinx of Egypt,
which, he says, 'watched over
the sepulchres,' and the כְּרוּב of
Holy Scripture, which he charac-
terises, first, as 'the harpy or
seizer,' and, then, by a transition
hard to follow, as 'symbolical of
the Divine presence,' and a 'sign
of warning to forbid a rash or
profane approach to the shrine of
inaccessible sanctity' (p. 355). It
may seem presumptuous to dis-
believe or controvert the etymology of *cherub*, here suggested;
but Dr. Donaldson knows, as well
as I do, that a multitude of other
guesses, quite as plausible, have
been in turn examined and rejected by Hebrew lexicographers.

clusive and prohibitory power; and if we seek, as we are bound, the fuller illustration of their form and import in the copious visions of Ezekiel, and especially among the wonders of the great Apocalypse, it is evident that whatever may turn out to be their true relation to the sphinx, they differed from the griffin absolutely and entirely. Both indeed were composite in structure, though the figures which make up the symbol were unlike in the two cases: and with this mere shadow of approximation ceases all affinity whatever.

Real nature of the cherubim.

How then, following in the steps of Holy Scripture, may we characterise the Hebrew cherubim? Each cherub was a group of figures, or was rather one compounded figure, consisting of four parts. The leading or most prominent shape resembled a human being, while the rest were like some portions of the ox, the lion, and the eagle. The whole emblem, it is true, might have been somewhat different at the different points of Hebrew history;[1] but two or more of these distinctive elements had always been the recognised members of cherubic combinations. Now we gather from Ezekiel that the fundamental thought embodied in such emblems was the property of *life:* they were emphatically the 'living ones';[2] they represented, therefore, several of the noblest forms of

---

[1] Bähr, I. 314. Hengstenberg (as before, p. 162), who, differing from Bähr, argues in favour of the original connexion between the sphinx and cherub, is of opinion that in the time of Moses the cherubic emblem consisted of two members only, the man and the lion, and refers in proof that such a double representation was oc- casionally continued in far later times, to Ezek. xli. 18—20. He urges also, from Exod. xxv. 20, that the Mosaic cherub had only *one* aspect.

[2] Ezek. i. 5, 13 sq.; x. 17. The LXX render ζῶα, which is also the word made use of in the Apocalypse, iv. 6, and generally.

creaturely existence, each excelling in its province, each contributing to the production of a group, in which the human form[1] predominated, and the four together constituting an ideal image of all animated nature.

So interpreted we readily understand not only *How connected with man's redemption.* their position in the sacred garden, but their office in the sanctuary of God on earth and also their proximity to God Himself in visions of the blessed. The planting of the cherub on the ground, which man had once inherited but failed ere long to cherish for his best possession, was suggestive of the truth that he and all whose fortunes had been linked with his had still, in virtue of some gracious mystery, a part and interest in Eden. The appearance of the cherub in the holiest of all was further proof of such an interest; it prolonged the hopeful pledge afforded to the Hebrew by traditions of his forefathers; it told him that the representatives of man and of creation generally had still their place allotted to them on the mercy-seat of the Most High; and in the glowing scenes of the Apocalypse when Adam's family have re-assembled round the throne of God to sing the praises of the great Redeemer, the same mystic creatures shew the ardour which that anthem has excited in their bosoms, by a rapturous 'Amen' (Rev. v. 14).

Whatever, therefore, may be urged in proof of *Relation to the sphinx.* some external correspondency in the Mosaic age between the cherub as already known to members of

---

[1] 'Out of the midst thereof came the likeness of four living creatures. And this was their appearance: they had the likeness of a man.' Ezek. i. 5.

the sacred family and the sphinx as sculptured in approaches to Egyptian temples, there can be no doubt that the two emblems were associated in those two systems with very different thoughts. The one might serve to symbolise the best conceptions which a pagan mind could form of properties possessed by favourite kings or by some nobler inmates of his crowded pantheon; while the other was designed to be a complex image of created nature in its highest, most ideal form, yet always bowing in distinct subordination to the great Creator, and as such ascribing 'glory and honour and thanks to Him that sat on the throne, who liveth for ever and ever' (Rev. iv. 9).

HOLY AND MOST HOLY PLACES.

Real import of the Hebrew sanctuary.   (3) It has again been frequently remarked that the division of the Hebrew sanctuary into a holy and most holy place was made to follow the Egyptian model; the idea in both those cases being that the special residence of the Divinity should form a kind of inner shrine, or adytum, secreted from the popular gaze by some mysterious curtain. Now the fact that the Egyptian temples *did* contain what was entitled a 'most holy region,'[1] as well as various courts conducting to it, is no longer open to dispute; yet with this solitary mark of outward correspondency, possessed in common by most other nations of the ancient world,[2] the parallelism in question seems to be exhausted.[3] As the Hebrew sanctuary was one, in

[1] Uhlemann, *Thoth*, p. 7, and above, p. 289.

[2] Bähr, I. 219.

[3] I have already called attention to the seeming parallelism between the 'ark of the covenant' and the sacred chests, or boats, of heathen nations, while discussing a ritual peculiarity of the Mexicans (above, pp. 149, 150); and the same re-

order to symbolise the absolute unity of God, so all arrangements there established had an eye to the surpassing purity and spirituality of His nature. There, as everywhere, the genius of the Hebrew system vindicated its true honour, as entirely and profoundly ethical. The migratory tent as well as the elaborate temple on Mount Moriah was a pledge to Israelites that God Himself, no mere abstraction, but a present, living, reigning God, had entered into fellowship with His elect, and though the heaven and the heaven of heavens were his (Deut. x. 14), had condescended to develope their religious sentiment by tabernacling in the midst of them. 'I will dwell among the children of Israel, and will be their God; and they shall know that I am the Lord their God, that brought them forth out of the land of Egypt, that I may dwell among them: I am the Lord their God' (Exod. xxix. 45, 46). The sanctuary had thus for them the kind of meaning which the Incarnation now possesses for the storm-tost spirit of the Christian; it presented to them one fixed point amid the fluctuations of the universe; it was the index of God's kingdom upon earth; it brought the infinite within the limits of the finite, it was raised into the meeting-place of human and Divine, and so became the feeble prelude to the mightiest of all facts. And as the holy-place was that to which the Israelite had access by his sacerdotal representatives, and where through them he could perform his ministry

---

marks may be applied at once to the Egyptian ceremony entitled 'the procession of shrines,' and described at length by Wilkinson, 2nd ser. II. 271 sq. The few external resemblances will only serve to bring out more clearly the internal contradictions. Cf. Orcurti, *Catalogo Illustrato dei Monumenti Egizii* (Torino, 1852), pp. 91, 92.

in the sight of God, so in the holy of holies, whence they all were equally excluded, there was imaged out the truth that even for the best of Israelites the way into the inmost presence of Jehovah 'was not yet made manifest.' Veils and barriers intercepted their approach to Him, whose glory, shining forth between the cherubim, was high above the mystic covering of the Ark; yet the admission of one single priest with the appointed offerings on the Day of Atonement was sufficient indication to the Hebrew who was truly bent on finding out 'the wonders of the Law,' that the condemnatory witness there deposited in the Ark might still be silenced and averted altogether by some absolute propitiation, symbolised in the arrangements of that annual solemnity.

Egyptian contrasts. It were superfluous to point out in detail how completely such ideas were absent from the goodliest temple of Mizraim, where the grovelling inmate of the holiest place was one or other of the sacred animals; and where the worship rendered by fanatic swarms of votaries was often no less gross and bestial than the object!

URIM AND THUMMIM.

Nature of the alleged parallelism. (4) Greater confidence has sometimes been expressed by theorisers on this subject as to the Egyptian origin of the mysterious symbol which the Hebrew commonly entitled the *Urim and Thummim.* We collect from Diodorus and other writers[1] that in

---

[1] See Wilkinson, 2nd ser. II. 28, and a fuller discussion of this point in Mr. Tomkins's *Hulsean Essay,* (1850) pp. 80 sq. Hengs-tenberg argues for the identity of the two customs, while Mr. Kenrick (II. 53, n. 1) seems to take the opposite view.

Egypt the chief judge engaged in listening to the cases brought before him wore about his neck a chain of gold and precious stones to which had been attached a small image of *Thmei*, the goddess of truth or justice, and that when the depositions of the litigants were heard, his practice was to touch the successful person with the image in token of the truth or justness of his cause. The drift of this Egyptian symbol is immediately apparent. It impressed on the administrator of public justice[1] that impartiality ought always to preside at his decisions, and the same idea of strict integrity was further hinted by the fact that Truth herself was pictured with closed eyes, and that the judges, in funereal rituals found at Thebes, were also represented 'without hands.' There is, however, far greater difficulty in ascertaining the precise complexion of the Hebrew usage which is frequently compared with this. The narrative respecting the institution of it will be found in Exod. xxviii. 30: 'And thou shalt put in the breast-plate[2] of judgment [*or*, righteousness], the Urim

---

[1] Diodorus (I. 48) mentions as a common interpretation that the ἀρχιδικαστής, who appeared on the tomb of Osymandyas with closed eyes and with the figure of truth suspended from his neck, was bound πρὸς μόνην βλέπειν τὴν ἀλήθειαν: cf. Ælian, XIV. 34. Hengstenberg, *Die Bücher Mose's und Ægypten*, p. 156, is almost alone in maintaining that the primitive signification of this emblem was rather 'promissory' than didactic, pointing to some special presence and inspiration of the goddess of Truth in the Egyptian courts of justice. He

[2] It has been urged (for example, by Mr. Tomkins, p. 83), as an admissible rendering of the Hebrew אֶל־חֹשֶׁן וְנָתַתָּ that 'these two mysterious names (Urim and Thummim) were *no visible part of it* (the breast-plate) *at all*, but attributes assigned to it emblematical of high moral qualities.' Yet as precisely the same phrase occurs in Exod. xxv. 16, 21, where the allusion is to the placing of the two Tables within the ark, we can hardly doubt that the Authorised Version refers in illustration to Deut. xxxiii. 8, 9.

and the Thummim; and they shall be upon Aaron's heart, when he goeth in before the Lord: and Aaron shall bear the judgment of Israel upon his heart before the Lord continually.' We read again (Numb. xxvii. 21) that on the designation of Joshua to the leadership which had been previously enjoyed by Moses: 'He shall stand before Eleazar the priest, who shall ask [counsel] for him, after the judgment of Urim before the Lord;' implying that the wonderful emblems here connected with the breast-plate of the high-priest were meant, as being one with it, to serve the purpose of an oracle, whatever be the right interpretation of the method in which responses were detected and delivered (cf. 1 Sam. xxviii. 6).

Points of difference.　The intimations, therefore, of a common parentage for the Egyptian and the Hebrew symbols, are restricted chiefly to the circumstance that both may be described as solemn badges, and that some *judicial* characteristics are attributed to their possessors in the two cases respectively. The chief judge, among his other decorations, wore about his neck the chain of office, with a precious seal, or effigy of truth, suspended from it: the chief priest, in asking guidance from Jehovah, wore the breast-plate of righteousness, containing in the precious stones of which it was composed an emblem of collective Israel; and armed with it he was directed to 'go in unto the holy place for a memorial before the Lord continually.' But the statement of this semblance of external approxim-

---

is here correct, and that the Urim and Thummim were something superadded, and materially separable from the breast-plate: cf. Bahr, II. 108, 109. In Lev. viii. 8, it is said expressly, 'And he put the breast-plate upon him; also he put in the breast-plate the Urim and the Thummim.'

ation, or rather of remote affinity in the *uses* of the two solemn symbols, is enough to make us thoroughly conscious of their general dissimilitude. The Aaronic breast-plate, for example, was not worn in any court of human judicature; it had no reference to the ordinary business of the individual Hebrew, but to special difficulties connected with the fortunes of the whole sacred corporation; neither was it meant to quicken in the spirit of the wearer a conviction of his personal frailty, or his need of more than ordinary watchfulness in executing his high office.

Whence, then, grew the prevalent notion that *Thummim* some very close affinity existed between the emblems *and Thmei.* now in question? It is clearly traceable to the rendering, which had been adopted in the Septuagint,[1] of the expression *Thummim.* That Hebrew word has there been made equivalent to 'Truth' (ἀλήθεια), and as the great Egyptian goddess, who presided over the courts of law, and aided the decisions of Osiris in the under-world, had also borne the name of Truth (*Thmei*), it was conjectured that the traces of a radical connexion between *Thmei* and *Thummim,* or in other words between the Hebrew and Egyptian

---

[1] Urim (אורים) is rendered δήλωσις in LXX, and (more literally) φωτισμοί in Aquila. The plural form is best explained as a plur. majest., so that it points to the idea of *Divine* illumination. The same account must be given of the plural form in Thummim (תמים) which the LXX, and Philo after them, have rendered ἀλήθεια, and Aquila (more literally) τελειώσεις. Wilkinson, who seems to accept the rendering of the LXX, thinks that the 'dual or plural word' (Thummim) corresponds to the Egyptian notion of the 'two truths,' (cf. above, p. 300), or two similar figures, marking a double capacity of the goddess (2nd ser. II. 28, 29). He also gives a drawing of a breast-plate, where both Ra (the Sun) and Thmei are represented together; which is doubtless a still closer parallel to 'Lights' and 'Perfections.'

customs, had been half-unconsciously attested by the
Alexandrine version of the Pentateuch. But this
conjecture has been seriously weakened, if not over-
thrown entirely, by other considerations: first, that
'Thummim' is a regular Hebrew form, grammatically
unconnected with the Coptic *Thmei;* secondly, that
in rendering 'Thummim' into Greek, the Seventy
have departed from the letter of the Hebrew text
and so confounded qualities which really differ; and
thirdly, that the error introduced by them may probably have had its origin, like others of the same
description, in their strong Egyptian bias.

*Probable
meaning of
the Hebrew
symbol.*   I may add that when the glorious properties of
light and of perfection had been thus ascribed emphatically to the Hebrew breast-plate by affixing to
it the significant symbols of the Urim and Thummim,
the high-priest was made to bear the whole of the
'oracular apparatus' with him as 'a memorial before
the Lord.' If, therefore, in accordance with some
other texts of Holy Scripture the inserted emblems
may be construed[1] as uniting into one the highest
moral qualities ascribable to God Himself, it is no idle
fancy to conclude that Aaron so adorned and bearing
on his heart the names of the children of Israel, was
to them a vivid image of the law of mediation (cf.
Numb. xvi. 47, 48), and to us a luminous shadow of
'*the* Mediator between God and man,' who having in
the fulness of the times obtained a more excellent
ministry, has gathered up into Himself the various
functions of the mediatorial office.

---

[1] See this point well drawn out   pp. 84 sq.
in Mr. Tomkins's Essay (as above)

THE RED HEIFER.

(5) In the law prescribed through Moses (Numb. xix.) for the cleansing of those Hebrews who had been defiled by touching a dead body, there is special mention of the colour of the victim to be offered up on such occasion; that its ashes, mingled with the lustral water, might conduce to the removal of the disability contracted, and so 'sanctify to the purifying of the flesh' (Heb. ix. 13). The victim was to be a *red* cow or heifer, without spot; and as no other valid reason seemed to be suggested[1] for the naming of one definite colour, fresh recourse was had by certain writers to the ancient usages of Egypt in the hope of thence extracting the desired elucidation. We have noted in the last chapter[2] that red was the Typhonic colour, and therefore, if full credit may be given to the account of Plutarch, the Egyptians 'never sacrificed any but perfectly red cattle.' It is plain, however, that if any foreign reference was intended, the idea of counteracting,[3] not of copying the Egyptian custom is involved in the selection by the Hebrews of a cow or heifer in the place of the more usual ox (Lev. iv. 14); since both those animals, as we have seen already,[4] were invested with peculiar sacredness throughout the Valley of the Nile. The truth will

Why the colour was specifically red.

---

[1] Maimonides wrote a special treatise *De Vacca rufa*, and the subject has been handled with singular frequency in all ages; yet the Hebrew doctors admit that even Solomon, who knew most other things, was in ignorance respecting the red heifer.

[2] Above, pp. 291, 292.

[3] This view is strongly urged by Spencer, whose work contains a very full discussion *De Vitula rufa Deo immolanda;* but Hengstenberg, as before, p. 182. while conceding the partial truth involved in it, has suggested that the offering was feminine to make it accord more fully with the common Hebrew word for sin, which is also of the feminine gender.

[4] Above, p. 291.

Chap. II. probably turn out to be, that the adoption of the
red colour in both cases corresponded only because
of its inherent fitness to express the thought which
it was made to symbolise in each community. It
was the colour of *blood*;[1] and while in Egypt this
idea was readily connected with the deadly, scathing,
sanguinary powers of Typhon, it became in the more
ethical system of the Hebrews a remembrancer of
moral evil flowing out into its penal consequences,
or an image of unpardoned sin (cf. Isa. i. 15, 18).

THE SCAPE-GOAT.

Hebrew ceremonial.   (6) A further instance of supposed affinity to
the Egyptian ritual is discovered in the ceremonies
appointed for the Hebrew nation on the greatest of
their annual celebrations,—the Day of Atonement
(Lev. xvi). It is there provided that the high-priest
of Israel, after making atonement for himself and for
his house, shall take two goats, and when they had
been solemnly presented shall cast lots upon them;
'one lot for the Lord and the other lot for the scape-
goat [*or*, Azazel]. And Aaron shall bring the goat
upon which the Lord's lot fell, and offer him for
a sin-offering: but the goat, on which the lot fell
to be the scape-goat [*or*, on which Azazel's lot fell],
shall be presented alive before the Lord, to make an
atonement with him, and to let him go for a scape-
goat [*or*, to Azazel] into the wilderness.' And in

---

[1] Hengstenberg, *Ibid.* p. 188.
Bähr adopts a different view:
'Das Thier war.....Antidotum
gegen den Tod und die Todes-
gemeinschaft, und musste eben
darum auf den Begriff Leben

hinweisen; das geschah nun schon
durch sein Geschlecht, noch mehr
und bestimmter aber durch sein
Aussehen, es trug die Lebens-
farbe' (ii. 500).

the following verses of the same chapter, where the ceremony in question is minutely sketched, we gather the additional information, that the high-priest was to 'lay both his hands upon the head of the live goat and confess over him all the iniquities of the children of Israel, and all their transgressions in all their sins, putting them upon the head of the goat, and shall send him away by the hand of a fit man into the wilderness.'

The practice of transferring, emblematically, the *Minor points of resemblance.* sins of the offerer to the innocent victim chosen by him as their representative had doubtless its analogy[1] among the Old Egyptians, who, in some at least of their oblations, prayed over the head of the victim that evils then impending might be all averted upon it; but there is no necessity whatever for supposing that a practice so graphic and so natural in itself was specially Egyptian, and not rather as primeval as the earliest dawn of the idea which prompted substitutionary offerings.

It is urged, however, that apart from any minor *Why an explanation is sought in Egypt.* proofs of correspondency, the whole conception of the two goats as there appointed, and the seeming dualism connected with their mode of treatment, indicate still deeper tinges of Egyptian influence.[2] On minute inquiry this interpretation of the Hebrew ceremonial

---

[1] Herod. II. 39; Kenrick, I. 443, 444. Wilkinson, referring to this practice, argues from the negative evidence of the sculptures that it was no more than occasional and exceptional.

[2] Spencer, II. 450 sq., has advocated this view in his usual manner, contending that while the Hebrew practice of sending away the second goat partly recognised the heathen theory of sacrifice, the whole rite was calculated to impress the truth that sin-offerings are due to God only, while the evil spirit, which he found in Azazel, was to be regarded as unclean, and as an object of abhorrence: cf. Bähr's criticism of these ideas, II. 693—695.

will be found to rest on the assumption that *Azazel* in the passage just recited is another name for Satan, and therefore that the final driving of the goat into the desert is, in Hebrew phraseology, a solemn renunciation of the powers of darkness, in the name of the whole reconciled community of Israel; or, in accordance with Egyptian forms of speech, a sending back of evil to the favourite haunts of its Typhonic author.

Who or what was Azazel?   Now the meaning of the word *Azazel* is confessedly involved in very great obscurity.[1] One ancient derivation, as attested by the version of the Seventy (ἀποπομπαῖος), makes the name equivalent to scape-goat ('hircus emissarius'); but how, it was demanded, passing by some other disputable matters, could the goat as mentioned in v. 10 be sent *to* or *for* Azazel, if Azazel were the goat itself? The force of this consideration led directly to the notion that Azazel meant either a person or a place; and as the parallelisms between some incidents, relating to Jehovah and to it, appeared in favour of the *personal* rendering, the alleged connexion of the word with evil spirits, or with Satan, came at length to be more generally accepted. Azazel was explained[2] as equal to 'the segregated,' 'the apostate,' 'the unclean'; and

---

[1] See the different interpretations of it in Winer, *Realwört.* s. v.

[2] Thus Hengstenberg, as before, p. 166, note; who revives the derivation of Bochart, according to whom the root of Azazel is עֲזַל = عزل = 'semovit,' 'dimovit,' &c. Ewald, who formerly espoused the Satanic theory in reference to *Azazel*, has of late years explained the word to mean 'das Unreine, Unheilige (eigentlich das Getrennte, Verabscheute), die Sünde' (*Ibid.* p. 176); but is there not something very harsh and unintelligible in saying, as v. 10 would then be made to say, that the second goat was sent forth as its destination *to sin*, or unholiness? On the contrary, the relation in which *Satan* here stands to the desert has some analogies in Matt. xii. 43, Luke viii. 29, Rev. xviii. 2.

although the title is not found elsewhere in Holy
Scripture,[1] nor the doctrine thus suggested capable
at first sight of reduction into harmony[2] with its
severe monotheism, this bold interpretation of the
chapter of Leviticus is on the whole perhaps more
justifiable than any other which has been proposed.

If, therefore, the identity of Satan and Azazel *Relation of*
be conceded, what is here revealed as to the true *Azazel to*
relation of Satan to Jehovah? How shall we ex- *Jehovah.*
plain the casting of lots upon the two goats, and the
devotion of the second to the powers of darkness?
That no actual sacrifice to Satan *could* have been
intended by the Hebrew ceremony, we may gather
most conclusively from the next chapter of Leviticus
(xvii. 7), where all offerings made to demons are
strongly interdicted. Nor will such a startling version of this incident be needed when the passage has
been duly weighed. The *two* goats, it will be seen,
were equally chosen to assist in the performance of

---

[1] *Azalzel* and *Azael* were, however, quite familiar to the later
Jews in the sense of 'evil spirit'
or 'fallen angel' (see Eisenmenger,
Entdecktes Judenthum, II. 155);
and from them, perhaps, the word
was handed over to Muhammadans.

[2] Bähr, it must be acknowledged, has stated his objections
to this view with very great
ability. After urging that the
vindication of the Divine Unity
was the leading, ever-prominent
aim of the Mosaic system, he
adds : 'Offenbar würde aber der
so strenge Mos. Monotheismus
gänzlich aus seiner Konsequenz
fallen, wenn er an dem heiligsten
und wichtigsten Festtag, bei einer

religiösen Feierlichkeit, in der
der ganze Cultus kulminirt, den
Teufel so neben Jehova gestellt
hätte, wie es nach dieser Deutung
v. 8-10 der Fall wäre' (II. 687).
He forgets, however, such revelations as those contained in Gen.
iii., and still more in Zech. iii.,
which latter passage also brings
together, in the closest juxtaposi-
tion, Jehovah, Satan, and the
high-priest. Bähr's own solution
of the difficulty is to derive
Azazel, as above, from עזל, and
to render 'zu völiger Hin-
wegschaffung' (II. 668), but in
attempting to construe the entire
passage on this hypothesis, the
difficulties appear to be only multiplied.

the one sin-offering; and as both were solemnly presented to Jehovah at the door of the tabernacle, both
were recognised by priest and people for His special
property. He it was who guided the lot by which
the one was destined to be offered, and the other sent
unoffered and alive into the dreary desert. It is also
most observable that the goat which was symbolically
destined to bear away the *pardoned* sins of Israel,
and so to bury them out of sight, had been already
'presented alive before the Lord,' and *in idea* had
been offered like the other goat 'to make atonement
with him' (v. 10); so that the duality of the offering
was most probably ordained to represent two different
aspects, or to carry on two separate stages, of the
same remedial process;[1] one of the twin victims dying
in the usual manner, and the second being spared to
shew the Hebrews in a striking figure, that iniquities
remitted by Jehovah on the Day of Atonement were
for ever hidden from their eyes,—remanded to the
sphere of the unclean Azazel, or the 'land not in-
habited' (v. 22). The most important truths, however, which the vivid ritual of that grand solemnity
had served to inculcate, were first and chiefly the
remissibility of human sin, and secondly the consequent call for its entire renunciation: and as truths
like these were lying at the core of the Mosaic system,
it alone of all religions had its Day of Atonement.

§ 2. *Doctrinal Contrasts.*

On passing forward from this necessarily brief examination of particular features, which are said to

---

[1] Hengstenberg, as before, p. 171.

characterise alike the Hebrew and Egyptian rituals,
we shall find that the alleged resemblances which
meet us on the surface are succeeded by a contrast
far more absolute and unmistakeable. 'With respect
to theology,' it is remarked by one[1] who proved himself as quick as others in discovering indications of
ritual sympathy, 'with respect to theology, no two
systems can be more directly opposed to each other
than the Mosaic doctrine was to that of the Egyptians.'
If resemblance to the latter *must* be sought among
contiguous nations of the ancient world, there is no
question, after what has been advanced in the preceding chapter, that the country whither we should
bend our footsteps is Phœnicia,[2] or the primitive land
of Canaan. Yet as every fundamental tenet of the
Hebrew had been always diametrically at variance[3]
with the tenets of his Canaanitish neighbours, it will
follow that so long as he was true to his own principles, he stood in no more friendly attitude to the
theology of Egypt. I shall make this point more
clearly manifest by choosing one or two examples,
where it might have been presumed that we should
trace, if not the positive marks of friendly interchange,
at least the general vestiges of common ancestry.

(1) Now both in Egypt and Phœnicia, during
the historic period, we shall look almost in vain for
recognitions[4] of the power and presence of one only
God, the spiritual Principle of the universe, distinct

---

[1] Prichard, *Egypt. Mythol.* p. 406.

[2] Above, pp. 265—269.

[3] Vol. 1. pp. 94 sq.

[4] Kenrick, speaking on this point (1. 438), goes further still, and while admitting that the highest order of monotheism was 'the clear doctrine of the Hebrew Scriptures,' urges that it cannot be traced in any pagan specula-tions older than the school of Anaxagoras.

from all material forms, and guiding by His legislative will the life and final destiny of all creation. Both countries, it is true, had long retained some glimpses of this grand idea in their knowledge, and some echoes of it, broken and confused by human passions, are still audible amid their wild ejaculations to Baal and Osiris, or are lurking here and there in epithets, by which they thought to honour their great female gods, as Neith or Astarte; but practically a belief in the Supreme Intelligence was disappearing from the earth, when Abraham received his summons from 'the God of glory' to set forth upon the wondrous pilgrimage which brought him as a witness for the truth delivered to his fathers from the eastern bank of the Euphrates. There his family were lapsing with the multitude and 'serving other gods' (Josh. xxiv. 2). They also, peradventure, learned to gaze upon the sun when it shined, or the moon walking in brightness, and their heart was secretly enticed and their mouth kissed their hand (cf. Job xxxi. 26, 27). And when descendants of the patriarch were similarly 'called' out of Egypt, their high mission was connected with the spread and conservation of the same great verity. The challenge which struck terror into their idolatrous enslavers was a proclamation of the sovereignty of God: 'Against all the gods of Egypt I will execute judgment: I am the Lord:' exactly as in later ages, one of the most haughty of the Pharaohs, glorying in the vast profusion of his foreign conquests and presuming on his godlike[1] strength, was doomed by the chastising breath of the Omnipotent, to utter and immediate

[1] Cf. Herod. II. 169.

ruin: 'The land of Egypt shall be desolate and waste, and they shall know that I am the Lord; because he hath said, The river is mine and I have made it' (Ezek. xxix. 9).

No account can here be taken of the 'esoteric' doctrines, which are said to have been handed down in Egypt by the help of her more sacred 'mysteries.' I speak of the religious creed of the Egyptian, either as inscribed upon his public monuments, or as recorded in funereal papyri of the many, or expounded by the treatise of an honest advocate like Plutarch; not as it was represented to us in the transcendental speculations of the Neo-Platonists, who breathing the fresh atmosphere of Christianity had often borrowed all their choicer and more spiritual ideas from the Gospel they were striving to uproot. That popular creed of Egypt, we have seen already, was in substance nothing higher than a deification of the various energies of nature; and in form was one of the least spiritual of the old polytheisms. 'Worship was paid in its turn to almost every object that revolves in the heavens, and to every creature which is possessed of locomotive powers on the earth.'[1]

The popular creed of Egypt.

What contrast, therefore, could be greater than the pure and absolute monotheism instilled into the mind of all the Hebrews? Far from being a mere sublimation of the pagan system, it was based throughout on the most opposite conceptions; it was penetrated by another spirit. God in it was everywhere revealed and worshipped as the one invisible Creator and Sustainer, as the only supramundane spirituality. I subjoin a single passage from the Pentateuch, in

Character of Hebrew monotheism;

[1] Prichard, as before, p. 407.

CHAP. II. proof of this assertion; and the passage, beautiful and touching in itself, is worthy of particular notice here, because it furnishes the most explicit condemnation not of stellar worship merely, which was shared by other Gentile nations both of East and West, but also of the vile zoolatry which flourished with portentous rankness on the soil of ancient Egypt:

'Take ye, therefore, good heed unto yourselves (for ye saw no manner of similitude on the day that the Lord spake unto you in Horeb out of the midst of the fire) lest ye corrupt yourselves, and make you a graven image, the similitude of any figure, the likeness of male or female, the likeness of any beast that is on the earth, the likeness of any winged fowl that flieth in the air, the likeness of any thing that creepeth on the ground, the likeness of any fish that is in the waters beneath the earth: and lest thou lift up thine eyes unto heaven, and when thou seest the sun and the moon and the stars, even all the host of heaven, shouldest be driven to worship them, and serve them, which the Lord thy God hath divided unto all nations under the whole heaven. But the Lord hath taken you, and brought you forth out of the iron furnace, even out of Egypt, to be unto Him a people of inheritance, as ye are this day' (Deut. iv. 15—20).

profoundly ethical.

But God as represented to us in the Hebrew Scriptures has not only been invested with an absolute mastery in all the realms of physical creation, which is therefore said to constitute 'His robe of glory' and to be 'expended in His service.' The few verses just recited lead at once to the idea of still more God-like characteristics. The Jehovah of the Hebrews is holiness itself. He is no expression fabricated by philosophy to denote the aggregate of all mechanical forces, active in the different provinces of nature; but the living, personal, holy God: and with a view to the diffusion of His holiness on earth, He chooses a peculiar people, who become the favoured nursery of religious truth, until endued with power from on high, the germs of life and godliness deposited with them, may fructify in every land and issue in the universal 'healing of the nations.' And the soul of the Mosaic system, which was meant to act as one of the more elementary exponents of God's will, is eminently ethical. It ever deals with man as with a free and strictly moral agent. Passing over all the speculative riddles, which perplexed the intellect or charmed the fancy of the Old Egyptian sages, it proclaims that God above us is our very King and Father, and as such constrains us to obey Him. Its grand purpose is, in other words, to cultivate the human *will*, to draw it into harmony with the Divine; and hence the key to all the homeliest of the Hebrew symbols will be found in the magnificent inscription, 'Holiness unto the Lord.' Here also I extract one single passage from the Pentateuch, to shew that all the ethical system of the ancient Hebrews was erected on their firm belief in the immaculate holiness of God, that holiness attracting to itself the homage, love, and adoration of a free and grateful people:

'And now, O Israel, what doth the Lord thy God require of thee, but to fear the Lord thy God, to walk in all His ways, and to love Him, and to serve the Lord thy God with all thy heart and with all thy soul; to keep the commandments of the Lord, and His statutes, which I command thee this day for thy good? Behold, the heaven and the heaven of heavens is the Lord's thy God, the earth also, with all that therein is. Only the Lord had a delight in thy fathers to love them, and He chose their seed after them, even you above all people, as it is this day. Circumcise therefore the foreskin of your heart, and

Chap. II. be no more stiffnecked. For the Lord your God is God of gods and Lord of lords, a great God, a mighty, and a terrible, which regardeth not persons, nor taketh reward: He doth execute the judgment of the fatherless and widow, and loveth the stranger, in giving him food and raiment. Love ye therefore the stranger: for ye were strangers in the land of Egypt. Thou shalt fear the Lord thy God; Him shalt thou serve, and to Him shalt thou cleave, and swear by His name. He is thy praise, and He is thy God, that hath done for thee these great and terrible things, which thine eyes have seen. Thy fathers went down into Egypt with threescore and ten persons; and now the Lord thy God hath made thee as the stars of heaven for multitude' (Deut. x. 12—22).

The moral sensibility of the Hebrew;

(2) In such a system of religion, where the spotless character of God Himself and the original goodness of the world which He had called into existence are beheld in their most perfect contrast to all that which had *become* evil, sin is in the same proportion a profound reality.[1] Grounded in that system on the moral freedom of the creature, it attains its true importance; it is recognised as flowing from perverted wills of personal beings, or rather every act of disobedience is the absolute refusal of the human will to stand in a receptive, creaturely relation to the Author and the Giver of all good. The fruit of this conviction had been ever manifested by the Hebrew; on the one side, in his abject self-renunciation and the frequent bitterness of his repentance; on the other, in his trembling hope of ultimate forgiveness. There is no period in the history of his race,[2] how dark soever be the clouds that menace the theocracy, how keen soever his own sense of personal shortcomings, when he ceases to take refuge

---

[1] Cf. Hävernick, *Introd. to the Pentateuch*, p. 100.   [2] Vol. I. pp. 140 sq.

in the thought, that in some latter day 'a fountain Chap. II.
shall be opened to the house of David and to the
inhabitants of Jerusalem for sin and for uncleanness'
(Zech. iii. 1). The feeling of imperfect reconciliation
in the present makes him yearn more deeply for the
'times of refreshing' and the bringing-in of true atonement.

But in Egypt we discover few, if any, traces of *contrasted*
a similar aspiration. There the want of clear con- *with the*
ceptions with regard to the surpassing holiness of *moral dul-*
God was followed by comparative deadness of the *ness of the*
moral intuitions. Sin was losing its inherent turpi- *Egyptian.*
tude, because the standard of integrity, which should
have been the holy character of God Himself, was
lowered with the gradual obscuration of that character. Most true it is that sacrifices had continued
to be offered on the altars of the Old Egyptian, and
that some at least of these oblations corresponded
in their outward form and import to sin-offerings of
the Hebrew; but we gather no less clearly from the
Rituals of the Dead and from abundant disavowals
of the spirits for whose benefit those Rituals were
compiled, that the prevailing consciousness of guilt
was very superficial: man was gradually arriving at
the thought that while obedience on the one side was
no arduous or impracticable task, all disobedience
would *inevitably* issue in the transmigration of the
erring spirit; and the offerings to the gods must,
therefore, have degenerated into mere routine, instead
of quickening the perception of demerit, or of leading
up the soul to God in acts of genuine self-devotion.
The indifference of the Old Egyptian to this deeper
view of sacrifice as well as the unspiritual tone per-

CHAP. II. vading all his moral precepts, may remind us of the
frigid self-complacency which we have witnessed in
the temper of the ancient China-man. We cannot
say that it was merely the outsidedness of ritual
worship, or the legal pressure by which it was enforced, wherein those nations differed so completely
from the Israelite; he also, in accordance with the
literal genius of the old œconomy, was required to
fix his eye upon the *body* as well as on the soul of
his religion: the chief difference had consisted rather
in the clearness of the spiritual insight, which enabled
all the members of the sacred family to perceive the
true relation even of the poorest of their ritual actions
to the holy will of God, by whom they were commanded.

Man's rela-
tionship to
God not
recognised
in Egypt.
     Their belief in such relationship to that exalted
Being had again been vivified by what they knew
of their own lofty origin. They were created in the
image of God; in that connexion therefore they could
see the basis both of present growth in habits of
obedience, and of restoration, through some mediatorial
system, to the likeness which they felt to be most
grievously impaired. But this conviction of man's
primal dignity had well-nigh faded from the sensuous
spirit of the Old Egyptian. He could dream of
dynasties of gods who occupied the earth anterior
to his own creation; yet the human sovereigns he
believed could never spring from such; the natures
of the two had no points of contact, or the fortunes
of the two could not be linked together; and accordingly the annals of the human period in Egyptian
history open, it has been remarked,[1] with kings of

---

[1] Lepsius, *Chronol.* pp. 26, 27, who also urges with more or less

purely human lineage, and contain no reminiscence of primeval virtues or of times when God and man were fully reconciled. And corresponding to this lack of faith in the harmonious meeting of the human and Divine is the remarkable absence from the Old Egyptian creed of the idea of incarnation. There *Bestial in-* was no reluctance, it is true, to welcome the chief *carnations.* gods as dwelling in the bestial Apis or in other sacred animals,[1] just as in the earlier *avatáras* of the Bráhman, Vishnu is beheld descending to the abject level of the fish, the boar, the tortoise: but in Egypt we shall find no counterpart of the exalted Krishna, stooping for a season to the semblance of a human body and the mean 'condition of the threefold qualities,' that he may help in the uplifting of mankind in general or reveal some method of escape from the necessity of repeated births. The only faint approxi- *Horus, no* mation to this thought of sympathy with human kind *mediator.* is traced in periodic conflicts of the irresistible Horus with the scorching blasts of Typhon; yet while all advantages derived to man from such encounters are entirely physical, Horus also acts throughout as an unmixed divinity; he never stands invested with a

propriety: 'Hier ist kein inniges Wechselverhältniss zwischen Gott und den Menschen, *wie im Alten Testamente,* kein Herabzaubern Olympischer Götter durch Dichter und Künstler unter die Heroen eines jugendliches Volkes, wie das der Griechen, noch auch nur ein zwitterhaftes Gemisch von menschlichen und dämonischen Gestalten einer trüben Phantasie, wie bei den Babyloniern und Chinesen:' cf. Herod. II. 142.

[1] Wilkinson, who mentions it as a merit of the Old Egyptians that they did not *humanise* their gods, has added (2nd ser. I. 176) that 'their fault was rather the elevation of animals and emblems to the rank of deities.' The heroes (ἡμίθεοι) of the Old Egyptians were consequently not demigods in the Greek sense (*i. e.* having one divine parent) but *gods* of an inferior rank: yet in the age of Manetho there was a disposition (Kenrick, I. 352, II. 92) to Hellenise on these points.

CHAP. II. human form in order to become the champion of the human species. Hence, indeed, it is that when the disembodied spirit of the Old Egyptian fights her way as far as the tribunal of Osiris, she has there no mediator and redeemer; and although she has the prospect of escaping and of floating with the glorious sun-god in celestial regions, it is only after she makes good her claim, as in some earthly court of justice, to the sentence of deserved acquittal.

Doctrine of a future life;

(3) But is there not one point,—the doctrine of a future life,—in which the creed of Egypt was confessedly superior to the teaching of the Books of Moses? This has often been asserted; and instead of pausing to appropriate the admission as an argument in favour of the independence of the Hebrew system, I proceed to ascertain how far the excellence *universally diffused:* ascribed to Egypt was possessed of real value. Now in seeking a true answer to the question, we should bear in mind that almost every tribe of man, wherever scattered or however brutalised, has had distinct conceptions of a life beyond the present; and the vividness with which such feelings are expressed is sometimes in inverse proportion to the intellectual culture of the people,—greatest in the savage, least in the philosopher. The Chayma, or the Esquimaux, the unimaginative Papuan, or the wildest rover in the forests of Central Africa, has never doubted that the spirits of departed ancestors still linger near the place of sepulture, retained in close connexion with the body they had once enlivened, and subsisting more or less upon the offerings made by the survivors. It need scarcely, therefore, be esteemed a matter of surprise, if the idea of an ulterior stage in man's

existence, stretching far beyond the term of natural
life, was quite familiar to the Old Egyptian. Such
idea was but a primary intuition which belonged to
him as *man*. Yet, as this doctrine in most regions *not necessa-*
had existed side by side with every phase of devil- *rily con-*
nected with
worship, and without involving any definite notion *sublime*
either of a moral order or a moral Governor of the *ideas of*
God.
world, the simple fact of its existence in the Valley
of the Nile can furnish no legitimate proof of spiritual
elevation.[1] Nor on analysing the accounts of the
Egyptian dogma, as presented to us by its warm
admirers, are we justified in treating it as something
either special or abnormal. The Egyptian seems to *The*
have imagined, when he introduced the custom of *Egyptian*
dogma.
embalming, that the progress of death itself might
finally be arrested and the past condition of the man
be closely imitated in all future time; and when with
this idea of simple prolongation, and the offerings to
the dead as prompted by it, was connected the more
ethical doctrine of a future judgment, for the grosser
crimes which man had perpetrated in his previous
lifetime, the acquitted spirit, freed at length from
the necessity of migrating to other animals, attained
no higher destination than was commonly awarded
to her by the wild tribes of America;[2] her heaven
was the resplendent sun himself, conceived of, it may
be, as personal, but certainly as undistinguished
from the centre of physical illumination.

---

[1] It is interesting to observe that De Wette, Vatke, and others (quoted by Hengstenberg, *Disser-tations*, &c. II. 460, 461) have begun to acknowledge that an entire silence respecting the doctrine of immortality may belong to a higher point of view than the belief in immortality where it exists only in this crude, unspiritual state. Such concessions undermine the cavils of the older race of Deists, who attempted to degrade the Mosaic religion below all forms of heathenism whatever.

[2] Above, pp. 129, 130.

Now, I grant, that these conceptions of futurity have no existence in the Books of Moses. They are foreign to the genius of revealed religion,[1] and accordingly when urged in a malignant spirit by the later Hebrew sceptics they were all repudiated by our blessed Lord Himself as proving ignorance 'of the Scriptures and the power of God' (Matt. xxii. 29). He told the captious Sadducee how some conditions and relations of the present life would *not* be simply and at once transferred into the future stage of being: just as the Apostle in discussing the objections of Hellenic sophists has proceeded to throw further light upon the mystery of our constitution, and has taught us how the resurrection-body will be very different from a bare resuscitation of the body once committed to the ground. 'It is sown a natural, it is raised a spiritual body' (1 Cor. xv. 44).

Part, indeed, of the transcendent excellence of Christianity, as compared not only with all heathen systems, but with Hebraism itself, consisted in the deep reality which it alone has given to *both* worlds. It never leads man to disparage his position and neglect his duties here, by preaching that the visible world is empty and illusive. Neither does it fashion for him a new sphere of being, modelled on the present life and reproducing all his animal enjoy-

---

[1] It has been reserved for Mr. D. I. Heath to discover (*Exodus Papyri*, p. 203) that 'with respect to the great subject of man's futurity, our present views in Europe are identical in principle, though not in detail, with those which were held by the *actual opponents* of Moses'! The true doctrine, according to Mr. Heath, (and here, he avers, is 'the one really distinguishing feature of Christianity') consists in proclaiming 'the human resurrection of each human being to a human kingdom of mutual human remission of sins'! (p. 103).

ments. Neither does it, in the third place, so restrain CHAP. II.
the human soul within the limits of the mundane
as to shade off many a motive to exertion which
is furnished by our clearer knowledge of the things
invisible. The Gospel has brought life and immortality *to light;* and blessedness, as there revealed,
is both the prolongation and transfiguration of our
present blessedness. How just soever be the statement that the germ of man's future self is lying in
his present self, the ripening and unfolding of that
germ so far exceeds our comprehension that we
measure it only by reflecting on the way in which
the Gospel has in fact transcended the best visions
of the old œconomy, or by noting how the Pattern-
Man Himself received unspeakable accessions to His
human dignity when, rising from the lowliness of
earth, He was 'crowned with glory and honour.'
But as life with Christ in glory must have always
for its precondition the accordance and assimilation *based on*
of the human will to God's, the training of that will *the revealed idea of*
must also be the first necessity in the education of *God.*
mankind. 'To walk *with* God' is that which ever
constitutes the basis of translation *to* God (Gen. v.
24). The true value, therefore, of belief in immortality arises from the ethical spirit of the system
upon which it is engrafted, and the nature of the
Person in whom it has subsistence. Where that
Person is the living, loving and Almighty God, there
is revealed in every glimpse of His exalted character
a strong assurance of continuous being[1] to His genuine

[1] 'That the Sadducees did not root of their unbelief in the re-
recognise this [the almightiness surrection. In the theology of
of God], our Lord marks as the the Pentateuch this hindrance is

worshippers. 'As many as believe that God truly is, believe that He is also 'a rewarder of them who diligently seek Him.' They *must* repose their confidence in Him for present and for future. Unto such He never can have been 'the God of the dead, but of the living.'

Elementary condition of the Hebrews, as explaining the way in which the future life is treated in the Old Testament.

Now it was the primary aim of the religion of the Hebrews to plant deeply in man's heart, and that by painful and protracted discipline, the grand conception of God's perfect truthfulness and the unswerving justice of His rule; and never till this object was attained could faith in immortality, as now unveiled to us by Christ and the Apostles, have been fostered in the Church of God to any salutary purpose. The Hebrews, it is true, like other nations of antiquity, were never left in total darkness with respect to the existence of the human spirit after death. Some intimations of their knowledge[1] on that subject are discovered even in the earliest of their sacred writings; and accordingly the absence of allusion to a future stage of being where as Christians we should have expected such allusion, or the vague and joyless terms in which a future life is sometimes mentioned, where as Christians we should use a more

fully overcome. He who created the world out of nothing—for whom nothing is too wonderful—death cannot obstruct *Him*, if He wills to preserve the soul. But in the theology of the Pentateuch, His will is pledged equally with His power. The God of the Pentateuch is love; He who reveals Himself so full of grace to His people, and enters into the most intimate communion with them, in doing so declares that He will preserve them to eternal life. To this foundation of the doctrine of the resurrection in the Pentateuch our Lord Himself refers (Matt. xxii. 31, 32).' Hengstenberg, *Ibid.* p. 469: cf. above, Vol. I. p. 99, n. 1.

[1] For some valuable remarks on this point, I would refer inquirers to a recent Essay by Mr. T. T. Perowne, *The Essential Coherence of the Old and New Testaments*, pp. 84 sq. Camb. 1858.

explicit phraseology, can only be adduced to shew
that Hades was to them more shadowy than to us,
or that ideas of immortality had been remanded to
the background in the admonitions of the Hebrew
doctors. And the explanation of this difference,
as of others like it, will be found in what has been
already more than once suggested,—the elementary
condition of the people. Their chief thoughts must
all be concentrated for a time upon the law of
temporal, visible retribution, as dispensed through
the arrangements of a theocratic system, in order
that when this idea was deeply rooted, faith in the
invisible and future retribution might spontaneously
grow up. The Israelitish worthy, confident that
God was with him, had been meanwhile going forward on his earthly pilgrimage, in a condition, as
to intellectual certainty, like that of Abraham himself, who, under the immediate eye of an unfailing
Benefactor, started on his journey to the land of
Canaan, 'not knowing whither he went.'

Before I bring these observations to a close, it
may be well to glance a moment down the stream
of Hebrew history, and ascertain the feelings of the
sacred writers at the period of the Babylonish exile
with regard to the admissibility of foreign notions
into their hereditary creed. An apt example may
be found among the visions of Ezekiel, who more
than other prophets was accustomed to revert for
imagery to the days of the Exodus and to events
which followed closely in its train. He thus becomes
a species of transition-link from Egypt to Babylon.
The flower of the two tribes who had been rescued

*The Baby-
lonish exile
the penalty
of indulg-
ing hea-
thenish
notions.*

from the scourge of the Assyrian spoiler were now smitten by a like calamity; and, refusing to be comforted, had hung their harps upon the trees that lined the banks of the Chebar, when a prophet, the partaker of their sad mischances, was commissioned to point out the moral agencies which had precipitated this catastrophe. How dark the contrast to a mind like his, between the coming up from Egypt and the going down to Babylon! There he saw a youthful people full of hope and ardour, marching with the Lord Jehovah at their head to occupy the soil which He had promised to their fathers. Here he sees them broken, joyless, and forlorn, a nation of mourners and of captives, driven from the homes which had been long preserved to them as by a miracle of mercy, and succumbing under the terrific curse which lighted on the wandering Cain. As contemplated by Ezekiel, the whole Hebrew race were going backward; they were exiles in a moral desert, in the 'wilderness of the people'; they were forfeiting the vantage-ground on which their fathers had been planted, and, abandoned to the grasp of a blaspheming power, were melting fast away into the heathen multitudes by whom they were surrounded. And the cause of this disastrous retrogression was declared to be the preference which the Israelite himself had manifested for all heathenish modes of thought. His craven wish had been to lose his sacred nationality, and so to be commingled and confounded with the world. 'We will be as the heathen, as the families of the countries, to serve wood and stone' (XX. 32).

To make Ezekiel more entirely conscious of the evils that were eating out the national life, he is transferred in spirit to the precincts of the Hebrew sanctuary (ch. viii.), the spot on which, if ever, might be found the lingering vestiges of unadulterated truth. But no: in rivalry or feigned alliance with the altar of Jehovah, he beholds 'the image of jealousy.' A nature-god of Canaan, viewed as Baal, the producer, or as Moloch, the destroyer, stands enthroned upon a level with the God of Abraham. 'Son of man,' is the inquiry, 'seest thou what they do, even the great abominations that the house of Israel committed here, that I should go far off from my sanctuary?' And then, as if to indicate the depth of the corruption now contracted by the Hebrew Church, Ezekiel has to witness, one by one, the other great idolatries, which, in despair of God and of her own religion (v. 2) she had borrowed from the heathen nations round about her. First of all he sees the grovelling rites of Egypt, imaged under 'every form of creeping things and abominable beasts.' The seventy elders of the house of Israel, faithless representatives of those who once had followed Moses to the holy mount (Ex. xxiv. 1) as witnesses of the more secret glory of Jehovah, are now impiously attempting to change that 'glory of the incorruptible God'; they stand before the image of Egyptian reptiles 'every man with his censer in his hand.' Another vision is unfolded to the prophet; he beholds in a fresh quarter of the sacred precincts that the old Phœnician worship of Adonis, the original type of the Osirian mysteries, has threatened to efface the purity of earlier generations. Women are assembled at the temple of Jehovah, to bemoan the loss of Tammuz, as the prelude to licentious revelry and

Chap. II. diabolic orgies. Last of all the prophet's eye is fixed upon the inner court of the Lord's house, to which the priests alone have access and which priests no longer blush to desecrate and to deride. It does not seem enough that the community at large are superadding the zoolatry of Egypt to the foul abominations of Phœnicia: men of priestly rank, the 'princes of the sanctuary,' though kneeling on the sacred threshold, have each turned his back upon the holiest of all, and, like the Old Parsee, whose superstitions they are now adopting, 'worship the sun toward the east' (v. 16). 'Then He said unto me, Hast thou seen this, O son of man? Is it a light thing to the house of Judah that they commit the abominations which they commit here? for they have filled the land with violence, and have returned to provoke Me to anger; and lo, they put the branch to their nose. Therefore will I also deal in fury; Mine eye shall not spare, neither will I have pity; and though they cry in Mine ears with a loud voice, yet will I not hear them' (vv. 17, 18).

CHAPTER III.

Characteristics of Medo-Persian Heathenism.

Μάγοι δὲ καὶ πᾶν τὸ Ἄριον γένος, ὡς καὶ τοῦτο γράφει ὁ Εὔδημος,
οἱ μὲν τόπον, οἱ δὲ χρόνον καλοῦσι τὸ νοητὸν ἅπαν καὶ τὸ
ἡνωμένον· ἐξ οὗ διακριθῆναι ἢ θεὸν ἀγαθὸν καὶ δαίμονα κακὸν,
ἢ φῶς καὶ σκότος πρὸ τούτων, ὡς ἐνίους λέγειν. Οὗτοι δὲ οὖν
καὶ αὐτοὶ μετὰ τὴν ἀδιάκριτον φύσιν διακρινομένην ποιοῦσι τὴν
διττὴν συστοιχίαν τῶν κρειττόνων· τῆς μὲν ἡγεῖσθαι τὸν Ὠρο-
μάσδην, τῆς δὲ τὸν Ἀρειμάνιον.—Damascius, *De Primis Principiis,*
c. cxxv. (p. 384, Kopp).

If the object of the present work had been to trace
the early growth of heathenism, without regard to
the contemporaneous fortunes of the sacred family or
the possible interchanges of religious thought between
the Hebrew and other systems, the true place of the
discussions opened in this chapter would have doubtless been immediately after the religions of Hindústán.[1]   For though it be impossible by means of
extant monuments to carry back the civilisation of
Persia to the same remote antiquity,[2] much less to

---

[1] This remark appears to have
been called for by complaints of
an intelligent and not unfriendly
critic in the *Colonial Church Chronicle,* who, in common with some
other reviewers of Part III., lost
sight of the original intention of
the present writer as expressed in
the title-page of his work.   Let

it be again repeated that these
chapters do not pretend to furnish
a complete and systematic history
of ancient heathenism; but rather
to exhibit the chief points of correspondency or contrast between
heathenism and revealed religion.

[2] 'The true historic period does
not commence till five generations

rank her with the great primeval empires of Babylon, of Egypt, or of China, facts are now at our command which will determine the exact position of the Persians proper in the ancient family of man. The region known as Persia (*Parasa* in cuneiform inscriptions) was a leading province of the 'pure Iran,' whose frontiers, reckoning eastward from the Caspian gates, extended to the very foot of the Hindú Alps; and therefore, as the name[1] itself will testify, the population which at length predominated was an off-shoot from the Áryan stock, who, after settling in the region of the Five Rivers, were the undisputed lords of Árya-vartta, and diffused their influence to the southernmost extremity of the Hindú Peninsula.

Related to India.   The proofs of this connection have been strengthened at all points by late researches and inductions of comparative philology. The language of the ancient Persian, or at least that one of many current languages, the Zend, in which the earliest of his 'sacred' books were written, is found to be most intimately related to the Sanskrit of the Védas: it deserves to be entitled second, if not eldest of the sister-tongues which form the Indo-European family. So close, indeed, is the affinity both in structure and in actual words, that we are justified on purely philological grounds in urging the protracted intercourse[2] of Persians and Hindús; who clung together as a

---

before Darius Hystaspis (or about B.C. 680), when Achæmenes founded a kingdom in Persia Proper.' Rawlinson, *Journal of As. Soc.* XV. 252.

[1] See above, Vol. I. p. 171, n. 2, and the references there. The form *Iran*, which has been already detected on coins of the Sassanian period, is undoubtedly equivalent to *Ariana*, *Airya*, and *Airyana*.

[2] M. Müller's 'Last Results of the Persian Researches,' as reported in Bunsen's *Phil. of Univ. Hist.* I. 112; Spiegel, *Avesta*, I. 5, Leipzig, 1852.

great community ages after the migrations of the Celt, the Teuton, and the Slave across the bounds of eastern Europe.

Fresh and still more definite information is reflected on this subject from the ancient books of the Hindús. The names of certain gods and heroes, who were strangers, it would seem, to the mythology of other kindred tribes, continued to be held in equal reverence by the Áryan on the Sutlej and his brethren on the Persian Gulf. The memory, for example, of a Hindú sun-god with the title *Vivaswat* is lingering[1] in the Zend *Vivanghwat*, whom the Persian honoured as the father of the mighty Yima, first and best of human rulers; and although in stories of the Indo-Áryan, Vivaswat had *two* sons, Manu and Yama, each investe[d] [w]ith transcendent dignity, and so inheriting a separate empire, one within the sphere of the living and the other of the dead, it is impossible to doubt the common parentage and ultimate identity of Yima and Yama. In like manner, the mysterious *soma* of the Védas, treated there not only as the best of sacrificial plants, but also as a true divinity,[2] had been reflected in the sacred *homa*[3]

---

[1] Lassen, *Ind. Alt.* I. 518, 519.

[2] Above, Vol. I. p. 178, n. 1; pp. 183, 322.

[3] Burnouf, *Études*, in the *Journal Asiat.* (1844), p. 475, and Spiegel, *Avesta*, I. 8. This change of a Sanskrit sibilant into a Zendic aspirate is of constant occurrence: *e. g.* the geographical name *hapta hendu* of the Avesta is the *sapta sindhu* of the Véda; both referring to the north of India, or the land of the 'Seven Rivers' (*i. e.* the Five of the Panjáb, together with the Indus and the Saraswati). The word Saraswati itself is also traceable in Haraqaiti. Rawlinson (*Journal of As. Soc* XV. 251, n. 1), who mentions this example, adds: 'The proper names of men, too, both in the Vendidad, in the cuneiform inscriptions, and even in the Greek notices of Persia, are in many cases Vedic or Puranic, and can almost always be referred to a Sanskrit etymology, thus authenticating the connexion of the races.'

whose enlivening juices, first expressed by Vivanghwat, were celebrated with a kindred fervour in the earliest of the Zendic hymns.

Religious differences one cause of the separation between Indo-A'ryans and Perso-A'ryans. But facts, which have thus tended to authenticate the old connexion of the Persians and Hindús, may also be adduced to illustrate the grounds of their eventual separation. It is not material for our present purpose to consider in what part of Asia the divergence had originated; whether (as some think) in the locality which formed the cradle of the human race, and so anterior to the first dispersion; or whether (as is far more probable) that schism was consummated at a period, when the Áryan character was fully formed beneath the glowing skies of India. But be this as it may, we have now ample reason for concluding that the final rupture in that primitive population was in part[1] at least connected with religious differences. Rebelling, it would seem, against the 'wild-grown nature-worship' which had characterised the earlier period of their history, or dissatisfied, perhaps, with the account there given of conflicts which they felt to be proceeding in the outer and the inner world, one section of the Áryans fell away from the society of their brethren, and in close analogy with later times and distant countries left the traces of the feud engrained in their religious phraseology.

Verbal traces of this schism. Thus, the Sanskrit name for god, *déva*, bearing witness to the ancient worship of the element of light,[2] is plainly kindred to the Zend *daéva;* and yet this latter tongue had ceased to use it of divini-

---

[1] 'Es finden sich nun auch Spuren, welche darauf schliessen lassen, dass die Trennung der beiden Völker *zum Theile wenig-* stens, aus religiösen Gründen erfolgt sei.' Spiegel, *Avesta*, I. 9.

[2] Vol. I. p. 177, n. 2.

ties in general, and confined it to a class of hostile CHAP. III. genii following in the train of the great Evil One. The highest also of the Vaidic gods, the glorious Indra,[1] whom the warm imagination of the early Aryan had been wont to picture as diffusing genial showers upon the earth, or chasing from the clouds the various ministers of evil, had become in Persia, as in later stages of Hindú mythology, a spirit of inferior rank; yet with the noticeable difference, that the Perso-Aryans had proceeded to invest their Andra with malevolent attributes. In further proof of this revulsion in men's thoughts, it is contended by some writers[2] that the first of good divinities among the Persians, viz. *Ahura,* or *Ahura-mazda* (Ormazd), is etymologically connected with *Asura* in the mythology of the Old Hindú; who was accustomed to employ the title as descriptive of the multitudinous demons dreaded by himself, or by his household, though it seems to have been treated by the earliest of the Vaidic poets as a word of no ill-omen.

Every fresh investigation into the degree of these *Reputed* divergences, as well as the distinct formation and *founder of Zoroas-* consolidation of the Perso-Aryan creed, is fitly pre- *trianism.'* faced by a question as to the antiquity and origin of its reputed founder. Not long after the Christian era[3] it was usual to ascribe the planting of the sacred

---

[1] Vol. I. pp. 173, 179.

[2] *e. g.* Spiegel, I. 9. followed by Dr. Donaldson, *Christ. Orthod.* p. 128: but cf. Burnouf, *Commentaire sur le Yaçna,* I. 78, Paris, 1833.

[3] See a list of the conflicting testimonies with respect to his age in Dr. John Wilson, *The Pársí Religion,* pp. 398—400, Bombay, 1843. Döllinger, *Heid-*

enthum, p. 352, staggered by these contradictions, has revived the theory of more than one Zoroaster, or at least distinguishes between Zarathustra the Perso-Aryan prophet and the Zoroaster, Zarades, or Zaratus of Greek writers, who was really, he thinks, a type, or mythical creation, representing a totally different

Chap. III. system of the Persians to an individual teacher, whom
they designated Zarathustra (Zoroaster); and the
scanty remnants of that people, who have found a
shelter from the fury of the Muslim, in the towns
of western India, or the wilderness of Yezd, look
up with reverence to the same Zartúsht as the great
prophet of Parseeism.[1] There is also evidence to
shew that in the judgment of at least some Persians,
he had flourished in the reign of king *Vistáspa*,[2] or
(according to a common change) *Gustásp;* and other
writers,[3] starting from this incident, have not unnaturally referred the ministry of Zoroaster, and the
earliest publication of the Zoroastrian tenets, to the
lifetime of *Hystaspes,* father of the great Darius.

Ormazd-worship older than the reign of Darius.

Now if it be meant that Zoroaster, a contemporary
of Darius, was the actual author of the system of
religion, in which *Ahura-mazda* (Ormazd) became
the principal object of men's worship, we have reasons
the most cogent and conclusive for rejecting such

(Hamitic) form of heathenism,
but ultimately confounded with
the historic Zarathustra, when the
fame of the latter had extended
to Western nations: cf. Westergaard, *Zendavesta,* 'Pref.' pp. 16
sq. Copenhagen, 1852—54.

[1] Dosabhoy Framjee, *The Parsees,* pp. 238 sq. Lond. 1858.

[2] See Spiegel, *Avesta,* I. 41 sq.
who quotes the traditional account
of the Bombay Parsees. A regular
history of their 'legislator,' the
Zartusht-Námah, written in the
13th century after Christ, has
been translated from the Persian
by Mr. Eastwick, and is appended
to Dr. J. Wilson's *Pársí Religion.*

[3] Ammianus Marcellinus (Lib.
XXIII. c. 6), of the 4th cent. after
Christ, is most explicit on this

point. He also says that Zoroaster was a Bactrian, that he
made additions to the creed of the
Magi, deriving these additions
'ex Chaldæorum arcanis'; and
further that he visited the north
of India, and reaching a secluded
spot among forests, conferred with
members of the Bráhmanical order.
The testimony of Agathias (of the
6th cent. after Christ) is more
valuable (II. 24), because he professes to give the opinions of the
Persians themselves; yet while
repeating the story that Zoroaster
lived at the court of Hystaspes,
he added, as the view of the
Persians, that it was very doubtful whether this Hystaspes was
the father of Darius (εἴτε καὶ
ἄλλος οὗτος ὑπῆρχεν Ὑστάσπης.)

interpretation. Ormazd had long been reverenced as
'the god of the Áryans,'[1] when Darius wrote the
history of his exploits upon the rock of Behistun:
indeed some passages in that magnificent inscription
will not suffer us to doubt that the great movement
headed by Darius was essentially *religious*,[2] aiming
at the restoration of an ancient faith which had been
threatened, and in part subverted, by the influence
of the Magus. The first care of the victorious prince
was 'to rebuild the temples which Gomates had
destroyed, and to restore to the people the sacred
chants and worship, of which Gomates had deprived
them ;'[3] and, as indicating both the nature and extent
of the corruption, he declares expressly that 'the *lie*
had become abounding in the land, both in Persia
and in Media, and in the other provinces.'[4] Supposing, therefore, the age of Zoroaster to have been
the fifth or sixth century before Christ, we are reduced to the necessity of concluding that his mission
had been rather to restore and purify, than to initiate
the sacred system which was afterwards connected
with his name. He must have been, as he indeed
is sometimes represented, nothing more than one
important member in a series of 'ancient *Persian
prophets*.'[5]

---

[1] 'The Median engravers, who executed the Scythic version of the great inscription of Bisitun (Behistun), so well understood the difference between Aryan Dualism and Scythic Magism, that when they had to speak of Ormazd in connexion with other gods, they interpolated after the name the distinctive epithet of "god of the Áryans."' Rawlinson, *Jour. As. Soc.* XV. 249.

[2] See Rawlinson's *Herod.* App. Bk. I. Essay v.; App. Bk. III. Essay II.

[3] *Behist. Inscr.* (as given, among other places, in the above work, Vol. II. p. 595); where Darius adds, 'As (it was) before, so I restored what (had been) taken away. By the grace of Ormazd I did (this).'

[4] *Ibid.* p. 593.

[5] Thus in the '*Desátír* or sacred

*Recent theo-
ries respect-
ing Zoroas-
ter.*

But the tendency of modern criticism, with only few exceptions, is to carry back the age of Zoroaster into pre-historic times, or representing him as the 'Vyása' of the Perso-Áryans to invest him with the dubious, half-impersonal character, which attaches to his Hindú prototype, the so-called author of the earliest Véda. While some (as Lassen[1]) have declared it utterly impossible to fix the period when he lived and so abandon the inquiry in despair, Sir H. Rawlinson has lately started an hypothesis[2] which finds in Zoroaster the personification of an old religious system, or in other words the sacred eponym of an adjacent, but non-Áryan race. To understand this view we must remember[3] that three different populations coexisted from an early date upon the plain of the Tigris and Euphrates, one descended from a Scythic, Cushite or Turanian stock; a second cognate with the Babylonians and Assyrians, or, in other words, Semitic; and the third consisting of the Medes and Persians proper who were members of the Indo-European family. Neglecting for the present the effects produced by the Semitic element, it seems that Scyths, the aboriginal owners of the soil, were

*Magism
and its
propaga-
tion.*

writings of the ancient Persian Prophets,' translated by Mulla Firuz Ibn Kaus (Bombay, 1818), Zirtúsht is the 13th prophet in the series, and the fifth Sassan (contemporary with the emperor Heraclius) the last. But the historical value of this work, which seems to have been fabricated as late as the 16th century, is very small indeed. It seems to have issued from the syncretistic movement, of which Akbar was the leading spirit: cf. Spiegel, *Avesta*,

I. 49, and Wilson, *Pársí Religion*, pp. 411, 412.

[1] 'Seine Zeit zu bestimmen wird nie möglich seyn.' *Ind. Alt.* I. 754.

[2] See his paper entitled *Notes on the Early History of Babylonia*, in the *Journ. As. Soc.* XV. 215—259, and the still more recent discussion of the subject in Rawlinson's *Herod.* as referred to in p. 367, n. 2.

[3] Cf. Vol. I. pp. 71 sq., and Rawlinson, as above.

strongly intermixed with Áryans in the whole of ancient Media, and that, owing to the higher civil- isation of the Scyth or to the witchery exerted by some features of his thaumaturgic system, the new- comers almost universally adopted the religion there established.[1] This, according to the present view, was genuine Magism,—the primeval faith associated far and wide with the time-honoured name of Zo- roaster, and at length erroneously ascribed to early 'Persians,' by Herodotus,[2] who represents it as 'purely and entirely elemental,' or a nature-worship of the simplest form, expressed in adoration of 'the sun and moon, of fire, of earth, of water, and of winds.' The same ideas, it might be not unreasonably contended, found acceptance in some parts of Persia proper; and when Cyrus was at length supreme in every province of Iran, he seems to have conciliated his Scytho- Median subjects by his patronage of Magi, and by placing Magism[3] on a level with the worship of the great Ormazd and other Áryan deities. This state- ment rests, indeed, on the authority of the *Cyropædia;* yet whatever value be assigned to it, there is now ample reason for concluding that such lenient measures were at once reversed on the accession of Cambyses,

[1] 'The Medes not only adopted the religion of their subjects, but to a great extent blended with them, admitting whole Scythic tribes into their nation. Magism entirely superseded among the Medes the former Aryan faith,' &c. Rawlinson's *Herod.* Vol. I. p. 430.

[2] I. 131.

[3] Xenoph. *Cyrop.* VIII. I, § 23, and Creuzer, *Symbol.* I. 189, n. 1. The conduct here ascribed to Cyrus will receive some illustra- tion from what Herodotus states respecting Xerxes, who, departing from the policy of Cambyses, and to some extent of his own father, did not scruple to consult the Magian soothsayers (VII. 19, 37). It was probably much later when the Magi as a body were installed as priests of Ormazd; for 'their name *Magu* occurs only twice in all the extant Zend texts.' West- ergaard, 'Pref.' p. 17.

Religious policy of Cambyses,

who, impelled by a fanatic spirit bordering upon frenzy, had extended his religious warfare into the Valley of the Nile. It is accordingly narrated that the old adherents of the Magian faith, emboldened by the absence[1] of the despot in the west, attempted to recover their importance by intriguing in behalf of the Pseudo-Smerdis; and as soon as the pretender had been planted on the throne proceeded to the

and Darius.

extirpation of established forms of worship. The avenging of this impious wrong became, as we have seen, a leading object in the policy of Darius. He declares repeatedly that 'by the help of Ormazd' he had confounded all the schemes of the insurgents, had abolished the reign of lies, had reared afresh the temples that were ruined by the Magians, had restored the several branches of the ancient liturgy. To this indeed we may ascribe the fact that king Darius was regarded by succeeding ages in the light of a religious reformer; hence the honourable mention of Gustasp (Hystaspis) in the sacred books of Persia; hence the feeling of respect with which his memory was long cherished by all classes of the Old Parsees.

Plausibility of the supposition that Zoroaster was at first a representative of Scythic Magism.

It must be granted that the difficulties attaching to this theory of Zoroastrianism are neither few nor inconsiderable; and yet some theory of the kind appears to be almost necessitated by the force of modern evidence, especially of that discovered on the cuneiform inscriptions. In favour of it is the circumstance that the religion of early 'Persia,' as described by Herodotus, has scarcely aught in common either with the religion of Persian monuments or Persian sacred books; and therefore we are driven

---

[1] *Behist. Inscr.* (Rawlinson's *Herod.* Vol. II. p. 593).

to suppose that his remarks apply to Magism, which may still have flourished in the western provinces, and not to the religion of Ormazd as patronised and practised at the court. In favour, also, of this theory, is the argument, that if the creed of the Magi had been merely a provincial variation of Ormazd-worship, no intelligible account is given of the religious movement strangled by Darius, and his own abhorrence of the Magian faith.

Yet, on the other hand, we have an almost equal difficulty in understanding how the Perso-Áryan people could in after-times have been induced to reverence the memory of Zoroaster, to accept a mere personification of Magism as the favoured organ of their own beneficent deity, and elevate what has been called the 'old heresionym of the Scyths' into the teacher of Gustasp, whose son became a champion of the Áryan gods.[1] This difficulty is relieved perhaps by taking into account the flexible and imitative genius of the ancient Persians, which extended also to religious matters;[2] and as positive proof will be adduced of minor amalgamations between the creed of Persia and other systems, it is possible that some such fusion was gradually effected on a larger scale, and that on the subsiding of the storm in which the festival of the Magophonia had originated, 'a mongrel

Difficulties attaching to this theory.

<hr/>

[1] 'Under the disguise of *Zara-thushtra*, which was the nearest practicable Áryan form, *Zira-ishtar* (or the seed of Venus) became a prophet and lawgiver, receiving inspiration from *Ahura-mazda*, and reforming the national religion.' Sir H. Rawlinson, *Journ. As. Soc.* xv. 254. This learned writer has elsewhere (p. 246) sought to justify his explanation of the word *Zarathushtra;* but does not seem to have noticed the verbal affinity of *Ishtar*, *Asteria*, and *Astarte* (this last representing the Aphrodite of Semitic tribes).

[2] Herod. i. 131, 135.

CHAP. III. religion grew up, wherein the Magian and the Áryan creeds were blended together."[1]

Decline and fall of Ormazd-worship.

But whatever might be the precise complexion of that older system it received its death-blow[2] at the period of the Macedonian occupation, or at least amid the sanguinary struggles of the Parthian conquest. From the former, we must date a large infusion of Hellenic thoughts and customs; while the latter was a fresh uprising of the Scythic population, banished or held down in bondage from the time of Cyrus.

Reaction under the Sassanian monarchs.

Owing to the strong persistence of these foreign agencies, the sacred language of the Perso-Áryan was depressed, neglected, and well-nigh extinguished; the old worship of Ormazd gave place again to Magism,[3] tinctured, it may be, with some Hellenic speculations; nor when Scyths were finally ejected by the daring of the native or Sassanian monarchs, and hurled back on one side into Georgia, and on the other to Afghanistan, could the religion of Cambyses and Darius be restored to its original purity.

---

[1] Rawlinson's *Herod.* Vol. I. p. 431. The vitality of Magism was evinced for ages after, in a form analogous to that already noticed (above, pp. 269 sq.) in discussing the animal-worship of the Old Egyptian, *viz.* by transfusing one of its more cardinal doctrines into the very soul of the new creed. This peculiarity consisted in the adoration of the element of *fire.* Hence the name 'fire-temples' and the title 'fire-worshippers.' I may mention that Mr. Dosabhoy Framjee (*The Parsees*, pp. 256 sq.), affecting to believe, like other Anglicised Parsees, that the religion of their own sacred books is pure theism, 'repels with indignation' the idea of worshipping any of the material elements. A Parsee, he says, while engaged in prayer, is merely 'directed to stand before the fire, or to direct his face towards the sun, as the most proper symbols of the Almighty.' But disclaimers of this kind are not easily reconciled with the express assertions of Parsee authorities; as indeed may be seen at length in Dr. Wilson's *Pársí Religion*, pp. 194 sq.

[2] Spiegel, *Avesta*, I. 16, 17.

[3] Sir H. Rawlinson, as before, p. 255.

Henceforth it bore the frequent traces of its intercourse with foreign creeds. Its sacred writings were indeed recovered, but no evidence survives to tell us, whether they were then collected and restored from extant manuscripts or from oral tradition. A new tongue (the Pehlevi or Huzváresh) was adopted as the vehicle of public worship, and the badge of the new dynasty; and since the Greek, the Jew, the Buddhist, and the Christian had all from various quarters penetrated to the banks of the Tigris and Euphrates, it is not so difficult to understand how the 'reformers, teachers, prophets' who sprang up with this fresh outburst of Persian nationality, should have all departed widely from the older standards, or should, speaking generally, have 'formed their language and the whole train of their ideas on a Semitic model.'[1]

And if the general history of the Medo-Persian were thus chequered and eventful, we shall be prepared to find no small variety in the tone of his religion and the texture of his sacred books. The whole collection of such writings, or at least of parts which have come down to us, is known as the *Avesta*, literally the 'Text.'[2]

One chief result of modern exploration in this region of philology has been to demonstrate, that whether as preserved in the original, or as translated by Parsees, the treatises of the Avesta *in their present*

---

[1] Max Müller, as before, p. 118; Renan, *Hist. des Langues Sémitiques*, i. 77, 78, Paris, 1858.

[2] Spiegel, p. 45: 'bei den spateren Parsen stets gebrauchte Bezeichnung für den Text der heiligen Schriften.' *Zand* or *Zend* properly means 'commentary' or 'translation' (*i.e.* of ancient texts): see Westergaard, *Zendavesta*, 'Pref.' p. 1.

Chap. III. *shape* can date no farther back than the Sassanian
revival, in the time of Artaxerxes, or the third century
of the Christian era (A.D. 226). Another of those
results has tended to confirm and justify suspicions
with regard to the antiquity of several writings which
are commonly adduced as high authorities by modern
Parsees. Of one important work (the *Bundehesh*) we
may affirm with certainty that it had never existed
in the Zend, or older dialect of Persia, but was first
compiled in the court-language of the restoration-
period; while some others (as the *Dabistán* and
Desátir) may be rejected absolutely as fabrications
of far later centuries. Such criticisms are not, of
course, intended to deny that many chapters of the
Persian sacred books are capable of being carried
back to a most venerable antiquity. Whole works
may have been actually committed to writing as
early as 400 B.C., for 'books of Zoroastrians' are related[1] to have perished at the time of Alexander's
expedition. Many also of the sacred chants and ceremonial precepts may, as now existing, have originated
at the epoch of the first migrations. Yet, while
granting this, our ablest scholars seem to be persuaded
more and more that works which have been brought
together in the Avesta, are not only the productions
of different ages, but have all been modified and
modernised by the intrusion of fresh matter. They
stand, in other words, to primitive documents of the
Ormazd-religion in substantially the same relation as
the Prayer-Book to the Use of Sarum.

In attempting to refer the several parts of the
Avesta to the different epochs which produced them,

---

[1] Cf. Westergaard's *Pref.* p. 18.

Spiegel, the most competent of living writers on this
subject,[1] draws attention to three separate stages of
progression or development. The earliest stage, he
thinks, is represented by the second part of the
Yasna,—the liturgy or sacrificial service of the
Persians, consisting of invocations to the 'pure'
Ormazd, to elements and energies of nature, to the
spirit of the worshipper himself, and also to beneficent
genii whose abodes are in the world invisible. The
mode of handling theological topics is there characterised by a remarkable absence both of order and
precision: every thing accounted pure and brilliant,
beautiful and salutary, is the object of half-conscious
homage and unreasoning worship, so that early invocations of the Yasna may be justly brought into
comparison with the oldest hymns of the Rig-Véda.
The next stage of that religion, according to the
same authority, is represented by the Vendidád, or
'Law Given,' in which, besides a most incongruous
list of remedies for earthly ills, has been narrated the
creation of the 'sixteen holy places,' the origin and
growth of evil and its partial overthrow as the result
of Zoroaster's mission; all communicated in the form
of a dialogue between that prophet and the great
Ormazd. As the theology of Persia has become at
this stage far more definite and distinctive, bearing
witness to the presence of the main ingredients which
compose the 'Zoroastrian' system, the transition may
perhaps be illustrated from the course pursued by
Hindú thought in passing from the simplest form of

Different parts of the Avesta in the probable order of composi- tion.

The Yasna.

The Vendi- dád:

---

[1] Spiegel's first notice of these
points was published in Weber's
Ind. Studien (1850), I. 313 sq.,
and he has since extended the inquiry in his edition of the *Avesta*
and elsewhere, arriving at the
same result.

Chap. III. nature-worship to the cultivated Bráhmanism of the heroic age. The third and most important step in the development here indicated led to the production of the first part of the Yasna, and the multifarious *The Yeshts or Yashts.* hymns and prayers collected in the *Yeshts.* The gods and genii of the Persian creed have now been classified in parallel ranks, according to their different properties: the attributes of each are clearly separated and dogmatically fixed: the system known as Zoroaster's has attained its full proportions; its whole 'character is unmistakeable': while the martial and intolerant spirit of Sassanian princes breathing in their sacred books will frequently remind us of the terrible Śiva-ism of later Hindústán, which, after scourging and extruding the disciples of the Buddha, left its dark and bloody trace on the Bráhmanical religion.

Who was Zervána-akarana? No sooner have we entered on a more minute investigation of the Perso-Áryan dogmas than allusions meet us, here and there, to a mysterious Being of transcendent dignity, yet one whose place in the construction of that system is most difficult to ascertain; enveloped as it is in clouds and controversies, which have long continued to obscure the character and parentage of Zarathustra himself. I am referring to a deity entitled *Zervan* or *Zervána-akarana*, who, strange to say, had sometimes been not only associated but identified[1] with Zoroaster, and described as both 'the origin of the Medians and the father of the gods.'

---

[1] As, for instance, by Moses of Chorene, a writer of the 5th century (Wilson's *Pársís*, p. 128). According also to this Armenian authority, the people of the East identified Zervan with Sim or Shem (cf. Rawlinson, in *Journ. As. Soc.* xv. 245, n. 2).

The old opinion was, that in this member of the Persian system proofs might be discerned of a conception bordering on the pure and spiritual monotheism inherited by members of the sacred family. *Zervána-akarana* was held to designate a personal god, to whom was given the appellation, 'Time without Bounds,' or 'Uncreated Time.'[1] Philosophy had also learned to speak of him as 'universal Being,' as the grand personification of eternity, as the primordial and illimitable void from which creation in its varying aspects is successively evolved. He was the basis of all other forms of being, whence conflicting powers of the phenomenal world had each derived its origin, and whither it was destined to revert on the expiring of the present strife, and the completion of the present cycle of existence. Zervan was, in other words, the Absolute, or primal essence, like the *Tae-keih* of the Confucianist, the Bythos of the early Gnostic, or the Ὤν of Neo-Platonism.

---

[1] While there is considerable unanimity in rendering *Zervan* either 'Old' or 'Time' (= Κρόνος), the precise meaning of the adjective *akarana* is still matter of dispute. Anquetil Duperron, the first translator of the *Avesta*, rendered the word by 'sans bornes;' but, as Schlottmann observes, against Spiegel (Weber's *Ind. Stud.* I. 378), it is not derivable from the Pehlevi root קנא, which gave rise to the old interpretation 'boundless.' It is rather (he thinks with Roth and others) to be explained by reference to the Sanskrit *akarana*, 'uncaused,' 'uncreated' (from *karana* 'cause'). That the Perso-Aryans were not only familiar with such epithets, but were in the habit of applying them to the heavenly bodies, is obvious from a remarkable hymn of the Yasna, which Burnouf translates as follows (*Comment. sur le Yaçna*, p. 559): 'J'invoque, je célèbre et ces lieux et ces pays, et les parcs des bestiaux, et les maisons, et les lieux où se gardent les grains, et les eaux, et les terres, et les arbres, et cette terre et ce ciel, et le vent pur, *les astres, la lune et le soleil, lumières qui sont sans commencement, incréés*, et toutes les créations de l'être saint et céleste, ceux et celles qui sont purs, (génies) maîtres de pureté.' It has been suggested to me that as one meaning of the Sanskrit *karana* is 'the time occupied by the moon in passing through a small part of her orbit,' *a-karana* might possibly have meant 'undivided.'

CHAP. III. Like them he was believed to have existed long before the contrariety of good and evil had been manifested in creation; and accordingly the practice was to represent him rather as a 'metaphysical abstraction'[1] dwelling in impenetrable void, than as an active and presiding deity; he was said to have been neither 'endowed with self-consciousness' nor 'possessed of moral perfections.' But here, as in some other cases,[2] a more critical knowledge of the language, and a juster estimate of the antiquity, of sacred documents has modified the first conclusions of speculative philosophy. It is found, for instance, that so far from Zervan standing out conspicuous in the creed of ancient Persia, the allusions to him in her sacred writings are extremely few, as well as cursory and indistinct. Thus, in the principal passage cited from the *Vendidâd*[3] in reference to this subject, Zarathustra, when the words are accurately rendered, has been merely made to say: 'What the holy-minded One (*i. e.* Ormazd) created, he created in the *boundless* (or, the uncaused) *Time.*' And in a subsequent verse, which forms the second important passage bearing on the character of Zervan, the favoured servant of Ormazd is bidden to 'invoke the self-created firmament, the *boundless* (or, the uncaused) *Time,* and the breeze that works in the high places.'[4] On a careful scrutiny of these and other like expressions, it appears that only one of two inferences is really justifiable,

Real nature of the evidence respecting Zervan.

Inference from it.

---

[1] *e. g.* Gibbon, ch. VIII.

[2] See above, pp. 64 sq., on the nature of the Chinese *Tao.*

[3] Farg. XIX. § 33 (*Avesta,* I. 245, ed. Spiegel). The original here is: 'dathat. çpentô. mainyus.

dathat. zrvânê. akaranê.'

[4] *Ibid.* § 44: cf. § 55, and Spiegel's essay in the *Zeitschrift der Deutschen morgenländ. Gesell.* (1851), v. 228, 229.

either, that some elementary substratum was here said
to have existed from eternity, and so to have preceded
the formation of the visible universe, or else, that
' uncreated Time' had been regarded as a species of
material, in and out of which was formed that definite
period of duration, which, according to the Perso-
Áryans, was allotted for the lifetime of the present
world. Such language does not, therefore, warrant
the hypothesis that Zervan was the principal god of
Persia, in the judgment of those writers who compiled
her sacred books.

It is again remarkable that the name of Zervan *Ultimate be-*
is never found upon the cuneiform inscriptions of *lief in some*
one Primal
Darius Hystaspis. Everything beneficent is there as- *Essence.*
cribed distinctly to the grace and succour of Ormazd,
—a circumstance which, owing to the constant repetition of the formula, could hardly fail to have impressed on the explorer his belief in the ' radical and
irreconcilable' divergence between Zervan-worship
and the genuine system of the Perso-Áryans. Still
there is no reasonable ground for doubting that in
subsequent centuries, when the feeling after unity
was re-awakened in the human spirit, and when men
were anxious to revert, in thought at least, to something permanent, illimitable, uncreated,—some existence underlying and reducing into harmony the painful contradictions of the visible universe,—a string
of texts like those surviving in the *Vendidád* were
eagerly appropriated by more philosophic thinkers,
till with such the name of *Zervan* was the recognised
expression of belief in some great Primal Essence.
I subjoin one extract from a later Parsee writing[1] of

[1] The work entitled *I'lmá-i- Islám* was composed about A.D.

considerable repute, in which this theory of Zervan has been formally developed. The opening sentence strikes me as containing an allusion to the passage of the *Vendidâd* above recited :

Example of such belief. 'In the religion of Zoroaster, it is to this effect declared, that God (*Khudâ*) created every thing from time; and that the Creator is *Time*. And for *Time* no limit has been made, and no height has been made, and no root has been made. And it always has been, and it will always be. He who has intelligence even will not be able to tell whence it has been made. So great is its glory that there is no other being who can be called Creator, because the creation was not then made. Afterwards, fire and earth were created; and from their union *Hormuzd* (Ormazd) was created. *Time* was the Creator, and this Lord has guarded the creation he has made.'

Probable connexion of Zervan with the Bel of Babylonia. Nor is the theory of Zervan, as here advocated, inconsistent with a second, which has recently proceeded from a different quarter, *viz.* that this god, whose worship had in later times been made to rest on rare and dubious texts of the Avesta, was in fact an early importation from some foreign and non-Áryan system. We have reason for supposing that the name of Zervan is related to the *ziru-banit* of Assyrian monuments.[1] The title there comes forward as an ordinary epithet of Bel, the Βῆλος ἀρχαῖος of Babylonian mythology, and therefore intimately connected with the thought of *time*.[2] It is accord-

---

1126, and contains the replies of a Parsee doctor to a Muslim inquirer: see the original in Wilson's *Pârsîs*, pp. 135, 136.

[1] See Sir H. Rawlinson's paper in the *Journ. As. Soc.* XV. 245, n. 2.

[2] The word *Zervâna*, according to Spiegel, I. 271, signifies *old* (not 'time' merely), and so would be a fair translation of the Semitic

ingly conjectured, that the knowledge of this great divinity, who, under the descriptive name *Bel-itan,* or 'Old Bel,' was once supreme in ancient Babylonia, had passed over to the Scythic magi, at a period when the different populations of that region were extensively intermingled. Thence the Zervan-dogma may have penetrated into Media, so that the divinity, connected by Herodotus[1] with 'the cycle of the heavens,' and incorrectly represented by him as of 'Persian' origin, might really correspond with the great Bel of ancient Babylonia: and at length, when the amalgamation was completed in the Magian and Persian creeds, and it was necessary to adjust the relative functions and positions of such gods as Zervan and Ormazd, a further precedent might be derived from the traditions of the Babylonian Semites, who had learned to venerate not only a supreme divinity (the $B \hat{\eta} \lambda o \varsigma\ \dot{a} \rho \chi a \hat{\iota} o \varsigma$), but also a reflection of him, called the $B \hat{\eta} \lambda o \varsigma\ \delta \epsilon \acute{\nu} \tau \epsilon \rho o \varsigma$, or the 'Assyrian Hercules.'[2]

In any case we are at liberty to argue that faint *The Parsee* glimmerings of one only God,—inert, indeed, if not *belief in* impersonal, but still the Primal Cause of all things— *unity;* are discernible here and there in the remains of Medo-

---

אֵיתָן, which is found distinctly in Bel-itan, or Old Bel. Spiegel in this matter has arrived at very much the same result as Rawlinson, but by a different process. He contends especially for the Semitic origin of the Zervan-dogma, from the fact that the name *Zerovanes* itself has been preserved in Berosus among the fragments of the Babylonian mythology.

[1] I. 131, where Mr. Blakesley suspects that the historian is following the 'account of some person who confused the genuine Persian with a Median [*i. e.* Magian] ritual.'

[2] 'Beide, der erste und zweite Bel, eben so wie Zarvan und Ormuzd, werden in einer Beziehung identificirt und in der andern unterschieden. Ahuramazda als der Absolute, Ewige, Ueberweltliche gedacht. . .ist der Zarvanakarana.' Schlottmann, in Weber's *Ind. Stud.* I. 378, 379.

CHAP. III. Persian heathenism; and certainly such a dogma, whether viewed as the reanimation of some patriarchal tenet, or as due to interchanges of religious thought with Scythic and Semitic tribes, or as the product of a speculative yearning to resolve all contrarieties of the visible world into an ultimate and higher unity, is often traceable in the literature of modern Parsees.[1]

not, how-ever, trace-able in the Avesta.

Yet, on the other hand, so long as our chief guides into this region are the sacred books of ancient Persia, and the monuments belonging to the age of Darius Hystaspis, we are no less under the necessity of urging in reference to *Zervána-akarana*,[2] that his worship was unknown to all the early generations of the Áryan settlers. He must therefore be eliminated from discussions of the Perso-Áryan theology; and the rather, since his name, whenever first admitted in that system, had produced in it no sensible effect. *Zervána* was from first to last a colourless abstraction,

[1] The following extract from Mr. Dosabhoy Framjee's work *The Parsees*, pp. 250, 251, will remind some readers of the strong assertions made by Ram-mohun Roy and other half-Christianized Hindús as to the primitive theology of the Védas: 'The religion propounded by him [Zoroaster] is a simple form of theism, recognising but one God, the Creator, Ruler, and Preserver of the universe, without form, invisible. To Him is assigned a place above all, and to Him every praise is to be given for all the good in this world, and all the blessings we enjoy. Zoroastrianism does not require any image of God to be made for the purpose of worship, as to Him is attributed no form, shape, or colour. He is an immense light, from which all glory, bounty, and goodness flow. He is represented as the mightiest, the most just, and the most benevolent. His mercies are as boundless as His being. The adoration or worship of any other object is blasphemous.' The author of such language would most probably explain the countless 'invocations' addressed in the Yasna to the various forms of created nature as no more than pious remembrances of high and noble objects: cf. Wilson, *Pársí Religion*, pp. 265 sq.

[2] Rawlinson and Spiegel are quite at one on this point. The latter writes (*Avesta*, Exc. I. 271): 'In dem ganzen persischen ursprünglichen Religionssysteme ist diese Lehre ein Misston.'

which Parsees are even now accustomed to esteem the mere equivalent of 'eternity.'

If we, accordingly, neglect this foreign and intrusive element, we find that the theology derivable from the pages of the Avesta[1] is, in form at least, completely *dualistic*. A belief in two great principles, of rival power and contradictory functions, is conspicuously set forth in every portion of those writings, or at least in all the portions where the language of the worshipper does not betray the influence of incurable polytheism. The rival principles of Medo-Persia are *Ahura-mazda*[2] (Ormazd), the good divinity, and *Aĝra-mainyus* (Ahriman), the 'Evil-minded.'

Ormazd and Ahriman.

Now with reference to Ormazd, it must be granted that he is not only, in accordance with his title, 'god of the Áryans,' but has also been at times invested with high honours and prerogatives which suffice almost to lift him to the rank of the Supreme Intelligence. He is the sovereign judge, the sovereign excellence, the sovereign knowledge: 'greatest, best, most beautiful, the strongest, most intelligent, most graceful, and most holy.'[3] Everything, so far as it is elevated in its aim, and noble in its nature, was the product of his hand: he is the 'Maker of

Attributes of Ormazd.

---

[1] The monuments are not included in this statement, because, with one exception where the 'god of lies' is glanced at, they contain no traces of the Persian dualism. Their silence, however, with regard to Ahriman is well explained in Rawlinson's *Herodotus*, Vol. i. p. 427, n. 4, where we are reminded that 'the public documents of modern countries make no mention of Satan.'

[2] On the various etymologies of this word, see Burnouf, *Commentaire sur le Yaçna*, pp. 70 sq.; Wilson, *Parsi Religion*, p. 110. Another name or title of Ormazd, viz. *Spento-mainyus*, 'the Holy-minded,' brings him into more direct antagonism with the 'Evil-minded.'

[3] *Vendidád*, Farg. xix. § 47.

Chap. III. the pure creation;' more exalted than the brilliant, fertilising Mithra, ruler of a spacious province, and gifted with ten thousand eyes; superior also to the holy Sraŏsha, the author of abundance, bearing in his hand the instruments of vengeance to chastise a multitude of evil spirits.[1] One example taken from the Yasna[2] will exhibit all these varied characteristics in a single group: 'I invoke and celebrate the creator Ahura-mazda, luminous, resplendent, best and greatest, excellent in strength and in perfection, most intelligent, most lovely, eminent in purity, possessing the good knowledge, source of pleasure, who created us, who fashioned us, who feeds us, most accomplished of intelligent beings.'

Amshaspands :

In the train of this divinity, or at times associating with him as possessors of the same exalted nature, are six other spiritual beings, genii of the world of light. The common name 'amshaspand' (*amesha-spenta*, or 'immortal holy one') is equally applied to all these seven intelligences; each has special days in every month devoted to his honour; though expressions, we must also grant, are never wanting where Ormazd is ranked indefinitely above the others, and regarded as the luminous chief and *their probable origin,* 'lord of the amshaspands.'[3] It is probable, as hinted in a previous chapter,[4] that this frequent limitation

---

[1] *Ibid.* §§ 51—53: cf. Spiegel's *Studien,* in *Zeitsch. Deutsch. morg. Gesell.* v. 223, 224. In a passage there translated from the *Minok-hired* (a work of the Sassanian age) we notice an endeavour to establish some original co-operation between Ormazd and Zervána-akaraua : 'Der Schöpfer Ormazd erschuf diese Welt und Creaturen und Amschaspande und den himmlischen Verstand *aus seinem eigenen Lichte* und mit dem Jubelrufe der *unendlichen Zeit.*'

[2] Burnouf, *Comment.* p. 146.

[3] Wilson, as above, p. 129. On the names of the *amshaspands,* see Burnouf, as before, pp. 147—174.

[4] Above, p. 267.

of the 'holy ones' to *seven* has reference to the
primitive worship of the heavenly bodies, the sun,
the moon, and the five planets. Light, in its most
elemental form, had fascinated the imagination of the
early Áryan, and at first, perhaps as the appropriate
symbol of the Godhead, had suggested the generic
name of his divinities.[1] The sun-god (Savitri) was
celebrated by the Hindú poet in the oldest of the
Vaidic hymns; and consequently, when his kinsmen
paid their homage to the gorgeous sky of Persia, it
was not unlikely that they all continued to associate
some ideas of the invisible world with the more
brilliant of the heavenly bodies. The great lord of
light, proceeding on his course in peerless dignity
and beauty, was the 'eye' of Ormazd himself; the
lesser lights were his attendants, shining by his
splendour and executing his behests; and thus, in
spite of all the systematising of the first mythology
which resulted in the formal 'dualism of Zoroaster,'
the old practice[2] of ascribing personality to sun and
moon and stars, and so exalting them to objects of
religious worship, was perpetuated in the Persian
system to the close of its existence.

But as physical light appears to be involved in
deadly strife with physical darkness, so the glory
of Ormazd was ever liable to diminution and eclipse
beneath the shade of Ahriman, his lying, 'evil-
minded,' and corrupting adversary. In the strength

---

[1] Above, Vol. I. p. 177.

[2] The following is M. Burnouf's version of a hymn in the *Yasna* (*Comment.* p. 375): 'Je célèbre, j'invoque Ahura et Mithra, élevés, immortels, purs; et les *astres, créations saintes et célestes;* et l'astre Taschter (Tistrya), lumineux, resplendissant; et la lune, qui garde le germe du taureau; et le soleil, souverain, coursier rapide, *œil d'Ahura-mazda;* Mithra, chef des provinces.'

CHAP. III. imparted to such contrasts by the Medo-Persian creed consists its grand peculiarity.[1]

Dualism not peculiar to Persia.

We must not suppose, indeed, with some living writers, that dualism was utterly unknown in all other heathen countries. Typhon's place in reference to Osiris was in many points analogous to that of Ahriman, the rival of Ormazd.[2] The Bráhman, also, could discourse of deep and irremediable antagonisms between the laws of matter and of spirit; and in some of the non-Áryan tribes of India,[3] to say nothing of American and other distant parallels, the two great members of the pantheon are the Sun, or light-god, and his wife, the Earth; the latter being adverse to the former as evil to good, yet both of them esteemed the fitting objects of religious worship. Still the shape assumed by Persian dualism is so peculiar, the antagonistic forces are so nearly balanced, and the contrast has been carried out so rigorously in its details, that we are justified in treating this as a distinctive feature in the history of religious thought.

Iran and Turan.

In Persia also, even more than Egypt,[4] the relations of the two chief gods reflect the physical circumstances of the country and the struggles of the early population. While their brethren on the Sutlej were invoking Indra and his host to aid in the ex-

---

[1] Sir H. Rawlinson has gone so far as to conjecture that it was the rise of this 'dualistic heresy' which led to the original disruption of the Áryan tribes.

[2] Plutarch, *De Iside et Osiride,* after describing the malignity of Typhon, proceeds (c. XLVI.) to speak of Zoroastrian dualism as something akin to that of Egypt: but Mr. Kenrick (*Anc. Egypt,* I.

419) argues that the contrast was less definitely established in the Egyptian system; for if not 'we should find other gods whose attributes are beneficent assailed by other Typhons.'

[3] See the extracts from Major Macpherson's paper on the religion of the Khonds, above, Vol. I. pp. 372 sq.

[4] Above, pp. 277—279.

pulsion of the dark-complexioned 'Dasyus,' the first settlers in Iran were waging a like contest with the 'hostile ones,' the *Tuíryas*[1] (Turanians). Every inch they rescued from the natives was a triumph won from Ahriman by timely succours of Ormazd; while in the lengthened fluctuations of that contest they beheld an image of the warfare ever raging in the spirit-world, where powers of good and evil, moral light and moral darkness, had alternate mastery. As from the fiat of Ormazd proceeded all the good things of creation, Ahriman had the terrific privilege of *creating* and transmitting evil.[2] Every thing that tended to impede the propagation of life and purity and light, or interrupted the benignant flow of order and prosperity, was imputed to the envious rage of the arch-demon, ever battling from a species of necessity within the borders of his rival. One of these co-ordinate powers was thus an object of desire and reverence, and as such received the willing homage of all worshippers, the frequent prayer, the grateful offering; while, on turning towards Ahriman, the object of men's dread and horror, prayer itself was changed to abject deprecation, and sacrifice became no better than a weapon or a charm for warding off

Evil created by Ahriman.

---

[1] Spiegel, in *Zeitsch. Deutsch. morg. Gesell.* v. 223. The Vaidic equivalent in *túrya*, 'hostile.'

[2] Thus in the opening Fargard of the *Vendidád*, as soon as it is mentioned that Ormazd had created any pure locality, the addition uniformly follows: 'Dann schuf eine Opposition desselben Agramainyus, der voll Tod ist.' After statements such as this, continually repeated in his own sacred books, it is difficult to understand how an intelligent writer like Mr. Dosabhoy Framjee (*Parsees*, p. 255) can argue that Ahriman 'should be taken in an allegorical sense, to denote the cause of the temptation under which man often falls into evil.' The *personality* of Ahriman is quite as clearly stated as the personality of Ormazd.

CHAP. III. calamity.[1] To illustrate the old ideas on this subject,

The homicidal serpent. I may mention that a hideous serpent, which in Egypt was connected with Typhonic malice,[2] was in Persia also the peculiar agent of the Evil-minded. Hence, indeed, arose the fancy that of salutary effects believed to flow in primitive times from the great homa-sacrifice the foremost was the generation of a warrior, who might slay 'the homicidal serpent, with three necks, with three heads, with six eyes, and with a thousand forces,—that remorseless god, who destroys purity, that sinner who ravages the worlds, whom Ahriman created the chief foe of purity, in the existing world, for the annihilation of the purity of the worlds.'[3]

Devs, the antagonists of amshaspands. Exactly as the projects of Ormazd were carried out by six immediate ministers or colleagues, Ahriman ere long was made the centre of a circle of malignant spirits, sons of darkness; six of whom, the *devs* (*daévas*), stand arrayed in deadly strife against the luminous *amshaspands*. The two orders had thus

---

[1] Plutarch, as before, c. XLVI. Among the other multitudinous objects invoked in the *Yasna*, frequent mention is made of the *Izeds*, a class of gods or genii which at times are scarcely distinguishable from the *Amshaspands*. They are saluted as 'the most worthy of the masters of purity, the most praiseworthy, the most pervading, the delight of the master, the pure master of purity.' The highest member of this order would appear to have been Mithra. We have again considerable difficulty in determining the precise nature and functions of another class of spirits mentioned in the *Yasna*, *viz.* the *Fervers* or *Fravashis*, which, although reminding us of guardian angels and good genii, are more properly considered as ideal prototypes of actual intelligences (cf. Wilson, *Pársí Religion*, pp. 130, 131). Every thing in nature, up to Ormazd himself (*Vendidâd*, XIX. 46), has its own special *Fervér:* and occasionally such model beings were supposed to form a vast spiritual army fighting on the side of the good Principle, passing also between earth and heaven, and carrying the devotions of 'pure' men to the feet of Ormazd (Döllinger, *Heidenthum*, p. 362).

[2] Above p. 284. n. 1.

[3] Translated by Burnouf, *Études*, 'Le Dieu Homa,' in *Journal Asiat.* (1844), IV. 493.

formed so many pairs of strong antitheses: they
personated in the one case high and salutary properties, as life and goodness, truth and plenty, and
the element of fire itself considered as a source of
happiness; they personated in the other case destruction, malice, lying, penury, and elemental fire that
shrivels and devours.

The question now is, Are we justified in speaking *Dualism,*
of the Persian form of dualism as absolute and eternal? *regarded as*
absolute or
Were the powers in conflict so equipotent, the ele- *as tempo-*
ments of good so hopelessly and so inextricably *rary.*
blended with the elements of evil, that mankind must
ever groan between the terrible contrariety?

Such is often said to be the character of genuine
' Zoroastrianism'; and little or nothing, I am bound
to mention, is detected in the ancient books of Persia
that necessitates an opposite conclusion. In those
writings, the two kingdoms almost uniformly stand
in harsh and absolute antagonism; on one side there
is primal Good producing and reviving good, and on
the other, primal evil, which, possessed of a co-ordinate power, is working, and must ever work, disorder
and decomposition. It appears, moreover, that belief
in this most rigorous form of dualism had been perpetuated in a Persian sect entitled Magusæans, while
the influence which it once exerted is perhaps still
more distinctly to be traced in the projection of the
Manichæan heresy.

Máni, we should here remember, lived and taught *Manichæ-*
at Babylon in the third century after Christ, and in *ism.*
the mythic names attributed to his pupils (Buddas,[1]

---

[1] The old reading *Addas* is now   *Ind. Alt.* III. 406).
corrected into *Buddas* (Lassen's

Thomas, Hermas) may be found not only proof of his reputed influence, but allusion to particular systems of belief which he attempted, not long after the Sassanian revival, to amalgamate with the Ormazd-religion.

Relation of Manicha-ism to Zoroastri-anism.

It is foreign to our purpose to inquire in what degree the Buddhist, Christian, and Hellenic elements were intermixed[1] by him with genuine 'Zoroastrianism'; but as none of those foreign systems can be charged with teaching the dogma of two opposite and co-eternal principles, we may conclude that in the view of Máni, who insisted ever on such dogma, it was held to be a genuine heirloom of the ancient Persian worthies. On the other hand, as Máni himself is said to have been barbarously put to death upon the charge of falsifying the pure religion of Zoroaster, we are not at once entitled to draw positive inferences, as to the early character of that religion, from accounts which have descended to us of the Manichæan heresy.

Fresh traces of the doctrine of unity.

It must, indeed, be granted that so far as our particular question is concerned, the language used by Persians in the fifth century after Christ again implied a prevalent disposition to reduce all contra-rieties of the physical and moral world into an abstract unity. For that Zervanism was then at least a primary article of their faith, the following extract from the proclamation[2] of a Persian general (A.D. 450) will abundantly establish:

---

[1] F. C. Bauer, *Das Manichäische Religionssystem*, followed, in the main, by Lassen, contends that in those particulars where Manichæism separated itself from the 'doctrine of Zoroaster,' it came nearer to Hindú systems and especially to Buddhism. On the strange way in which Zoroaster (Ζαράδης), Buddha, Christ, and Máni were associated on a level by some of the Mediæval Manichæans, see Vol. I. p. 34, n. 2.

[2] The author of it was Mihr

"Before the heavens and the earth were, the great god Zruan (Zervan) prayed a thousand years, *Mythe con-* and said, 'If I, perhaps, should have a son named *necting Zervan* *Vormist* (Ormazd), who will make the heavens and *with Or-* the earth.' And he conceived two in his body, one *mazd and Ahriman.* by reason of his prayer, and the other because he said *Perhaps.* When he knew that there were two in his body, he said, 'Whichever shall come first, to him will I give over my sovereignty.' He who had been conceived in doubt passed through his body and went forth. To him spake Zruan: 'Who art thou?' He said, 'I am thy son Vormist.' To him said Zruan: 'My son is light and fragrant breathing; thou art dark and of evil disposition.' As this appeared to his son exceedingly harsh, he (Zruan) gave him the empire[1] for a thousand years. When the other son was born to him, he called him Vormist. He then took the empire from Ahriman, gave it to Vormist, and said to him, 'Till now I have prayed to thee, now thou must pray to me.' And Vormist made heaven and earth; Ahriman on the contrary brought forth evil."

Nerseh, grand vizier of Iran. It was addressed to the Armenians, and has been preserved in the *History of Vartan* by an Armenian bishop Eliseus (pp. 11, 12, translated by Neumann, Lond. 1830). The account respecting Zervan and the two derived intelligences (Ormazd and Ahriman) agrees substantially with that transmitted by another Armenian writer of the 5th century after Christ: see the *Réfutation des Sectes,* par Eznig, pp. 75 sq., (translated into French by De Florival, Paris, 1853). Döllinger (p. 360, note) has also pointed out distinct allu-

sions to the same mythe in Theodore of Mopsuestia, who says, in speaking of Zervan (ἀρχηγὸν πάντων), that while making a libation (? of the homa-plant), ἵνα τέκῃ τὸν Ὁρμίσδαν, ἔτεκεν ἐκεῖνον καὶ τὸν Σατανᾶν.

[1] The priority of birth and empire here attributed to the Evil One has a most striking parallel in the dualistic system of the Bogomiles (of the 12th century after Christ): see Hardwick's *Middle Age,* pp. 303 sq. There also Satanael is the first-born, and is entrusted for a season with the chief administration of the world.

CHAP. III.

Moral import of such mythes.

In accordance with the hopeful spirit that gave being, both to this and other kindred mythes, the reign of the good Principle, though subsequent in point of time, was represented as far mightier and more lasting than the reign of evil. Ahriman, the child of doubt, shall be hereafter superseded.[1] On the expiration of some dark millenium, he shall cease to be the terror of all pure and upright beings, while his rival, raised to the administration of the kingdom, shall create a second order of superior spirits, or at least initiate some remedial process, by which all things now existing may revert to their original condition. In other words, the ancient Persian could descry beneath the manifold contradictions of the actual world an aboriginal unity, nay, could hear amid them all the promise of some blessed restoration.

Hope of ultimate triumph.

Faint, indeed, and broken were the whispers of that promise. Often the mere echo of instinctive longings under which the heart of man had ached in every region of the ancient world, it was devoid of all historic basis, and was pointing onward to no definite fulfilment; yet in spite of its intrinsic weakness, and in spite of all the clouds in which it was involved by desperate speculations on the origin of evil, a belief in some such promise,—a belief in the superior majesty of truth and her eventual triumph,—

---

[1] These peculiarities of the later Persian creed are fully established in passages brought to light by J. Müller, in 1843, and subsequently considered by Spiegel, in the *Zeitschrift der Deutsch. morgenländ. Gesellschaft* (1851), v. 225. One of such passages affirms in reference to Ahriman: 'Aber es wird eine Zeit sein, wo sein Schlagen aufhört.' And in a second, after describing the effects of the Evil Principle, it is added: 'Es war (eine Zeit), da er nicht war in diesen Geschöpfen, und es wird sein (eine Zeit), da er nicht sein wird in den Geschöpfen.' The same idea of Ahriman's eventual overthrow occurs in Plutarch, *De Isid. et Osir.* c. XLVII.

had been always lingering in the Persian mind. We
may hereafter have occasion to observe that under
the Sassanian monarchs, some at least of the more
popular traditions on this subject bore no slight resemblance to the Messianic prophecies transmitted in
the Hebrew Church.

As special virtue had been constantly ascribed to *Armour of*
words of Ormazd, it was by these, as parts of his *the holy man of*
offensive armour, that the good man was commissioned *Persia.*
to do battle with the swarming hosts of darkness.
For example, when the Evil One demanded[1] of Zarathustra ' By whose word wilt thou smite, by whose
word wilt thou destroy?' the 'holy man' is said to
have replied: 'A mortar and a bowl, the *homa* and
the words which Ormazd has spoken, these are my
best weapons.' Nor did victory over Ahriman consist
in mere escape from present physical suffering, and
in larger and more sparkling cups of temporal prosperity.[2] Here the Persian, of historic times at least,
was far superior to his kinsman whose importunate
prayer for cows and horses and the like was heard
pervading all the oldest invocations of the Véda. In
the measure of her moral sensibility, Persia may be
fairly ranked among the brightest spots of ancient
heathendom.

The 'holy man,' indeed, of the Avesta, is often *Largeness*
a mere synonym for 'worshipper of Ormazd,' yet ex- *of spirit, a distin-*
cellence, it should not be forgotten, is confined no *guishing*
longer to descendants of a priestly class dissevered *feature of the Ormazd-*
by impassable gulphs from all below them: not to *religion.*

---

[1] *Vendidâd*, xix. 28—32, where   sind die Worte, welche alle Dae-
I follow Spiegel's version: cf. x.   vas schlagen.'
25, sq. In § 28 we are told 'Dies   [2] Cf. above, Vol. I. p. 181.

the possessor of recondite knowledge, and the lordly founder of some philosophic school; not even to the ardent devotee recoiling from the din and business of the world, and seeking in the silence of the jungle a sure refuge from its perils and seductions. Purity is there made possible for all: in all it is connected with incessant warfare, and in all dependent on exact conformity to the Ormazd-religion, ' in thought, in word, in deed.' Deflection from its precepts is the only cause of permanent disaster. Servants of Ormazd, unfortified by prayer and sacrifice, may yield to the temptations of the Evil One, and as the fruit of their misdeeds may undergo a lengthened term of penance. The body also must in every case eventually succumb beneath the iron yoke of death, the ruthless minister of Ahriman, and then communicate a portion of its own 'impurity' to all who come in contact with it. Still so long as any man was held to have continued in the number of the ' pure,' it was believed that saving efficacy issued to his spirit from the law of Ormazd; that law 'taking away all the evil thoughts, words and actions of a pure man, as the strong fleet wind purifies the heaven.'[1]

Persian ideas of purity. A cursory glance at precepts and prescriptions of the *Vendidád* will serve, however, to convince us that in Persia, as in Egypt, the idea of 'purity' had always been extremely superficial and unspiritual. It involved but little more than a punctilious compliance with established rites and ceremonies. Starting from the thought that every thing in nature was intrinsically either ' clean' or ' unclean,'—a production either of Ormazd the good divinity, or else of the impure

[1] *Vendidád*, III. 149.

arch-demon,—the Old Persian was at least as anxious to escape from bodily defilement,[1] or from contact with material things possessed by Ahriman, as to exemplify the higher moral qualities of which that Evil One had introduced the hideous negations. On *Practical character* the other hand, it is apparent that the consciousness *of the Old* of an unceasing conflict in the spirit-world had kept *Persian.* alive the habit of discriminating between moral light and moral darkness, and produced in many hearts a deep abhorrence of the evil, and a resolute yearning after good. The Persian had been commonly one of the least compromising, if not also the most active and most truthful, nations of antiquity.[2] Accustomed to regard the universe in general as one mighty battle-field, the genuine worshipper of Ormazd had also tenanted his own immediate sphere with foes innumerable: his mission was to aid in counteracting the unwearied malice of the *devs*, to vindicate the cause of right and truth against the advocates of wrong and falsehood; and the stern intolerant spirit breathed by despots like Cambyses indicates the natural product of that system of religion, when directed by unflinching hands.

Indeed the Persian monarchs may be fitly taken as at once the visible centres and the highest practical

---

[1] On this subject, see, for instance, *Vendid.* VII. 193—196. Rhode (*Die heilige Sage des Zend-volks*, pp. 453 sq. Frankfurt, 1820) in discussing such passages attempts to establish an absolute identity of view in the Avesta and the Old Testament: but whatever may be urged with regard to some particulars, there is certainly not a word in the Books of Moses to justify the supposition that any creature is *essentially* unclean, or that certain animals are produced by the creative energy of an Evil Principle.

[2] Burnouf, *Études*, in the *Journ. Asiat.* (1840), p. 324, regards the importance assigned to the 'sentiment of human personality and morality' as the best feature of 'Zoroastrianism.'

illustrations of the Medo-Persian theology. Un-

High posi- checked alike by the intrigues and admonitions of
tion of the
Persian a dominant priesthood, such as that which flourished
kings. at the ancient court of Oude, or Thebes, or Memphis,
they stood forward the supreme reflections, if not

King-wor- actual incarnations, of the glory of Ormazd.[1] The
ship. warm and flexible polytheism of their subjects had
been earnestly directed towards them.[2] They seemed
to be entrusted with the sole administration of the
light-kingdom, as the Pharaohs of an earlier period
were the children of the Sun.[3] Their court was an
inferior copy of the court of Ormazd: on grand or
critical occasions they convoked a solemn council,
the idea of which, in form and number, had been
borrowed from the brilliant circle of divine amshaspands; and as 'words of Ormazd' himself were deemed
most sacred and oracular, the law of ancient Persia
had been taken from the lips of her great despot,
who by placing his own signet on the harshest of
decrees could render them irrevocable.

---

[1] Thus, when Themistocles (Plutarch. *Them.* c. xxvii.) wished to be presented to the king, he was told by the Persian Artabanus that he must first submit to offer worship 'to the image of god the preserver of all things,' (*i. e.* of Ormazd). Curtius (VIII. 5) in like manner says expressly, 'Persas reges suos inter deos colere:' see Hengstenberg, *Genuineness of Daniel*, pp. 103 sq., Edinb. 1847.

[2] Arrian, *Alex.* IV. 11, mentions a report that this προσκύνησις began with Cyrus: Λέγεται τὸν πρῶτον προσκυνηθῆναι ἀνθρώπων Κῦρον καὶ ἐπὶ τῷδε ἐμμεῖναι Πέρσαις τε καὶ Μήδοις τήνδε τὴν ταπεινότητα.

[3] Above, p. 252.

CHAPTER IV.

Alleged Affinities of the Medo-Persian Creed to Hebraism and Christianity.

Οὕτω λέγει Κύριος ὁ Θεὸς τῷ χριστῷ μου Κύρῳ, οὗ ἐκράτησα τῆς δεξιᾶς. . .Ἐγὼ Κύριος ὁ Θεὸς, καὶ οὐκ ἔστιν ἔτι πλὴν ἐμοῦ θεός. ἐνίσχυσά σε, καὶ οὐκ ᾔδεις με. ἵνα γνῶσιν οἱ ἀπ' ἀνατολῶν ἡλίου καὶ οἱ ἀπὸ δυσμῶν, ὅτι οὐκ ἔστι θεὸς πλὴν ἐμοῦ. ἐγὼ Κύριος ὁ Θεὸς, καὶ οὐκ ἔστιν ἔτι. ἐγὼ ὁ κατασκευάσας φῶς, καὶ ποιήσας σκότος, ὁ ποιῶν εἰρήνην, καὶ κτίζων κακά. ἐγὼ Κύριος ὁ Θεὸς, ὁ ποιῶν πάντα ταῦτα. Isa. xlv. 1—7. (LXX.)

THE second period in her lifetime when the Hebrew Church was forced into more lasting and direct communication with the heathen of surrounding countries must be dated from the middle of the eighth century before the Christian era. As the prelude to a general deportation of the Ten Tribes, the settlers in the Trans-Jordanic province had been carried captive to Assyria under Tiglath-Pileser (2 Kings xv. 29); and at length, about the year 600, a large portion of the feeble remnant, stricken by a like calamity, had run the risk of being quite extinguished under the tremendous despotism, which formed in every age a vivid type of the ungodlike and unchristianlike,— Babylon the Great.

The exile was itself, however, the effect,[1] and not

---

[1] See above, pp. 357—360.

the cause, of cravings after 'all the abominations of the heathen.' From the period of the Exodus the leaders of the Hebrew nation had been ever struggling with this downward, retrogressive tendency. 'The Lord God of their fathers sent to them by His messengers, rising up betimes and sending...but they mocked the messengers of God and despised His words and misused His prophets, until the wrath of the Lord arose against His people, till there was no *Effects of* remedy' (2 Chron. xxxvi. 15, 16). Yet penal though *it.* it was, the isolation of the Hebrews in the 'wilderness of the nations' had been also meant as a corrective discipline, and actually conduced by visible stages to the culture and the exaltation of the Church. Henceforth, as Jew and Christian have alike acknowledged, there was far less disposition to relapse into the bondage of the old polytheism. Closer contact with the creed and institutions of his heathen taskmasters had wakened in the spirit of the Hebrew exile a more deep and passionate longing not for Salem only, but the worship of his fathers' God. He bowed no more in adoration of the graven image, nor of elements and heavenly bodies: he no longer substituted a personification of recurring processes in animal or vegetable nature for the 'God of the spirits *New phases* of all flesh.' It is again observable that the trying *of doctrine.* period of captivity, when the Hebrew could no longer celebrate the ritual worship of his fathers, was selected as the aptest time[1] for inculcating lessons of Divine wisdom on the subject of a new œconomy and a truer service of the heart: while prophecies of the Messiah, in accordance with the law of progress and expansion

---

[1] Vol. I. pp. 151 sq.

which obtains in all their earlier stages, had been now detached more plainly from the thought of national triumph or disaster, and invested with their fullest form and their most spiritual expression.

But while sacred writers on the one hand trace *Modern* that exile to the heathenish temper of the chosen *theories respecting* people, and attribute on the other hand the restoration *the effect of* of the Hebrews to a signal act of mercy following *the Captivity.* their profound repentance, the assailants of revealed religion have persisted in affirming that the sojourn of the Jews in Babylonia was the time when, most of all, they had deflected from the creed of Abraham and David, when the priest and prophet also, equally besotted by the popular love of heathenism, had joined in the adulteration of the choicest truths committed to their keeping. With the sole exception of a faithful remnant, whose descendants must be sought for (it is now discovered) in the sect of the Sadducees, the great community returned from Babylon, so infected with the superstitions of the foreign despot, that the doctors of the subsequent period (not excepting Christ and the Apostles) had been all unable or unwilling to shake off the dominant delusion. As the traces of Egyptian heathenism were freely pointed out, by this class of critics, in the ritual institutions of the ancient Hebrew, they proceed to argue that a worse corruption in respect of doctrine had resulted from his long familiarity with the Zendic literature of Medo-Persia.

Now in estimating this momentous question it is *With what* doubtless of the first importance to observe that any *form of heathenism* influences exerted on the Hebrews by the votaries *were the* of the Ormazd-religion must have always, in the *Hebrews brought in contact?*

CHAP. IV. period of the exile, been extremely slender and in-direct.   The principal scene of transportation was *not* Persia Proper; and although the natives of some Median cities where those exiles were dispersed might then have been, in part at least, related ethnologically to their Perso-Áryan neighbours, the religion which prevailed in Media,[1] before the accession of Darius Hystaspis, and perhaps still later, was the element-worship of the Scythic Magi,—not the formal and elaborate dualism connected with the name of Zoro-aster and proclaimed at large in the Avesta.   It would further seem that actual conquerors of the Hebrew nation, the Assyrians or Chaldæo-Babylo-nians, *not* the Medo-Persians, are the people to whose creed we should most reasonably turn in searching for an explanation of the change alleged to have

General character of Baby-lonian my-thology.

passed over the theology of the conquered.   Is there, then, enough of general similarity in the ideas of ancient Babylonians and of Hebrews after the Cap-tivity, to warrant us in carrying this investigation far into details?   I answer, that no contrast could have well been greater.   The mythology of Babylonia from the oldest period to the Achæmenian conquest[2] will exhibit scarcely any trace of dualism, which forms, as we have seen, the most distinctive property of the Persian system, and which Hebrews are sup-

---

[1] See above, pp. 368, 369.

[2] Its main identity at very dif-ferent periods is affirmed by Sir H. Rawlinson, *Journ. As. Soc.* XV. 253, n. 3.   In a special Essay on the subject (Rawlinson's *Herod.* I. 584 sq.,) the absence of all trace of dualism is more distinctly pointed out.   Perhaps one of the most remarkable features of the Babylonian mythology is the high rank there awarded to the Moon-god: see above, p. 132, where moon-worship, as exemplified in old religions of America, *is* con-nected with the thought of some great evil principle.

posed to have eventually adopted. That religion, on the contrary, had ever been 'a very gross polytheism,' which is said in general grouping to have borne no small resemblance to 'the mythological systems of Greece and Rome;'[1] and therefore must have differed *toto cælo* from the creed of the Old Testament, alike before and after the Babylonish captivity. I shall accordingly dismiss at once the oft-repeated fallacy which professes to connect the Hebrew exiles with the advocates of the Ormazd-religion, or, despairing of this pretext, throws together[2] into one the motley tenets of Magi, of Perso-Aryans and of Babylonians, gives the general name of 'dualism' to the incongruous compound, and concludes by arguing that the Jews who 'spent the long years of their captivity' in the midst of it 'returned not unimbued with the superstitions of their masters.'

The unfairness of such arguments must not, however, tempt us to deny the fact that striking parallelisms do really exist between traditions now surviving in the sacred books of Persia and some doctrines of the Hebrew and Christian Scriptures. What may be the real ground of such resemblances, the age when they are first apparent, and the aspect they are calculated to assume in reference to the character and claims of Christianity, are questions calling for minute investigation : but since no competent scholar is prepared to say that the Avesta *in its present shape* is clearly traceable further back than the third

Existence of resemblances between the Hebrew and Persian systems.

---

[1] Rawlinson's *Herod.* I. 586.

[2] This is done, for instance, in Dr. Donaldson's *Christian Orthodoxy*, p. 102, where, unconscious, it would seem, of the confusion, he informs the reader that 'dualism was the creed of the Medes, Persians, and *Babylonians*.' If by 'creed of the Medes' we are to understand pure 'Magism,' the assertion is still further incorrect.

century after Christ, and since the fact is growing more indisputable every year that a variety of Semitic, if not Christian, elements were intermingled with the faith as well as with the language and literature of the Sassanian period, we are surely not at liberty to urge, before a strict examination of particulars, that traces of revealed religion which exist in sacred books of Persia must be treated as in every case original, and as proving the existence of an imitative spirit only in the Jewish nation. It is antecedently as probable that the Persian borrowed largely from the Hebrew as that the Hebrew borrowed from the Persian.

Possible accounts of such resemblances. If resemblances in question should be found too many or too minute to be regarded as entirely accidental,—such, that is, as men might, under similar circumstances, have originated independently of each other,—three suppositions can alone be urged in explanation of the strange phenomena. We may hold that the traditions common to the Persian and Hebrew (1) are equally a portion of 'original truth,' which both alike inherited from fathers of the human family: or (2) the Persians, at the period of the exile, and still more in later and post-Christian times, when their own system reached its full proportions, were conversant in some degree with Hebrew and Christian learning: or (3) the Jewish doctors in the course of their dispersion at, and after the Captivity, contracted an unnatural fondness for the sacred books of Persia.

Were they due to primitive traditions? (1) The first of these three suppositions may of course be held concurrently with the second; yet by many Christian writers of our own and foreign countries, it alone has been regarded as the key to Chap. IV. the affinities we are considering. When the genuine works of the Avesta, and still more the *Bundehesh*[1] itself, a Pehlevi compilation, were first brought to light by the adventurous Duperron, men were startled by the suddenness and brilliance of the grand disclosure. They beheld in it a series of most venerable relics, each at least coeval with the Persian monarchy. Nor at present, when it is completely ascertained that some of the results to which Duperron pointed with especial satisfaction were due to his inaccurate version of the sacred texts he had assisted in recovering, is there any lack of Christian writers who affirm that the traditions of the Avesta are well-nigh commensurate with those of the Old Testament. 'Of the King of Heaven' it is asserted[2] 'and the Father of eternal light, and of the pure world of light, of the eternal Word by which all things were created, of the seven mighty spirits that stand next to the throne of Light and Omnipotence, and of the glory of those heavenly hosts which encompass that throne; next, of the origin of evil and of the Prince of darkness,

[1] See above, p. 374.

[2] F. von Schlegel, *Phil. of History*, pp. 173, 174, where it is added: 'That with all these doctrines much may have been, or really was, combined, which the ancient Hebrews, and even we, would account erroneous, is very possible, and indeed may almost naturally be surmised; but this by no means impairs that strong historical resemblance we here speak of.' Dr. Mill (*Christ. Adv. Publ.* for 1841, p. 62) in alluding to the preservation of original truth in various parts of heathendom, agrees with Schlegel in ranking Persia far above most other regions: 'Such we find in nations most infected with polytheistic error: and much more we might well conceive to exist in one by which the grosser forms of idolatry were ever held in peculiar abhorrence: a nation whose greatest Prince is signally honoured by Divine prophecy [cf. the motto at the head of this chapter] in being named as the future restorer of God's people to their ancient seat: and whose sages were summoned from afar, before the great and wise of Israel, to adore the infant Redeemer.'

CHAP. IV. the monarch of those rebellious spirits—the enemies of all good; they [the Persians] in a great measure entertained completely similar, or at least *very kindred*, tenets to those of the Hebrews.' We may see hereafter that all statements of this kind are both exaggerated and overcoloured; yet no student of the question who considers the proximity of Persia to the cradle of the human race and the existence of a similar cluster of traditions[1] in the kindred tribe of Indo-Áryans, will be likely to relinquish the belief that there, as well as in the darker depths of gentilism, the echoes of primeval truths had lingered ages after they had lost all practical effect.

Were those resemblances due to the action of the Hebrews on the Persians?

(2) The next hypothesis accounting for those common elements of thought and worship was at first supported mainly by insisting on the synchronism of Zoroaster and the Hebrew prophets of the Captivity; a further supposition being that if Daniel and Zoroaster had not actually communicated with each other, as doctor and disciple, the reputed author of the Avesta had at least been versed in 'sacred writings of the Jewish religion.'[2] It was felt by the adherents of this view, especially when regard was had to the minute disclosures of the *Bundehesh*, that many representations so closely resemble 'those of the Hebrew Scriptures, as to leave no doubt of their real origin,

---

[1] See Vol. I. pp. 294 sq.

[2] See, for instance, Prideaux, *Connection*, I. 216, Lond. 1718, who adds that the whole system was extracted thence; 'only the crafty impostor took care to dress it up in such a style and form, as would make it best agree with that old religion of the Medes and Persians, which he grafted it upon.' It is curious to observe, in connexion with the prophet Daniel, and his influence on the heathen world, that persons are not wanting who identify him with the Hindú Buddha, and ascribe the appearance of Buddhism in Central India to the captivity and dispersion of the Jews. (*Journ. As. Soc.* XVI. 233).

through whatever channel ideas so analogous, or almost identical, can have been derived. The analogy is not of that kind which may be attributed to a similar derivation of tradition from a common source. It is more precise, and evidently belongs to a period not very remote."[1] So long, however, as the history of Zarathustra is involved in the obscurity thrown over it by recent criticism, we are unable to refer the introduction of Semitic thoughts among the Medo-Persians to supposed effects of his communication with the Hebrew exiles. Like uncertainty is felt when we compare some striking texts of the Avesta with the kindred language of the Old Testament; for owing to the numerous gaps in Persian history and the changes which the Persian writings have undergone, there is good reason for suspecting the antiquity of certain passages on which our predecessors had implicitly relied. If, on the other hand, we start from the idea that many of the Persian stories which resemble Hebraism were not the product of remote ages, but obtained their earliest credit in the first three centuries after Christ, the history of the period will be found in many different ways to favour such hypothesis.

That age was characterised far more than all before it by a spirit of religious syncretism, an eager thirst for compromise.[2] To mould together thoughts which differed fundamentally, to grasp if possible the common elements pervading all the multifarious religions of the world, was deemed the proper business

Peculiar state of religious feeling in the first three centuries after Christ.

---

[1] Prichard, *Researches*, IV. 45, where, however, the so-called 'mythus of the Zendavesta' is taken chiefly from Rhode's un- critical work entitled *Die heilige Sage des Zendvolks* (Frankfurt, 1820).

[2] Cf. Vol. I. pp. 31, 32.

CHAP. IV. of philosophy both in East[1] and West. It was a
period, one has lately said, 'of mystic incubation,
when India and Egypt, Babylonia and Greece, were
sitting together and gossiping like crazy old women,
chattering with toothless gums and silly brains about
the dreams and joys of their youth, yet unable to
recall one single thought or feeling with that vigour
which once gave it life and truth. It was a period
of religious and metaphysical delirium, when everything became everything, when Máyá and Sophia,
Mithra and Christ, Viráf and Isaiah, Belus, Zervan
and Kronos were mixed up in one jumbled system
of inane speculation, from which at last the East was
delivered by the positive doctrines of Muhammad,
the West by the pure Christianity of the Teutonic
nations.'[2] Out of this remarkable ferment of the
human spirit issued both the *Bundehesh* and the
Minokhired, which though strongly Persian in their

[1] Speaking of Eastern Syria, Uhlhorn remarks (*Die Homilien und Recognitionen des Clemens Romanus,* Göttingen, 1854, p. 411): Kein Land war der Religions-mischung so gelegen wie dieses. Hier haben sich von den ältesten Zeiten an die verschiedensten Völker gedrängt, berührt und vermischt. Judenthum und Parsismus, der noch in der ersten Zeiten der christlichen Zeitrechnung sich stark nach Westen zu verbreitete, wie seine zahlreichen Anhänger selbst in Kleinasien beweisen, berührten und vermischten sich hier. Dazu war Griechische Bildung gekommen, selbst Einflüsse des Buddhaismus erstreckten sich bis hieher, wie solche später in Manichäismus wohl kaum bezweifelt werden können. Auf diesem Boden erstarkte nun das Christenthum rasch und brachte eine mächtige Gährung hervor. Dazu kamen dann nach dem Untergange des Jüdischen Staates die aus Palästina auswandernden Juden und Judenchristen, welche die Keime der Zersetzung mit hinüberbrachten. So schoss hier eine reiche Saat von Sectenbildungen, die alle mehr oder minder einen Mischcharakter an sich tragen und in denen wir überall wieder unsern Homilien ähnelnde Elemente erkennen, die ein näheres oder ferneres Verwandtschaftsverhältniss bezeugen.'

[2] M. Müller's 'Last Results of the Persian Researches,' as before, p. 119; although I cannot acquiesce entirely in some of the expressions.

tone, are also strongly tinctured by Semitic and Hebraic notions. For Jews[1] on the destruction of the holy city planted some of their chief schools in Babylonia, and even were at times promoted to high places in the Persian court; in learned centres, like Edessa, were discussed the various tenets of all known religions, Christianity in the number; and the Gnostic Bardesanes, writing from that city in the time of Marcus Aurelius, draws attention to the early progress of the Gospel,[2] not in Parthia and in Media only, but in Persia Proper and in Bactria. Passing by the other traces which the new religion left behind it in those far-off regions, we may notice as of vast importance the long-thriving sect of Manichæans, who accepted Christianity as the groundwork of their composite belief: while stress may equally be laid upon the fact that one favourite writing of the later 'Zoroastrians' is only a Parsee adaptation[3] of the apocryphal or quasi-Christian work entitled the *Ascension of Isaiah;* where the prophet, on recovering from his rapture, narrates a journey to the 'seventh heaven,' in which his eyes were gladdened by the vision of Christ and of the Holy Spirit, and beheld inscribed upon a roll the wondrous story of the birth and passion of the Saviour.

(3) In exact proportion to the strength of the

Chap. IV.

Influence in Persia of Jews,

of Christians,

and of early heretics.

---

[1] Spiegel, *Avesta,* I. 17, 25.

[2] Euseb. *Præpar. Evangel.* VI. 10 (Vol. II. pp. 92, 93, ed. Gaisford): cf. Neander, *Ch. Hist.* I. 111.

[3] See the comparison between the two works (the *Arda-viráf-náme* and the 'Αναβατικὸν 'Ησαίου) in Spiegel, as before, pp. 21 sq. His closing remark is: 'Die Verwandtschaft der beiden Bücher wird wol Niemand ableugnen, doch scheint die christliche Gestaltung die ältere zu sein. Die Lehre von sieben Himmeln ist nicht parsisch, die spätere Parsenlehre kennt blos drei, über ihnen ist der *Gorothmán,* die Wohnung Ahura-mazdas.'

Were the Hebrews guilty of corrupting their old religion?

hypothesis just mentioned is the weakness of a third account which has been rendered of resemblances between the Persian and the Biblical traditions. Assuming even that the captive tribes were brought into familiar intercourse with the Ormazd-religion; assuming also that the Hebrew people as a body, still unweaned from old corruptions, had come back to Zion lusting after 'their fathers' idols;' in other words, assuming two positions which both militate against a long array of well-authenticated facts; we notwithstanding offer violence to all the probabilities of the question by supposing that Hebrew doctors, such as Daniel or Ezekiel, in whose eyes the exile was itself a penalty provoked by heathenish tendencies, should slide away into the superstitions either of their patrons or their taskmasters. The sentiment possessing them had always been: 'How shall we sing the Lord's song in a strange land? If I forget thee, O Jerusalem, let my right hand forget her cunning;' and notable instances may be adduced where men of constancy like theirs could brave the fiercest rage of Babylon, the lions' den, the blazing furnace, rather than renounce their sacred nationality or 'worship any other god.'

Conclusions to be established.

But with the view of justifying this main inference more completely, I propose to shew, by strict examination of particulars, that where a truly old relationship exists between the Hebrew and Persian systems, it is naturally explained on the hypothesis of aboriginal unity; and that in other cases there is either no true parallelism at all, or else that points of doctrine said to be imported by the later class of sacred writers, had been actually current in the Hebrew Church for centuries anterior to the Babylonish exile.

§ 1. *The Fall of Man.*

According to the 'Persian Genesis' (the *Bundehesh*), *The primi-tive Bull.* the earliest representative of animal creation[1] was the primitive Bull (Goshurun), from whose right shoulder, as he fell beneath the stroke of the malignant Ahriman, proceeded Kaiomorts, the first of human beings. This grand prototype of men, including in himself the properties of both the sexes, was in turn assaulted by the Evil One, and finally destroyed by machinations of the *devs;* but from the vital force inherent in him there sprang up a plant which yielded as its fruit the true progenitors of the human family (Meshia *Meshia and Meshiane;* and Meshiane),[2] or at least became the author of their bodily framework; for the soul itself was held to draw its origin directly from nothing short of heaven. Endowed with noble qualities, man was bidden to approve himself the lord of this lower world, by cultivating 'purity' in thought, in word, in action, *their tempt- ation;*

[1] The different passages of the *Bundehesh* relating to this point are brought together in Rhode, *Die heilige Sage*, etc., pp. 383 sq.: cf. Döllinger, p. 367. It is also worthy of remark, that in the Persian story the account of man's fall is intimately connected with the cosmogonic theory which pervaded most other countries of the ancient world both Old and New (see above, pp. 162, 163). In Persia (at least according to one version of the matter) we have first a cycle of 3000 years, when Ormazd is absolute (cf. however, above, p. 391); then, a cycle of the same period, when Ahriman commences his attack upon the light-kingdom, but, abashed by the exceeding purity of the *fervers* of holy men (above, p. 388, n. 1), falls back into the dark abyss, and lies quiescent during 3000 years. At the expiration of this time, Ahriman becomes more bold and active; and in the fourth period of 3000 years, completing the 'magnus annus' of the later Persians, Ahriman is, on the whole, ascendant and predominant.

[2] With these names compare the Sansk. *mánusha*, the Germ. *mensch*, and the *mannus* of Tacitus, *German.* c. 2 ('Tuisconem deum, *terra editum*, et filium Mannum'). On the Egyptian *Menes*, and other similar forms, see above, p. 232, n. 1, and Diefenbach, *Vergl. Wör- terbuch der goth. Spr.* II. 32, 33, Frankfurt, 1851.

and by keeping up a constant warfare with his enemies the *devs*. At first the parents of mankind were humble, and, devoted to the service of Ormazd, were innocent and happy; they were destined also to enjoy more perfect happiness; but Ahriman, the sleepless enemy of man and 'purity,' descending *and fall.* earthwards in the fashion of a serpent, plotted their corruption, and ere long by means of fruit derived from his own province of creation, he seduced them from their true allegiance : they declared that all they saw was Ahriman's, and therefore grew, it is narrated, as wicked as himself.

The form of the Tempter. Without dwelling[1] on the obvious kinship which exists between this story and the sacred narrative, it is worthy of especial notice that one form attributed in Persia to the Evil Principle, or at least one favourite organ used by him for man's undoing, is the serpent, of whose guile and malice traces are continually recurring in the farthest wilds of gentilism.[2] Nor is this representation only to be met with in chapters of the *Bundehesh* : in genuine works of the Avesta also, the great 'homicidal serpent'[3] is the object of men's dread and horror: while the Evil One himself is sometimes called 'the Serpent,' in

---

[1] I deem it quite superfluous, now that we can speak more positively about the age and origin of the *Bundehesh*, to answer such objections as those of Rhode and the older Rationalists, who used to affirm not only that the Mosaic version of the Fall was unintelligible without the Persian commentary, but also that the Hebrews had derived their knowledge of the whole tradition from a Persian source. Precisely the same kind of hardihood was shewn by Holwell and other sceptics, when they ventured to derive both Hebraism and Christianity from the 'Hindú scriptures' : see Vol. I. p. 168, n. 1.

[2] See, for instance, the *Prose Edda*, § 34 (Mallet's *North. Antiq.* p. 423, Lond. 1847), where the second child of *Loki* (the Ahriman of Scandinavia) is the Midgard serpent, and the third Hela (Death).

[3] Above, p. 388.

direct allusion to his power of counteracting the Good
Principle. Thus, Ormazd is heard declaring in the
Vendidâd :[1] 'I am Ahura-mazda, I am the giver of
good things. When I formed this dwelling-place,
the beautiful, the brilliant, the note-worthy, saying,
I will go forth, I will go over, then the Serpent
beheld me. Thereupon the Serpent Âgra-mainyus,
who is full of death, created, with an eye to *my*
creation, nine sicknesses, and ninety, and nine hundred, and nine thousand and ninety thousand.'

§ 2. *Doctrine of the Evil One.*

This extract brings us to a question of very grave *Satan and*
importance: Is the doctrine of a personal, super- *Ahriman;*
human Tempter, as now current in all branches of
the Christian Church, the product of religious intercourse which Hebrews had maintained with their
enslavers at the time of the Captivity? Is the Satan
of the Old and New Testament, in other words, a
modern copy of the Ahriman of the Avesta? In
replying to this question I shall not survey afresh
the main historical probabilities arising on the one
side from the nature of the Babylonic (as distinguished
from the Medo-Persian) creed, and on the other from
the stern, uncompromising spirit of the Hebrew worthies who were sharers in the exile of their nation.
On internal grounds alone I hold it to be far more
likely that the Persian dogma, as it stands conspicu-

---

[1] Farg. xxii. §§ 1—6, where
Spiegel's note is: 'Dass Âgra-
mainyus eine *Schlange* genannt
wird, kann nicht befremden, da
er ja bekanntlich auch im Bundehesh unter dieser Form erscheint.'

ous in the *Vendidâd*, was the corruption and distortion of a primitive truth bequeathed by the first parents of the human family. For no one who is able to discriminate at all, will question that under the more obvious features of resemblance there is lying also a most vital contrariety between the Hebrew and Old Persian theories on the nature of the Evil One.

how different from each other. As Satan in our sacred books is far from being the seductive spirit of the world, or of man's lower nature, 'conceived of in concrete personality';[1] so neither is he there esteemed an absolutely evil being, like the Ahriman of the Avesta, coeternal and coequal with the Good, and like the Good an independent centre of creative energy. Satan is a fallen *creature*, his fall involved like man's fall in impenetrable mystery, and yet a fall which in results which it entailed on the creation has its dark analogy in the first great fall of man, as well as in that fiendish satisfaction which the fallen still experience in communicating their own misery to others. In neither case, however, is the sovereignty of God at all impugned by the existence of ungodlike passions in the

---

[1] See Dr. Mill's masterly sermons 'On the Temptation' (Camb. 1844), especially Serm. III.: in which the place and power of the arch-fiend are accurately determined. On the contrary, Dr. Donaldson's work, entitled *Christian Orthodoxy*, is devoted in no small measure to the maintenance of a theory, which involves our Lord Himself, and with Him the whole Christian community of every period, in the charge of swerving from the old (or ante-Babylonic) doctrine of the Hebrew Church in reference both to fallen and unfallen angels (cf. Vol. I. p. 100, n. 2). The same tendency (strange to say) is manifested at the same time by the intelligent Parsee writer, above quoted (p. 387, n. 2); who in the teeth of the most cogent evidence is able to declare that the Ahriman of his forefathers was really impersonal, or, as some scholastics would express it, 'was merely the evil of the world *hypostasised*' (precisely Dr. Donaldson's own position with regard to Satan).

creature, and the partial triumph of the powers of evil. Jew and Christian, equally possessed by a belief that there is One, and only one, true Principle of Existence, would alike recoil with horror from the notion which exalted the arch-demon to equality with the supreme and unapproachable Jehovah. The feeling of them both, in later as in earlier times, has been, that Satan is a 'murderer' and a 'liar,' *not* because he is the necessary antithesis of God, but simply because 'he *abides not* in the truth'[1] of his original creation (St. John viii. 44).

A most ample opportunity for testing both the genuineness and depth of this conviction had been offered on the rise and early progress of the Manichæan heresy. No countenance was given in East or West to figments of the Persian misbeliever. Then it was that St. Augustine, who amid the moral and intellectual tempests of his youth had learned to fathom the abyss of human depravity, stood forward to unmask the sophistries beneath which Mani sought to introduce into the Church the dogma of Two Principles ; and worthy of our special notice is it, that the arm which levelled the proud system of Pelagius when he ventured to extenuate the malignity of moral evil, was uplifted with the same gigantic vigour for the overthrow of Faustus, the great champion of the Manichæans.[2]

St. Augustine and the Manichæans.

---

[1] See Dean Alford on this passage, who remarks that it is 'one of the most decisive testimonies for the *objective personality* of the devil. It is quite impossible,' he continues, 'to suppose an accommodation to Jewish views, or a metaphorical form of speech, in so solemn and direct an assertion as this.'

[2] See, especially, the treatise *Contra Faustum, Manichæum* (Opp. x. 221 sq., Bassani, 1807), where several of the Manichæan arguments are also given at length.

Scriptural notices of the Tempter :

Turning, then, directly to the books of Holy Scripture, what can we detect in it to justify the charges of its modern adversaries? Is there any discernible variation in the language used at different periods with regard to the existence of diabolic agents and the personality of the Tempter? Now I find no difficulty whatever in admitting, just as when the elementary conceptions of a future life were made the subject of discussion,[1] that a steadier light may have been gradually thrown upon this question in successive stages of the Church's growth. The revelations of the Old Testament, and therefore more particularly of the earlier portions of it, were not absolute and ultimate. As centuries went over, many large accessions may be clearly dated in the measure of man's sacred knowledge. It is found accordingly that truths pertaining to the spirit-world have also gained a greater prominence and greater clearness of expression in 'the fulness of the times,' nay, even in the latest writings of the New Testament.[2] It was our blessed Lord Himself, who in delivering the grand parable of the wheat and tares has singled out, for His direct antagonist, *the* wicked one; who told us also in His exposition that this wicked one is the Devil (St. Matth. xiii. 39), and the reapers holy 'angels.' In like manner, one chief object of the Saviour's mission is declared to be the 'stripping from Himself of prin-

more vivid in the New Testament.

---

[1] Above, pp. 352 sq.

[2] 'In the spiritual world, where the lights are brightest, the shadows are deepest; and instead of hearing less of Satan, as the mystery of the kingdom of God proceeds to unfold itself, in the last book of Scripture, that which details the fortune of the Church till the end of time, we hear more of him [Satan], and he is brought in more evidently and openly working than in any other.'—Dean Trench, *On the Parables,* p. 84, Lond. 1844.

cipalities and powers,' (Col. ii. 15)—the subjugation of those more than human adversaries, with which the Christian in his turn is summoned to do battle (Eph. vi. 12). 'The Son of God was manifested that He might destroy the works of the Devil' (1 St. John iii. 8),—the works of that 'old serpent, which is the Devil and Satan' (Rev. xx. 2). It is true that reasons might exist alike in the prevailing tendencies of Asiatic thought, and in the moral status of the Hebrew Church itself, explaining the comparative absence of allusion to such topics in the early writings of the Bible; 'till the mightier power of good was revealed we were in mercy not suffered to know how mighty was the power of evil:'[1] yet to say that nothing is recorded of Satanic influence till the period of the Babylonish exile is the arbitrary assumption of determined theorisers, aided in this matter by a rude and vulgar spirit of destructive criticism, which, guiding in old time the hands of Mani, could not rest till it had torn away the passages, and even books, of Holy Scripture[2] where resistance had been offered to his shameless innovation.

---

[1] *Ibid.* p. 83.

[2] Thus St. Augustine aptly remarks (*De Utilitate Credendi*, c. 7), just after his own extrication from Manichæan errors: 'Nunc vero postea quam mihi sunt exposita atque enodata multa, quæ me maxime movebant, ea scilicet in quibus illorum plerumque se jactat, et quo securius sine adversario eo effusius exsultat oratio, nihil mihi videtur ab eis *impudentius dici*, vel (ut mitius loquar) *incuriosius* et *imbecillius*, quam Scripturas divinas esse corruptas; cum id nullis in tam recenti memoria exstantibus exemplaribus possint convincere. Si enim dicerent, eas sibi *penitus accipiendas non putasse*, quod ab his essent conscriptæ, quos verum scripsisse non arbitrarentur, esset utcumque tergiversatio eorum rectior vel error humanior.' He then goes on to mention that they did reject the whole of the Acts of the Apostles, not for any critical reasons, but *because* the account there given would not square with their notions about the descent of the Holy Ghost on Mani: cf. Tertull. *De Præscript. Hær.* c. xvii., where

Chap. IV.

Satan's connexion with the Fall :

In pointing to the earlier intimations of some diabolic agency, I need not touch again[1] upon the ancient passage in Leviticus (xvi.), where *Azazel* is commonly believed to be another name for 'demon,' and is so indeed interpreted by modern writers, who, as soon as the admission has been made, resolve that being into 'a liturgical idea.' Neither shall I urge at length that he who finally bore the title of 'adversary' and 'calumniator' of the human race is called '*the* Satan,' and invested with peculiar guile and malice, in the opening of the Book of Job (i. ii.), no less than in the kindred vision of Zechariah (iii.), which belongs, unquestionably, to the age succeeding the Captivity. My present stand is rather on the sacred narrative of the Fall, which few, if any, even of our most daring critics, venture to bring down as low as the sixth century before the Christian era.

how understood by Jews and Christians.

Now if the true meaning of that narrative can be determined by consentient verdicts of Jewish and Christian writers, in all ages, it imports that man, through the extraneous solicitations of a personal seducer, and not merely through the motions of inborn concupiscence, was urged to the commission of the first dark sin which wrought disorder in himself, his children, and his species. That the visible agent of man's ruin was an *agent* merely in the hands of the great Evil One, St. Paul has plainly intimated where he writes that the serpent who beguiled our first mother was the subtle, self-transforming potentate who is still active in the Christian Church

---

allusion is made to the arbitrary additions and subtractions of heresy, 'ad dispositionem instituti sui.'

[3] See above, pp. 339 sq.

(2 Cor. xi. 3, 14); and when the same Apostle turned
with ardent hope to the eventual triumph of the
Woman's Seed, his comfort flowed from a conviction
that 'the God of peace will bruise *Satan* (not the
serpent) under our feet shortly' (Rom. xvi. 20).

But excluding once again both these and other *Heathen*
Christian testimonies, all of which, it is pretended *testimony*
on this
by the modern sceptic, have been deeply tinctured *point.*
with foreign superstitions, I appeal to universal heathendom itself in favour of the ancient exposition of
the sacred record. There is found to be a singular
consent,[1] in East and West, in North and South, in
civilised and semi-barbarous countries, in the Old
World and the New, not only to the fact that serpents
were somehow associated with the ruin of the human
family, but that serpents so employed were vehicles
of a malignant, personal spirit, by whatever name
he was described.

As, therefore, the Old Persian is but one of a *Most rati-*
large cluster of cognate stories, it were surely far *onal con-*
clusion.
more rational to explain them all on the hypothesis
of common parentage anterior to the primitive migrations, than to argue, *first*, that Hebrews only had
been left without traditions on this subject till comparatively modern times; and *secondly*, that the age
in which they finally contracted their belief in Satan
and his angels, and so consummated, in the view of
the objector, their portentous lapse into the eastern
dualism, was, strange to say, the age, when, as a
body, they are known to have imbibed far stricter
tenets on the unity and monarchy of God.

---

[1] See, for instance, Vol. I. p. 308; Vol. II. pp. 147, 410.

§ 3. *Doctrine of Holy Angels.*

Angelology attributed to heathen influence.

The spirit which impelled some modern writers to explain the scriptural notices of Satan, the great Tempter, by referring to the influence exercised upon the Jew by Persian dualism, is shewn afresh in their impatience of all statements with respect to the existence of the 'holy,' or unfallen, angels. These also we are told 'belong to a class of conceptions no longer possible in the world,'[1] and *therefore* (such is the conclusion of philosophy) they must all of them be proved to have originated in some thoroughly pagan system. The abettors of this startling argument have had recourse especially to effects supposed to have been wrought upon the Hebrews by the 'Zend religion of the Persians;'[2] and they point triumphantly, in confirmation of their view, to the existence of the Sadducees,[3] a high and philosophic order, who are thought to have preserved the purer creed of earlier generations with remarkable fidelity,

The Sad-ducees.

---

[1] Dr. Donaldson's *Christ. Orthod.* p. 349 (following Schleiermacher).

[2] Here Dr. Donaldson accepts the dictum of Strauss without the least qualification: *Christ. Orthod.* p. 137.

[3] The author of *Christian Orthodoxy*, p. 372, affirms that 'their disbelief in angels and devils is passed over [by New Testament writers] in guarded silence, as far as any censure is concerned.' He then adds, 'In many respects our Lord seems to have approved and recommended their views;' and again (p. 373), 'It is difficult to resist the impression that Jesus [our blessed Lord] and His brother James, being known by the characteristic title of this sect, openly allowed many of the fundamental doctrines of the Sadducees'! Such language has not unnaturally exposed its author to the animadversions of the last Bampton Lecturer (Mr. Mansell), who, after pointing out the real origin and affinities of Dr. Donaldson's hypothesis, declares that 'by this method of exposition,' according to which our Saviour lent His high authority to the dissemination of religious falsehood, 'Christian Orthodoxy may mean anything or nothing' (p. 419).

—in so far at least as they dissented from the superstitions of the Pharisees, in confessing neither angel nor spirit. Efforts have again been made in this particular instance to support the theory of extensive amalgamation between Hebrews and Babylonians by adverting to the fact that various forms of error and exaggeration in the sphere of angelology *did* spring up, as it would seem, spontaneously among both Jews and Christians of succeeding times.

The chief reliance has been placed, however, on one definite testimony of the Jerusalem Talmud. In that passage,[1] it is written: 'R. Simeon Ben-Lachish saith, The names of angels went up by the hand of Israel out of Babylon. For before it is said, "Then flew one of the seraphim unto me:" "The seraphim stood before him," Isa. vi.; but afterward, "the Man Gabriel" [Dan. ix. 21] and "Michael your prince" [Dan. x. 21].' Now whatever else may be implied in such assertions, we are doubtless pointed by them to a circumstance, which cannot fail to have arrested the attention of all Biblical scholars, viz. that after the great exile, *personal appellations* had begun to be assigned in some few cases (Michael, Gabriel, Raphael, Uriel) to the ministering angels of the Hebrew Church. But equally apparent is the fact that these angelic designations are in no way borrowed from the titles of gods and genii which abound in writings of the Medo-Persians, as indeed of every other ancient people; they have no apparent relation, etymological or otherwise, with the element-worship of the East; in thought as well as grammar

Inference to be drawn from Rabbinical testimony.

Character of angelic designations.

---

[1] Lightfoot's *Heb. and Talmud. Works*, xii. 24, ed. Pitman. *Exerc. upon St. Luke* (ch. i. v. 26):

CHAP. IV. they are all of them the purest Hebrew ; *Michael*, for example, signifying ' who is as God ?' and so protesting in its very form against approaches to polytheism.[1]

Real points under discussion.

On looking, therefore, with a critical eye upon the question now before us, we discover that the chief external evidence in favour of supposing that the angelology of the Hebrews was of heathen parentage, is totally unconnected with the point at issue; for I feel no obligation to analyse the many wild conceits, which, in the dotage of the Hebrew nation, urged men to ' intrude into the things not seen,' and build their visionary systems of ' celestial hierarchies.' The questions[2] fairly brought into the present investigation

[1] See Dr. Mill's examination of this very point in his *Christ. Adv. Publ.* for 1841, pp. 55, 57. Hengstenberg, *Genuineness of Daniel*, p. 138, remarks with justice that ' both Gabriel and Michael [the two names peculiar to Daniel] occur only in such visions, as from their dramatic character demand the most exact description possible of the persons concerned, and the bringing of them out into stronger relief.'

[2] I cannot, for example, be expected to discuss the general question, opened more than once by Dr. Donaldson, as to whether angels, in the *Christian sense*, are ever mentioned in the old (or ante-Babylonic) Scriptures. Dr. Donaldson seems to be persuaded (*Christ. Orthod.* p. 348) that the received doctrine of good angels is somehow incompatible with the doctrine of the Holy Spirit. He may well, on such hypothesis, be anxious to get rid of what he feels to be a horrible superstition ; but surely the argument which he employs is equally fatal to belief in *all* intermediate agencies whatever; for example, in the institution of a Christian ministry, who, like the angels, act in God's behalf, and by authority derived from Him. All theories apart, I cannot help expressing my amazement how any person of average ability can study the Old Testament without discovering at every turn the flattest contradiction of Dr. Donaldson's assertions. Were the two angels, for example, who had been despatched to Sodom other than personal beings, acting as the veritable messengers of the Most High God Himself? They say expressly, 'The Lord hath sent us to destroy it' (Gen. xix. 13). Dean Milman (*Hist. of Christ.* I. 70, Lond. 1840), who also traces the systematising of Hebrew angelology to the residence in Babylon, is notwithstanding ready to admit that ' the earliest books of the Old Testament fully recognize the ministration of angels.' It is, indeed, remarkable that the *only* historical books of the Old Testament where such allusions do *not* appear, are exactly those which were written *after* the Babylonish captivity,—the books of Ezra and Nehemiah.

will relate, (1) to a distinction between higher and lower angels, *i. e.* the existence of orders or *gradations* in the spirit-world; and (2) to the specific number of intelligences who occupy the loftiest rank in these angelic orders.

Now that some distinction of the sort existed long *Early traces* before the Babylonish exile can be satisfactorily *of angelic orders.* evinced from the magnificent passage in the sixth chapter of Isaiah. There the prophet's eye is riveted upon the glory of the six-winged seraphim, who constitute the 'angel-princes' of that early period, and as such are stationed foremost in the ministry of heaven; while one of them by issuing forth (vi. 6, 7) upon a message to Isaiah, and so offering proof of independent personality, enables us to answer the absurd objection that the primitive angels were but passive vehicles or manifestations of God Himself. The vision of Micaiah, in like manner, brings before us in still older times 'the Lord sitting on His throne, and all the host of heaven standing by Him on His right hand and on His left' (1 Kings xxii. 19—22). Nay, traces of angelic orders, such as meet us in the New Testament and later writings of the Old, are pointed out as early as the age of Moses and of Joshua; for the 'prince,' or captain of the Lord's host (Josh. v. 13—15) who then comes forward to conduct the family of God into the land of promise, has been held to correspond[1] with the created angel

---

[1] This subject also is discussed at considerable length by Dr. Mill, as above, pp. 92—99. The rival theory is, that the Angel in Josh. v. was none other than the Second Person of the Blessed Trinity,—identical, therefore, with the Angel of the Lord, in Exod. xxiii. 20—23, and other places: see Ode, *Commentarius de Angelis*, pp. 1032 sq. Traject. 1739; who, with many modern critics, goes farther still, identifying Michael himself with the un-

CHAP. IV. (Exod. xxxiii. 2, 3), who replaced the glorious Angel of the Presence (Exod. xxiii. 20—23) in administering the Sinaitic dispensation, after Israel had most grievously offended in the matter of the calf. But be this as it may, the close affinity that exists between the language of the book of Joshua and descriptions of the prince of angels, who, as Michael, reappears for the protection of the Israelites in visions of the book of Daniel, may be fairly pleaded as a proof that the familiarity of the Hebrew Church with such conceptions is not due to her reputed intercourse with the Ormazd-religion.

Amshas-pands and archangels.

It was easy to foresee that the amshaspands of the Persian system[1] would be quoted as the nearest parallel to the archangels of the Holy Scriptures. Those beings, we have learned already,[2] were six in

created Word of God; while others add again to these supposed identifications by representing the *Gabriel* of the prophet Daniel as a reappearance of the created, or inferior, angel of Exod. xxxii. 34.

[1] *e. g.* the author of *Christian Orthodoxy* declares (p. 135) with reference to the Book of Daniel: 'In this book we find the celestial hierarchy of amshaspands fully recognised.' Other speculators of the same school have sought to bring the *fervers* of Persia into connexion with the 'guardian angels' both of Jews and Christians (see St. Matth. xviii. 10; Acts xii. 72; and Dean Alford on the former passage); but the Persian *ferver*, where we are not forced to understand it of the *spirit* of the individual man, was rather the ideal prototype or archetype of some actual being: see above, p. 388, n. 1. With regard to the conception of angels, specially allotted to watch over

the affairs of particular *nations*, Hengstenberg (*Daniel*, p. 140) affirms that no trace of it occurs in the Avesta, except that Bahman, the first of the amshaspands, 'who stands in about the same relation to Ormazd as Gabriel here does to the angel of the Lord,' is called the 'protector of all animals' who are there said to constitute his people (Rhode, p. 323), while Ormazd himself is the patron of men. The version of the LXX in Deut. xxxii. 8, will perhaps bear witness to some old tradition of the Jews with respect to the allotting of particular nations to particular angels: ὅτε διεμέριζεν ὁ ὕψιστος ἔθνη, ὡς διέσπειρεν υἱοὺς Ἀδάμ, ἔστησεν ὅρια ἐθνῶν κατὰ ἀριθμὸν ἀγγέλων Θεοῦ, where the Hebrew is לְמִסְפַּר בְּנֵי יִשְׂרָאֵל: cf. Prof. Selwyn's *Notæ Criticæ*, 'Deuteron.' p. 65, Cantab. 1858.

[2] Above, p. 384.

number; or, including Ormazd himself, who also
is invested on some rare occasions with the title of
amshaspand, the whole number may be raised to
seven.[1] We saw, moreover, that the probable origin
of such specification must be sought in the primeval
worship of the heavenly bodies, when the shining
multitude above were substituted by man's vain
imagination for the Lord of hosts Himself: and as
the influence of that ancient superstition was far from
being peculiar to the Persians, the allusion to 'seven'
principal objects of esteem and worship is continually
recurring in all parts of heathendom.[2] It is, however, a mistake to argue that the later Hebrew people,
and much less the Hebrew prophets of the exile,
manifested any disposition to deify the orbs of light.
There is indeed one solitary passage in the book of *Number of*
Tobit, where the speaker, Raphael, describes himself *archangels.*
as of the number of the '*seven* holy angels who enter
in before the glory of the Holy One' (xii. 15; cf.
Rev. viii. 2); but, according to a different method
of enumeration, the archangels of the Hebrew are
more frequently reduced to *four* (Michael, Gabriel,
Raphael, and Uriel), each presiding over one of the
four armies of ministry who sing praises to the Holy
and the Blessed.[3] Still if we had higher reasons

---

[1] Rhode, p. 365; Mill, as before, p. 59.

[2] Above, pp. 267, 384, to which
examples may be added the seven
rishis of Hindústán, who, at least
in the Puranic period, were represented as 'seven primeval per-
sonages, born of Brahmá's mind,
and presiding, under different
forms, over each Manwantara.'

[3] See the passage from the

Pirke of Rabbi Eliezer (who, according to Fürst, *Bibliotheca Ju-
daica*, i. 232, flourished about A.D.
70), in Dr. Mill's work, as before,
p. 58, n. 10. Dr. Donaldson (p.
136) breaks through this difficulty
at once by urging that when the
Jews limited the number of 'attendant spirits' to *four*, they did
so 'probably from some confusion
between the amshaspands and the

for accepting the account of Tobit as an illustration of the general state of knowledge on this subject at the period when he wrote, it would be running counter to the sacred usage, both of the Old and New *Scriptural use of 'seven.'* Testament, to argue that the number *seven*, as there employed, contains the slightest reference to the worship of celestial luminaries, or to any phase whatever of gentile superstition.[1] 'Seven,' alike before and after the Captivity, had its own specific import for all members of the Hebrew Church. It was the signature of fulness, union, manifoldness, perfection; and therefore the 'seven spirits of God' in the Apocalypse (i. 4; iv. 5) are understood as pointing us directly to the diverse operations of the One allgracious Spirit;[2] while the 'seven stars' are the 'angels of the seven churches,' and the 'seven candlesticks' a grand collective symbol of the whole Christian body (i. 20).

§ 4. *Doctrine of the Resurrection of the Body.*

Importance attached to this doctrine in the New Testament. To foster a belief in the awakening of man's body from the sleep of death, and in the final glorification of his whole humanity, was a primary object in the teaching of St. Paul and of apostles generally. In their view 'the redemption of the body' at the re-appearing of our Lord and Saviour, was the crowning-point in a succession of stupendous acts which dated from His own ineffable assumption of our weak

seraphim of Isaiah on the one hand, and the four creatures of Ezekiel on the other'!
[1] Cf. Bähr, *Symbolik*, I. 189 sq.

[2] Hengstenberg, *Die Offenbarung des h. Johan.* I. 91, 92, Berlin, 1849.

and dying flesh. Yet writers are not wanting who assure us that the doctrine of the resurrection, so specifically and profoundly Christian, is a relic only of primeval barbarism which passed into the Hebrew creed, like others of the same description, at the period of the Babylonish exile.[1] Observing, it would seem, that fuller light is thrown upon the mystery of our future being, in proportion as the 'mystery of godliness' itself was gradually unfolded, those irreverent critics have not scrupled to conjecture that instead of such ulterior light proceeding from the supernatural source, it must have had an earthly origin among the ancient votaries of Ormazd.

And here, as in some other cases, the supposed 'discovery' of the doctrine in the Zendic books had been facilitated by the mistranslations of their first editor. It is since established by more competent scholars,[2] that in passages where Anquetil Duperron rendered 'till the resurrection,' the words really signify 'for ever,'—an important rectification, which, as soon as it is generally made known, will silence not a few of the objections borrowed from this quarter. Like results have also followed from the critical examination of some other Zendic texts; until at present all who are entitled to pronounce a judg-

No trace of it in the Avesta.

---

[1] *e. g.* Wegscheider does not blush to affirm that this opinion unquestionably grew up 'e notionibus mancis et imperfectis hominum incultiorum,' and that it finally passed over to the Jews from the school of Zoroaster (quoted in Mr. Mansell's *Bampton Lectures*, 1858, pp. 417, 418).

[2] Burnouf, *Études*, in *Journ. Asiat.* (1840), pp. 7 sq., was the first scholar who pointed out this mistake. His conclusions have been since corroborated by Spiegel, *Zeits. Deutsch. morg. Gesell.* (1847), I. 260, 261; *Avesta*, I. 15, 248, n. 2. According to the *Vendid. Farg.* XIX. 89 sq., as there translated, the good or 'pure' spirits are removed on the *third day after death* to a place of perfect happiness, and the bad spirits to a place of torment : cf. Wilson's *Pársí Religion*, pp. 337, 338.

CHAP. IV. ment on the question may be heard affirming that no glimpses of a resurrection of the body can be traced in extant books of the Avesta.

Statements of Theo-pompus.

Still that Persians did not long continue strangers to the thought of some ulterior re-embodying of the souls departed, may be argued with great shew of reason from the testimony of the historian, Theo-pompus,[1] who died about the year 300 B.C. He has declared that in accordance with the Persian creed, as soon as the great struggles of Ormazd and Ahriman are all exhausted, Hades will become a void; and that mankind attaining to true happiness will then 'require no nourishment and will cast no shadows.' And elsewhere his language is still more explicit; for he says that if we may believe the Magi, men will come to life again and be immortal:—both which statements fairly indicate that at the close of the 'great year' of Persia, every thing, it is believed, will have reverted to the primitive condition, and that the human body, no exception to this general law, will have itself experienced the refining and exalting process.

Two theo-ries of the body.

There are reasons, it is true, for urging[2] that two different lines of thought existed in the schools of

[1] The testimony of this writer has been examined at some length by J. G. Müller, *Theol. Studien und Kritiken* (1835), pp. 482 sq. in an article entitled 'Ist die Lehre von der Auferstehung des Leibes wirklich nicht eine alt-persische Lehre?' The discussion turns in a great measure on the force of ἀναβιοῦν in the following passage: Θεόπομπος, ἐν τῇ ὀγδόῃ τῶν Φιλιππικῶν, καὶ ἀναβιώσεσ- θαι, κατὰ τοὺς Μάγους, φησὶ τοὺς ἀνθρώπους καὶ ἔσεσθαι ἀθανάτους (in Diogen. Laert. 'Procem.' § 9). The other passage of importance is preserved in Plutarch. *De Iside*, c. XLVII. the chief words being: τέλος δ' ἀπολείπεσθαι τὸν ᾅδην, καὶ τοὺς μὲν ἀνθρώπους εὐδαίμονας ἔσεσθαι, μήτε τροφῆς δεομένους, μήτε σκιὰν ποιοῦντας.

[2] See Döllinger, *Heidenthum*, p. 381.

ancient Persia: one, proceeding from a rigorous form of dualism,[1] akin to that of Mani, and so, as in the convents of northern India, making of the human body a mere prison-house in which the soul was doing penance for her past misdeeds; the other mourning over the dissolution of the body as a victory won by Ahriman, and so including the idea of re-embodiment among the blessings that would ultimately flow from the subversion of his empire. But the testimony of Theopompus may be viewed as an expression of the 'orthodox' belief, especially when we bear in mind that subsequent language of the *Bundehesh*[2] is strikingly in favour of the resurrection theory.

On the other hand, assuming, as in previous *The Hebrew doc-* instances, that Hebrew prophets would have seen no *trine ante-* difficulty in borrowing novel tenets from the creed *Babylonic.* of their enslavers, it appears to me indisputable that the doctrine of the resurrection of the body was believed to some extent among the members of the sacred family long before the period of the Babylonish exile. I shall lay no stress at present on debateable texts;[3] of which, however, it is no exaggeration to affirm that while incapable of *proving* that the doctrine of a resurrection was fully or definitely held, they nevertheless bear witness to the fact that the idea of resurrection had never been repugnant to the feelings of the ancient Israelite, but rather coincided with the expectations that arose in

[1] Above, p. 389.
[2] The passages are collected in Rhode, as before, pp. 465 sq.; but, as Spiegel remarks, a correct and critical edition of the *Bunde-* *hesh* will doubtless modify the old assertions on this point also.
[3] Cf. Fairbairn's *Ezekiel*, pp. 356—359.

him from a belief in God's redemptive and restoring mercy. It will here suffice to mention that the words which Daniel is said to have indited under the inspirations of the Medo-Persian system are in perfect unison with declarations of Isaiah two centuries before. For instance, if the prophet of the Captivity was pointing onward to a crisis when 'many of them that sleep in the dust of the earth shall awake' (Dan. xii. 2); the jubilant prophet of the reign of Ahaz had already comforted his audience by the promise that the Lord 'will swallow up death in victory' (Is. xxv. 8); nay, the words which, in a second passage, are employed by him have found their literal echo in the words of Daniel just recited; for Isaiah also has proclaimed in no ambiguous language 'Thy dead men shall live, together with my dead body shall they arise; awake and sing, ye that dwell in dust' (xxvi. 19).

§ 5. *Doctrine of a Benefactor and Mediator.*

Early mention of Sosiosh.

(1) Connected with the re-awakening of the dead, at least in some of the more recent, or post-Christian, writings of the Persians, there is frequent mention of a glorious hero-prophet, by whose ministry, as one chief organ of Ormazd, the empire of the *devs* shall be subverted, earth herself shall be restored to something of her pristine glory and the wrongs of man redressed. The name of this expected champion of the Perso-Áryan race is Sosiosh (*Saŏshyaṅs*,[1] 'the

---

[1] Spiegel, *Avesta*, I. 244, n. 1, informs us that the root of the word is *su* ('to profit'), to which it is related as the future participle: hence 'der nützen werdende' 'der Helfer.' It was not,

Benefactor'). He is first of all presented to our notice in a passage of the *Vendidád*,[1] which, if the new translation of it be accepted, is found to run as follows: 'Zarathustra gave warning to Aĝra-mainyus (and said): "Base Aĝra-mainyus! I will smite the creation, which is fashioned by the *devs:* I will smite the *Nasus*, whom the *devs* have fashioned. I will smite the *Pari* whom men worship (?), until Sosiosh the Victorious, is born out of the water *Kañsaõya*, from the eastern clime, from the eastern climes.'"

Expansion of the idea.

The meagre hint of Sosiosh, thus communicated in the early part of the Avesta, was expanded and embellished in the works of the Sassanian epoch and especially in the *Bundehesh*.[2] That benefactor was from first to last a *man;* and like two other beings, his precursors, now associated with him in the work of liberation and each reigning in succession for a thousand years, he was distinctly held to be the off-

however, a proper name nor limited to an individual worthy, but rather marked a series or *class* of benefactors, and as such it occurs also in the plural number.

[1] Farg. XXI. 16—19: cf. *Zeits. Deutsch. morg. Gesell.* (1847), I. 261, 262, where the old translation was first corrrected.

[2] See the passages in Rhode, pp. 465 sq. Spiegel (*Avesta*, I. 32 sq.) has also drawn attention more especially to the full-blown eschatology of the Persians and compared it with that of the later Jews, which, in his opinion, it strongly resembles (p. 35). The main points, according to his representation, are as follows: 'Die Erwartung eines sowol *weltlichen* als geistlichen Herrschers, der sowol sein Volk zum herrschenden macht, zum Regenten über alle seine Bedrücker, der aber auch die Religion wieder reinigt. Dass das Reich *tausend Jahre* dauern soll, ist überall bestimmt ausgesprochen :'—points indeed which may remind us not only of the Messianic tenets prevalent among the later Jews, but also of the modified Judaism which in the form of Chiliasm (or sensuous Millenarianism) was current more or less in various branches of the early Christian Church, and only repressed with great difficulty: see Neander, *Ch. Hist.* II. 395—401.

spring of the holy Zoroaster; yet the name of Sosiosh alone, as greatest or as last in order of the hero-prophets, was the rallying-point where Persians were accustomed to find refuge from the miseries of their present lot. The time assigned for his appearance (say the authors of the story) is the time when evil and impiety of every kind have grown to an appalling magnitude. Approaching with a noiseless step, he will evince the greatness of his mission by destroying death itself, and by recalling all the dead to life. *Persian eschatology.* The first to rise again will be the prototype of men (or Kaiomorts), and after him the earliest pair of human beings (Meshia and Meshiane); then, in seven and fifty years, the long array of their descendants. All of these have been appointed to receive the gift of immortality by drinking of the sacred *homa*. Next will follow a grand separation of the pure and impure, of the righteous and unrighteous; friend will lose the sweet companionship of friend, the husband will be severed from his spouse, the sister from the brother. They who stand the sifting of that day are borne aloft to the peculiar dwelling of Ormazd: the rest are driven back to the abodes of misery and torment which had also been their portion from the third day after death. The change, however, thus effected is not destined to be ultimate. A blazing comet (Gurz-sher), hitherto held in fetters by the moon, will break away from his confinement, and, rushing wildly on the earth, will be converted into the agent of Ormazd for purging out the dross that now adheres to all created nature; Ahriman himself will vanish in the flames, and hell, the dark abyss of Duzakh, with its godless tenants, being purified and renovated by the final conflagration, the whole family of man will be assembled on the new-born earth to sing the glory of Ormazd and the amshaspands.

CHAP. IV.

(2) But the later history of religious thought in Persia introduces us to one more being who has not unfrequently been placed in close comparison with the Founder of Christianity. His name is *Mithra;* and so paramount are claims which he advances, in the estimation of some modern writers, that the Gospel is itself pronounced by them a branch of Mithraism.[1] No small confusion, it is true, exists among the older notices of Mithra even in the Persian sacred books;[2] yet there, as elsewhere, the prevailing image represents to us a wakeful and beneficent divinity,[3] 'lord of life and head of all created beings,' active, luminous, fertilising, purifying, and invincible. His place and functions in relation to the highest god appear to have resembled those of the Greek

Early place and character of Mithra.

---

[1] This, for instance, was one of many self-contradictory views propounded by Dupuis in his *Origine de tous les Cultes* (see Vol. I. p. 37, n. 3): and even Creuzer, while rejecting the theory with something like contempt (*Symb.* I. 238, n. 2; cf. p. 341), is induced to look favourably upon another oft-repeated story which ascribes the origin of some ecclesiastical usages (*e. g.* the institution of the Christmas festival) to the influence of Mithraism (*Ibid.* p. 261). Christ, according to this notion, was, in a spiritual sense, the *Sol Novus,* and His birth was therefore celebrated at the period of the year, which Mithraism assigned to the new birth of the celestial luminary. See, on the general question of Mithra-worship, Von-Hammer, *Mémoire sur*

le culte de Mithra, Paris, 1833.

[2] The same remark applies equally to the Greek writers: for Herodotus (I. 131), in speaking of the imitative genius of the Persians, is thought to be guilty of confusing the Venus of Assyrian mythology, *Mylitta,* with the Persian *Mithra* (cf. Xenoph. *Cyrop.* VIII. 13, § 12). The real representative of Venus in the later Persian system was Anahita (Anaitis); Mithra and Anahita corresponding in the main to Baal and Astarte: see Rawlinson's *Herod.* I. 271, 272; Döllinger, *Heiden.* pp. 384, 385; Burnouf, *Sur le Yaçna,* pp. 351 sq.

[3] For instance, in the *Yasna* (Burnouf, p. 222), 'J'invoque, je célèbre Mithra qui multiplie les couples de bœufs qui a mille oreilles, dix milles yeux,' &c.

CHAP. IV. Apollo; and at periods when Ormazd sinks back into comparative quietude, the old connexion with the creature-world and the administration of the light-kingdom, are dependent on the energy of Mithra, who is thus the living and abiding link between the visible and the invisible. Associating intimately and well-nigh upon a level with Ormazd[1] himself, this secondary principle of good is also from his very nature the antagonist of the Evil One. He marshals the bright army of beneficent genii[2] in their conflict with the *devs;* in him the soul departed finds her best conductor to the bridge of Chinevad; while bodies of the dead, though captured by the prince of darkness, are the objects of his sympathy and care.

Mithra as a mediator.
It may have been the service rendered to the votary of the Ormazd-religion in the daily war with Ahriman, that made the later Greek of Plutarch's[3] age, assign to Mithra the peculiar title 'Mediator' ($\mu\epsilon\sigma\acute{\iota}\tau\eta\varsigma$); for although a somewhat similar class of functions was awarded to other beings, as Sraŏsha and Ráshne-rást,[4] who both were thought to super-intend the great judicial process after death, in order that the soul of man might then receive her fitting recompence, 'not a hair too little nor too much,' it was to Mithra, most of all, that subjects of the light-kingdom were instructed to address their homage. Some were even ready to contend that if the first

[1] See the passage from the *Yasna,* quoted above. 385, n. 2.
[2] Hence his rank as chief of the *Izeds;* above, p. 385, n. 2.
[3] *De Isid.* c. XLVI. Plutarch himself seems to regard Mithra as partaking of the natures both of Ormazd and Ahriman ($\mu\acute{\epsilon}\sigma o\nu$ δ' $\dot{\alpha}\mu\phi o\tilde{\iota}\nu$): cf. Dr. Donaldson's *Christ. Orthod.* p. 131, and Creu-zer, I. 292, the latter of whom supposes that Mithra was a kind of chemical mean or 'Liebesfeuer,' harmonising two antagonistic Principles.
[4] Spiegel, *Avesta,* I. 31; Bur-nouf, *Sur le Yaçna,* p. 200.

man had sung the praise of Mithra, or had ever Chap. IV.
named that name, his soul would forthwith have
ascended to the mansions of ultimate felicity.

In proportion as Ormazd himself receded from the *Virtual*
active visible sphere of being, or, in different lan- *substitution of Mithra*
guage, was abstracted more and more from his con- *for Or-*
nexion with the Sun, that luminary was appropriated *mazd.*
as the home or symbol of his younger representative.
Originally placed, as it would seem, midway between
the sun and moon, and so perhaps identified on some
occasions with the planet Venus,[1] Mithra was ere long
a potent and invincible sun-god,[2] author of the light,
dispeller of the darkness ; and in subsequent stages
of the mythe, he rose completely to the rank of a
supreme divinity, corresponding in the vastness and
the splendour of his attributes to the Osiris of the
later Pharaohs. Mithra was *the* sun-god of the
Medo-Persian system. Drawing his existence no *Post-Chris-*
longer from Ormazd, of whom in the Avesta he was *tian repre-*
sentations
ever made a creature and a tributary, he is pictured *of Mithra.*
to us in post-Christian writings as the preternatural
offspring of a rock, or of the soil.[3] According also

---

[1] See above, p. 431, n. 2.

[2] Strabo is the first Greek writer who says this expressly : Πέρσαι.. τιμῶσι δὲ καὶ ἥλιον, ὃν καλοῦσι Μίθρην (xv. 13). Ἀπόλλωνα δὲ ἥλιον τὸν περιπολοῦντα εἶναι νόμιζε, γονὴν ὄντα τοῦ Διός, ὃν καὶ Μίθραν ἐκάλεσαν. *Homil. Clem.* III. 50, ed. Dressel. It is further worth noting that the name does not occur on the Achæmenian inscriptions until the reign of Artaxerxes Mnemon (Rawlinson's *Herod.* Vol. I. p. 272, note) : yet there can be no doubt as to its ancient usage in connexion with

the *Sun*, in both the branches of the Áryan family. To pass by Medo-Persian names *Mithradates* (or Μιτραδάτης, Her. I. 110), as importing 'given by the Sun' (cf. *Hormisdates* 'given by Ormazd'), we have continual examples in the Rig-Véda, where *Mitra* is used as the equivalent of *Áditya*, 'the sun,' or one at least of twelve personifications of the Sun corresponding to the signs of the Zodiac.

[3] St. Jerome, who followed a history of Mithra by Eubulus (now lost) informs us (*Adv. Jovinian.* Opp. IV. col. 149, ed. Bened.) :

to the numerous sculptures of him still surviving he has been invested with distinctly human properties. He is a young man, clothed with a tunic and a Persian cloke, and having on his head a Persian bonnet or tiara. He kneels upon a prostrate bull; and while holding it with the left hand by the nostrils, with the right he plunges into its shoulder a short sword or dagger. The bull is at the same time vigorously attacked by a dog, a serpent, and a scorpion. The ideas embodied in the suffering animal are at once elucidated when we call to mind,[1] that in the old mythology of Persia all organic life, the human and the bestial, issued from the shoulder of the primitive bull; and therefore astronomic and other symbols here employed are probably to be expounded of the action of the sun-god on created nature, his far-piercing beams awakening all its latent energies, opening the fresh veins of life and drawing thence a large supply of fructifying virtue. The key, however, to Mithraic mysteries, all of which are said to have been celebrated in a species of 'cave,' was not entrusted to the vulgar and unlettered, but reserved, as in the other kindred rites and orgies, for the few who underwent a solemn initiation. Here indeed the worship of the Persian sun-god lost all traces of its old resemblance to the creed of the Avesta. It fell off into the whirl of mystic and ascetic faiths, wherein the laxer party, such as Commodus and monsters like him, reconciled the adoration of Serapis and of Mithra with the foulest vio-

Meaning of those symbols.

Mithraic mysteries.

'Narrant et Gentilium fabulæ Mithram et Erichthonium, vel in lapide, vel in terra, de solo æstu libidinis esse generatos.'
[1] Above, p. 409.

lations of the law of conscience; while the genuine devotee was eagerly accepting the severe prescriptions of the mystagogue,[1] who told him that by passing through a lengthened ordeal of torture and privation, he was able to escape from the necessity of repeated births, and consummate his union with the glorious Mithra, 'his god and his crown.'

There is no doubt that while the visions of the *Bundehesh* derived their colouring, and in part their substance also, from Semitic or from quasi-Christian influences, the advocates of Mithra-worship in the earlier centuries of our era were engaged with more or less of system in retarding the triumphant march of Christianity.[2] At a period when the claims of our religion were put forward with an irresistible charm alike in the unspotted lives and the heroic deaths of its true-hearted converts, many of the heathen, still unwilling to embrace it, so far yielded to vibrations it excited in all quarters, as to recognise in it the hidden working of a supernatural virtue. We discern this tendency amid the swarm of startling heresies that sprang up in its track; for most of them were anxious to embody one or more dissevered doctrines of the Gospel with their wild and heathenish specula-

Opposition between Mithraism and Christianity.

---

[1] 'At the time of the final agonies of Paganism, the only portions of the old religion which retained any vitality, at least among those of Greek race and language, were the mysteries. Here alone persons agitated by religious hopes and fears, distracted by doubt, oppressed with a sense of sin, found pleasing excitement in dark riddles and symbolic rites, and consolation in the promised immortality.' Clark, *Peloponnesus,* p. 112.

[2] This is one of Von Hammer's conclusions, in which Creuzer (I. 329) apparently acquiesces, extending the remark to other heathen 'orgies' and 'mysteries' of the post-Christian period. Yet, as various writers have complained, there was occasionally a disposition in apologists of the early Church to lay undue stress on some points of resemblance between Mithraism and Christianity.

CHAP. IV. tions; and others have been also charged with mim-
icking the smaller details of its ritual system.[1] We
discern this tendency still more in one particular instance, bearing on the present theme, for 'almost
every thing that Zoroaster taught of Mithra' was
perpetuated in the school of Mani, with the noticeable
difference that the Persian misbeliever did not scruple
Wide dif- to transfer it all directly to his Christ.[2] And, strange
fusion of though such an issue may appear, not Mani's system
Mithraism. only, but the heathen form of Mithraism as well, was
able, in the breaking up of old religions, to attract
unto itself a multitude of followers both in East and
West. It flourished in alliance with some kindred
systems in the mother-city of the Roman empire:
it was planted, by the ardour of the foreign legion-
aries, in the Roman capital of Britain.[3]

Christ the   Vain, however, and unfruitful was the zeal put
True Light forward in transplanting these fantastic shadows of
of the Gen- exhausted paganism. The western world, excited
tiles.

---

[1] *e.g.* Tertullian (*De Præscript. Hær.* c. xl) alludes to such ap-
parent mimicries in speaking of Mithraism itself: 'Sed quæritur, a quo intellectus intervertatur eorum, qui ad hæreses faciant? A diabolo scilicet, cujus sunt partes intervertendi veritatem: qui ipsas quoque res sacrament-orum divinorum in idolorum mys-teriis æmulatur. Tingit et ipse quosdam, utique credentes et fide-les suos [referring to the ceremony of initiation when water was pour-ed by the mystagogue on the aspirant's head]: expositionem delictorum de lavacro repromittit: et si adhuc initiat Mithra, signat illic in frontibus milites suos; celebrat et panis oblationem' (re-ferring perhaps to a kind of Parsee

communion, where bread was blessed by the priest and eaten, in conjunction with draughts of the homa-plant: cf. Döllinger, p. 373).
[2] Neander, *Ch. Hist.* II. 177.
[3] See Wellbeloved's *Eburacum*, pp. 80—86, York, 1842; and, for some very curious matter with regard to this and kindred sub-jects, *An Essay on the Neo-Druidic Heresy in Britannia* (ascribed to the late Mr. Algernon Herbert), pp. 29 sq. Lond. 1838. The 'Druidizing Mithriacs, referred to in this essay, are supposed to be an offshoot from 'a sort of magical association' that 'had grown up in the eastern parts of the Roman dominions, founded upon the doc-trines and mysteries of the Persian Magi.'

by the general 'shaking of the nations,' was now
yielding to the voice of the celestial Charmer: it
was gazing on the silent march of that obscure yet
glorious, of that suffering yet majestic system, to
whose birthplace the inquiring Magi came of old,
the first-fruits of the Gentile harvest. 'When they
saw the young child, with Mary His mother, they
fell down and worshipped Him.' And Christians of
all future times have counted it their highest glory
to prolong that wondrous act of love and adoration.
They are conscious that in Christ are fully satisfied
the cravings of a spiritual hunger which religions
of the world may stimulate but have no power to
appease. While Bráhmans, in despair of all the
helpers whom their own imagination had created,
were still dreaming of some future and more permanent *avatára;* while the Buddhist, equally in north
and south, abandoned the original Buddha and sought
comfort now in picturing to himself the distant paradise of Amitábha 'the unmeasured Light,' and now
in praying for the gracious intervention of some
Buddha of the future; while the primitive vision
of the helper Sosiosh, dim and fluctuating at the
best, was blotted from the Persian mind entirely, or
was fading under the augmented brilliance of the
younger Mithra;—Christ and Christ alone, expected
in the old œconomy and made manifest in the new,
the living, reigning, and historic Christ, the brightness of the Father's glory and the 'first-born' of
a human brotherhood, was everywhere imprinting
on the world an image of His love, which neither
time nor space could deaden. He 'lighteth every
man' by shining down into the heart. He is the

true Sun, of which all heathen mediators are but transient and confused *parhelia;* for while Mithra, once his mighty rival and as such rejoicing in the name of 'the Invincible,' has left no traces, save in monumental sculptures, of the homage rendered to him in the early centuries of our era, Christ, the sovereign Lord of all, is going forward on His peaceful conquest of the nations, 'the same yesterday and to-day and for ever.'

APPENDIX I.

Alleged connexion between Coptic and Hebrew.

(See above, p. 235, n. 3).

(See above, p. 235, n. 3).

Through the kindness of my friend, Professor Jarrett, I am now in a position to supply the following brief comparison of ordinary words in Coptic and Hebrew. It seems to shew that so far as *vocabulary* is concerned, the relationship between the two languages can hardly be established.

Comparison of common words in Coptic and Hebrew.

Numerals.		
1	ⲞⲨⲀ	אחד
*2	CⲚⲀⲨ	שנים
3	Ⲩ̣ⲞⲘⲦ	שלש
4	ϤⲦⲞ	ארבע
5	ⲦⲒⲞⲨ	חמש
6	CⲞⲞⲨ	שש
7	Ⲩ̣ⲀⲨ̣Ϥ	שבע
*8	Ⲩ̣ⲘⲞⲨ̣Ⲛ	שמונה
9	ⲮⲒⲦ	תשע
10	ⲘⲎⲦ	עשר
20	ⲬⲰⲦ	עשרים
30	ⲘⲀⳠ	שלשים
40	ϨⲘⲈ	ארבעים
50	ⲦⲀⲒⲞⲨ	חמשים
60	CⲈ	ששים

*70	Ⲩ̣ϤⲈ	שבעים
*80	ϨⲘⲘⲚⲈ	שמנים
90	ⲠⲒCⲦⲀⲞⲨ	תשעים
100	Ⲩ̣Ⲉ	מאה
1000	Ⲩ̣Ⲟ	אלף

Nouns.		
Father	IⲰⲦ	אב
*Mother	ⲘⲀⲨ	אם
Brother	CⲞⲚ	אח
Sister	CⲰⲚⲒ	אחות
Son	Ⲩ̣ⲎⲢⲒ	בן
Daughter	Ⲩ̣ⲈⲢⲒ	בת
Man	ⲢⲰⲘⲒ	אדם, איש
Woman	CϨⲒⲘⲒ	אשה
Head	{ⲀⲠⲈ, ⲀⲪⲈ, ⲬⲰ, ⲬⲰⲬ}	ראש

APPEND. I.

English	Coptic	Hebrew	English	Coptic	Hebrew
Eye	ⲃⲁⲗ	עין	Wind	ⲛⲓⲃⲉ	רוח
Mouth	ⲣⲟ	פה	†River	ⲓⲁⲣⲟ	נהר, יאר
Tooth	ⲛⲁϫϩⲓ	שן	Tree	ϣϣⲏⲛ	עץ
Nose	ϣⲁ	אף	Leaf	ϫⲱⲃⲓ	עלה
Beard	ⲙⲟⲣⲧ	זקן	Ox } Cow }	ⲉϩⲉ	בקר, פר
Neck and Shoulder	ⲕⲉⲛϩⲉ and ⲙⲟⲧⲓ	ערף and שכם	*Sheep	ⲉⲥⲟⲟⲩ	צאן, שה
Arm	ϣⲱⲃϣ	זרוע	Horse	ϩⲧⲟ, ϩⲑⲟ	סוס
Hand	ⲧⲟⲧ, ϫⲓϫ	יד	Ass	ⲉⲱ	חמור, אתן
*Finger	ⲧⲏⲃ, ⲑⲏⲃ	אצבע		Verbs.	
Belly	ⲑⲏ, ⲛⲉϫⲓ	בטן	See	ⲛⲁⲩ	ראה
Heart	ϩⲏⲧ	לב	Hear	ⲥⲱⲧⲉⲙ	שמע
Knee	ⲡⲁⲧ	ברך	Eat	ⲟⲩⲉⲙ, ⲟⲩⲱⲙ	אכל
Foot	ϭⲁⲧ	רגל	Drink	ⲥⲉ	שתה
Ear	ⲙⲁⲁϫⲉ	אזן	Go { ⲓ, ⲙⲟϣⲓ, ⲛⲁ, ϣⲉ }		הלך, יצא
Flesh	ⲁϥ	בשר	Run	ⲡⲏⲧ	רוץ
Skin	ϣⲁⲣⲟⲙ	עור	Take	ⲁⲙⲟⲛⲓ, ϭⲱⲛⲓ	לקח
Day	ⲉϩⲟⲟⲩ	יום	Give { ⲙⲁ, ⲙⲏⲓ, ⲙⲟⲓ, ⲧⲏⲓ }		נתן
Night	ⲟⲩϣⲏ	לילה	Do	ⲉⲣ	עשה
Light	ⲟⲩⲱⲓⲛⲓ	אור	Say	ϫⲉ, ϫⲱ	אמר
Darkness	ⲕⲁⲕⲉ	חשך	Love	ⲙⲉⲣⲉ	אהב
†Water	ⲙⲱⲟⲩ	מים	Hate	ⲙⲉⲥⲧⲉ	שנא
†Sea	ⲓⲟⲙ	ים	Touch { *ⲙⲁϣ, ϣⲓ, ϫⲱϩ }		משש נגע
Fire	ⲕⲗⲱⲙ, ⲕⲣⲱⲙ	אש			

(1) Of the above words those marked † are *identical:* יְאֹר being used of the Nile.

(2) The words marked * have considerable resemblance, which *may* point to a common origin.

(3) The remainder, a vast majority, appear to have no connexion whatever.

The following is a short list of accidental *resemblances which* APPEND. I.
have also occurred to Professor Jarrett (the Coptic words
meaning the same as the words set against them):

CⲀⲂⲈ = sap-iens.

IⲰⲦ = آتا *Turkish;* atta,
    Gothic, 'father.'

CⲀⲬI = sag-en.

OⲨOⲚ = van, 'is,' 'are,' *Mag-
    yar.*

OⲨOⲢⲠ = werf-en.

KOⲖⲠ = κλεπ-τειν.

ⲀOϤ = ὄφις.

ⲰOⲚⲦI = sentis.

ⲘOⲱI = مشي, 'walked,'
    Arab.

ⲰⲈⲘⲰI = שִׁמְשׁ.

ⲪⲰⲦ = fut-ni, 'to flee,' *Mag-
    yar.*

OⲨⲬⲀI = ὑγιης.

ⲰⲂⲰⲦ = שׁבׁב

CHϤI = سيف, 'sword,' *Arab.*

ⲬⲰⲬ = coq-uere.

I = ι-εναι = i-re.

ⲰⲈⲘⲘHⲢ = חמר, 'leaven.'

IHC = חש, 'hasty.'

The use of pronominal affixes is not confined to Hebrew and
Coptic, but is found also in Welsh and Magyar; of which the
former is an A'ryan language, and the latter Turanian. Of the
sixteen affixes used in Hebrew, the Coptic coincides exactly in only
two, the Welsh in *one;* while in the use of *n* for בנ, the Welsh
agrees with the Coptic, and the Magyar differs only by the
addition of *k,* which is in that language the regular affix to mark
the plural in all cases. The Magyar agrees also with the Hebrew
in the insertion of י = *i,* when the pronominal affix is added to
a plural noun. The Welsh uses *t,* and the Magyar *d* as the
characteristic of the second person.

On this latter question of pronominal affixes, as pointing to some
close analogy between the Coptic and the Hebrew, M. Renan,
Histoire des Langues Sémitiques, I. 83 sq. (Paris, 1858), has
made the following observations:

'Il est, je le sais, des analogies plus profondes et beaucoup plus
considérables aux yeux des linguistes, qui semblent rattacher la
langue copte aux idiomes sémitiques. L'identité des pronoms,
et surtout de la manière de les traiter dans les deux langues, est

APPEND. I. assurément un fait étrange. Cette identité s'observe jusque dans les détails qui semblent les plus accessoires : plusieurs irrégularités apparentes du pronom sémitique (le changement du ת en ך à l'affixe, par exemple) trouvent même dans la théorie du pronom copte une satisfaisante explication.

PRONOMS ISOLÉS.

Copte.		Hébreu.
1re p. sing. ⲀⲚⲞⲔ	....	אָנֹכִי
2re p. sing. ⲚⲦⲞⲔ et en baschmourique ⲚⲦⲀⲔ...	אַתָּה pour	אַנְתָּה
1re p. pl. ⲀⲚⲞⲚ et en baschmourique ⲀⲚⲀⲚ ...		אֲנַחְנוּ
2e p. pl. ⲚⲦⲰⲦⲚ	....	אַתֶּם pour אַנְתֶּם

PRONOMS SUFFIXES.

Copte.		Hébreu.
1re p. sing. Ⲓ	....	י
2e p. sing. Ⲕ ⲭ	....	ך
3e p. sing. Ⳁ	....	ו
1re p. pl. Ⲛ	....	נוּ
2e p. pl. ⲦⲈⲚ	....	כֶם

Les analogies des noms de nombre, signalées par M. Lepsius, ne sont pas moins frappantes. Exemples : ⲤⲚⲀⲨ = שנים ; ϢⲞⲘⲦ = שלש ; ⲤⲞ = שש ; ⲤⲀϢϤ = שבע ; ϢⲘⲞⲨⲚ = שמנה, etc. L'agglutination des mots accessoires, l'assimilation des consonnes, le rôle secondaire de la voyelle, son instabilité, qui la fait souvent omettre dans l'écriture, sont autant de traits qui rapprochent singulièrement la grammaire égyptienne de la grammaire hébraïque.—La conjugaison elle-même n'est pas sans quelques analogies dans les deux langues : le présent copte, comme le second temps des langues sémitiques, se forme par l'agglutination du pronom en tête de la racine verbale ; les autres temps se forment au moyen d'une composition semblable à celle qu'emploient les langues araméennes. On trouve, en copte, l'emploi d'une forme causative analogue à l'*hiphil*, et la voix passive y est marquée,

comme dans les langues sémitiques, par une modification de
la voyelle du radical.—La théorie des particules offre aussi,
de parte et d'autre, quelques ressemblances; la conjonction
copte, comme la conjonction arabe, est susceptible de régime;
ⲅⲱϥ = *etiam ipse;* ⲁⲅⲡⲟⲕ = *cur tu.* Enfin, une en-
tente analogue de la phrase et une conception presque identique
des rapports grammaticaux établissent entre les deux systèmes
de langues d'incontestables affinités.

Mais ces affinités suffisent-elles pour ranger dans une même
famille les langues entre lesquelles on les observe? Sont-ce
de simples ressemblances comme on en remarque entre toutes
les langues, ou des analogies tenant à une commune origine?
C'est ici que le problème devient délicat et, à vrai dire, presque
insoluble. Il implique une question de méthode sur laquelle,
dans l'état actuel de la linguistique, on ne peut rien dire de
bien précis. L'histoire naturelle a des signes parfaitement
déterminés pour établir les embranchements, les classes, les
genres et les espèces; la linguistique n'en a pas: c'est une
question de degré, sur laquelle l'appréciation individuelle de
chaque linguiste pourra varier. Si l'on veut attribuer à la
classification des langues en familles un sens positif, on doit
faire correspondre cette division à un fait réel et historique.
Elle doit vouloir dire qu'à l'origine de l'humanité le langage
apparut sous un ou plusieurs types qui ont produit, par
leur développement, toutes les diversités actuelles. Or nous
n'avons pas assez de lumières sur les temps primitifs pour
aborder ce difficile problème. Le naturaliste n'est pas obligé
de décider si chaque genre représente une forme de création
primordiale: il se contente de dire que les genres, dans l'état
actuel de notre planète, sont irréductibles. Le linguiste, dont
les hypothèses impliquent, quoi qu'il fasse, une assertion historique, serait tenu à quelque chose de plus: et pourtant il
ne possède qu'un seul criterium pour établir la distinction des
familles, c'est l'impossibilité d'expliquer comment le système
de l'une a pu sortir du système de l'autre par des transformations régulières. De là au fait primitif, qui seul pourrait offrir
aux classifications linguistiques une base solide et clairement
intelligible, il y a un abîme qu'aucun esprit sage ne se décidera
jamais à franchir.

APPEND. I.   Du moins, à la question ainsi posée : peut-on expliquer par
un développement organique comment le système des langues
sémitiques a pu engendrer le système de la langue copte, ou
réciproquement ? il faut répondre sans hésiter d'une manière
négative.   Des rapprochements comme ceux que l'on signale
sont tout à fait insuffisants pour établir une parenté primitive.
Un système grammatical va tout d'une pièce, et il est absurde
de supposer que deux groupes de langues possèdent en commun
une moitié de leur système grammatical sans se ressembler par
l'autre.   Certes il nous est difficile d'expliquer l'identité d'éléments en apparence aussi accidentels que les pronoms et les
noms de nombre.   Quelle raison a pu déterminer les races di-
verses à prendre le *t* pour caractéristique de la seconde personne
du singulier, l'*n* pour caractéristique de la première personne
du pluriel ?   Il serait puéril de le rechercher.   Avouons pourtant
que les premiers hommes ont pu se laisser guider en cela par
des analogies qui nous échappent.   La théorie du pronom tient
d'une manière si intime à la constitution même de l'esprit humain, qu'elle appartient presque aux catégories de la logique,
et doit, comme ses catégories, se retrouver partout la même.
Les noms de nombre se rattacheraient de très-près aux pronoms,
s'il fallait ajouter foi aux vues ingénieuses que M. Lepsius lui-
même, dans la seconde des dissertations précitées, a émises sur
ce sujet.   Enfin, quelque étrange que puisse paraître un *emprunt*
portant sur des éléments linguistiques aussi essentiels, on n'ose
regarder un tel emprunt comme impossible, quand on voit le
pehlvi (dont la réalité comme langue parlée n'est pas, il est
vrai, bien certaine) offrir des pronoms, des noms de nombre, des
prépositions, des conjonctions sémitiques, à côté d'éléments non
moins fondamentaux appartenant aux idiomes iraniens.'

APPENDIX II.

Religions of the barbarous tribes of Africa.

(See above, p. 237).

THE special interest attaching at the present day to explorations in that mighty tract of unknown country, which is vaguely termed the highlands and lowlands of Central Africa, induces me to add a few brief notes on some remarkable analogies which may be traced between the aspects of religion there and in the other parts of heathendom. I do so from a further wish to illustrate, as far as may be, the religious condition of Egypt anterior to the coming of that second race of immigrants who stamped a widely different character on many of her sacred institutions.

The great work of Dr. Livingstone has pointed here and there to some remote connexion in primeval ages between Egypt and South-Central Africa.[1] Thus, the animal-worship of the Old Egyptians, which had ever formed their strongest and most startling peculiarity in the eyes of Greece and Rome (see above, pp. 270 sq.) is traceable as far southward as the Bechuana tribes. These tribes are also named after certain animals. 'The term *Bakatla* means, "they of the monkey;" *Bakuena*, "they of the alligator;" *Batlápi*, "they of the fish," each tribe having a superstitious dread of the animal after which it is called...*A tribe never eats the animal which is its namesake*, using the term *ila*, "hate" or "dread," in reference to killing it' (*Missionary Travels*, p. 13: cf. above. pp. 271, 285). Prichard, in like manner, has collected observations bearing upon this point from earlier travellers in South Africa: 'If a person has been

[1] See also Brosses (Ch. de), *Du Culte des Dieux Fétiches, ou Parallèle de l'ancienne Religion de l'Égypte avec la Religion actuelle de Nigritie*, Paris, 1760.

APPEN. II. killed by an elephant, they offer a sacrifice, apparently to appease the demon supposed to have actuated the animal. One who kills by accident a *mak'em*, or Balearic crane, or a *brom-vogel*, a species of tucan, must offer a calf in atonement. Sometimes they imagine that a *shulúga*, or spirit, resides in a particular ox [cf. the *Apis* of Egypt, above, p. 272, and n. 2], and propitiate it by prayers when going on hunting expeditions:' *Researches,* II. 289. From the Rev. J. Shooter's *Kafirs of Natal and the Zulu Country,* Lond. 1857, we have learned, again, not only that serpents and some other reptiles are there regarded as 'incarnations of spirits departed' (p. 162), but also that Zulus are very scrupulous in abstaining from the flesh of a particular group of animals (p. 215), some of which, however, as in different nomes of ancient Egypt, are eaten freely by their neighbours.

Dr. Livingstone has further drawn attention to the fact that striking coincidences exist between the customs of Egypt and Central Africa, *e.g.* in pounding maize (p. 196), in dressing the hair (pp. 304, 443), in spinning and weaving (pp. 399, 400), and other matters: but one of the most important links supplied by him for drawing together the first populations of the two districts will be found in his comparison of the African dialects with the language of the Old Egyptians. He thinks it nearly certain (1) that all the tongues now spoken to the South of the Equator, with the exception of the Bush or Hottentot, are strictly *homogeneous,* and (2) that the Sichuana tongue, as now elevated by the powerful Bechuana chieftains, bears, in structure, very close resemblance to the language of Egyptian monuments. He has handled this subject in a small unpublished work, for some knowledge of which I am indebted to the valuable edition of *Dr. Livingstone's Cambridge Lectures,* by the Rev. William Monk (Camb. 1858), pp. 106—121.

But, to my own mind, the most conclusive testimony flowing from late researches of Dr. Livingstone may readily be brought to bear upon a somewhat larger question, *viz.* the affinity in thought and feeling and traditions between the natives of Central Africa and the primitive layer of human population, not in Egypt only, but in other and far-distant countries. As Dr. Livingstone was himself, apparently, unconscious of any

such relationship, his observations will of course possess the
greater value. I shall cite a few examples; at the same time
illustrating Dr. Livingstone's account by references to the Third
Part of this work, and by adducing, here and there, the testimony
of other writers.

The African idea of God. According to the verdict of early
travellers in Southern Africa, the natives of that region were
esteemed 'the most brutal and barbarous in the world, neither
worshipping God nor any idol;' and the general absence of all
forms of public worship, both among the Kafirs and the Bechuanas of the present day, has caused the charge of atheism to be
continually repeated (Livingstone, pp. 158, 159). Such also, we
have seen already (Vol. II. p. 180), was precisely the condition
of the Papuan Family, exposing them to similar charges. Yet
in neither case are we at liberty to argue that the thought of
a superior race of beings, superhuman and invisible, had been
quite obliterated from the native mind. With reference to
South Africa, Dr. Livingstone appears to be at variance on this
point with Mr. Moffat, his friend and predecessor (*Missionary
Labours*, p. 245): for, writing of the people towards the mouths
of the Zambesi (pp. 641, 642), he affirms that they have a clear
idea of a Supreme Being. That being 'is named *Morimo,
Molungo, Reza, Mpámbe*, in the different dialects spoken. The
Barotse name him *Nyámpi*, and the Balonda *Zámbi*. All
promptly acknowledge him as the ruler over all.' Dr. Livingstone, however, confesses plainly in another passage (pp. 158, 159),
while speaking of the Kafirs and Bechuanas, that this notion
of the deity, though present, seems to be inoperative at the
best; and since the form *Morimo* is probably identical with
Barimo, and both the nouns are also used in the *plural* number
as equivalent to 'spirits,' we are fully entitled to infer that
there, as in the wild tribes of America, *the* Morimo is only
a Great Spirit, acting as the highest member of a group,—in
other words, 'the brightest inmate of a crowded pantheon'
(above, p. 130). I may observe that *Morimo*, as the nearest
possible approximation, has been hitherto adopted by missionaries in rendering the name of the Supreme Being. We further
ascertain that in the Kafir tribes some memories are still linger-

APPEN. II. ing of a 'Great-Great' and a 'First Appearer'; and in one single
district of Natal the Great-Great is actually worshipped, 'though
the recollection of him is very dim' (Shooter, p. 160).

Offerings to and for the dead. Hegel seems to fancy (*Phil.
of Hist.* p. 99, Lond. 1857) that this kind of worship was the
special characteristic of the African negroes, their idea being
that departed 'ancestors exercise vengeance and inflict upon
man various injuries.' We have seen, however, that the practice
was all but universal in China (Vol. II. pp. 34, 35), among the
wild tribes of America (p. 127, n. 1), among the Papuans
(p. 179), and the Maori (p. 200); and was further recognised
as one chief part of the religion of the Old Egyptians (p. 292).
The soul of the deceased was commonly believed, in Asia,
Africa, America, and Oceanica, to linger for a certain period
near the place of sepulture, and also to derive while there a sort
of gratification from the offerings which were made in her
behalf. Thus, to take one striking specimen from Dr. Livingstone's work (p. 434; cf. pp. 319, 641, 642): 'The same superstitious ideas being prevalent through the whole of the country
north of the Zambesi, seems to indicate that the people must
originally have been one. All believe that the souls of the
departed still mingle among the living, and partake in some
way of the food they consume. In sickness, sacrifices of fowls
and goats are made to appease the spirits. It is imagined that
they wish to take the living away from earth and all its enjoy-
ments. When one man has killed another, a sacrifice is made,
as if to lay the spirit of the victim. A sect is reported to
exist who kill men in order to take their hearts and offer them
to the *Barimo.*' Mr. Shooter also, speaking of the Kafirs of
Natal, has made a similar observation (p. 161): and when he
adds that the attention of departed spirits is thought to be restricted to their own relatives,—a father caring for the family
and a chief for the tribe, which they respectively left behind
them,—we need only turn to China or New Zealand to discover
a most vivid and exact resemblance (above, p. 36, p. 200).

Slaughter of servants in honour of their chiefs. The
horrible practice of burning widows which had long prevailed
in Hindústán, and which was also found by early missionaries
in the Wendic tribes of northern Europe (see the letter of

Boniface, *Opp.* ed. Giles, I. 132 sq.) had extended southward APPEN. II.
to the Vítí islands (above, p. 185, n. 1), where slaves and even
children of the deceased were put to death at his funeral (cf.
Herod. IV. 71, 72). Dr. Livingstone, while speaking of the
negroes of South-Central Africa (p. 318), produces the same
gloomy picture : ' When a chief dies, a number of servants are
slaughtered with him to form his company in the other world.'
He then adds : ' As we go north, the people become more
bloodily superstitious.'

Transmigration. We have seen that both in civilised and
barbarous countries the idea of immortality was always prone to
clothe itself in more or less elaborate theories on the transmigration of the human soul. Such theories, we have further seen,
prevailed in all the polished circles of Hindústán and Egypt, but
the traces of them were observable as well among the wild tribes
of America (above, p. 135). It is probable that in almost every
case the spirit was supposed to linger for a time in the vicinity
of her old dwelling, and then to start upon her wanderings
through the different animal forms which she was destined to
inhabit. And substantially the same account is brought us by
the missionary who has studied the religion of the southern
tribes of Africa : ' They believe in the transmigration of souls ;
and also that while persons are still living they may enter into
lions and alligators, and then return again to their own bodies '
(Livingstone, p. 642). Mr. Shooter (*Kafirs of Natal,* p. 162)
corroborates this statement also, adding that ' departed spirits
are believed to revisit the earth and appear to their descendants
in the form of certain serpents.'

Bondage to fear. The gloomy terror everywhere inspired
alike by the religions of the wild American and by those of
Oceanica (above, pp. 133, 134, 188), has found its counterpart
again among the various tribes of Central Africa : ' Their religion, if such it may be called, is one of dread. Numbers of
charms are employed to avert the evils with which they feel
themselves to be encompassed. Occasionally you meet a man,
more cautious or more timid than the rest, with twenty or thirty
charms hung round his neck ' (Livingstone, p. 435). Again :
' There is nothing more heart-rending than their death-wails.
When the natives turn their eyes to the future world, they have

APPEN. II. a view cheerless enough of their own utter helplessness and hopelessness. They fancy themselves completely in the power of the disembodied spirits, and look upon the prospect of following them, as the greatest of misfortunes. Hence they are constantly deprecating the wrath of departed souls, believing that, if they are appeased, there is no other cause of death but witchcraft, which may be averted by charms' (p. 440).

Circumcision. I have already had occasion to notice the prevalence of this rite in Southern Africa, and also pointed out some traces of it in the Egypt of the Pharaohs, as well as in far distant parts of heathendom: see above, pp. 321, 322, and the references there given.

Black and white men. The following declaration of a 'rain-doctor,' as recorded by Dr. Livingstone (p. 24) is identical with a tradition already noted (above, p. 189) in speaking of the Víti islands: 'He made black men first, and did not love us, as he did the white men. He made you beautiful, and gave you clothing and guns, &c.; but toward us he had no heart. He gave us nothing, except the assegai and cattle and rain-making; and he did not give us hearts like yours. We never love each other.' A legend of precisely the same import (above, p. 197, n. 2) is still preserved among the Tongans (and not improbably among some other of the Polynesian islanders). There too it is the elder son who is depraved and idle, and his children who are destined to change colour, and to pass from white to black, by reason of some moral delinquency of their progenitor,—'because the heart is bad.'

Veneration of the Ficus Indica. Attention has been drawn already to the marvellous frequency with which the nations of South-Eastern Asia and the wilder tribes of Oceanica have betrayed their reverence for the banyan-tree or Indian fig (above, pp. 182, 183): but, strange as this may seem, the regions of Central Africa explored of late years by Dr. Livingstone have yielded further testimonies of precisely the same kind. In speaking of the Balonda, he says (290): 'They regard this tree with some sort of veneration as a medicine or charm.' And again, referring to a village in the Barotse valley, he writes (p. 495): 'At this village there is a real Indian banyan-tree, which has spread itself over a considerable space by means of roots from its branches...It is curious that trees of this family are looked upon with veneration, and all the way from the Barotse to Loanda are thought to be preservatives from evil.'

The examples here adduced of some original tie connecting the barbaric tribes of Southern and Central Africa, not only with the earliest masters of the land of Egypt, but with primitive layers of population in Asia, in America, in Oceanica, will serve a highly moral purpose, if they tend to silence the suspicions now again in circulation with regard to the admissibility of Africans into the family of man. I deem it a most cruel falsehood to maintain that any even of the lowest negro tribes are unsusceptible of mental and moral culture; but instead of urging my own opinion, I transcribe the words of one who, by his long and patient study of the question, earned a fairer claim to speak about it than a multitude of philo-slavers : ' The civilisation,' writes Prichard, ' of many African nations is much superior to that of the aborigines of Europe during the ages which preceded the conquests of the Goths and Swedes in the north, and the Romans in the Southern parts. The old Finnish inhabitants of Scandinavia had long, as it has been proved by the learned investigations of Rühs, the religion of fetishes, and a vocabulary as scanty as that of the most barbarous Africans. They had lived from immemorial ages without laws, or government, or social union ; every individual the supreme arbiter, in every thing, of his own actions; and they displayed as little capability of emerging from the squalid sloth of their rude and merely animal existence. When conquered by people of Indo-German race, who brought with them from the East the rudiments of mental culture, they emerged more slowly from their pristine barbarism than many of the native African nations have done. Even at the present day there are hordes in various parts of Northern Asia, whose heads have the form belonging to the Tatars, and to Slavonians and other Europeans, but are below many of the African tribes in civilisation.'

INDEX.

Cambridge:
PRINTED BY JONATHAN PALMER, SIDNEY STREET.

WORKS BY CHARLES HARDWICK, M.A.

Late Archdeacon of Ely, and Christian Advocate in the University of Cambridge.

1.
CHRIST AND OTHER MASTERS.

A Historical Inquiry into some of the Chief Parallelisms and Contrasts between Christianity and the Religious Systems of the Ancient World: with Special Reference to Prevailing Difficulties and Objections. Revised, with the Author's latest Corrections, and Prefatory Memoir, by FRANCIS PROCTER, M.A., Vicar of Witton, Norfolk, Author of "History of the Book of Common Prayer."
Second Edition, 2 vols. Crown 8vo.

CONTENTS: Part I. INTRODUCTION. Part II. RELIGIONS OF INDIA. Part III. RELIGIONS OF CHINA, AMERICA, and OCEANICA. Part IV. RELIGIONS OF EGYPT AND MEDO-PERSIA.

"Never was so difficult and complicated a subject as the history of Pagan religion handled so ably, and at the same time rendered so lucid and attractive."—*Colonial Church Chronicle.*

2.
HISTORY OF THE CHRISTIAN CHURCH
DURING THE REFORMATION.
459 pp. (1856). Crown 8vo. *cloth,* 10s. 6d.

This Work forms a Sequel to the Author's Book on The Middle Ages. The Author's wish has been to give the reader a trustworthy version of those stirring incidents which mark the Reformation of the Church throughout Europe.

"The utility of this work consists in bringing the greater and minor histories connected with the Reformation into a single volume and a compact shape, as well as presenting their broad features to the student. The merit of the history consists in the penetration with which the opinions of age, the traits of its remarkable men, and the intellectual character of the history are perceived and the force with which they are presented."—*Spectator.*

3.
HISTORY OF THE CHRISTIAN CHURCH
DURING THE MIDDLE AGE, A.D. 590—1520.

With 4 Maps, constructed for this work by A. K. JOHNSTON.

Second Edit. Cn. 8vo. (1861) 10s. 6d.

Edited by the Rev. FRANCIS PROCTER, M.A.

This history of the Mediæval Church commences with the time of Gregory the Great, because it is admitted on all hands that his pontificate became a turning-point, not only in the fortunes of the Western tribes and nations, but of Christendom at large. A kindred reason has suggested the propriety of pausing at the year 1520,—the year when Luther, having been extruded from those Churches that adhered to the Communion of the Pope, established a provisional form of government and opened a fresh era in the history of Europe.

"As a manual for the students of Ecclesiastical History we know of no English work which can be compared to this." —*Guardian.*

THE DECALOGUE

Viewed as the Christian Law with Special Reference to the Questions and Wants of the Time. By RICHARD TUDOR, B.A., Curate of Helston.

Crown 8vo. (1860) 10s. 6d.

"The Decalogue occupies so prominent a part in the Service of the Church, that it demands our consideration, and yet we fear it is too often thought lightly of or explained away as being in many respects unsuitable to Christian times. This volume treats the subject more fully than we remember to have seen it done before; the author has met every objection, pointed out the particulars in which its rules admit of adoption to ourselves in the place of an exact obedience, and applied the whole to current opinions and feelings."—*Clerical Journal.*

Crown 8vo. cloth, 10s. 6d.

HISTORY

OF

CHRISTIAN MISSIONS

DURING THE MIDDLE AGES.

BY

GEORGE FREDERICK MACLEAR, M.A.

Classical Master in King's College, London; Late Scholar of Trinity College, Cambridge.

SPECTATOR.

"He tells with great calmness and with great impartiality the story of at once the strangest and the most successful of missionary enterprises."

PATRIOT.

"A most admirable book * * * and supplies a vacant place in our ecclesiastical and missionary literature. We are not aware of any other work in the English language that brings together into one view the missionary enterprises and achievements of the Middle Ages. His book is one that will be indispensable not only to the ecclesiastical student, but also to every practical worker who would understand how the various missions of the Modern Church have their prototypes and roots in the Christian enterprise and zeal of a millenium and a half ago."

JOHN BULL.

"Written in an easy style, and almost every statement verified . . . the interest is well kept up, and we are carried on continuously, the connexion of one mission with another being well brought out . . . we have said enough to induce many of our readers who are interested in Missions to get the book for themselves, and we are sure that they will not think the time ill-spent that has been devoted to its perusal."

MACMILLAN AND CO., LONDON AND CAMBRIDGE.

www.ingramcontent.com/pod-product-compliance
Lightning Source LLC
Chambersburg PA
CBHW052350110726
47901CB00005B/1425